SIGHTSEEING

London Transport run a circular guided sightseeing tour of London, which if it is your first visit to London or you are not familiar with the capital, is an excellent way to get your bearings and see at least the exterior of famous buldings to which you may return at your leisure. Tours, which take 1 1/2 hours and run at least every hour from 10am to 5pm (even later in the summer), start from Victoria (near Underground Station), Piccadilly Circus (Haymarket), Marble Arch (Speaker's Corner) and Baker Street Station: fare £6, children £4. There is a discount of £1 if you purchase your ticket from a London Transport Travel Information Centre.

Additional places of interest near to main sights

When visiting:

– **St Paul's,** don't forget to walk round the precinct and spot the steeples of nearby City Churches.
– The **Guildhall,** don't forget the Clock Museum.
– The **Tower,** take time also to visit (i) All Hallows to see the model ships, the Grinling Gibbons font cover, the brasses (on request); (ii) St Olave's Church. Relax afterwards in St Katharine Dock.
– **Greenwich,** in addition to the Maritime Museum (including paintings) and RN College (chapel and refectory), allow time for the Queen's House, Flamsteed House and the Old Observatory, (even if not astronomically minded!); continue to the Ranger's (or Chesterfield) House and allow time to explore Blackheath and/or Greenwich town and riverside.
– **Southwark Cathedral,** visit also Guy's Hospital and St Thomas's Operating Theatre, then the pubs down Borough High St and Trinity Church Sq or Clink St and Bankside.
– **Westminster Abbey,** don't forget to look into Dean's Yard and St Margaret's.
– The **Silver Vaults,** allow time to see Lincoln's Inn and at least look into the Public Record Office.
– **Westminster Cathedral,** cross the road and explore Queen Anne's Gate.
– **Fleet St,** turn off to Dr Johnson's House and the Temple Church, hall and gardens.
– The **Nash Terraces,** go afterwards to sit in Queen Mary's Gardens in Regent's Park.
– **Sadler's Wells Theatre** (even after dark), make sure you see Myddelton Sq.
– The **British Museum,** approach by different routes, in time to take in Bedford and all the surrounding squares and St George's Church.

Children's half-term outing or a day in town

– The Tower; St Katharine Dock; Tower Bridge; the *Belfast.*
– Museum of London (not Mondays); St Paul's dome (view); Monument. At Christmas go first to Leadenhall Market to see the poultry.
– Greenwich by boat: Maritime Museum, Old Observatory, Cutty Sark; foot tunnel under the Thames.
– Changing the guard at Buckingham Palace or mounting the guard at Horse Guards Parade; Trafalgar Square to see Nelson's Column, the pigeons, Standard Measures, point from which mileages are measured, King Charles' statue; Christmas Tree and carol singing.
– At Christmas: shop windows and decorations in Oxford St; pantomime or children's play.
– The Polka Children's Theatre, Wimbledon; The Little Angel Marionette Theatre, Islington; Unicorn Children's Theatre; Shakespeare Globe Museum and St Thomas's Operating Theatre, Southwark.
– Pollock's Toy Museum; The London Toy and Model Museum; Bethnal Green Museum of Childhood – dolls, doll houses, costume, toys. Brass rubbing (St Martin-in-the-Fields or Westminster Abbey).
– Museum of Mankind via the Burlington Arcade; British Museum (Egyptian mummies, coins).
– Science and/or Natural History and/or Geological Museum.
– Westminster Abbey (older children); Palace of Westminster (when open – older children); Westminster Cathedral campanile (view).
– Mme Tussaud's Waxworks and/or the Planetarium/Lazerium; London Dungeon; Space Adventure.
– RAF Museum, Hendon; Imperial War Museum; National Army Museum and Chelsea Hospital; Royal Artillery Museum, Woolwich and Woolwich ferry.
– Wembley Stadium tour; Wimbledon Lawn Tennis Museum.
– Wimbledon Windmill Museum; Kew Bridge Steam Engines; Musical Museum; Heritage Car Museum, Syon.
– The National, National Portrait and Tate Galleries – special holiday arrangements for children; ICA special films.
– Canal boat trip from Little Venice to the Zoo or Camden Lock.
– The Zoo (picnics); Children's Zoo, Battersea Pk; pelicans and wildfowl in St James's Park.

A London Calendar on p 30 lists a selection of annual attractions.

Suggestions for simple outings at different seasons

A grey or wet **winter's day:** the British Museum – the Nereid Monument against its blue sky! (Greek wing), the rooms of treasure and riches or the manuscripts and illuminations (British Library). The National Portrait Gallery. The Tower of London. Wallace Collection.

An early **spring day:** crocuses in Hyde Park (Marble Arch and Knightsbridge); daffodils in Green Park, Hyde Park (Knightsbridge), Hampton Court, Kew.

Mid and **late spring:** bluebells at Kew; rhododendrons and azaleas in Battersea, Dulwich and Crystal Palace Parks, at Kenwood, Kew, in the Woodland Garden, Bushy Park, and Isabella Plantation, Richmond Park; chestnut avenue, Bushy Park; cherry blossom in Battersea Park and at Kew.

A **summer's day:** roses in Queen Mary's Gardens, Regent's Park, at Kew and Hampton Court; the houses to London's west – Osterley, Ham House, Syon Park, Strawberry Hill, Marble Hill, Orleans House (and Montpelier Row).

An **autumn day:** Kensington Palace followed by a walk to see the autumn tints in the park.

For page references (with visiting hours) turn to final index.

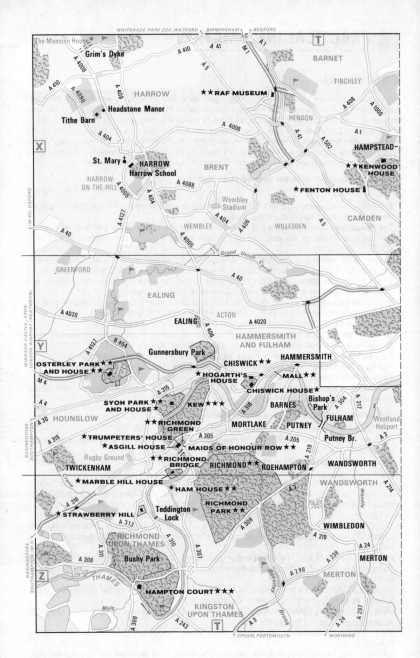

FACILITIES

Information. – Details of **exhibitions, concerts, theatrical performances** and **special events** are available from:

- the daily and weekly press and the weekly magazines *What's On, Time Out*
- the London Tourist Board, Victoria Station *(9am to 8.30pm - November to Easter to 7pm, Sundays 5pm)*, Tourist Information Centre, West Gate, H.M. Tower of London *(April to October, 10am to 6pm daily)*, Heathrow Information Centre Terminals 1, 2, 3 *(9am to 6pm)*, Harrods and Selfridges, *(open during store hours)*; enquiries by phone ☎: 01-730 3488 *(Mondays to Fridays 9am to 6pm)* and, for written enquiries only, 26 Grosvenor Gardens SW1. City of London Information Centre, St Paul's Churchyard, EC4, ☎: 01-260 1456/7/3456.
- the venue or the organiser (including commercial galleries)
- the theatre box office, a ticket agency (20% surcharge)
- Leicester Square Ticket Booth *(open Monday to Saturday, noon to 2pm for matinees and 2.30 to 6.30pm for evening performances)*: 1/2 price theatre tickets (if available) for same day performance (£1 surcharge)
- local public library or town hall for a local event.

Walks. – For information on **guided walking tours** of London consult the London Tourist Board, *The Times* and *What's On* etc.

The **Silver Jubilee Walkway,** created in 1977, covers 10 miles in the heart of London (marked by special markers in the pavement) but can be taken in 7 separate sections. At eight selected points are metal indicators identifying the neighbouring buildings. Maps are available from LTB Information Centres *(35 p)*.

Cycle Hire. – Consult *Time Out* or *Cycling in London* produced by British Tourist Authority.

CONTENTS

KEY

★★★   **Highly recommended**

★★   **Recommended**

★   **Interesting**

■ **Sights described**

⛪ ⚱	Church		Tube station	⊖
■	Statue		Fountain	◎
	Gardens, parks		Motorway, interchange	═══
⸸	Cemetery		Racecourse	🐎
●	Pub		Golf course	⚑
	View		Tennis courts	🎾

SIGHTS AND MAPS IN THE GUIDE

CHELSEA★★ . . . . . Sight or area headings
Royal Hospital★★ . Individual starred sight
CZ . . . . Reference letters on the appropriate general map
45 . . . . Page number of the local map in the guide

CENTRAL LONDON
General map pages 5-8

THE CITY
General map pages 9-12

OUTER LONDON
General map pages 14-15

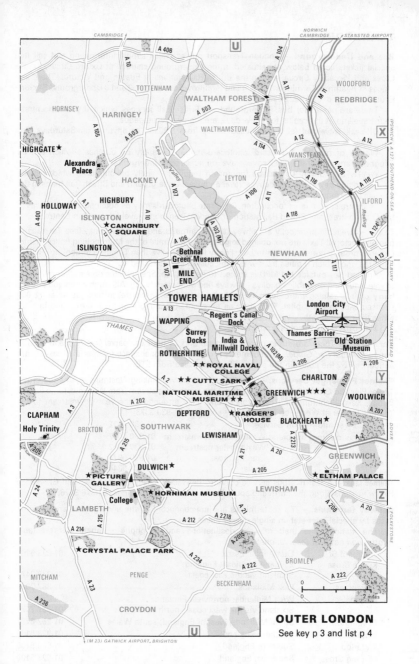

OUTER LONDON

See key p 3 and list p 4

Accommodation. – See *Michelin Greater London*, hotels and restaurants Red Guide; published annually and available from bookshops (an excerpt from the *Michelin Great Britain and Ireland* annual Red Guide). For the stranded there are commercial hotel accommodation agencies at Heathrow and Gatwick and at Victoria Station.

Youth Hostels: there are five hostels in central London:
– Holland House, Holland Park, Kensington W8
– 84 Highgate West Hill, N6
– 4 Wellgarth Road, NW11
– 38 Bolton Gardens, Old Brompton Rd, SW5
– 36 Carter Lane, St Paul's, EC4.

Disabled People. – Facilities are gradually being provided for those in wheelchairs (toilets, lifts in museums, theatres and public buildings). For details see *Access in London,* available from PSHP, 39 Bradley Gardens, W13 8HE *(£4 inc p/p).* Information about arts venues is available from Artsline ☎ 01-388 2227/8.

Information by telephone. – Kidsline – 01-222 8070.
– Weatherline – 01-246 8091.

Lost property. – In the street – enquire at the local police station,
– on trains – enquire at the local station,
– in taxis — contact the Metropolitan Police Lost Property Office, 15 Penton St N1 (written enquiries only),
– on London Regional Transport – enquiries at the Lost Property Office, 200 Baker St, NW1 5RZ, Monday to Friday 9.30 am to 2 pm (no phone calls). Alternatively enquiry forms may be obtained from any LRT bus garage or Station.

TRANSPORT

Bus and Underground. – London Transport offices which supply information and sell the special tickets listed below are situated in the Underground stations at Oxford Circus, King's Cross and Piccadilly Circus, also in the British Rail stations at Euston and Victoria. There are offices at Heathrow Terminals 1, 2, 3, 4 and Heathrow Terminals 1, 2 and 3 Underground Station. Enquiries by phone: 01-222 1234.

There are passes for bus, Underground and British Rail services, which, if you concentrate your travelling in the capital for a few days, are highly advantageous:

Off-peak Travelcard (all Zones) valid 1 day from 9.30am, or anytime on Saturdays and Sundays.

Weekly or monthly **Travelcard** (photocard required – apply on purchase) which can be bought on any day of the week cover travel on buses and Underground trains.

Weekly or monthly **Capitalcard** (photocard required – apply on purchase) which can be bought on any day of the week cover travel on buses, Underground and British Rail trains in the Greater London area.

There are special fares for children. Child-rate photocards may be obtained at Post Offices in the London area, any British Rail station or London Transport Travel Information Centre.

Taxis. – Available principally at railway termini, airports and on a few ranks (see Taxicabs in phone directory). Taxis are not obliged to go beyond the limits of the Metropolitan Police District (an area broadly corresponding to but slightly less extensive than Greater London) nor, within that area, more than 6 miles from where the customer was picked up.

Any journey outside the MPD is subject to negotiation. Special rates obtain after midnight, at weekends and on public holidays – always find out before hiring. Although when you are in a hurry or it is raining there seem to be no taxis for hire, there are, in fact, just over 12 000 licensed cabs in the capital. They have an excellent steering lock and can turn round in 1 1/2 times their own length.

Mini-cabs – see telephone directories.

Car parks. – There are street meters, daytime and 24 hour car parks *(see Michelin Greater London annual Red Guide)*. Arrangements providing additional space for special occasions are announced by the police in the press; information also from LTB.

Thames Passenger Services. – Daily throughout the year linking Westminster, Charing Cross, Tower Pier and Greenwich; daily throughout the summer upstream from Westminster to Putney Bridge, Kew, Richmond and Hampton Ct and daily throughout the year downstream to the Thames Barrier at Woolwich (no landing – enquiries 01-930 3373).

LTB: River Information Service:		01-730 4812
Information from the piers:	Westminster downstream	01-930 4097
	Westminster upstream	01-930 2062
	Charing Cross	01-930 0971
	Tower	01-488 0344

Thames Line. – A fast riverbus service operates between Chelsea Harbour Pier and Greenwich Pier with stops along the north and south banks of the river. Enquiries: 01-376 3676.

Railway terminals. – The six terminals are interconnected by the underground and in some cases by special inter-station single decker buses.

The stations and their relevant destinations and telephone numbers *(for timetable information* not seat reservations) are:

Liverpool St	East Anglia, Essex	01-928 5100
King's Cross	East and northeast England; Scotland via the east coast	01-278 2477
St Pancras	East Midlands	01-387 7070
Euston	West Midlands: northwest England; Scotland via the west coast; north Wales	01-387 7070
Paddington	South Midlands, west of England; south Wales	01-262 6767
Victoria	Southern England	01-928 5100
Waterloo	Southern England	01-928 5100
Charing Cross	Southeast England	01-928 5100

Information and tickets can also be obtained from British Rail Travel Service offices at:

407 Oxford St, W1;　　　　　　　　　　Bank Buildings, 87 King William St, EC4;

12 Lower Regent St, SW1;　　　　　　　Terminals 1, 2, 3, 4 Heathrow Airport.

14 Kingsgate Parade, Victoria St, SW1;

Airports. – London is served by three airports:

London City Airport. – Access by car by A13 and A1011 (car park at airport); by train from Stratford to Silvertown; by riverbus hourly from Charing Cross, Swan Lane to London City Airport pier and courtesy bus from the pier to the terminal building.

Heathrow, Middlesex. – Access by car by M4 or A4 (car parks at airport); by underground (Piccadilly Line) to Heathrow; by airbus: Route A1 every 20 mins from Victoria Station, stopping at Hyde Park Corner and Cromwell Road (Hotel Forum), 60 mins; Route A2 every 30 mins from Euston Station, stopping at Russell Sq, Bloomsbury (Bonnington Hotel), Marble Arch, Bayswater Rd, Lancaster Gate Station, Queensway Station, Notting Hill Gate and Holland Park Ave (Kensington Hilton Hotel), 80 mins.

Gatwick, Crawley, W Sussex. – Access by car by A23 (car parks at airport) and by train from Victoria.

Passenger Immunisation Centres: British Airways, 75 Regent St. Phone in advance: 01-439 9584/5.

For **reservations, tickets** and **flight enquiries** contact the individual airlines.

British Airways: Flight Enquiries, Heathrow 01-759 2525, Gatwick 0293 518033.
　　　　　　　Reservations 01-897 4000

NB: *The stations, London Regional Transport, the airports are equipped with automatic incoming storage telephone call systems – hang on, therefore, and your turn will come!*

ENTERTAINMENT

Theatres, Concerts. – For programmes and times of performances, see Sunday, daily and evening papers and *What's On*. Notices include phone nos. *See map below for situation.*

Cinemas: for programmes and times see evening and other papers and *What's On*. Notices include phone nos and addresses.

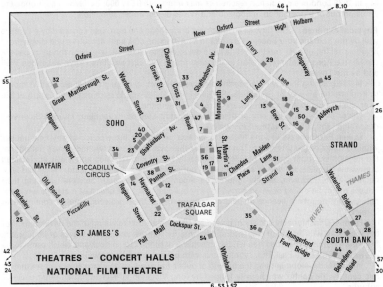

THEATRES – CONCERT HALLS
NATIONAL FILM THEATRE

Shopping. – Magnitude of turnover and competition serve the central London shopper in providing a fantastic number of small specialist shops where he or she may hunt for the exotic, the particular, the luxurious version of an everyday article, handmade still by craftsmen. At the other extreme there are big multiple stores with full ranges of a diversity of branded goods from whitewood furniture to raincoats, from tin mugs to fine glass and china and also with their own lines, made up in their own workrooms or imported especially from abroad, whether couture clothes or carved rose quartz figurines.

The big stores, with prices as disparate as their situations, are located along Oxford St, in Regent St, at Piccadilly Circus, in Bond St, Sloane Sq and King's Rd and at Knightsbridge, with furniture also at the north end of Tottenham Ct Rd.

Don't forget the London Silver Vaults *(qv)* in Chancery Lane.

The small shops traditionally and still radiate from Bond St. They extend north across Oxford St into Wigmore St and Marylebone High St (St Christopher's Place includes within its 50 yds, a picture dealer, a military memorabilia shop and an antiquarian), east to Regent St, particularly along Brook (Halcyon Days) and Maddox Sts, and west to Park Lane across the parallel Davies, Duke, Audley and Park Sts, intersected by Mount St. Still in the same quarter are South Molton St, a pedestrian precinct with summer pavement cafés, and Burlington Arcade with glittering windows beneath rose coloured arches.

In St James's, silk shirts, bespoke hats and shoes, tobacconists, gunsmiths, are as numerous as the furniture and fine art shops; in Belgravia (Motcomb St and Halkin Arcade) the emphasis is more on antiques. Beyond are the outer groups, particularly of antique shops, in Hampstead, Kensington (Church St), the west end of King's Rd, in Camden Passage. Every group, whether in one of the outer villages or at the centre, is widely assorted so that antique dealers neighbour silver shops, porcelain shops, print and secondhand bookshops and the would-be purchaser may have far to travel. In other cases the shops will be within walking distance as are the four major antiquarian booksellers, Quaritch (Lower John St), Francis Edwards (Marylebone High St), Sotheran (Sackville St) and Maggs (Berkeley Sq). There is probably a shop for everything, whether one requires cooking utensils, David Mellor (Sloane Sq), Divertimenti (Marylebone Lane), Christmas presents (General Trading Co, Sloane St) an umbrella (from that perfect example of Victorian shop design, James Smith & Sons, New Oxford St), Christmas cards (at the museums and HMSO, 49 High Holborn, where there are also posters, maps and monographs), books and booklets on special areas and aspects of London (Tourist Information Centre bookshop, Victoria Station forecourt), a special pasta (Parmigiani, Frith St), brass fittings (Beardmore, Percy St)...

GROWTH OF THE CAPITAL

A capital grows in three ways: visibly in the increase in its population and in its physical expanse and cumulatively through the continuous activities of its inhabitants which make it the historical centre of the country.

Population. – There may have been as many as 25 – 30 000 souls by the time the king, courts of law and parliament were established at Westminster, the City was a rich port and 12-13C London had become the **capital** of the kingdom.

It is from Tudor times that numbers begin to grow apace: in 1558, at the death of Mary Tudor, the London population was 100 000; at the death of Elizabeth in 1603, 200 000 out of a total for England and Wales of approximately 4 million. (The three other biggest towns of the period, York, capital of the north, Norwich, centre of the wool trade and Bristol, a flourishing mercantile and inland port, numbered 20 000 each.)

In 1700 there were 670 000 people living in London; in 1801 the first census showed there to be 1 100 000 out of a population of just under 9 million in England and Wales together. By the year of the Great Exhibition it was 2 700 000 and in the next 50 years it more than doubled to 6 600 000 (1901) owing to the influx from the provinces to industry and commerce in the capital and to improved housing.

In 1939 London's population reached its maximum with 8 610 000: by 1975 it had dropped to 7 million out of a population in England and Wales of just under 50 million.

Physical expanse. – The City, as an important bridgehead and port, was encircled by a defence wall by the Romans after Boadicea's attack in 61 AD; in the dark ages assaults came chiefly from invaders sailing upriver and the wall fell into decay only to be rebuilt largely on the same base in the Middle Ages with an extension to the west (north and east sections visible at London Wall and by the Tower).

In 1643, during the Civil War, earthworks were thrown up ringing the capital from Wapping to Rotherhithe by way of Spitalfieds, St Giles-in-the-Fields and Westminster and, south of the river, circling Lambeth and Southwark to reach Rotherhithe.

Never at any time did any of these barriers stop London expanding: in 1598 Stow was describing "the suburbs without the walls".

Queen Elizabeth passed the first of many acts prohibiting the erection of any new houses within 3 miles of the City gates. The reason for the royal alarm was twofold: it was feared that the newcomers, poor country people, might easily be led into rebellion and it was appreciated that water supplies, as well as sewerage and burial grounds, were inadequate. These and later decrees were, however, largely ignored or circumvented. The poor builders, knowing their houses might be pulled down, resorted to jerry-building using the cheapest materials while the rich usually bought a licence or paid compensation for their projects. London continued to spread.

From 16C fashionable society migrated steadily westwards resulting in the development of the West End with its life of elegance and leisure. By contrast successive waves of immigrants from both home and abroad had tended to settle east of the City in dockland which came to be known by 19C as the East End, synonymous with poverty and overcrowding.

Industrial development and the growth of public transport in the Victorian era meant that by this century the centre was heavily fringed by long Victorian streets within an outer circle of suburbs.

Only in 1930s was a visionary solution proposed and enacted (1938): a **Green Belt,** in itself 840 sq miles in area, was designated to run through the home counties encircling London at a radius of between 20 and 30 miles.

Although the belt does not completely contain the metropolitan sprawl – in some sections it has disappeared completely and exceptional buildings have been erected on it in others – yet it has had some success in defining the limits of London.

The historical centre. – In the second half of 20C the Port of London shifted down river to Tilbury; for the first time in 2 000 years cargo ships are no longer a common sight in the Pool, moored in midstream or tied up along the banks or in 19C docks.

Ships began to sail out of the estuary in 5C BC, to arrive and drop anchor, when London, a Celtic derived name, was a riparian settlement congregated at the river's first ford, a place where the gravel subsoil proved suitable on which to build a bridge. They came in greater numbers under the Romans who transformed the village into a major town, erecting in it some of their largest buildings north of the Alps and traversing the river with a permanent stone bridge. Most important of all the Romans made it the hub of their road system, through which legionaries and merchandise alike, after coming ashore in the auxiliary Kentish and south coast ports or in London itself, passed on the way to Verulamium (St Albans), the early capital, or Camulodonum (Colchester), the later capital, and to the cities and settlements of the north.

In the Dark Ages, the time of Germanic and Danish invasions, of siege and fire, of **Alfred** briefly uniting the kingdom and constituting London a major city, of the unsuccessful attempt to establish the metropolitan see in London, of no mention for scores of pages in the *Anglo-Saxon Chronicle* – in the face of oblivion, trade went on; London in 8C was the "mart of many nations by land and sea".

The **City** was an ordered and rich community: in 1016 the gemut or assembly of London elected Edmund Ironside as king. When he died his successor, Canute, exacted tribute and the citizens rendered £10 500 – an eighth of the total paid by the whole of England. Edward the Confessor was also elected king by the people of London but once named he did not remain in the City; he went upstream to **Westminster,** an area quite apart, to rebuild the abbey, build a royal palace and thus lay the foundation for London's double centre – a feature unique to London in all the world's capital cities.

Jealous of its independence the City obtained **charters** affording it privileged status from William I, Henry I and John. It elected its own mayor, held its own courts of law; it lent money to kings to wage war abroad but did not get involved. It traded. In the age of exploration it raised loans, it fitted out and financed merchant venturers. Queen Elizabeth knighted her navigators but it was the City which raised the funds for Drake, Frobisher and Hawkins to sail the Spanish Main, singe the King of Spain's beard and defeat the Armada, for Raleigh to sail to Virginia. The aim of the adventurers was to make their fortune, of the City to establish trading posts, of parliament, in later times, to found colonies. The results were quite unforeseeable: in 1600 Queen Elizabeth, under a charter of incorporation, granted a monopoly of trade between England and India to a new undertaking, the **East India Company;** by 18C the larger part of India was being ruled by the company; in mid 19C, after the Mutiny (1858), it passed to the crown. In 1670 the Hudson Bay Company was founded with a monopoly in the fur trade with the Red Indians (monopoly ended 1859). All company head offices were in the City.

In England the medieval wool trade had given way to a trade in cloth; the agricultural life of centuries, began, in mid 18C, with ever increasing momentum, to be transformed into the most intensely industrialised economy ever known.

As the spinning wheel and loom in the cottager's room gave place to the flying shuttle (1733), the spinning jenny, Arkwright's spinning frame, Crompton's mule and Cartwright's power loom, the population moved into towns to work in factories and textiles and other products poured out on to the home and export markets.

The **roads,** never remade since the departure of the Romans in 4C, were improved by the establishment of Turnpike Trusts, which by mid 19C had constructed 20 000 miles of good turnpike roads and nearly 8 000 toll gates and bars (including one at Marble Arch, another at Hyde Park Corner and one still remaining at Dulwich). Canals were excavated and in 1825 the first **railway** was opened.

All roads (and railways), literally and metaphorically, led to London.

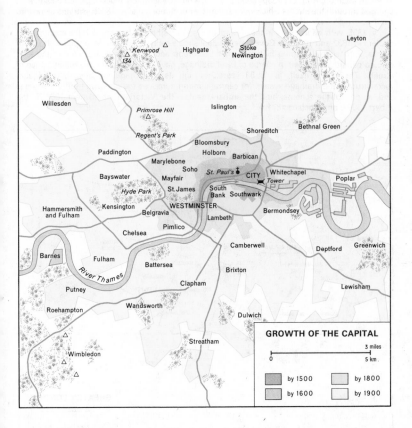

GROWTH OF THE CAPITAL

3 miles
0
5 km

by 1500 — by 1800
by 1600 — by 1900

The City at no time encroached on Westminster and, with a few notable exceptions, citizens held no office under the crown or parliament. Many of the merchants and, as time went on, insurance brokers and bankers who took over more and more from the actual commodity dealers, particularly in earlier times, were related to landed families – Richard Whittington, the younger son of a Gloucestershire squire, like many, was sent to seek his fortune in the City. As they made their pile they built houses in the West End and further out, founding new dynasties in their turn.

The **Industrial Revolution** produced a new type of MP after the Reform Bill of 1832, industrial working class with no feudal manorial connection such as had existed for better or worse with earlier landowners. The new members were far apart from the City men but brought new blood to London.

In the second half of 20C the capital is still growing – not in the size of the population, not in extent, but historically. The City and Westminster as ever remain distinct; the villages, coalesced in places to the outward eye, are claimed with individual pride by their inhabitants. Fired, blasted, blitzed as never before the City remained blackened but upright in 1945 – and, as before, was rebuilt. As in previous periods new museums, concert halls, houses have been built; new schools and new amenities in tune with the age.

It is, of course, Londoners and adopted Londoners who make "London town" – refugees, 14-17C Flemish and French Huguenots, 20C Chileans, kings and princes, political theorists from Marx and Engels to the man now sitting in K12 in the British Museum (or British Library) Reading room, philosophers such as Voltaire, painters such as Holbein, capital citizens of genius, architects, painters, writers, musicians, doctors, scientists and lawyers and the nameless millions who, if they are true cockneys, ply their daily trade with wit and humour.

GOVERNMENT OF THE CAPITAL

The City has been administered since the early Middle Ages by the Corporation but after the Dissolution Westminster and Southwark were given into the care of newly appointed parish vestries. These differed in character and probity, their powers overlapped and were insufficient to control, even where they thought it necessary, such men as the speculators jerrybuilding in the centre of London and the outskirts of the City, who erected tall houses with inadequate sanitation which thus polluted the water supplies and who let off each room to one or often several families. Hogarth illustrated the scene in 18C, Mayhew and Dickens described it in the press in 19C.

Conditions, of course, were not uniform: the "good life" was being led with considerable elegance in St James's and Whitehall, in Mayfair, St Marylebone, Knightsbridge, Kensington and further west.

By the late 17C the river was ceasing to be the capital's main highway and as the volume of traffic increased the roads in all areas became appallingly congested: where once there had been only walkers, riders, costermongers with their barrows and an occasional coach, there appeared in 17C sedan chairs and hackney carriages and in 18 and 19C curricles and gigs, phaetons, barouches and landaus, broughams and hansom cabs (7020 were plying for hire in 1886). In addition, from the 1830s company horse buses alternately blocked or, in fierce rivalry, charged through the streets which were still further encumbered after 1870s as trams came into service.

In 1855, with reform long in the air and spurred or frightened by considerable epidemics of cholera in 1832 and 1848, the Government established a central body, the Metropolitan Board of Works, with special responsibility for main sewerage and to act as coordinator of the now elected parish vestries left in charge of local drainage, paving, lighting, and the maintenance of streets. The board itself, in its 33 years, through its chief engineer, Joseph Bazalgette, reconstructed the drainage system for central London, removed the outflows from the Thames and, as part of the scheme, built the embankments – the (Victoria) Embankment 1864-70, the Albert 1866-9 and Chelsea 1871-4.

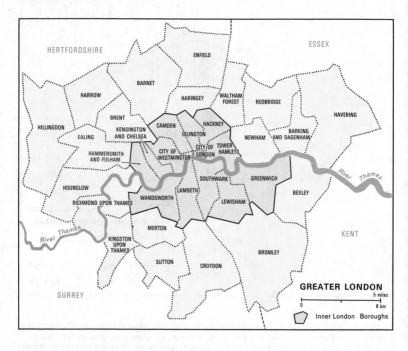

In 1888 the County of London was created with an area equivalent to the present 12 inner London boroughs with the LCC as the county authority. In 1965, in the newly defined area of Greater London, the LCC was superseded by the GLC, a regional authority. Greater London comprised the former County of London and former local authority areas surrounding London, in all a total of 610 square miles, with a population of about 6.7 million.

Following the 1983 general election the government was committed to reforming the structure of local government and the necessary legislation was passed for the abolition of the GLC and other metropolitan councils on 1 April 1986. The GLC's functions have devolved largely to the borough councils. New statutory bodies have been created to take over control of local services such as transport, fire, drainage, waste disposal and flood control to be provided on a wider basis. The London Residuary Body is charged with the task of winding up the GLC's affairs within five years. A London Consultative Committee of all the boroughs has been set up to discuss and advise on strategic planning matters affecting more than one borough. The London Boroughs Grants Scheme to which all participating boroughs pay a levy on population is headed by a Committee comprising one representative from each borough. The amounts raised are allocated as grants to voluntary organizations previously funded by the GLC. A new trust will be set up to give grants to charities. The research and intelligence unit which provides essential information on every aspect of London life and the scientific services have been retained. The Greater London Enterprise Board which invests in small businesses is now funded by twelve boroughs.

London's services and amenities

The origin and extent of some of the capital's major facilities are as follows:

Rates. – Rates were first exacted from householders under a statute of 1601, a measure instituted to provide a dole for vagrants and the destitute after the Dissolution of the monasteries had removed the traditional almoners! For centuries the major part of the levy was employed for the relief of the poor – in 1813 out of £8 1/2 million raised in local taxation throughout the country, £7 million went in relief and £1 1/2 million only on all other local necessities.

The statutory bodies' finance today derives from a proportion of the rates collected locally through the borough councils and City Corporation, payments for services and specific government grants and subsidies. The Block Grant received from the government is passed to the borough councils and to the statutory bodies.

Water. – The Thames Water Authority, successor to, among other bodies, the Metropolitan Water Board (1903), was constituted in 1974; it levies its own rate and is responsible for the management of the Thames throughout its length and for London's water supply, sewage disposal and pollution control.

Medieval supplies came from the Thames itself, its tributaries and from wells – Clerkenwell, Sadler's Wells, Muswell Hill; after 1285 conduits of leather or hollow tree trunks were provided by the City fathers to bring water from the Tyburn, Westbourne and Lea to lead cisterns in the City where it was collected by householders and by water carriers who later formed a guild; there were three conduit heads in Cheapside (qv).

During the next 300 years these provisions were augmented by private enterprise. Six tidal water wheels were licensed under the northern arches of London Bridge between 1582 and 1822; the first pump driven by horses was set up in Upper Thames St in 1594. The most elaborate undertaking, however, was the cutting of the New River (qv) from 1609 to 1613.

The industrial revolution brought steam pumping (p 112), first tried unsuccessfully in 1712 but gradually introduced from 1750 together with cast iron pipes since wooden mains could not sustain the higher pumping pressures. The widespread introduction of the water closet after 1820 resulted in sewage being discharged into the streams and rivers, polluting the water supply and bringing epidemics of typhoid and cholera. In 1858 the Thames was so foul that sheets soaked in disinfectant were hung at the windows of Parliament to keep out the stench.

Filtration (1829), the requirement to draw water from the non-tidal river above Teddington (1856) and chlorination (1916) have made London's water safe to drink. Reservoirs also played a part, by allowing the sediment in river water to settle, but they chiefly serve as storage capacity to meet fluctuations in supply and demand. Datchet (8 300 million gallons), Staines, Chingford and Walthamstow among others supply London with 436 million gallons of water daily –double in summer if necessary – roughly the volume of the Serpentine.

Pollution of the tideway has now greatly reduced and many fish are descending the stream and re-entering the estuary; so far over 100 species have been identified. Salmon, which were once so cheap and plentiful that people complained of eating them daily, have now returned in quantity after an absence of more than 150 years and new licences are being issued for eel fishing. The Thames Water Authority is also responsible for the Thames barrier (qv) and piers.

The Streets: paving, lighting, numbering. – The so-called Improvement Acts of 1762 were well named in that they began the transformation of every street in the capital; many were in a worse than medieval condition, while others, although fine and handsome, were rough surfaced and ill-lit.

Paving became the responsibility of vestries who, though often corrupt, found it in their interests to relay the streets which previously had been in the hands of individual householders each paving his frontage, or not, with stone or rubble at a level convenient to his house without regard to the general course.

The vestries abolished the kennels or deep central drains replacing them with shallow underground sewers and lateral gutters; they provided scavengers and sweepers to clear the streets of night soil and garbage which were still thrown out of doors.

Houses in 17C were being built of brick and tile and were no longer advanced so bridging narrow alleys with their upper storeys; new streets were wider. Legislation called for the removal of balconies and projections, of coal shoots and lean-tos at pavement level and of house, inn and trade signs, to let in light and air.

The small stagnant alleys and courts, however, were not reformed, slaughterhouses remained adjoining private dwellings, rookeries continued and the problems of the overcrowded burial yards remained with "poor's holes" or open pits, earthed over only when full in non-epidemic as well as plague years.

Progress in all but the worst areas was nevertheless marked: the streets were cleaner, the squares were cleared of accumulated refuse and were enclosed and planted.

House numbering and street lighting were instituted under the same 1762 acts. Since 1416 householders had been required to burn a candle nightly outside their doors, since 1716 those in the City had been ordered to burn lights on the 18 dark nights of each winter moon, but snuffers and lampholders outside the 18C houses of St James's and Mayfair are a reminder of how, in the circumstances, every man carried his own flaming torch, and link boys walked ahead of sedans and carriages.

Revolution began in 1738 when the vestries installed in such main thoroughfares as Oxford St, 15 000 oil fed lamps with cotton wicks which burned from sunset to sunrise. In 1807 there was a second advance when after a preliminary demonstration outside Carlton House, 13 gas lamp-posts were set up in Pall Mall. Seventy years later, in 1878, electricity had arrived and the first major street lighting project was inaugurated with the illumination of the Embankment.

Today, the inner boroughs are responsible for 895 miles of metropolitan thoroughfares and the outer boroughs for 6 800 miles of local roads. They liaise with the Departments of Transport and Environment regarding traffic and road planning through the Joint Planning Committee.

The corollary to the 1762 Improvement Acts has come within the last 35 years with the passage of the Clean Air Acts (1956, 1962) controlling the burning of coal in furnaces and open grates, so banishing for ever the notorious London pea-soup fogs.

Housing. – Out of a total of 2.7 million houses and flats in the Greater London area, rather more than 1.7 million are privately owned, some 820 000 belong to the boroughs. The 'new town' of Thamesmead *(qv)* initiated by the GLC is now run by a private Community Trust.

Historical note. – Municipal housing is a modern phenomenon: from the late Middle Ages the City Companies and a few endowed charities provided almshouses for a small number of old employees but working citizens lodged in their own houses or rented what they could – in the case of the very poor a room or part of a room; many lived on the streets, orphan children especially sleeping and finding shelter where they could.

The first major housing scheme was financed by the American philanthropist, George Peabody who in 1864 had constructed in Commercial St, Spitalfields, a massive 5 storey building of 3 room flats with running water, sanitation and laundry facilities available at 5s a week. As twenty-nine other blocks were erected, charitable bodies began to follow suit. Octavia Hill, in 1845, with financial help from Ruskin and later from others, began a different type of enterprise; on a small scale she reconstituted run down houses and let them at modest rents.

Slum clearance, which began in the Victorian era with the driving of new roads to ease traffic congestion: Victoria St, Northumberland Ave, Trafalgar Sq, Shaftesbury Ave, Charing Cross Rd, New Oxford St, Queen Victoria St and Southwark St, was continued by LCC clearances in 1920-30, by war time bomb damage and by large-scale demolition of terrace housing in 1960s for the construction of tower blocks. Current planning policy favours renovation of existing properties or lowrise high-density developments.

Housing associations, first founded in 1253, have provided specialist rented accommodation since 1964 for the single, elderly and disabled, supplemented since 1974 by central government funds through the Housing Corporation.

The first garden suburbs – Merton Park (1870), Bedford Park (1875), Hampstead Garden Suburb (1906) – offered a variety of houses to let in tree-lined streets.

Fire service. – Frequent fires, a "London inconvenience" as Fitzstephen termed them in 12C, raged unchecked until the Great Fire stirred invention and engines were built which forced a jet of water on burning buildings. From the same calamity fire insurance so increased that companies organised private brigades for the protection of the property which they advertised as covered by means of their own firemarks *(see opposite)*.

By 1833 ten major companies had combined to form the London Fire Brigade but even it was powerless to prevent the total loss of the Houses of Parliament in 1834, the Royal Exchange in 1838, the burning out of the Tower armoury in 1841, and the devastation of three acres of warehouses worth £2 million in Tooley St. Finally in 1866 the government recommended that a Fire Brigade should be established, at public expense, by the Metropolitan Board of Works.

The London Fire Brigade (under the London Fire and Civil Defence Authority) today numbers nearly 7 000 firefighters, based on 114 stations. It has 600 vehicles, 350 of which are specialised appliances for fighting fires and dealing with rescues. The total annual cost (including fire prevention – 50 000 visits...) is £157 million; the number of calls over 158 000.

Police. – Thieves, miscreants and the innocent, footpads and murderers alike were seized by paid informers, thief-takers and hired strong men until the mid 18C; malefactors were brought before so-called "trading justices" and thrown into one of the infamous jails or, if convicted on any one of the then 156 capital offences, were hanged, often at Tyburn where there were, on average, 12 public hangings a month – some 50 000 in all between 1170 and 1783 when the gallows were removed to Newgate.

Reform began in Bow Street under the honest magistracy of the Fieldings, Henry, the novelist, and his younger half-brother John, the Blind Beak, who recruited the first band of six honest men to apprehend villains – the Bow St Runners.

So great was the fear of the institution of a national police body that it was not until 1829 that Sir Robert Peel's bill was passed, founding the Metropolitan Police Force. (The River Police had been formed in 1800.) When the "Peelers" or 'Bobbies' first appeared on the streets they wore navy serge frock coats and top hats to attract as little attention as possible and, as now, were unarmed, except for a discreetly concealed truncheon.

Unlike the Metropolitan Police, who are under the jurisdiction of the Home Secretary, the City Police, founded in the same decade, are a separate body under the Corporation. The combined forces (men and women) number 28 242.

Transport. – Commuting, which began in 1836-8 with the inauguration of the London Bridge – Deptford – Greenwich Railway, increased with every new line laid to a London terminal and took on phenomenal proportions when the connecting Metropolitan Railway (Paddington to Farringdon St) opened in 1863. On its first day the line carried 30 000 passengers and in the first year 9 1/2 million – in open carriages behind steam engines through the tunnels.

London Transport, established in 1933 as a public corporation to co-ordinate and modernise the underground, railway and bus companies then in existence, was from 1970 to 1984 under the overall policy and financial control of the GLC. A new body, the London Regional Transport has been set up and reports to the Secretary of State for Transport. To cater for some 2 000 million journeys made by Londoners and visitors each year, there are 4 100 red buses (80% one man operated) and 4 400 railway carriages.

Education. – A century ago there were in the capital only the schools of ancient foundation such as Westminster (1371) and St Paul's (founded by the Dean, John Colet, in the cathedral churchyard – 1510), charity schools, Sunday schools and a few groups run by the Ragged Schools' Union organised by Lord Shaftesbury in 1844. The government had the right of inspection in 258 of these institutions and in 1854 reported attendance by 57 000 or an estimated 12 1/2 % of the child population.

Change came with the Education Acts of 1870 and 1876 which provided schools and laid upon parents the duty of seeing that their children "received elementary education in reading, writing and arithmetic" – the 3Rs. Responsibility has since devolved on the LCC (1903) and subsequently on the Inner London Education Authority (ILEA) for Inner London (the old LCC area). The outer London boroughs provide education in their own areas.

In 1985-6 the ILEA budget of £1 025 million provided for over 286 000 pupils in 1 057 nursery, primary, secondary and special schools and Sixth Form colleges as well as maintaining 5 polytechnics, 18 further and higher education colleges, 20 adult education institutes and 78 youth centres and various ancillary services.

The Arts. – Support and patronage, as necessary today as in Handel's, Shakespeare's, Dryden's times, are supplied in 20C London by the government through the Arts Council, the City Corporation (Barbican Centre) and the BBC (Promenade Concerts). The Arts Council administers and aids the South Bank concert halls, gallery and theatre besides giving grants to the four symphony orchestras – the London Symphony, London Philharmonic, New Philharmonia and Royal Philharmonic – which, with chamber orchestras, ensembles, academies, quartets and quintets, have made London the music capital of the world. Ballet, opera, museums (the London, in conjunction with the City Corporation) and galleries (Whitechapel and Dulwich) are aided, besides no less appreciated concerts and entertainments in the parks and a host of other undertakings to a total of nearly £6 million a year.

Open Spaces. – At the centre of London and on the west and east boundaries are the Royal Parks and still ringing the capital the age-old commons, some 3 500 acres in extent despite encroachment by peasants, manorial farmers, larger landowners and, in 19C, by land speculators, builders and local authorities constructing roads. Among those of considerable size north of the river are Hackney Marshes (340 acres), Hampstead Heath (208 acres), Wormwood Scrubs (200 acres; reduced by the construction of the prison) and on the south side Wimbledon and Putney Heath (1 200), Clapham (205), Wandsworth (175, again reduced by the prison), Streatham (58), Tooting Bec (218), the last four probably continuous originally and, further east, Peckham Rye (64), Plumstead (104), Woolwich (240) and historic Blackheath (271 acres), a rallying point for Wat Tyler, Jack Cade and the Kentish rebels, where James I introduced golf to England...

Parks are in another category – a countless number are tended by the 32 borough councils and some have more than local interest – Kenwood (English Heritage), Lesnes Abbey Woods (12C ruins, Bexley), Crystal Palace (Bromley), Alexandra Park and Palace (Haringey) and, the latest addition, next to County Hall on the South Bank, Jubilee Gardens (South Bank Board). These and many of the commons and gardens, besides their natural or landscaped features and flowers, have sports facilities – football and cricket pitches, bowling greens, golf courses, tennis and other courts; bands; children's summer zoos and playgrounds.

In 1977 the first ecological park was created out of inner city wasteland, turning it into a renewed natural refuge where urban wild life could thrive, bringing nature to the city dweller for serious study or simple enjoyment.

The City has no room within its square mile for parks but since 1878 has acquired superb tracts of land "for the recreation and enjoyment of the public": Epping Forest (6 000 acres), Burnham Beeches (504 acres), Coulsdon Commons (430),

Victoria Embankment bench.

Highgate Wood (70), Queen's Park, Kilburn (30), West Ham Park (77) and Spring Park and West Wickham, Kent (76). The Corporation has converted Bunhill Fields into a garden, maintains a bowling green at Finsbury Circus, has created gardens and courts in churchyards (Postman's Park by St Botolph's) and in the shells of blitzed and deconsecrated churches – in all 142 patches of green with over 2 000 trees. There are "open spaces" in the City not two yards square, pavements charged with modern statuary and summer window boxes bursting with colour. Such an abundance of open spaces makes London the most luxuriantly green capital in the world, much appreciated by inhabitants and visitors.

Iron street furniture. – In 19C design and iron casting complemented each other highly successfully in the production of street furniture, notably the Egyptian inspired bench ends along the Embankment by Cleopatra's Needle, the cannon barrel and ball bollards marking among other places the Clink in Southwark, the pair of George III lampposts in Marlborough Rd, St James's and the beautiful dolphin lamp standards of 1870 which line the Albert Embankment from Westminster Bridge.

Also to be noted, although of earlier date and of wrought not cast metal, are the gold crowned bracket lanterns at St James's Palace.

Pillar boxes, invented by Anthony Trollope, are a subject apart. The first to be erected in London, fifteen years after the introduction of the penny post in 1840, were in Fleet St, the Strand, Pall Mall, Piccadilly, Grosvenor Place and Rutland Gate; they were rectangular with a solid round top crowning the pyramid roof. Designs, hexagonal, circular, fluted, conical and flat roofed have followed, crowned and plain, most emblazoned with the royal cipher. Hexagonal boxes (1866-79) can still be

Dolphin lamppost.

seen in London today, also some of the 1880s "anonymous" series when the Post Office forgot to put its name on the box! They were first painted red in 1874.

Firemarks date from 18-19C when they were issued by insurance companies to policy holders – the early ones are numbered – as tokens of identification for the fire brigades, receipt and advertisement. Among the 150 companies which issued tin, copper and cast iron marks were the Sun Fire Office (f 1710), Hand-in-Hand (f 1696), Royal Exchange Assurance (f 1720).

CAPITAL CITIZENS AND THEIR PURSUITS

ARCHITECTS AND ARCHITECTURE

Only from 17C do the names of architects become known – before the only signatures to endure appear in the idiosyncratic fashioning of walls or columns, in the grace of rounded or pointed arches... highly distinctive in the case of Master William, Henry III's chief mason and builder of large areas of Westminster Abbey and of Robert Vertue, master mason to Henry VII and builder of his chapel.

The bare sequence of styles followed by the early constructors and later designers, as still exemplified in London churches dates back 1 100 years.

ECCLESIASTICAL ARCHITECTURE

Norman. – Although found in parts of Westminster Abbey as rebuilt by Edward the Confessor and therefore preceding the arrival of William, Duke of Normandy, Norman is now most beautifully extant in St Bartholomew the Great and in St John's Chapel in the White Tower.

Gothic. – Gothic arrived in England from the continent in the 12C and remained the predominant style for 400 years, the centuries being marked by three distinct phases: **Early English** in 13C, when the original style took on an English idiom; **Decorated,** in late 13-14C, notable for the richness and variety of design of the geometrical and later, curvilinear, tracery in ever widening windows – as in Westminster Abbey but most successfully in cathedrals such as Lincoln; and **Perpendicular,** which for 50 years overlapped the previous style and inspired architects, on occasion, to abandon the quadrangular for the polygonal, so as to give greater visual play to the windows as in Westminster Abbey Chapter House. The style continued to evolve with increased emphasis on the vertical line, outside in ever taller spires, flying buttresses and finials and inside as clusters of attached columns sweeping to overhead ribbed vaulting. Surfaces were divided into tiers of panels, blind and cusp arched on walls, framed by mullions and transomes in windows; the vaulting was lierne and tierceron ribbed before being supplanted by fan vaulting, the hallmark of Late Perpendicular and of which there are three great examples in southeast England: St George's Chapel, Windsor (1474 crossing and aisles), King's College, Cambridge (1446, 1508-15) and Henry VII Chapel (1503-19).

By 16C the capital contained Old St Paul's Cathedral (rebuilt in 12C-14C Gothic), Westminster Abbey, hundreds of parish churches, particularly in the City, and former conventual churches such as St Helen's Bishopsgate and St Bartholomew the Great which had been allowed to continue after the Dissolution of the religious houses. Ecclesiastical building then came to a halt.

One hundred and fifty years later it was re-instituted on a scale never attained before or since. The Great Fire had destroyed four fifths of the City, St Paul's and nearly 180 churches. In the next 45 years Wren rebuilt the Cathedral and 51 of the churches.

Renaissance. – Although the style never came to England except in decoration, Wren might be considered a Renaissance man who took into his architectural embrace ideas from Italy, France and the Netherlands, combining designs inspired by the ancient Roman architect, Vitruvius, with those of his own time, to produce, for example, in St Paul's, a classical dome and Baroque west towers.

Classical. – The reaction to Wren's last decorated, Baroque, period was a return to the Classical as seen in Hawksmoor's Christchurch, Spitalfields, St Anne's, Limehouse, St George's, Bloomsbury. The principles remained but by the late Georgian period had begun to be freely adapted as in John Nash's design for All Souls (1822-4).

19C. – This period also produced a wave of church building to serve the new suburbs. A profound respect for the past, coupled with painstaking erudition, produced the neo-Gothic style – Perpendicular spires spiked the sky, every element was accurately and skillfully included in the detailed designs of Gilbert Scott and Augustus Pugin – only inspiration was lacking as it was also in the neo-Norman, neo-Early Christian and neo-Italian Romanesque of the mid century.

20C. – Not until the 1920s did Edward Maufe make the break with the neo-Gothic tradition and begin the line of thought which has produced the new cathedrals outside London (Coventry, Guildford, Liverpool RC, Bristol RC) and the rebuilt or new churches in the capital such as St Columba's, Pont Street, St John's, Peckham, the churches of the Annunciation and Resurrection, Beckenham...

SECULAR ARCHITECTURE

It begins boldly with the White Tower by Norman William and continues with Westminster Hall, constructed by his son, William Rufus, and given its great hammerbeam roof by Richard II, then divides into two categories: the royal, official and public domain and that of the private house, in and out of town.

Construction materials were stone, quarried first in Kent or imported from Normandy and later brought from Portland (St Paul's in 17C was the first building to be constructed in London of Portland stone) and Yorkshire (Houses of Parliament), brick (from local fields in Kensington and Islington) and timber. Roofs in the City were for the most part thatched until 15-16C and were only uniformly tiled or slated after the Fire.

Tudor and Jacobean Gothic. – In the public domain the greatest examples (despite later additions) are St James's Palace and Hampton Court; both have archetypal gateways, but the latter also displays decorative chimney stacks and internal courts as well as a great hall with a hammerbeam roof such as can be seen in the Middle Temple, the Charterhouse and at Eltham.

17 and 18C, Early Classicism or Palladianism, Classical Baroque and the Classical Revival. – The long period is characterised by the architecture of Inigo Jones, Wren, his followers Hawksmoor and Vanbrugh (whose principal works, however, were respectively at Oxford and Cambridge, Blenheim and Castle Howard), George Dance Senior and finally Sir William Chambers. Their monuments include the Palladian inspired Queen's House at Greenwich and Banqueting House, Whitehall (Jones), the Royal Naval College, Greenwich (Wren, Hawksmoor and Vanbrugh), the Royal Hospital, Chelsea, Hampton Court and Kensington Palace (Wren), the Mansion House (Dance), Somerset House and, in lighter vein, the Pagoda at Kew (Chambers).

Late 18, early 19C or late Georgian-Regency. – The period which should have been marked by Henry Holland's Carlton House and Sir John Soane's Bank of England and other central London buildings, is now represented only by lesser buildings: Nash's Haymarket Theatre, the garden front of Buckingham Palace, Decimus Burton's screen at Hyde Park Corner, the Athenaeum, the domed building of University College by William Wilkins...

1830-1911, Victorian and Edwardian. – The public buildings of the period display a wide variety of materials, techniques and styles; it was a period of prosperity when expense was not spared, particularly in ornament. The dominant styles were Classical and Gothic but architects often combined elements from different styles. Brick in various colours was as popular as stone with terracotta and glazed tiles employed primarily for ornament. Iron frame construction began to be used not only for railway stations and glass houses. The period produced such contrasting buildings as the Classical British Museum (1804-48) by Sir Robert Smirke, the Gothic Houses of Parliament (1836-65) by Sir Charles Barry and Augustus Pugin, the Crystal Palace (1851) by Joseph Paxton, the Foreign Office (1873), a cinquecento palazzo by Gilbert Scott, a mixture of Baroque and Scottish baronial for New Scotland Yard (1871) by Richard Norman Shaw, the Baroque Central Hall, Westminster (1905-11) by Lanchester and Rickards and County Hall (1908-31) by Ralph Knott.

The astonishing complex of museums built in South Kensington with funds arising from the 1851 Exhibition includes the Natural History Museum (1873-80) by Alfred Waterhouse and the Victoria and Albert Museum (1909) by Sir Aston Webb.

The Modern Period. – The austere lines of post-war architecture, which too often result in monotonous office blocks, have also produced more dramatic effect in the BBC (1929-31) by Val Myer, Simpsons Piccadilly (1935) by Emberton, Peter Jones, Sloane Square (1935-6) by Slater & Moberly, the Royal College of Art, Kensington (1961-2) by Casson & Cadbury-Brown, the South Bank and Barbican Arts Centres and Lloyd's building (1986) in the City by R. Rogers.

English houses have always had a remarkable beauty and sense of ease whether in town or country, whether mansion, terrace house or cottage. It is a category in which named and unnamed architects alike have delighted.

Tudor and Jacobean. – Staple Inn, Holborn, comprises a short range of half-timbered houses with advanced upper floors beneath pointed gables such as one sees in old prints. Although late 16C, they are among the capital's oldest domestic buildings, fire having swept the City, Westminster and Southwark so often that only street courses, not the houses that lined them, remain. Other single houses of the period are no 17 Fleet St comprising the gateway to the Inner Temple with Prince Henry's Room beneath a crowning gable, the 16C house over the 13C gateway to St Bartholomew the Great in Little Britain and houses in nearby Cloth Fair. Many pubs also date from Tudor-Jacobean times: the Cheshire Cheese, Old Wine Shades, The Anchor, London Apprentice...

No 7 Adam St.

16C was also the age when City financiers and great merchants, often the younger sons of landed families, in addition to their town mansions (Crosby Hall) began to build themselves country houses of such splendour that they were able to accommodate the queen on her summer tours – Sir Thomas Gresham received Elizabeth I at Osterley Park.

A new style evolved with gables influenced by the Dutch (Kew Palace), the timber frame was displaced by brick and stone, windows enlarged after the Gothic technique, a greater symmetry designed on either side of full height, decorated, porches to afford the Jacobean style of Audley End, Charlton and Hatfield Houses. The interiors were as impressive with panelling, musicians' galleries and screens, long galleries, strapwork decorated plaster ceilings and stairs with carved balustrades and newel posts around a square well.

17-18C Classical, Queen Anne and Georgian. – Palladianism was a long standing influence: Marble Hill House, built in 1720s, was a direct descendant of Inigo Jones' Queen's House of 1616; Chiswick House in 1725-29, the manifestation of inspiration from the same source. Classicism in other hands brought the apparently effortless simplicity that comes from perfection of proportion in individual houses and terraces such as those round Richmond Green, notably Maids of Honour Row (1724), Sion and Montpelier Rows, Twickenham, and in central London, the earlier Bedford Row (1700), Queen Anne's Gate and the streets off Smith Sq.

It was also the period of the early squares of which there remain complete Bedford Sq (1774) and Fitzroy (1793-8). This last was by Robert Adam and is all that remains of his work in the centre apart from single houses in St James's Sq (no 20), in Chandos St and in what was once the Adelphi area. His conversion and decoration of large houses is splendidly displayed at Kenwood, Syon Park and Osterley Park.

Regency House, Wilton Crescent.

1800-1837, Late Georgian, Regency. – The period is typified by two men, John Nash architect, planner and developer, and Thomas Cubitt, quality builder and developer. The interest of both was the private house which Nash realised superbly in the terraces surrounding Regent's Park, in the course, if no longer the buildings, of Regent St and in the monumental Carlton House Terrace, as well as such projects as Buckingham Palace, the Brighton Pavilion and country houses. Working from George Basevi's designs Cubitt erected Belgrave Square, followed by Belgravia (1825), Pelham Crescent (1820-30) and squares, crescents and streets from Putney to Islington.

19C Victorian. – Fashion changed bringing in an eclectic style, inspired by Gothic, in which turrets, gables, pointed windows and stained glass proliferated in the architect-designed estates and the anonymous streets of the expanding suburbs. Its most successful exponent, who succeeded E. W. Godwin at Bedford Park, was Richard Norman Shaw (Lowther Lodge, Kensington 1873, now the Geographical Society, and Swan House, Chelsea 1876).

Contemporary with him were Sir Edwin Lutyens, best known for his country houses, and the members of the Arts and Crafts movement: William Morris, Philip Webb, C. F. A. Voysey and W. R. Lethaby; the latter's influence can be seen in the first municipal housing, Millbank (1899) built by the LCC.

20C Post-war. – Distinctive modern housing is rare: 64-66 Old Church St, Chelsea (c 1934) by Mendelssohn and Chernayeff, the Sun House, Hampstead (1935) by Maxwell Fry, Highpoint One and Two, Highgate (1936-38) by Lubetkin and Tecton. Lillington Gardens, Pimlico (1960s) and Aberdeen Park, Islington (1980s) by Darbourne and Darke show that council housing need not be unattractive.

Belgrave Square.

Victorian House, Cadogan Sq.

PAINTERS AND SCULPTORS

What has become the great tradition of portrait painting in this country was started, and for several centuries was led, by artists who came here from Germany and Holland: Holbein in 16C who painted Sir Thomas More and his family in Chelsea, Henry VIII, his court and the great merchants of the day; van Dyck in 17C who portrayed Charles I, his queen, children and the nobility of the period; Sir Peter Lely, who after Commonwealth personalities, went on to paint those of the Restoration, Charles II, his queen, children, mistresses, the *Hampton Court Beauties* and the *Admirals;* and Sir Godfrey Kneller who at his academy school completed hundreds of political and other figures of the reign of William and Mary and Queen Anne among them the *Windsor Beauties* and the *Kit Cat Club.*

In 18C portraiture was reborn under Sir Joshua Reynolds, who was successfully emulated by Gainsborough and followed by Ramsay and Raeburn, so that there remain splendid likenesses of a great number of the major figures and, in the paintings of Gainsborough, also of the beautiful women. In 19C tradition, competently pursued, was enlivened by the sophistication of Sir Thomas Lawrence and, at the turn of the century, by Sargent's portrayal of Edwardian High Society. The new century brought Augustus John and a new style.

Topographical painting, exemplified by the van de Veldes in 17C in their wonderful seascapes and by Canaletto in his views of London (1746-56), was transformed by Gainsborough into landscape painting and advanced into art by Constable (18-19C).

Outside the mainstream have been Hogarth in 18C, Blake and, in 19C, Turner.

In sculpture the evolution from Gothic tombal effigies to modern abstract form begins with William Torel, citizen and goldsmith of London, who modelled Henry III and Eleanor of Castile (1291-2), and Torrigiano, the visiting (1511-20), early Renaissance, Florentine, who cast the gilt bronze figures of Henry VII, his queen, Elizabeth, and mother, Margaret, Duchess of Richmond. Actual portraiture appears in 17C in the works of, among others, Nicholas Stone (John Donne), the French Huguenot Le Sueur (bronzes of Charles I and James I) and Grinling Gibbons (statues of Charles II and James II), although it is as a wood-carver of genius that he is celebrated.

In 18C, as a Classical style began to appeal to graduates of the Grand Tour, the Flemings, Michael Rysbrack and Peter Scheemakers, the Frenchman, François Roubiliac, the Englishmen John Bacon, John Flaxman and Nollekens executed hundreds of figures, many with considerable strength of character, until the genre became stylised and empty in 19C.

Vigour began to return in 20C, in portraiture and religious sculptures with works by Jacob Epstein, in human, near abstract and abstract themes with Henry Moore, and pure abstract with Barbara Hepworth.

WRITERS

Not all have felt with William Dunbar "London thou art the flower of cities all", nor even with Dr Johnson that "there is in London all that life can afford" but at some point in their careers the great majority of writers have lived in London.

Dramatists have come to play before the necessary audiences – Marlowe, Shakespeare, Ben Jonson, Wycherley, Congreve, Sheridan... Oscar Wilde; others were held by their daily work – Chaucer, Donne, Milton, Fielding, Lamb, Disraeli, T S Eliot; many were journalists and wrote outside the daily stint – Johnson, Addison and Steele, Dickens, Bernard Shaw, Edgar Wallace; others devoted themselves to writing and always lived in London like John Galsworthy. With lyric and other poets the attachment has been more tenuous – Keats came to study medicine, Wordsworth mused on Westminster Bridge but lived by the Lakes, Byron enjoyed high society...

For many it has been the logical next step – Arnold Bennett, J B Priestley this century – although with the development first of radio, then of television and faster travel, the tendency seems to be to move away.

Despite their numbers there has been no regular forum for writers down the years – groups have shifted from the pubs near Blackfriars theatre to those on Bankside and down the Borough High St close to the Globe; to Highgate, to Chelsea and, for a charmed circle, to Bloomsbury; at the turn of the century a band around Oscar Wilde which included Aubrey Beardsley and Max Beerbohm and artists of the day met at the Café Royal. Since many have begun or earned a living as journalists, the first regular haunts were the coffeehouses around Fleet St: Addison and Steele frequented the George and Vulture, then doing greater business in tea, chocolate and coffee than in ale, and subsequently Button's, at both of which they wrote copy for the *Tatler* and *Spectator;* Dr Johnson called at many coffeehouses and taverns but nearest his own house was the Cheshire Cheese, where tradition has it, many of the great conversations took place.

Some have detested the capital, some indulged in a love-hate relationship, some known that for them it was the only place in the world to live; in consequence, English literature from detective stories to diaries, from novels to biographies and histories, is permeated with scenes of London life.

MUSICIANS

The light airs of Tudor England (*Greensleaves* attributed to Henry VIII) developed into rounds, cannons and finally a golden age (1588-1630) of madrigals by Thomas Morley, who published the first collection, John Wilbye, Thomas Weelkes, Orlando Gibbons and Thomas Tompkins. Much instrumental dance music was written with variations to display the performer's virtuosity whereas John Dowland excelled at solo songs accompanied by lute and viol. At the same time Thomas Tallis and William Byrd were composing religious music for the organ and voice in masses and anthems, set to the Latin or English liturgy; only in Elizabeth's reign did a distinctive Anglican style emerge.

In the latter half of 17C composers extended their range with *Te Deums* and secular airs, songs and incidental music for the theatre.

Henry Purcell (1659-96) who despite his brief life dominated his own and subsequent generations produced the first full length opera (*Dido and Aeneas* 1689). Italian opera then became popular and was firmly established with *Rinaldo* (1711) by Handel who had arrived in England that year shortly before the future George I to whom he had been *Kapellmeister* in Hanover.

Handel remained in England until his death in 1759 and in that time poured out operas (satirised by John Gay in *The Beggar's Opera,* 1728), occasional pieces such as the *Fireworks* and *Water Music* and his great succession of oratorios, *Esther, Israel in Egypt, Messiah* (1742 – ms presented to the Foundling Hospital), *Judas Maccabaeus...*

Mozart visited England as a *protégé* of 8 in 1764, Haydn in 1790s when he was the greatest musical figure in Europe. Mendelssohn came early in 19C (although the *Scottish Symphony* and *Midsummer Night's Dream* were not completed until some 20 years later).

(National Portrait Gallery)

Handel.

English music entered an entirely new phase at the end of 19C: it started to become widely popular – through the operettas of Gilbert and Sullivan (1875-99) and through the inauguration, under the conductor, Henry Wood, of the Promenade Concerts (1895). From 1936 as radio became widespread and the BBC began to broadcast the Promenade Concerts, music entered people's lives as never before. The post war period has seen the establishment of permanent centres of opera at Covent Garden and the London Coliseum, the construction of concert halls on the South Bank and at the Barbican and the birth of numerous provincial festivals.

The opening of the 20C also saw the appearance of a host of new British composers: Elgar (*Enigma Variations* 1899, *Dream of Gerontius* 1900), Delius, Vaughan Williams (9 Symphonies, the ballet *Job*) and Gustav Holst (*The Planets*, 1914-16). These were joined in 1920s by Bantock, Bax, Bliss (*Checkmate* 1937) and William Walton (*Belshazzar's Feast* 1931).

After the war they were reinforced by Michael Tippett (*A Child of Our Time* 1941, *The Midsummer Marriage* 1955) and Benjamin Britten who produced a magnificent series of operas – *Peter Grimes* (1945), *Albert Herring, Let's Make an Opera, Billy Budd, Turn of the Screw, Noye's Fludde, Midsummer Night's Dream, The Burning Fiery Furnace, Prodigal Son,* and the operetta *Paul Bunyan.*

CABINET MAKERS AND FURNITURE DESIGNERS

The great transformation in English furniture making occurred in 18C when in place of oak, imported mahogany was used and later tropical satinwood, before a return to native walnut. To these new woods were added, besides carving, enrichments of brass in the form of inlays and gilded mounts, hardwood veneers and marquetry. The great English names of the period were Thomas Chippendale, the leader with a classical sureness of style which he illustrated in *The Gentleman and Cabinet Maker's Director* (1754) and who produced pieces for the great houses being designed or remodelled by Robert Adam and his contemporaries; John Linnell, executor of Adam's designs and his follower who left mirrors and especially chairs of delightful form and William Vile, cabinet maker to George III, who made superbly finished, massive library tables and bureau cabinets.

Carolean: 1680.

George Hepplewhite marked a new departure with a characteristic lightness and delicacy in every piece, achieving this effect not only by slimming down but by delicate inlays and carving. Elegant simplicity attained a peak in his shield back chairs. A thoroughbred's lightness was the hallmark of Thomas Sheraton, who frequently used satinwood for richer pieces besides carving and inlay. Among his favourite subjects are small worktables, beautiful sideboards, secretaires and full height bookcases. He also produced, many "harlequin" or dual purpose items such as library tables containing hidden step ladders...

Chippendale: 1755.   Adam lyre back: 1770.   Hepplewhite: 1775.

In 19C William Morris, whose work was based on craftsmanship, set up his firm of Art Decorators at Merton Abbey supplying not only furniture, mostly designed by Philip Webb, but wallpapers, carpets, curtains and other furnishings.

DOCTORS AND LAWYERS

The population of London which in 1700s was 670 000 had doubled to 1 274 000 by 1820 owing, in no small measure, to a sudden advance in medical knowledge. The 18C brought the decline of practice by apothecaries and barber-surgeons (the Royal College separated from the City guild in 1745) and the establishment, in addition to the two medieval foundations of Bart's and Thomas's, of five new hospitals between 1720-45: Guys, Westminster, St George's, the London and Middlesex, of Thomas Coram's Foundling Hospital and the Lying-in Hospital. Anatomy schools existed in the universities but those who wished to practise came to the capital, to hospitals and private laboratory and dissecting rooms often set up in their own houses for research by men of science in the tradition of Thomas Linacre, physician to Henry VII and VIII and founder of the Royal College of Physicians in his house in 1518. William Harvey, a century later, gave his early lectures to members of the college on the circulation of the blood.

In 18C, William Hunter, after studies in Glasgow and Edinburgh where there had been advanced medical schools since 1505, came south to become the first great teacher of anatomy and later of obstetrics. He was joined in 1748 by his younger brother, the anatomist and physiologist, John Hunter, who was elected surgeon at St George's in 1758. They were succeded by other Scots and Englishmen (Jenner, Gray – *Gray's Anatomy* 1858) in ever widening fields.

By late 16C when *The Comedy of Errors* was staged in Gray's Inn and *Twelfth Night* beneath the hammerbeam roof of Middle Temple Hall, the four Inns of Court and dependent (now defunct) Inns of Chancery had been established for nearly 300 years as the country's great law societies. Many advocates were employed in the courts in Westminster Hall, in the Court of Star Chamber, in the adjoining palace, where, before it became a royal instrument in 17C and was abolished, were heard cases of "riot, rout and misdemeanour" and in White Hall, the future Lords' chamber, where there was a Court of Requests for poor equity. Litigation was a serious business: there were endless disputes on land entitlement and inheritance while actions for slurs and insults, real or imagined, were also a fashionable and obsessive pastime indulged in by many. They offered a lucrative field which was also a good stepping stone to high office: from 16C there were some 2 000 students dining in the halls.

The legal fraternity has always formed a close-knit group with traditional attachment to plays, masques and revels; among their number have been found many of the most learned men in every age: Thomas More, Thomas Cromwell, Francis Bacon, William Cecil (Lord Burghley), H H Asquith, F E Smith (Lord Birkenhead), Lord Justice Birkett, Lord Denning...

Francis Bacon.

LEARNED SOCIETIES AND UNIVERSITIES

The Royal Society, founded as the Philosophical Society in 1645, granted a royal charter at the Restoration and incorporated in 1662, took as its province the whole field of human knowledge. Founder members were from all walks of life: Robert Boyle – natural philosopher and chemist, Abraham Cowley and Dryden – poets, John Aubrey – antiquarian and John Evelyn – diarist and the society's first secretary. Meetings were held in Gresham College, the City institution founded in 1597 under the will of the Elizabethan financier, Sir Thomas Gresham, to which Christopher Wren was appointed Professor of Astronomy in 1657.

Since the early days members have been men of wide experience and interest, such as Pepys, who was president from 1684-5 and Sir Hans Sloane, president 1727-40, or specialists such as Wren, Newton, and in later years, Humphry Davy, T H Huxley, Lister, Rutherford and Florey all of whom presented original papers to the Society.

Unlike the continental academies and societies of the same period (the Académie Française was founded in 1635), London's learned societies were assigned no special task by the government of the day; royal patrons sought no reflected glory. Other societies formed at the time, or later in the same spirit, include the Society of Antiquaries (1717), the Linnean Society (1778), Geological Society (1807), Royal Geographical Society (1830) and the British Association for the Advancement of Science (1831).

The societies, therefore, in a city where there was no university until 19C, provided a meeting place where men in all branches of knowledge could publish and exchange ideas and, by attracting those working in and beyond the capital to attend conferences, did much to make London the centre of knowledge throughout the kingdom.

There were only two universities in England – Oxford and Cambridge, both Church of England establishments – until 1828 when a group of radicals and dissenters founded University College *(qv)* in London to give education in arts, sciences and medicine in a non-residential and non-sectarian milieu. It was referred to as 'that Godless institution in Gower Street' by supporters of the Anglican Church who reacted by founding Kings College in the Strand (1831) with a strong theological faculty. Neither was allowed to grant degrees but the University of London was incorporated as an examining body by charter in 1836 and as a teaching body in 1900. There are now some 72 800 registered students (51 965 internal, 16 948 external and part-time) in colleges all over London and beyond.

The City University *(qv)* was created in 1966 out of the Northampton Polytechnic (founded 1896). It works in association with Gresham College *(qv)* and has close links with the City financial institutions; many students are on sponsored sandwich courses.

FASHIONS

Fashions, which at their peak greatly affected London and influenced taste and architecture, include coffeehouses, clubs and the Grand Tour.

Coffeehouses, which were introduced to the capital during the Commonwealth (1652) and, serving originally as meeting places, in the City for the exchange of shipping news (Lloyd's), multiplied in number and spread to Covent Garden and the Strand, St James's, Mayfair and Westminster, until by 1715 there were more than 500.

Customers of like interest would foregather regularly, in many cases daily, in the same houses or call at several houses at different times to pick up messages and even mail, to auction a cargo, a ship, raise a loan in any of the lounges around the Exchange. To gossip and hold literary talk one went to Will's, to gather news and write reviews to Button's, to talk of law and art to the Grecian, to discuss Tory politics to the Cocoa Tree, Pall Mall, to embroil in Whig intrigue to the St James's; ... a major attraction was the news sheets which at first circulated from one house to another and the later newspapers (*Daily Courant,* 1702) which were available to customers for the price of a single cup of hot chocolate or coffee.

At the end of 18C the City coffeehouses reverted to being pubs and the West End houses disappeared, except Boodle's and White's which became clubs.

A new fashion developed for **clubs** where men could indulge in gaming, drinking, conviviality and display of the latest masculine attire. They became the setting for legendary wagers placed on a throw of dice, the turn of a card; some took on a literary or political character, others were patronised by the Services; they acquired spacious premises built by the architects of the day in Waterloo Place, Pall Mall and St James's. They were also a haven for the younger sons of large Victorian families who, if in neither the army nor the church and without a town house, found themselves living in rooms; the obvious place to repair to for the day was the club with its library, dining room, smoking room and famous attentive servants.

In Edwardian days there were more than 150 clubs; today the number decreases annually, as they merge, so that there remain only a few 19C palazzos along Pall Mall and 18C houses in St James.

The London Season dates from 1705. It was an indirect result of the growing intellectual and social curiosity which had always brought men to the capital and, with the newly improved roads and development of carriages, brought their families also. Travel to London was however only the first step: the **Grand Tour** became the fashion.

Artists had long been going to Italy and by 17C were followed by individual collectors and patrons: Inigo Jones went alone on his first visit (1601) when he studied Vitruvius and Palladio; on a second visit in 1613-4 he went as adviser to the collector, Thomas Howard, Earl of Arundel.

The exile of royalist families during the Commonwealth familiarised many with the continent and continental taste including Charles II himself. From the time of the Restoration, painters began to work in Rome as part of their training and often stayed on to study; the sons of the wealthy were sent on journeys of a year or two to France and Italy. It was in Rome that the 3rd Earl of Burlington *(qv)* met William Kent.

Collecting, by the knowledgeable – Soane – and the knowledgeable but eclectic – Horace Walpole – developed to such lengths that some, like Sir William Hamilton, even commissioned vessels to ship home statuary, vases and thousands of items for their country and town houses. In 1775 when Edward Gibbon was in Lausanne, he learned that there were estimated to be 40 000 English "milords" and their servants abroad in Europe; gentlemen who did not possess a title took one, it was said, for the occasion.

Thomas Cook organised his first grand circular tour of Europe in 1856.

A LONDON CALENDAR

Listed below are a few of the most popular annual events; for full details, for the special and commemorative exhibitions held by all museums, commercial gallery exhibitions and sporting and other events, consult the daily and weekly press, the **Tourist Information Centre,** (Victoria Station Forecourt, SW1) or the **London Tourist Board** (26 Grosvenor Gardens SW1; ☎ 01-730 3488).

Floodlighting: in summer the most rewarding and important monuments in Westminster, the City and especially along the river are floodlit.

Thames Boat Services: downstream all year; upstream summer only; pp 16, 150.

JANUARY	Boat Show	Earls Court
	Rugby: Triple Crown + International Championship England v Scotland (Calcutta Cup) and France, odd years, differing months	
	England v Wales and Ireland even years, differing months	Twickenham
	Charles I Commemoration	Charles I statue, Whitehall
FEBRUARY	Cruft's Dog Show	Earls Court
	Chinese New Year celebrations	Soho
MARCH	Ideal Home Exhibition	Earls Court
	Chelsea Antiques Fair	Old Town Hall, King's Rd
	Oxford and Cambridge Boat Race	Putney to Mortlake
EASTER	Service and distribution of purses (Maundy Thursday)	
	Service and distribution of Hot X buns (Good Friday)	St Bartholomew the Gt
	Carnival Parade (Easter Sunday)	Battersea Park
	London Harness Horse Parade (morning Easter Monday)	Regent's Park
	Fairs on Hampstead Heath, Blackheath, Wormwood Scrubs, etc.	
APRIL	Royal Horticultural Society Spring Flower Show	RHS Westminster
	London Marathon	Greenwich to Westminster
MAY	Royal Windsor Horse Show	Home Park, Windsor
	Chelsea Flower Show	Royal Hospital, Chelsea
	F.A. Cup Final	Wembley
	Mind-Body-Spirit Festival	RHS Westminster
	29: Oak Apple Day Parade: Chelsea Pensioners	Royal Hospital, Chelsea
JUNE	Beating Retreat	Horse Guards Parade, Whitehall
	Royal Academy Summer Exhibition	Burlington House, Piccadilly
	Trooping the Colour (second or third Saturday)	Horse Guards Parade
	The Derby	Epsom
	Royal Ascot	Berkshire
	Antiquarian Book Fair	Park Lane Hotel
	Stella Artois Grass Court Championships	Queen's Club, West Kensington
	All England Lawn Tennis Championships (2 weeks)	Wimbledon
	Cricket – The England team usually play 2 Test Matches during June – July – August against a touring team from Australia, NZ, India, Pakistan or the West Indies	Lord's and The Oval
	Open Air Theatre Season	Regent's Park
	Royal Regatta	Henley
JULY	Royal Tournament	Earls Court
	Promenade Concerts (mid July for 8 weeks)	Royal Albert Hall
	Benson and Hedges Cup Final	Lord's
	Swan upping	The Thames
	Doggett's Coat and Badge Race (rowed by 6 new freemen of the Watermen and Lightermen's Company)	London Bridge to Chelsea Bridge
	The City Festival	City Churches and Halls
AUGUST	Hampstead Heath Fair (also Blackheath, etc. (holiday Monday weekend)	Hampstead
	Westminster Horse Show	Hyde Park
	Summer Flower Show	RHS Westminster
	Outdoor Theatre Season	Holland Park
	Notting Hill Carnival	Ladbroke Grove
SEPTEMBER	NatWest Trophy Final (1st Saturday)	Lord's
	The Burlington House Fine Arts and Antique Dealers' Fair (odd years only)	The Royal Academy
	Chelsea Antiques Fair	Old Town Hall, King's Rd
	Farnborough Air Show (even years only; in first week)	Farnborough, Hants
	Thames Day	South Bank
OCTOBER	Horse of the Year Show	Wembley
	Motor Fair (odd years)	Earls Court
	Opening of Michaelmas Law Term: Procession of Judges in full robes carrying nosegays	Westminster Abbey
	National Brass Bands' Championship	Royal Albert Hall
NOVEMBER	Remembrance Sunday (11 am service; Sunday closest to 11th)	Cenotaph, Whitehall
	London to Brighton Veteran Car Run (1st Sunday)	from Hyde Park Corner
	Lord Mayor's Show (Saturday closest to 9th)	The City
	London Film Festival	NFT
	State Opening of Parliament	Westminster
	Caravan-Camping-Holiday Show	Earls Court
DECEMBER	Royal Smithfield Show	Earls Court
	International Showjumping Championships	Olympia
	Lighting of the Norwegian Christmas Tree; carols nightly (middle of the month)	Trafalgar Sq
	Carol services	

LONDON SIGHTS

Listed alphabetically

ALEXANDRA PALACE (Haringey)

Set atop a hill in a 480 acre park, **Alexandra Palace,** known as the People's Palace, was built in 1873 as a counterpart to Crystal Palace *(qv)* and twice burned down (1873, 1980). The Great Hall with its single-span glass roof and rose window, the West Hall and the Palm Court have been attractively restored and provide a venue for exhibitions, concerts and sporting events. Extensive views of the city from the top of the hill.

The first live television transmissions were made in 1936 by the BBC from Alexandra Palace.

APSLEY HOUSE ★ (Westminster)

Map p 99.

Apsley House stands on the site of the old lodge of Hyde Park and an older public house. As the first house beyond the turnpike it became known in 19C as No 1, London.

The House. – Wellington bought the house, designed nearly 40 years before by Robert Adam for Baron Apsley, in 1817: views on porcelain in the Plate and China Room show Adam's construction as small, square and built of brick. Later the duke and his architect, Benjamin D. Wyatt, transformed it: outside they added the pedimented portico and refaced the walls entirely with Bath stone; inside, excepting the Portico and Piccadilly Drawing Rooms, all was re-arranged and, in 1828, a west extension added containing the Muniment or Plate and China Room below and the Waterloo Gallery above. In 1947 the 7th duke presented it to the nation. In 1982 the house was redecorated and the public rooms recreated to the original designs.

The Wellington Museum★. – *Open 11am to 5pm; closed Mondays (except Bank holidays), 1 January, Good Friday, May Day Bank holiday, 24, 25, 26 December; £2, child £1.*

The exhibits have the dual interest of association and high artistry: porcelain from Meissen, Berlin, Sèvres; gold and silver plate; jewellery, orders of chivalry, field marshal's batons, snuffboxes; paintings by English, Spanish, Dutch and Flemish masters including more than 100 captured in 1813 following the Battle of Vitoria from Joseph Bonaparte who had appropriated them from the Spanish royal collection. The chandeliers are 19C English.

Entrance hall and inner hall. – These rooms are devoted to the Duke : busts, sculptures, portraits of himself and his military contemporaries.

Plate and China or Muniment Room. – Among the orders and decorations, note the silver Waterloo Medal, the first ever campaign medal. There are 10 batons of seven different armies, swords and daggers, the Egyptian service and the Prussian service (Berlin: 1819), two of the 5 porcelain and one of the 3 silver and gilt services (most of several hundred pieces); there are rich gold, enamelled and jewelled snuffboxes, field equipment and silver and gilt plate, most notably in figured relief, the great Wellington Shield and the great gold Waterloo Vase.

Basement. – In a new gallery are displayed the Duke's death mask, a panorama and a programme, printed on silk, of his remarkable funeral and a commentary on his political career by newspaper cartoonists of the day (1852). Also on view are despatches, maps and memorabilia, and his uniforms and garter robes.

Staircase Vestibule. – Wellington never met Napoleon but here is the Emperor himself in sculpted likeness, an 11ft 4in Carrara marble statue by Canova.

Upper Staircase Landing. – Portraits of Charles X, John VI, Napoleon and Frederic III.

Piccadilly Drawing Room and Portico Room. – *(First floor).* The rooms are beautiful examples of interior Adam decoration. The drawing room in gold and white is hung with 17C Dutch paintings – David Teniers II, Nicolas Maes, Pieter de Hooch, Jan Steen. The portico room contains four Raphael copies by Bonnemaison and portraits of *Napoleon* by Lefèvre and Dabos, of the *Empress Josephine* and *Pauline Bonaparte* by Lefèvre.

The Waterloo Gallery. – The early Waterloo Day (18 June) reunion dinners, with only the generals present, were held in the dining room. By 1829, with Wellington now premier, the guest list had grown so he added the 90ft gallery, decorated in 18C French style which set a fashion favoured until the end of the Edwardian era. The ceiling decoration combines the Wellington arms and the George within the Garter collar, The paintings, renovated and rehung in 1980, are dominated by the portraits of Charles I after van Dyck, and the Goya portrait of the duke himself in the classic Spanish pose on horseback – so standard, in fact, that recent x-rays have revealed that it was painted somewhat prematurely and the head of Joseph Bonaparte had to be overpainted with that of the ultimate victor. Also hung here are Murillo, Rubens, Reynolds, Ribera, Mengs, Bruegel, Velasquez – *Water Seller of Seville* and *A Spanish Gentleman* – and the Duke's favourite, *The Agony in the Garden* by Correggio.

(By courtesy of the V & A)

The Wellington Boot.

APSLEY HOUSE*

The windows are fitted with sliding mirrors which enhanced still further the already glittering gold decoration, chandelier, silver centrepiece and plate, the uniforms...

Yellow and Striped Drawing Rooms. – The first, hung with yellow damask resembling that originally in the Waterloo Gallery, is dominated by a portrait of William IV by Wilkie, flanked by portraits of Joseph Bonaparte and the Empress Josephine by Lefèvre and the Duke of Wellington looking at a bust of Napoleon. The striped drawing room is devoted to The Battle of Waterloo by Sir William Allan (about which the Duke commented 'Good – very good; not too much smoke'), the Duke of Wellington by Lawrence and portraits of his generals.

Dining Room. – The amazing portrait of George IV in Highland dress by Wilkie overlooks the banquet table set with the 26ft silver centrepiece from the Portuguese service.

BARNES (Richmond upon Thames)

Barnes remains incredibly countrified in character: the **Green,** ringed with trees, possesses a pond, the weatherboarded early 19C Sun Inn and the former village school.

St Mary's Parish Church. – *Open 10.30am to 12.30pm, Saturdays 9.30 to 11am.*

The church, said to have been consecrated in 1215 by Archbishop Langton after the signing of *Magna Carta,* was burnt out in 1978 but reopened in 1984 after sensitive rebuilding to Edward Cullinan's designs to include elements of former structures. The medieval tower, nave and chancel, with its triple lancet windows and frieze, form the narthex of the much enlarged new church. The nave extends northwards to a high wall containing a delicate Gothic revival east window (1852) and rose window and to the east and west to the round turret and old vestry.

Near the church are three early 18C houses: *(east)* The Homestead (no 113), *(west)* Strawberry House and the Grange *(corner of Grange Rd).* Henry Fielding lived in Milbourne House *(Station Rd)* in the 1750s; Rose House (no 70) in the **High Street** is the oldest in Barnes.

Two adjoining riverside inns typify 19C pub architecture before **Barnes Terrace,** which runs upriver as a line of 18C residences, terrace houses and cottages.

BATTERSEA (Wandsworth)

Battersea's transformation into an industrial town of 151 000 inhabitants took just 100 years. In 1782, 2 160 souls were engaged in growing strawberries and asparagus, herbs (Lavender Hill) and vegetables for seed and transporting their produce over the wooden bridge, erected in 1771, to Westminster; by 1845 the railway had extended to Clapham Junction and the population explosion begun. Local street names recall the St John Bolingbroke family and their successor, Earl Spencer, Lord of the Manor since 1763.

Battersea Old Church, St Mary's. – *Open Mondays to Fridays 9am to noon.*

Since Saxon times there has been a church well forward at the river bend. The current building with a conical green copper spire dates from 1775 (portico 1823); the 14C east window encloses 17C tracery and painted heraldic glass. The aisle windows commemorate famous people with local connections: the 18C botanist William Curtis who is buried here, William Blake who married here and Turner who sketched the river from the vestry window and whose chair now stands in the chancel. Amusing epitaphs and memorial busts of the St John – Bolingbroke family, lords of the manor in 17/18C.

Vicarage Crescent. – **Old Battersea House,** a two storey brick mansion with a hipped roof and pedimented doorway, dates from 1699 when it was built by Sir Walter St John; it houses the **William de Morgan collection** of ceramics and paintings. *Open by arrangement: apply to the De Morgan Trust, 21 St Margaret's Crescent, London SW15 6HL.* **Devonshire House** is an early 18C stucco house of three storeys with a Doric porch, small curved iron balconies and a contemporary wrought iron gate. St Mary's House is a late 17C mansion.

High Street. – **The Raven,** with curving Dutch gables, has dominated the crossroads since the 17C. **Sir Walter St John's School,** founded in 1700, was rebuilt in 19/20C on the original site in Tudor Gothic style. Note the St John motto surmounted by helm and falcon at the entrance.

Battersea Park. – The marshy waste of Battersea Fields was popular in 16C for pigeon shooting, fairs, donkey racing and duels; by 1828 however, when Wellington and Lord Winchelsea exchanged shots over the Catholic Emancipation Bill, they had become illfamed. In 1843 **Thomas Cubitt** suggested that a park be laid out; a bill was passed in 1846 and 360 acres purchased. The site was built up with land from the excavation of the Victoria Docks. The funfair built for the Festival of Britain in 1951 had to be demolished in 1976. The park includes a boating lake, a garden for the handicapped, sculptures by H. Moore and B. Hepworth and sports facilities. A Japanese Peace Pagoda (1985) with gilded windbells and statues overlooks the Thames.

East of the park, a gleaming white building with rounded arches and tinted glass panels houses the offices of the Observer newspaper.

Battersea Power Station. – This familiar landmark built in 1932-34 by Giles Gilbert Scott shut down in 1983. Work to convert the massive structure into a leisure park while retaining the Art Deco interiors of the turbine hall and control room, is under way and it is due to open in 1990.

The Dogs Home, Battersea. – *4 Battersea Park Rd. Open 10.30am to 4.30pm; closed Sundays and public holidays; 50p, child 20p.* The home, established in 1860, moved to its present site in 1871. The number of dogs and cats brought in annually runs into thousands.

BLACKHEATH ★ (Greenwich)

Blackheath★. – Blackheath is ringed by stately **terraces** and **houses★** mostly built of brick relieved by stone dressings or of sparkling white painted stucco. They date from the 18C and early 19C when merchants newly rich from the expanding docks began to build in the vicinity.

The present calm gives the lie to the rumbustiousness and pageantry of the past. Blackheath Rd, Blackheath Hill and Shooters' Hill mark the course of the Roman Watling Street between the coast and London. In the 18C the area was notorious for highwaymen and earlier as a rallying ground for rebel forces: Wat Tyler – 1381; the Kentishmen under Jack Cade – 1450; the Cornishmen under Audley – 1497. It has also always been a fairground, meeting place and encampment: citizens greeted Henry V on the heath on his victorious return from Agincourt in 1415; Charles II was met there by the Restoration Army; James I is said to have taught the English to play golf on it when in residence at Greenwich in 1608.

Among the almost unbroken circle of buildings overlooking the green from the south are **Colonnade House,** South Row – a big early 19C house with a Tuscan portico decorating the front along its full length; **The Paragon,** a late 18C shallow crescent by Michael Searles, of seven brick villas linked by white, Tuscan columned arcades; All Saints Church – built of Kentish ragstone in neo-Gothic style – an oddity by Furley with even the tower in a peculiar position crowning the south wall. Lindsey House, Lloyds Pl, is all in brick with white trims; Grotes' Buildings, a mid 18C terrace; Heathfield House, early 19C, stucco with a Tuscan columned, paired bow window. Dartmouth Row *(west side)* is notable for the early 18C Spencer and Perceval Houses with eleven bays, several Georgian groups and survivals of the original 1680-90s houses.

Blackheath Village, the main street, and traffic noisy, Tranquil Vale, lead off the heath to the south; the more modern estates by Span and others lie farther back.

Morden College. – *St German's Place, SE 3. Open by appointment for small groups; apply at least one month in advance.* The college, designed by Wren in 1695, stands in 18C landscaped parkland, an attractive low, two storeyed building in mellow brick with stone dressings. An ornamented central stone gateway which rises to a double niche contains the figures of the founder, the city merchant, Sir John Morden, and his wife, and leads to an inner, collegiate style, quadrangle.

Charlton. – The parish church, the big house, the Bugle Horn Inn, a rebuilt post-house, the 18C White Swan, mark the length of the main street still characteristically rural and appropriately named The Village.

St Luke's. – *Charlton Church Lane. Usually open; key obtainable from rectory.*

The brick church with its square tower and Dutch gable doorway, dates, in the main, from 1630 when it was rebuilt by Sir Adam Newton *(see below).* Inside are a memorial tablet to Master Edward Wilkinson (d 1567), Yeoman of the Mouth to Henry VIII and Edward VI and Master Cook to Queen Elizabeth, a 17C heraldic north window, the hatchment (west wall) of the Spencer Percevals and Spencer Wilsons, who in the 18C owned Charlton House, the royal arms of Queen Anne and the tablet and bust of Spencer Perceval, assassinated in the House of Commons when prime minister in 1812. The church, a landmark from the Thames, served as a navigational aid in the early 18C and so flies the white ensign on St George's and St Luke's days.

Charlton House. – *View by appointment with the warden:* ☎ 01-856 3951

The house, the finest extant example of Jacobean architecture in London, was built between 1607 and 1612 for Adam Newton, Dean of Durham and tutor to Prince Henry, eldest son of James I. Characteristically of deep red brick with stone dressings, it has a shallow H shaped plan with symmetrical bays at the end of each wing and balustrades lining the crest and terrace. At the centre is the door with a surround dated 1607, and two storey bay above in stone, exuberantly decorated in an inexplicable German style.

Features inside include the plasterwork, particularly the ceiling with pendants in the Grand Saloon over the two storey hall, the fireplaces, Long Gallery and typical staircase with square well and carved newel posts. The gateway, stranded on the front lawn, is the original Tuscan pillared entrance with an added 18C crest. In 1608 at James I's request a mulberry tree was planted in the north-east corner of the garden near the gazebo.

Eltham Palace*. – *Off Court Road. Open Thursdays and Sundays only, March to October 11am to 7pm (4pm November to February).*

Eltham, described as a manor in *Domesday,* became a favourite with the Plantagenets and by the 14C was described by the chronicler, Froissart, as "a very magnificent palace". In 1390 under Richard II Geoffrey Chaucer was Clerk of the Works. Edward IV added the Great Hall in 1479-80; the foundations of Henry VI's royal apartments still remain; Henry VIII resided there until a growing interest in his ships made him prefer Greenwich. During the Commonwealth, according to John Evelyn, it fell into "miserable ruins" and was finally valued only as building material (£2 754). At long last, in 1931, it was let to Mr Stephen Courtauld who restored the Great Hall. Excavations have revealed the plan of the medieval and Tudor buildings.

The Great Hall. – The hall, 101ft long, 36ft wide and 56ft to the roof apex, is built of brick, faced with stone along its length and decorated with grotesque heads. Inside is the hall's chief glory, in all but the technical sense since the posts are tenoned, a **hammerbeam** roof of four centred arches, with braces, open traceries, cusped spandrels, elaborate pendants, and massive main timbers, intricately moulded. Note the canopy, screen and Minstrels' Gallery.

Outside the Tudor House, on the right was "My Lord Chancellor's lodging" or the occasional residence of Cardinal Wolsey, who was installed as Lord Chancellor in the palace chapel.

Well Hall. – *Well Hall Rd.* Half a mile north of Eltham Palace lies Well Hall estate, the home of the Roper family *(qv)* until 1733. All that now remains are the site of the medieval house surrounded by a moat and reached by a 16C bridge, a Tudor barn *(restaurant and art gallery)* and the Pleasaunce – a garden surrounded by old red brick walls.

BLOOMSBURY ★ (Camden)

The once residential area with its many squares is dominated by two major learned institutions, the British Museum *(p 36)* and the ever expanding London University.

The development of Bloomsbury Sq in 1661 brought a new concept in local planning: the 4th Earl of Southampton, descendant of the Lord Chancellor to whom Henry VIII had granted the feudal manor in 1545, erected houses for the well-to-do around three sides of a square, a mansion for himself on the fourth, northern, side and – the innovation – a network of secondary service streets all around, with a market nearby, so ordering, in Evelyn's words, "a little town". He was successful: by 1667, when he died, he had a magnificent residence, the focus of fashion had transferred to his estate and he had made a fortune. His only daughter, Lady Rachel, married the future 1st Duke of Bedford, uniting two great estates.

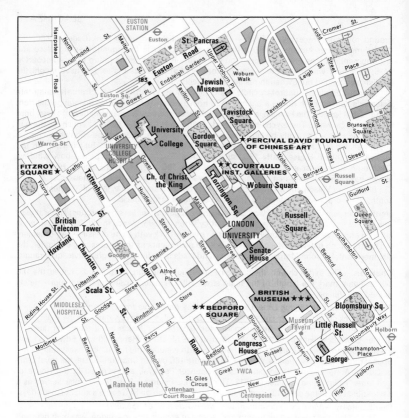

THE SQUARES

Bedford Sq, the most elegant, was developed by Gertrude, widow of the 4th Duke, with Thomas Leverton as architect in 1775. The other squares, all different and now partly or totally incorporated in the university precinct, followed in 19C: **Russell** 1800, **Tavistock** 1806-26, **Torrington** 1825, **Woburn** 1829, **Gordon** (originally by Thomas Cubitt) 1850.

Bedford Sq★★, still complete, with three storey brick terrace houses with rounded doorways, delicate fanlights and first floor balconies, is relieved halfway along each range by a pedimented stucco centrepiece. Bloomsbury Sq contains none of the original houses but in the south-west corner are two mid 18C houses, one, with a cherub decorated plaque, the residence from 1818-26 of Isaac and Benjamin Disraeli.

The squares' most famous residents were the **Bloomsbury Group** of Virginia Woolf, Vanessa Bell, Roger Fry – the art critic who in 1910 organised the first Post-Impressionist Exhibition to be held in London, Clive Bell, E.M. Forster, Lytton Strachey, Duncan Grant, Maynard Keynes, David Garnet and Wyndham Lewis. The group were joined in Gordon Sq, Fitzroy Sq and neighbouring streets by Rupert Brooke, D.H. Lawrence, Bertrand Russell, Lady Ottoline Morrell... By the early 30s their ideas and works, literary, critical and artistic, had become widely known and accepted, their influence absorbed into the artistic tradition.

LONDON UNIVERSITY

London University (qv) moved to Bloomsbury only after the second war, although the **Senate House,** a cold Portland stone building with a tall square tower (library) by Charles Holden, had been under construction since 1932. Colleges, faculties and new institutes are now housed throughout the local streets and squares in the old 18/19C houses and in the ever extending, heterogeneous complex of brick, stone, concrete, steel, mosaic and glass (in blue on plan).

University College. – The central range of this, the oldest of the university buildings, designed by William Wilkins, is marked by an imposing pedimented portico, behind which rises a high dome (1827-9). Guarding either side of the courtyard are a pair of miniature, domed, observatories. The college houses the **Flaxman Sculpture Galleries,** renowned Egyptology Galleries and the figure of Jeremy Bentham (1748-1832), inspiration of the college's founders. Opposite is the red brick, gabled University College Hospital (1897-1906) by A. Waterhouse.

Courtauld Institute Galleries★★. – Courtauld-Warburg Building, Woburn Sq. Open daily 10am to 5pm, Sundays 2 to 5pm; closed 1 January, Easter, May Day holiday, holiday Mondays, 24, 25, 26 December; £1.50, child, student, OAP 50p.

Its collections comprise the major art bequests to London University: Paintings of the Italian Primitives and of the Renaissance to the 18C donated by Thomas Gambier-Parry and Viscount Lee of Fareham; paintings by the Bloomsbury Group gifted by Roger Fry (1866-1934); the private collection assembled by Samuel Courtauld of Impressionists, with canvases by Manet (Bar at the Folies-Bergère), Degas, Bonnard, Gauguin (Tahitian scenes), Van Gogh (Peach Trees in Blossom, Self-Portrait with Bandaged Ear), Seurat and Cézanne, including the celebrated Lake at Annecy; and the Princes Gate Collection, bequeathed to the nation by Count Antoine Seilern and including 30 oils by Rubens and six drawings by Michelangelo as well as works by Breugel, Leonardo, Tiepolo, Dürer, Rembrandt, Bellini, Tintoretto and Kokoschka. Furniture, carpets, sculpture and china create an intimate setting. The galleries are scheduled to move to Somerset House (qv) in 1989.

Percival David Foundation of Chinese Art*. – *53 Gordon Sq. Open Mondays to Fridays 10.30am to 5pm; closed 1 January, Easter, 25, 26 December and holiday Mondays.*

The Foundation displays the world famous collection of Chinese porcelains assembled between the wars by the late Sir Percival David, scholar and connoisseur of great distinction, complemented by the Elphinstone bequest. The collection reflects Chinese imperial taste and includes the finest classic wares of the Sung dynasty together with splendid blue and white porcelains, monochrome and polychrome wares of 14C to 18C. It also contains important dated blue and white and celadon pieces that are remarkable for their sophistication and beauty.

Church of Christ the King. – *Gordon Sq.* The church, built in 1853 in the Early English style to cathedral proportions – the interior is 212ft long – is now the University Church.

■ ADDITIONAL SIGHTS

Jewish Museum. – *Upper Woburn Place, Tavistock Sq. Open Tuesdays to Fridays and Sundays 10am to 4pm (Fridays in winter 10am to 12.45pm); closed Mondays, Saturdays, Jewish Holy Days, holiday Mondays, 1 January, Good Friday, Easter Sunday, 25, 26 December.*

Crowded into a single room, overlooked by the portraits of 17/19C worthies, are ritual objects including a 16C Venetian Ark of the Law, scrolls in embroidered silk, beaten silver covers, bells, lamps, Ram's Horns, historic wedding rings and 18/19C miniatures.

Tottenham Ct Rd. – The road, named after the feudal manor of Tottenhall, is known especially for the interior decoration and furnishing shops at its northern end – Maple's no 149, Habitat and Heal's no 191-199 – and for the American Church (no 79) and the 1970s YMCA *(112 Gt Russell St)*. Centrepoint, an office block of 34 storeys by Richard Seifert, erected in the 1960s, towers over St Giles' Circus.

More interior decoration showrooms are to be found in Berners St: at no 19 Parker Knoll (furniture and textiles) and at no 53 Sandersons (wallpaper and fabrics) where the William Morris blocks for hand printed wallpapers are still in use. The interior decor of the former Berners Hotel (now Ramada Hotel) dates from 1809: elaborately carved plasterwork, hand painted glass, marble pillars and staircases have all been faithfully restored.

Pollock's Toy Museum and Shop. – *1 Scala St. Open Mondays to Saturdays 10am to 5pm; closed Sundays, 25, 26 December; 80p, child 40p.*

Toy theatres, that 19C delight made from sheets described by Robert Louis Stevenson as "one penny plain and twopence coloured" can be seen amidst a mass of 19 and 20C toys: wax, porcelain, peg and spoon dolls, teddy bears, carved wooden animals, optical toys...

The Wellcome Museum of the History of Medicine. – *183 Euston Road. Ask at the reception desk to view the pharmacies.*

The museum is open to specialists only but in the entrance hall are reconstructions of three historical pharmacies – English *c* 1680, 17C Italian, Hispano-Mauresque *c* 1790 – displaying vividly decorated drug jars, pestles and mortars, original decor... *The Wellcome Historical Medical Museum is in the Science Museum, South Kensington.*

British Telecom Tower. – *Cleveland St.* Once London's tallest building (620ft including the mast), now topped by the Nat West bank in the City, the Post Office Tower, as it was originally known, has been a dominant, if undistinguished, landmark since 1965 when it was erected to provide an unimpeded path for the capital's telecommunications system.

Fitzroy Sq*. – The square, almost at the foot of the Telecom Tower, is now a paved pedestrian precinct on three sides. Development began in 1793 when the east and south sides in Portland Stone designed by **Robert Adam** were erected; 40 years later the square was completed but with stucco facing not stone. Note the giant columned centrepiece on the east side repeated in miniature at either end and as the centrepiece of the south terrace.

The quarter was frequented by artists and writers from late 18C to early 20C: Madox Brown, Bernard Shaw and Virginia Woolf (no 29; 1887-98), in Fitzroy Square; Whistler and Sickert in Fitzroy St; Verlaine and Rimbaud in Howland St; Richard Wilson, Constable (no 76) in **Charlotte St,** well known for its restaurants; Wyndham Lewis in Percy St...

Congress House. – *Great Russell St.* The structural mass of the T.U.C. headquarters is lightened by a glass screen at ground level on the east side, giving a view of an inner court and hall, distinguished by a war memorial before a high green marble screen, carved on the spot from a 10 ton block of Roman stone by Jacob Epstein (1958).

St George's Bloomsbury. – *Open Mondays to Fridays 10am to 3pm; closed 1 January, Good Friday, 25, 26 December and holiday Mondays.*

Hawksmoor's church (1716-31) externally makes the most of a difficult site, with a grand pedimented portico at the top of a flight of steps and a stepped stone tower surmounted by a spire. Topping the steeple, to the contemporary public's derision, is a classical statue of the unpopular George I. Inside the problem of orientation on such a cramped site, resolved by Hawksmoor by hollowing out a small apse in the east wall, has since been settled by the transfer of the high gilded and inlaid reredos (1727) to the north wall. At the centre of the flat rectangular ceiling is a flower 5ft in diameter in richly gilded plaster and in the shell over the east niche another delicate gilded relief, both by the master plasterer, Isaac Mansfield.

St Pancras Parish Church. – *Upper Woburn Place, Euston Rd.* The church was built in 1819-22 at the time of the Greek Revival and the design, selected from 30 submitted in response to an advertisement, echoes the Erechtheon in the caryatids supporting the roofs of the square vestries to north and south, the Tower of the Winds in the columned, two stage elevation of the octagonal west tower and in the Classical colonnade, and the Elgin marbles in the columns supporting the gallery in the spacious interior.

The caryatids are a prime example of ladies who have withstood being sawn in half: they were made too tall and a middle section had to be removed from each to make them fit!

Woburn Walk, to the rear, is lined by small shops behind early 19C shopfronts in colour washed, three storey houses.

Foundation. – It was the bequest in 1753 by **Sir Hans Sloane,** physician, naturalist, traveller, of his collection to the nation which finally spurred Parliament to found the BM. Already acquired (1700), but left in vaults in Westminster, was the priceless collection of medieval manuscripts of Sir Robert Cotton (1570-1631), and deposited with them, the old Royal Library of 12 000 volumes, assembled by monarchs since Tudor times (officially presented to the museum by George II in 1756); elsewhere mss, charters and rolls collected by Robert Harley and his son Edward, Earls of Oxford (dd 1724, 1741) and made available in 1753. The collections were so magnificent, so extensive, that a building apart was necessary. A lottery was launched, money raised, and for £21 000 Montagu House, built in 1675 for the Duke of Montagu, ambassador to the court of Louis XIV, and rebuilt in 1686 after a fire, to designs by the French architect, Puget, was purchased and altered. Although access, when the museum opened in 1759, was limited to certain weekdays and, until 1810, was by ticket only – always free – attendances soon mounted to 10 000 a year. Arrangement in the main rooms and on the staircase landing was miscellaneous; engravings show stuffed giraffes, portraits, fossils and mss, books, dried plants, Classical marble statues and coins, pots and Buddhas, against a background of heroic frescoes and plasterwork ceilings. There were no labels – Cobbett christened the institution "the old curiosity shop".

Collections. – Acquisition was by presentation, bequest and special parliamentary purchase: it was in this period that the foundations of the present museum were laid. Chief among the acquisitions were: Thomason Tracts, pamphlets published during the Civil War and Commonwealth 1642-1660 (presented by George III, 1762): David Garrick Library (1 000 printed plays including First Folios, 1779), Sir William Hamilton collection of antique vases (£8 400; 1772): Cracherode collection of books, fine bindings, great master drawings, Greek and Roman coins (1799): Egyptian antiquities including the Rosetta Stone (under the Treaty of Alexandria, 1802, following Nelson's victory on the Nile); Greek and Roman sculptures, bronzes and terracottas, the Townley Marbles (1804; £20 000); sculptures from the Temple of Apollo at Bassae, 1815: sculptures from the Parthenon, the Elgin Marbles (purchased 1816; £35 000)... In addition, there were purchases of mss, minerals (Grenville), libraries (Hargrave, legal), music collections (Burney), natural history collections, French Revolution tracts and ephemera. In 1823, George IV presented his father's library of 65 000 volumes, 19 000 pamphlets, maps, charts; in 1824 came the Payne-Knight bequest of Classical antiquities, bronzes and drawings; in 1827 the Banks bequest of books, botanical specimens and ethnography.

(By courtesy of the BM)

Lewis Chessmen.

The building. – To house the burgeoning collections, temporary buildings were erected (1804-8) until, in 1824, **Robert Smirke,** appointed to design a permanent extension, produced plans which, beginning with a wing projecting from the northeast corner of the old house, culminated in the replacement of the decayed Montagu House itself by a new, Greek inspired, colonnaded façade. It took 20 years to complete and, with three later additions, the Reading Room (1857), the Edward VII (1914) and Duveen Galleries (1938), is the building we know today.

Extensions. – In 1880-83 renewed pressure on space brought about the removal of the natural history departments to South Kensington; in 1905 of the newspapers to Colindale. In December 1970, the ethnographic collections transferred to 6 Burlington Gardens *(p 116)*. In 1978 a new extension on the last remaining space on the Bloomsbury site was opened. The museum is now engaged in re-arrangement whereby, in the main, primary collections (or key items) are on display in the galleries, secondary collections are held in reserve stores.

Bequests have greatly influenced the museum's immense variety; the early sequence of acquisitions, increased in the later 19 and 20C by finds by archaeologists attached to the museum, brought the BM the reputation it has as the greatest centre of world antiquities.

The British Library. – The museum's library departments since 1973, have been vested in a separate authority and will eventually move into a new building at Somerstown *(p 112)*.

The round **Reading Room** *(escorted tours on the hour from 11am to 4pm Mondays to Saturdays)* in the museum, came about through many factors: rooms, at first in the basement, later on the ground floor, were available to "men of letters", but Antonio Panizzi, refugee Italian revolutionary appointed Keeper of Printed Books in 1837 and Principal Librarian (Director) in 1856, was determined that the library should be open equally to "the poorest student". Robert Smirke's King's Library, splendid in appearance and size, could not provide sufficient seating nor was there room to house the Grenville Library, bequeathed in 1847. Panizzi and the architect, Sydney Smirke (Robert's younger brother) planned the present Reading Room to fill the damp and gloomy courtyard at the centre of the building. It was opened in 1857 beneath a 40ft wide dome. It seats 400 readers with 25 miles of shelving (1 300 000 books) surrounding the circular room. Less spectacular, but equally if not more fundamental, was Panizzi's compilation of the catalogue.

Practical Information. – *Open Mondays to Saturdays 10am to 5pm, Sundays 2.30 to 6pm; closed 1 January, Good Friday, May Day holiday, 24, 25, 26 December. Coffee Shop and Restaurant. Special facilities: Readers' and Students' tickets available on application to the Keepers of Departments.*

To help you find what you want to see:

Named objects – look in the right hand column; note the gallery name and colour in left column; find corresponding colour and gallery on plans p 38;

The table is divided into 5 area sections: ground and upper floors, east and west and the King Edward VII Galleries, listed in sequence and colour keyed to the plans.

Special Exhibitions are now also shown in a new gallery on the ground floor.

GALLERY		CONTENTS	SELECTED OBJECTS
Ground Floor West and Basement			
Assyrian Transept	26	Colossal human headed winged lion gates from Nimrud (9C BC).	Balawat gates, steles and statue of Ashurnasirpal, Ishtar lion.
Egyptian Sculpture Gallery	25	Obelisks, steles, statues of the kings, sarcophagi, colossal red granite statues (1360 BC), small bronzes of gods.	**Rosetta Stone;** Lions of Amenophis III; Rameses II; King Amenophis III (1400 BC).
Nineveh Gallery	21	Low reliefs of the Assyrian Army; the building of Sennacherib's palace.	White Obelisk (9C BC).
Nimrud Gallery	19-20	Low reliefs; coronation and other scenes with spade bearded, winged or bird headed men (Palace of Ashurnasirpal II).	Black Obelisk (9C BC).
Khorsabad Entrance	16	Colossal winged bull and god (8C BC).	Floral pavement.
Assyrian Saloon	17	Low reliefs of hunting and war scenes.	
Assyrian Rooms (by staircase 18)	89-90	Low reliefs of the wars of Ashurbanipal, Ishtar Temple reliefs.	
Cycladic Room	1	Marble figurines.	Treasury of Atreus.
Bronze Age Room	2	Vases, bath-tub and chest coffin (1400 BC); bronze and terracotta figurines.	Aegina and Elgin jewellery.
Archaic Greek Room	3	8-6C BC; statues; figurines; vases.	Sculpture from Sanctuary of Apollo at Didyma.
Andokides Room	4	Athenian vase painting.	Black-figured amphora signed by Andokides.
Room of the Harpy Tomb	5	Tomb monuments, vases and figurines.	Strangford Apollo; Harpy Tomb; "Chatsworth" Head of Apollo.
Bassae Room	6	High relief frieze – Centaurs and Lapiths, Greeks and Amazons – from temple of Apollo at Bassae(c 400 BC).	
Nereid Room	7	Nereid Monument; statues of the Nereids (breezes); lion gate guardians.	
Duveen Gallery	8	Frieze, metopes of the battles of the Lapiths and Centaurs and pediments from the Parthenon (5C BC).	**Elgin Marbles; the Horse of Selene.**
Room of the Caryatid	9	The statue and a fluted Ionic pillar – both Pentelic marble; terracotta figurines; a recumbent bull; Greek jewellery and seal stones (480-330 BC).	**Caryatid** from the Erechtheon on the Acropolis 5C BC.
Payava Room	10	Tombs, kraters, minute bronzes; clay vessels 4C BC, terracotta figures.	Payava Tomb 350 BC.
Greek Room (mezzanine by staircase 23)	11	Athenian red figured vases (c 440 BC).	
Mausoleum Room	12	Statues, friezes (battle of Greeks and Amazons) from the Mausoleum at Halicarnassus; column drum from the temple of Artemis at Ephesus.	Forepart of a horse (from chariot group on crest of the tomb); Cnidus lion tomb monument.
Hellenistic Room	13	Statues, bronze and marble heads, jewellery; the Choragic Monument of Thrasyllos 320 BC.	Goddess **Demeter** from Cnidus; bronze head of **Sophocles** 3C BC; jewelled sceptre.
First Roman Room	14	Gold jewellery; silver, glass and clay vessels; figures in silver, bronze and terracotta.	Marble head of Vestal Virgin, mosaics, wall paintings; **Portland Vase;** Apollo with a lyre.
Second Roman Room	15	Mosaic floor from Gaul and statues; portraits, sculpture.	
Greek and Roman Rooms (downstairs from Rooms 12, 16)	77-85	Temple fragments, documents, epitaphs, sculpture, sarcophagi, statues, caryatids, portraits.	Elgin collection, Inscription to Alexander the Great 334 BC, Townley Vase.
Northwest Staircase (to Room 59)		Mosaics of animals, birds, hunting scenes from 4-6C Carthage and Utica.	
Ancient Palestine	24	Jericho rock tomb (late 3C BC), Nicanor ossuary, jewellery, pottery.	Gold pendant, fertility goddess.
Ground Floor East			
Grenville Library	29	English and continental illuminated mss.	Books of Hours.
	30	Historical documents, literary autographs, maps, early music mss, modern caligraphy, bibles and psalters.	Lindisfarne Gospel, Codex Sinaiticus, **Magna Carta,** Essex's death warrant, Nelson's last letter.
King's Library	32	Oriental illuminated mss., early printing, famous books, handmade books, children's books, postage stamps, George III's library, special exhibitions.	Gutenberg Bible, Caxton and Wyken de Worde's books, Henry Davis' Gift (fine bindings); Shakespeare's signature and first folio (1623).
Northeast Staircase		Canadian Totem pole, 88 steps high; mosaic pavement.	
Upper Floor West			
Terracottas, Bronzes	68	Greek; Etruscan and Roman.	Tanagra figurines (330-200 BC).
Greek and Roman Life Room	69	Farming tools, writing materials, weights and measures, games counters; jewellery; sandcore, moulded, carved, blown glass.	1/4 of a Roman wooden waterwheel; Greek (600-1BC) and Etruscan (700-200 BC) jewellery, gold wreaths.

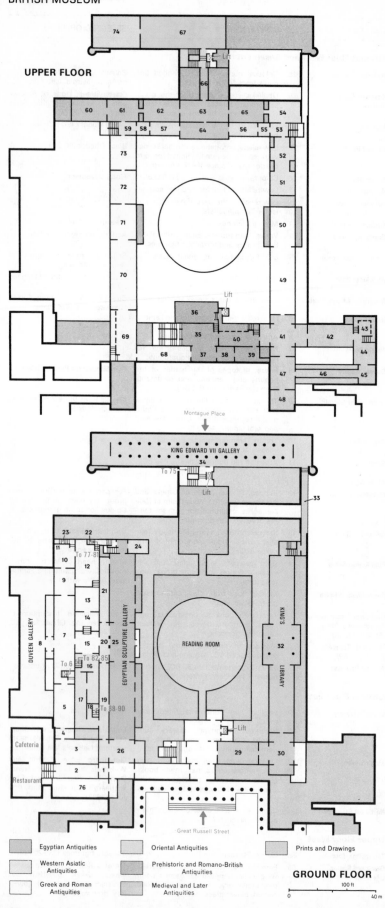

BRITISH MUSEUM★★★

UPPER FLOOR

King Edward VII Gallery — 34
To 75
Lift
33

Duveen Gallery
Egyptian Sculpture Gallery
King's Library
Reading Room
Cafeteria
Restaurant

To 77-81
To 6
To 82-85
To 38-90

Montague Place

Great Russell Street

GROUND FLOOR

Egyptian Antiquities
Western Asiatic Antiquities
Greek and Roman Antiquities
Oriental Antiquities
Prehistoric and Romano-British Antiquities
Medieval and Later Antiquities
Prints and Drawings

100 ft
0   40 m

GALLERY		CONTENTS	SELECTED OBJECTS
Third Roman Room	70	Portraits – coins, heads, busts – of Augustus *(until 1989)*.	
Etruscans – Iron Age Cultures in Italy	71	Cinerary urns, sarcophagi, pottery, bronze figurines.	Head of athlete with a leather cap 300-200 BC; stone sarcophagus from Tarquinia *c* 250 BC; bronze horse bit and bridle ornaments early 7C BC.
A.G. Leventis Gallery of Cypriot Antiquities	72	Objects illustrating Cypriot civilisation and culture *c* 4500 BC - AD 300: vases with incised and painted decoration.	Terracotta figurine with earrings 1400-1200 BC; flat limestone statue 575-550 BC.
The Greeks in Southern Italy	73	Marble sculpture, bronze statuettes and vessels, gold jewellery, coins, decorated pottery, terracottas.	Jewellery from Tomb of Taranto priestess *c* 350-340 BC; bronze cauldron and red figured cup from Berone tomb 5C BC.
South Arabia	59	Bronze figurines, funerary monuments 2C BC-1C AD, alabaster head 2-1C BC.	
Ivory Room	58	Nimrud carved ivories (*c* 9-7C BC).	
Syrian Room	57	Stelae and antiquities from Syria (4000 BC to the Roman period).	Phoenician obelisk 4-3C BC; Palmyrene tomb 50-217 AD.
Ancient Writing	56	From 2280 BC – Inscriptions on cylinders, tablets, seals.	Date stamps in reverse for imprinting bricks; the Flood Tablet.
Prehistoric Room	55	Pottery, figurines, stone seals.	
Neo-Hittite Landing	53	Sculptures from Carchemish 10-8C BC.	Cult statue of goddess Kubaba.
Ancient Babylonia – Royal Tombs of Ur	54	Headdresses with gold leaves; earrings, gold goblets, a silver lyre, a harp; animal masks; (reconstructed) shrine.	Early Sumerian jewellery; the Chaldees treasure from the city of Ur.
Ancient Anatolia	52	Miniature figures of Hittite Gods; coins, bronzes, arms and armour.	The Gold Tomb 605 BC.
Ancient Iran	51	Luristan bronzes, gold objects and jewellery, Parthian pottery, Achaemenian art, Sassanian vessels.	The Oxus Treasure.
Upper Egyptian Galleries	60-65	Mummies bandaged in cases and coffins; mummified cats, a crocodile; domestic objects; mirrors, clothing and hairstyles; musical instruments; furniture; papyri; wall paintings, portraits.	The **Mummies;** the Book of the Dead.
Coptic Corridor	66	Reliefs and paintings of Roman and Coptic periods in Egypt, 1-9C AD; linen, rugs, tapestry.	Wax Portrait of Artemidorus 2C AD.

Upper Floor East

GALLERY		CONTENTS	SELECTED OBJECTS
Prehistory and Roman Britain	35	Early Christian mosaic: 4C AD, central male head before Chi-Rho monogram thought to be Christ.	**Pavement** from Hinton St Mary, Dorset.
The Stone Age	36	10 500-1600 BC, farm implements, flint axes, pottery.	The Folkton Drums; the Sweet Track *c* 3900 BC; the Meare Bow *c* 2700 BC (replica).
Later European Prehistory	37-39	Earliest human societies; advance from 2000 BC – 1 AD; pre-Roman metalwork; early Celtic jewellery.	Lindow man; Rillaton cup; Witham and Battersea shields; Welwyn Garden city burial 1C BC; Basse Yutz flagons and jars *c* 400 BC.
Roman Britain	40	Daily life (1-4C AD) portrayed through common objects – trade, religion, the army, the home (tableware, mosaics, wall paintings).	Vindolanda tablets; **Mildenhall Treasure** (4C silver). Water Newton treasure. Thetford treasure; Lullingstone wall paintings.
Early Medieval and Medieval Art	41-42	Anglo-Saxon and Romanesque ivories, enamel work, reliquaries, jewellery, religious art and secular utensils.	**The Royal Gold Cup,** *c* 1380; The Lycurgus Cup; the Franks Casket; **Sutton Hoo** treasure; **Lewis Chessmen** (12C); the Westminster Sword of State, 15C; the Savernake horn, Royal Gittern.
Medieval Pottery and Tile Room	43	English and continental pottery and ceramics.	The Canynges Pavement *c* 1461.
Horological Room	44	Clocks before and after the introduction of the pendulum; watches.	The Ship Clock (Nef).
Waddesdon Bequest	45	Renaissance jewellery, plate, enamels, bronzes, majolica.	**Thorn Reliquary; Lyte Jewel** (James I miniature); Limoges enamels; 1554 iron shield.
Renaissance and Later Corridor	46-47	Jewellery, glass and porcelain arranged to compare British craftsmanship with contemporary foreign work.	Royal seals; Battersea enamels, **Huguenot silver;** Hull Grundy gift.
Modern Gallery	48	Vases, tiles, plate and silver ware.	

King Edward VII Galleries

GALLERY		CONTENTS	SELECTED OBJECTS
Ground Floor	34	Chinese porcelain, jade, bronze, terracotta, ivory; Central Asian bronzes; Buddhas; Persian, Syrian metalwork, enamelwork, porcelain; glass; cloisonné ware; Syrian astronomical instruments, Japanese netsuke.	**T'ang horses** and camels; guardian figures; Judge of Hell (16C Chinese); Yuan blue and white porcelain; Sambas Treasure of Buddhist images.
Oriental Art	75	Islamic pottery.	
Upper Floor	67	Prints, drawings displayed in special exhibitions only; portrait drawings; water-colours; modern lithographs.	Michelangelo, Rubens, Rembrandt, Blake, Dürer, Piper, Sutherland...

Mulberry Garden to Royal Palace. – In 1703, John Sheffield, newly created Duke of Buckingham, received from his queen, Anne, a grant of land planted the previous century by James I as a mulberry garden at the west end of St James's Park. His Grace built himself a town residence of brick which he named Buckingham House. Little more than half a century later, in 1762, the mansion was purchased for £28 000 by **George III** and presented to his bride, Charlotte. Although renamed Queen's House, few major alterations were made except the construction in the south wing of George III's octagon library, demolished and replaced in 1854 by the Ball Room (the library was presented to the British Museum).

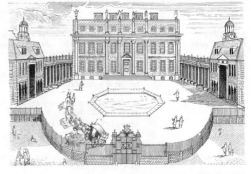

In 1825 George IV summoned **John Nash** and their imaginations fired each other as they had for the recently completed Brighton Pavilion. The architect produced around the core of the old brick mansion, a palace clad in Bath stone. The king however died in 1830 before it was complete and Nash, although technically exonerated from blame for the extravagant expenditure, was discredited

(After engraving, Pitkin Pictorials)

Buckingham House *c* 1710.

and retired, the work in hand being taken over by Edward Blore and completed only in 1837, by which time William IV had also died.

Victoria took up residence three weeks after her accession; the royal standard, at last, was flown on the Marble Arch designed by Nash as a state entrance to the open forecourt. Ten years later came the construction of the east face, linking the advanced north and south wings, enclosing the forecourt in a quadrangle and including what has since become the palace's focal point on public occasions, the balcony. The grand entrance remained in its original position and is approached through arches in the east front; Marble Arch was rendered superfluous and was removed. Finally, in 1912, the east front was heightened and refaced in Portland stone to harmonise with the Mall and new Victoria Memorial.

The West Front and the Gardens. – The west front of golden Bath stone, stepped from an attic frieze at the centre, descends to twin pedimented pavilions from which the eye returns along the line of the white stone terrace balustrade to the central steps and the great bow, balconied and columned at first floor level, balustraded and green saucer domed above. As achieved, the front is a reduced version of Nash's extravaganza: the stone, the strong horizontal lines, the bow, however, were his in essence.

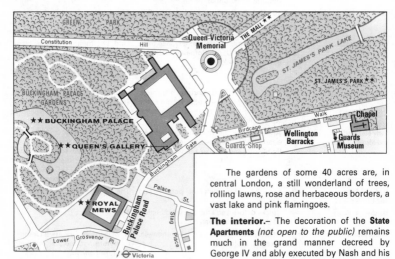

The gardens of some 40 acres are, in central London, a still wonderland of trees, rolling lawns, rose and herbaceous borders, a vast lake and pink flamingoes.

The interior.– The decoration of the **State Apartments** *(not open to the public)* remains much in the grand manner decreed by George IV and ably executed by Nash and his followers in columned proportion with tall windows, coved ceilings, flowing staircases, emphasised in coloured marbles, bronze, ivory, highlighted everywhere with gold and reflected in splendid mirrors and chandeliers.

The areas of the palace familiar to the public are the **Ball Room** where investitures and large state banquets are held and the **Bow Room** through which pass the 8-9000 invited to the garden parties.

The Ball Room, with ivory coloured walls, is 123ft long by 60ft wide and has the canopied royal dais as a focal point in scarlet and gold at the west end. Beneath the canopy, domed, gold fringed and embroidered with the crown, are the thrones and royal arms. On either side gold capitalled pilasters and candelabra; above, supporting emblematic figures, recessed covings outlined in gold as are the compartment ceiling, the corbelled and pedimented doorways, cornice, panelling, wainscoting... In summer, the focus of the Bow Room, also with a decoration of ivory and gold, is the garden seen through tall windows framed by deep crimson curtains.

The apartments of the Royal family are in the north wing.

The Queen's Gallery★★. – *Buckingham Palace Road. Open Tuesdays to Saturdays and holiday Mondays, 10.30am to 5pm, Sundays 2 to 5pm; closed Mondays, Good Friday, 24, 25 December and between exhibitions; £1.20, children, students, OAPs, 60p.*

Details of exhibitions, which run for considerable periods, are to be found in the press.

Built on the site of a former domestic chapel, the gallery presents temporary exhibitions of the portraits, paintings, drawings and furniture in the superb Royal Collection.

Changing of the Guard★★. – *Time 11.30am daily (alternate days September to March) affairs of state and weather permitting – ask the police on duty or telephone 01-730 0791.*

This colourful ceremony takes place in the forecourt when the sovereign is in residence (Royal Standard flying over the palace).

The guard is mounted by the five regiments of Foot of the Guards Division whose uniform of great bearskin, scarlet tunic and dark blue trousers is distinguished by badges, buttons and insignia: the Grenadiers (f 1656), by a white plume, buttons evenly spaced, Coldstreams (f 1650), scarlet plume, buttons by twos, Scots (f 1642), no plume, buttons by threes, Irish (f 1900), blue plume, buttons by fours, Welsh (f 1915), green and white plume, buttons by fives.

Wellington Barracks. – *Birdcage Walk.* Built in 1833 by Sir Francis Smith and P. Hardwick, they are occupied by the 2nd Battalion of the Coldstream Guards.

The Guards Museum. – *Open 10am to 4pm; closed Fridays, 1 January and 25 December; £2, children, OAPs £1.*

Situated under the parade ground of the barracks the museum presents the history of the Guards Regiments from the Civil War origins to the present day. Dioramas, weapons, trophies, uniforms, memorabilia, documents and paintings tell the story of their military campaigns and of their historic role in guarding the sovereign.

The Guards' Chapel. – The chapel arose in 1962-3 from the devastation of a direct hit by a flying bomb in June 1944 when more than 120 died. The lofty clean lined interior is of white marble with clear glass lancet windows opposing brightly lit memorial chapels aligned in a cloister along the south wall. Above hang regimental colours. Note the dark, mosaic lined, apse – all that remained of the 19C church – the screens in the choir arch, the engraved side chapel windows and the terracotta frieze in the Household Cavalry chapel.

The Royal Mews★★. – *Open Wednesdays and Thursdays 2 to 4pm; closed on state occasions, Royal Ascot week in June and bank holidays; £1, OAPs, children 50p.*

The mews which, apart from the earlier Riding House (1764), were built by Nash around a square courtyard are entered through a lion and unicorn gate then a Classical archway, topped by a small clock tower. The blocks around the tree shaded court are occupied by the stables, harness rooms and coach houses where the equipages vary in splendour from modest, covered two wheelers to the open state landau, the Glass Coach in which royal brides and bridegrooms return from their weddings, the Irish Coach in which the Queen rides at the State Opening of Parliament and the Gold State Coach (1762) which has been used at every coronation since 1820.

No 25 **Buckingham Palace Rd** is the HQ of the Guides.

CHELSEA ★★ (Royal Borough of Kensington and Chelsea) _____

The completion of the embankment in 1874 removed for ever the atmosphere of a riverside community – boats drawn up on the mud flats, trees shading the foreshore, people walking along a country road – as painted by Rowlandson in 1789 *(Chelsea Reach)*, watched in his old age at sunset by Turner and luminously captured by Whistler *(Old Battersea Bridge)*.

Chelsea has a Royal Hospital but no "big houses", a few squares, terraces, attractive houses of all periods and 19 and 20C blocks of flats.

By the late 19C, of course, the roads and bridge were constructed and the river no longer served as Chelsea's main access as it had when **Sir Thomas More** came upriver and bought a parcel of land at the water's edge west of the church (approximately on the site of Beaufort St). The house he built was large enough to contain his extensive family, portrayed vividly by **Holbein** on his first visit to England (National Portrait Gallery). Another regular guest in the twelve years More lived in Chelsea, before sailing down river to his execution in 1535, was **Erasmus** and another, who came informally, appearing unannounced at the river gate, was Henry VIII himself. Reminders of More, that "man of marvellous mirth and past-times and sometimes of as sad a gravity, (that) man for all seasons", remain in the memorial inscription he composed himself in the church *(see opposite)* and the statue, a seated, black robed figure with gilded face and hands, on the pavement outside.

(After photograph, Pitkin Pictorials)

Sir Thomas More.

Since those times a varied cavalcade has lived in the village: Nell Gwynn, Ellen Terry, Sybil Thorndyke; Sir Joseph Banks (botanist, explorer and PRS); Sir John Fielding, Sir Marc Isambard Brunel and his son, Isambard Kingdom; Charles Kingsley (Old Church Street); Mrs. Gaskell; the **Pre-Raphaelites** – Dante Gabriel Rossetti, his sister Christina, Burne-Jones, William and Jane Morris, Holman Hunt, Swinburne, Millais. Other artists include William de Morgan, Wilson Steer, Sargent, Augustus John, Orpen, Sickert. Mark Twain, Henry James, T S Eliot are among Chelsea Americans. Smollett lived in Lawrence St, **Oscar Wilde** at 34 Tite St. There were also Hilaire Belloc, the Sitwells, Arnold Bennett... **Thomas Carlyle** in Cheyne Row.

Chelsea has frequently been the setting for a new or revived fashion – the smart and cosmopolitan crowds in the Ranelagh and Cremorne Gardens, the exclusivity of the Pre-Raphaelites and the individuality of Oscar Wilde's green carnation. The opening of Bazaar in

CHELSEA★★

1955 by the designer **Mary Quant,** led to a radical change in dress – the mini skirt; the **King's Road** became a Mecca and Chelsea in the '60s was the "navel of swinging London". More recently the gaudy cockscomb hairstyles of the punk rock craze have dominated the scene.

■ CHEYNE WALK★
Downstream towards the Royal Hospital

The terraces of brick houses standing back from the river front are rich with memories of artists, writers... even the Restoration monarch – the riverside pub, the King's Arms, is named after the arms of Charles II in whose reign it was founded and who is reputed to have been a frequent visitor. Turner spent his last years in near seclusion at 119 Cheyne Walk (restored to the same tall narrow form with a rooftop studio); Brunel House, 105 Cheyne Walk, commemorates the engineers, father and son, who lived at no 98.

Lindsey House. – *96-100 Cheyne Walk, west end.* The house, from 1752 the London headquarters of the Moravian Brethren (their burial ground to the right of Milman's St can be seen from the rear of the flats), was built for the 3rd Earl of Lindsey in 1674 on the site of Sir Thomas More's farm. The 17C Lindsey mansion (since subdivided) of brick, is centrally pedimented and quoined. Whistler resided at No 96.

Nos 92 and 91 Cheyne Walk. – The houses, built in 1771, are rich in Venetian windows – 2 in 92 and 5 (2 blind) in 91; other characteristics are parallel arches over the garage (formerly a passage) and front door in 92, a modestly fine entrance to 91 and a conservatory on the first floor, with a commanding view of the river. Nos 93 and 94 date from 1777.

Crosby Hall. – *Open daily 10am to noon, 2 to 4pm; closed 1 January, Good Friday, Easter, 25, 26 December and holiday Mondays.*

A regrettable post-war annexe and a neo-Tudor building of 1926, the premises of the British Federation of University Women, look puny beside the great hall of the 15C wool merchant, **Sir John Crosby,** whose residence, built between 1466-75, stood in medieval Bishopsgate. The panelled hall, with its painted hammerbeam roof, three-tier oriel window and a fireback stamped with an early version of the wool mark, was transferred to its present site in 1910.

Roper's Garden. – This walled garden, once part of More's orchard, is named after William Roper, his son-in-law. An upstanding stone relief of a woman walking against the wind by **Jacob Epstein** commemorates the artist's years in Chelsea (1909-14).

Chelsea Old Church. – The church dates from pre-Norman, possibly Saxon times, evolving until by 20C it appeared with a nave and tower of c 1670, 13C chancel and early 14C chapels of which the south one had been remodelled by Sir Thomas More in 1528. In 1941 it was badly bombed except for the More chapel; in 1950-8 it was reconstructed on the old foundations so that it looks substantially as in old prints and paintings. Inside, the nave divides beneath three arches at the east end into the chancel, the Lawrence and More Chapels; the monuments, rescued from the rubble, are old; the furnishings old supplemented by modern replacements – the altar and rails are 17C, the small marble font dates from 1673, the **chained books,** presented by Sir Hans Sloane and the only ones in a London church, consist of a Vinegar Bible (1717), a prayer book (1723), *Homilies* (1683) and two volumes of Foxe's *Book of Martyrs* (1684).

Quite new are the kneelers, embroidered 1953-8, to commemorate by coats of arms or symbols, those associated with the church – among the 400 are Elizabeth I, Holman Hunt, Sir Hans Sloane, Sir Thomas More... Among the monuments are the reclining figure of Lady Jane Cheyne (1699), Sarah Colville with aghast expression and upraised hands (1631; Lawrence Chapel), the massive Stanley monument of 1632 and, near the squint, the small alabaster group of Sir Thomas Lawrence, City goldsmith and merchant adventurer, at prayer with his wife and eight children. More's self-composed inscription stands against the south wall of the sanctuary by the arch with capitals dated 1528, designed by Holbein. The novelist Henry James is also buried here while in the churchyard an urn marks the grave of Sir Hans Sloane.

It was in **Lawrence Street** that the Chelsea China Works flourished in the 18C before being transferred to Derby. Among 18C houses to remain are the early Georgian, Dukes and Monmouth Houses, sharing a pedimented porch on carved brackets (nos 23-24).

Carlyle's House. – *24 Cheyne Row. Open April to end October, 11am to 5pm; closed Mondays, except holiday Mondays, Tuesdays, Good Friday, £1.60, children 80p. NT.*

Thomas Carlyle lived in this modest Queen Anne house for 47 years, working, walking, dour and apart, though his young wife loved company. The "Sage of Chelsea" is commemorated in a statue by Boehm in Cheyne Walk gardens.

On the southwest corner of Oakley Street is a bronze of a boy poised high above a dolphin by David Wynne. The Antarctic explorer, Captain R.F. Scott, lived at No 56.

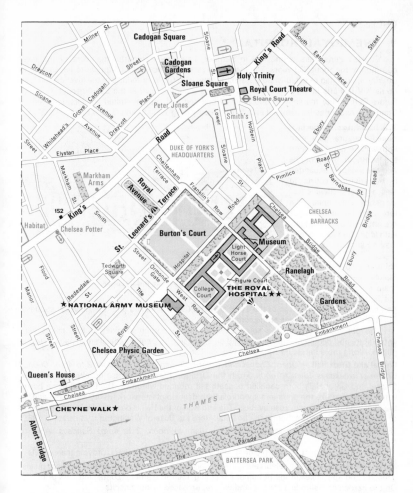

Henry VIII's Chelsea Palace.

Henry VIII's Chelsea Palace. – Nos 19-26 Cheyne Walk, dating from c 1765, occupy the site of Henry's riverside palace. Built in 1537 and known as the New Manorhouse (the Old Manorhouse, demolished in 1704, stood where Lawrence St is), the two storey Tudor brick mansion included "three cellars, three halls, three parlours, three kitchens... a large staircase, three drawing rooms, seventeen chambers"; water was brought by conduit from Kensington. Here resided the young Prince Edward, Princess Elizabeth and their cousin Lady Jane Grey, followed at the king's death first by Catherine Parr (d 1548) and then by Anne of Cleves (d 1557). It was owned by the Cheynes in 17C and then by **Sir Hans Sloane,** who retired to Chelsea with his two daughters and his collection *(p 36)* from 1712 until his death in 1753 when the house was demolished.

No 18 was the popular Don Saltero's coffeehouse and museum. No 16, named the **Queen's House** after Catherine of Braganza, although it was not built till 1717 twelve years after her death, was the home of the poet and painter D.G. Rossetti and where the Pre-Raphaelites used to meet; the house is, apart from the bay window, unaltered with a central pediment, segment headed windows, brick corner pilasters and the finest among several contemporary iron gateways. A fountain in the gardens opposite includes a portrait bust of Rossetti by Seddon.

No 6 is remarkable for the Chippendale-Chinese gate and railings before the large plain parapet while no 5 has beautiful, conventional, railings. A Corinthian pilastered and entablatured entrance marks no 4 where the painter Maclise lived and George Eliot spent her last weeks. Old Swan House, no 17 on the Embankment (1876), is a town house by Norman Shaw.

Chelsea Physic Garden.

Chelsea Physic Garden. – *Open early April to late October, Wednesdays and Sundays, 2 to 5pm; closed holiday Mondays; £1.50.*

The garden was founded in 1673 by the Worshipful Society of Apothecaries of London on land leased from Sir Hans Sloane who in 1722 granted the Society the lease in perpetuity. The record of the garden, overlooked at the centre by a statue of Sir Hans, is remarkable: Georgia's cotton seeds came from the South Seas via the Physic Garden, India's tea from China, her quinine *(cinchona)* from S America, Malaya's rubber from S America...

National Army Museum*.

National Army Museum*. – *Royal Hospital Rd. Open weekdays 10am (Sundays 2pm) to 5.30pm ; closed 1 January, Good Friday, May Day holiday, 24, 25, 26 December.*

The museum tells the story of the British Army from the formation of the Yeomen of the Guard by Henry VII on Bosworth Field in 1485, of the Indian Army and of colonial forces. The Story of the Army gallery illustrates campaigns in every continent, the evolution from armour to khaki and tin helmets. A new gallery continues the story from the First World War to the present day : reconstructions, models, dramatic audio-visual displays and dioramas. The domestic life of the soldier is also recreated.

The Weapons gallery demonstrates the development of hand held weapons from pikes and swords to revolvers and repeating rifles, pistols and machine guns. The Uniform gallery displays buckskin breeches, helmets, caps and hats; also notable honours and decorations, many very beautiful in their coloured enamelwork and craftsmanship. The Art gallery contains mainly portraits by Reynolds, Romney, Gainsborough, Lawrence and others.

■ THE ROYAL HOSPITAL★★

Chelsea Pensioners, some 400 in number, have been colourful members of the local community for about 300 years. The idea for a veterans' hostel would appear to have come to Charles II, who had re-established a standing army in 1661, from reports of the Invalides built by Louis XIV in Paris in 1670. The next ten years are summarised in the Latin inscription in the Figure Court: "For the support and relief of maimèd and superannuated soldiers, founded by Charles II, expanded by James II and completed by King William and Queen Mary – 1692".

The buildings. – Wren produced a quadrangular plan with a main court open on the south to the grounds and the river. He expanded it by abutting courts to east and west always leaving one side open. The long, regular brick ranges are marked at the angles with stone quoins and midway by stone centrepieces pierced at ground level, colossally pilastered and plainly pedimented. The main entrance is beneath the lantern crowned octa-

Figure Court, Royal Hospital.

gon porch in the north range of the original **Figure Court,** so-called after the Classical statue of Charles II by **Grinling Gibbons** at the centre.

The porch emerges on the south side beneath a portico of giant Tuscan pillars with entablature and pediment, which is flanked on either side by a colonnade of small paired Tuscan pillars. Along the entablature runs the historical Latin inscription *(see above).*

Chapel and Great Hall. – *Open: Chapel and Great Hall daily 10am to noon, 2 to 4pm; Council Chamber weekdays 10am to noon.* From the Octagon Porch steps rise on either side to the Chapel and Great Hall, both panelled beneath tall rounded windows. The Chapel has a barrel vault, decorated like the piers and spandrels with delicate plasterwork (Henry Margetts) and, at the end, a domed, painted, apse by Ricci. The end wall of the Hall is decorated with an 18C mural of Charles II on horseback before the hospital. Here the Duke of Wellington lay in state in 1852.

The Museum. – *Open Monday to Saturday, 10am to noon, 2 to 4pm; Sundays, April to September, 2 to 4pm; closed holiday Mondays.*

Wellington mementoes, the history of the hospital and its members, provide the exhibits.

Ranelagh Gardens. – The celebrated gardens opened in 1724, offering patrons *al fresco* meals, concerts and spectacles in the Rotunda, a building 150ft in diameter containing tiers of boxes. On the garden's closure in 1805 the land was repurchased by the hospital.

The **Chelsea Flower Show** *(p 30),* displaying flowers, plants and everything else imaginable for a garden, has been held in the grounds by the Royal Horticultural Society since 1913.

Royal Avenue, (planted in 1692-4), leads north from the Royal Hospital across the fields known as **Burton's Court** to King's Rd – it was planned to extend to Kensington Palace but was never completed. The terrace houses on either side date from the early and mid 19C. **St Leonard's Terrace** is Chelsea's most attractive mid 18C, Georgian row (14-31), the small streets off the north side of King's Rd, lined by former artisans' cottages, its most traditional.

■ ADDITIONAL SIGHTS

Sloane Sq is notable for several reasons: architecturally – Peter Jones (1936) remains one of London's most successful shop exteriors; historically – it was where William Willett invented daylight saving or **summer time** (adopted 1916); theatrically – the **Royal Court Theatre** has twice, since it opened in 1870, launched a new vogue: in 1904-07 when Harley Granville Barker put on Arthur Pinero farces, and plays by Bernard Shaw and Somerset Maugham and in 1956-8 when the English Stage Co under George Devine presented Osborne's *Look Back in Anger.*

Residential development can be traced in the squares: **Paultons** (1830-40), **Carlyle** (mid 19C), **Chelsea** (18/19/20C), the architectural style of the area centred on **Cadogan Gardens** and **Square** (19C) goes by the 20C nickname of 'Pont Street Dutch'.

Holy Trinity. – *Sloane St.* The church was rebuilt in 1888 when the Pre-Raphaelites were at their height. **Burne-Jones** seeing it under construction proposed the design with flowing tracery of the 48 panel east window of the saints for which the glass was made by William Morris. All decoration is of the period and harmonises with the architect, Sedding's, own designs for the High Altar crucifix and candlesticks. Note also the variously coloured marbles, the pulpit stair rail, the bronze panels in the choir and the singular railings outside on Sloane St.

King's Road. – Originally a path taken by Charles II to visit Nell Gwynn in her house at Fulham, the King's Rd was closed, except to those holding a royal pass, from 1719 to 1830 owing to its attraction to footpads. It is now famous for its shops, antiques, restaurants and pubs.

The Pheasantry. – *No 152.* Only the façade and portico remain of the building erected in 1881 on the site of an 18C pheasantry and later used as a dance school and artists' meeting place.

St Luke's. – *Sydney St.* The Bath stone church of 1820, an early example of the Gothic Revival, is tall and lanky both outside and in. The pinnacled and slimly buttressed 142ft west tower is pierced at the base to provide a porch which extends the full width of the west front.

New Cremorne Gardens. – *Lots road junction.* The pleasant 1 1/4 acre gardens (1982) on the southeast corner of the former pleasure gardens (1843-92) include the original gates, a pool and a weighbridge from neighbouring wharves. Views of the river.

Chelsea Harbour. – This riverside development built around a marina and comprising luxury housing, offices, a hotel, shops and restaurants, is enhanced by its fortunate setting. Fine views of the Thames and of St Mary's, Battersea *(qv)* on the south bank.

Chiswick remained a country village until the 1860s when within 20 years the population increased from 6 500 to 15 600. But whereas neighbouring Ealing, Acton, Brentford, in the same circumstances, became suburbs, Chiswick has retained its individuality. Georgian houses remain in roads leading down to the river such as Church St and most notably on the attractive riverside reach overlooking the Eyot, Chiswick Mall. Even within a stone's throw of such 20C monuments as the Gt West Rd roundabout, there are enclaves like Chiswick Sq (on Burlington Lane) where a forecourt, flanked by low, two storey houses of 1680 precedes the three floor Boston House, built in 1740, where Thackeray had Becky Sharp throw away her dictionary.

Chiswick House★. – *Burlington Lane. Open 15 March to 15 October, daily 9.30am to 6.30pm; 16 October to 14 March Wednesday to Sunday, 9.30am to 4pm; closed 1 January, 24, 25, 26 December; £1, children, OAPs 75p.*

Chiswick, a Jacobean mansion set in extensive acres, was purchased by the first Earl of Burlington in 1682; in 18C Richard Boyle, 3rd **Earl of Burlington** (1695-1753), connoisseur, and generous host-patron (Kent, Rysbrack, Campbell, Pope, Swift, Gay, Thompson, Handel...), first made alterations and additions. Fashion had changed from Wren's ebullient Baroque to the classically inspired and Burlington on his return from his second Grand Tour (1714, 1719) designed a Palladian villa (1725-9) in which to display his works of art and entertain his friends.

William Kent (1686-1748) a follower of Inigo Jones and Burlington's protégé, was responsible for much of the interior decoration and the gardens. (18 and 19C additions made by Georgiana, Duchess of Devonshire and queen of society and her successors who entertained Charles James Fox, Canning, Edward VII, the tsars... have since been demolished, as was the Jacobean mansion in 1788, leaving only Burlington's villa.)

Exterior. – The villa, approached up an avenue of terms (busts carved in one with short base pillars) and less than 70ft square, has all the grace of classical proportion. Paired dog-leg staircases – statues of Palladio (left) and I. Jones (right) by Rysbrack (*c* 1730) – ascend to a portico behind whose pediment is a raised octagonal dome, guarded on either side by obelisks.

Interior. – The lower floor – octagon hall (with wine cellar below), lobbies and library – now displays drawings and other material about the creation and restoration of the house and garden. A door in the north east corner of the library leads through the pillared link building to the Summer Parlour (*c* 1717) originally connected to the 17C mansion. The grisaille paintings are by Keller (1719).

On the principal floor (staircase to the left of the library), the public rooms follow a square plan of intercommunicating rooms around a central octagon which itself communicates with the oblong shaped room on each of the three sides and the gallery opposite the entrance. The **Dome Saloon,** its eight walls punctuated alternately by pedimented gold highlighted doors and classical busts, rises by way of an ochre coloured entablature to a windowed drum and diamond patterned dome. The Red, Green and Blue Velvet Rooms are rich with gilded highlights on ceiling coffering, Venetian windows and pedimented door casings, carvings, chimneypieces (the flues lead out through the roof obelisks). Note the roundels in the Blue Room of Inigo Jones (by Dobson) and Pope (by Kent). The **gallery,** on the garden front consists of three rooms: the apsed, oblong centre room, communicating through arches to circular and octagonal end rooms, gilded and endlessly multiplied in mirrors. From the octagonal room a passage leads north into the upper storey of the link building which is adorned with Corinthian columns.

The Gardens. – The gardens were landscaped, including the giant cedars, in the main, by William Kent. He modified Burlington's earlier, geometrical, plan of avenues and formal vistas, so that the canal became serpentine and temples, obelisks and statues were so placed that one came on them unawares. Later owners left their mark: Georgiana made the design even freer and had Wyatt build a bridge across the water; Joseph Paxton probably came from Chatsworth to erect the greenhouse: Italian formal gardens were laid out providing a brilliant pattern of colour. The Inigo Jones Gateway *(northeast of the house)* was erected in 1621 outside Beaufort House in Chelsea and presented by Sir Hans Sloane to the 3rd Earl in 1736.

Hogarth's House★. – *Hogarth Lane, Great West Rd. Open 11am to 1pm (Sundays, bank holidays 2pm) to 6pm, October to March to 4pm; closed Tuesdays, 1 January, Good Friday, 25, 26 December, first two weeks in September and last three weeks in December.*

William Hogarth was 52 and well established when he acquired his "box by the Thames", a three storey brick house, to which he added a hanging bay window above the front door, in a small garden shaded by a still flourishing mulberry tree. He spent not only the summers, but ever longer periods at Chiswick although a Londoner born, apprenticed (in Leicester Fields now Sq) and famous as a commentator on contemporary 18C London life. "Conversation pieces", collected by contemporaries who recognised in them personalities of the day, can be seen in the house: *the Election, London Scenes, The Harlot's Progress, Marriage à la Mode* and many more.

St Nicholas Parish Church. – *Open Sundays 10am to 7pm.* The church, last rebuilt in 1884 on a site dating back to 1181, has a buttressed and battlemented west tower of 1436. The list of vicars, with a few gaps, traces incumbents by name from 1225.

In the burial ground are the tombs of Hogarth, Lord Burlington, William Kent, Whistler and P. de Loutherbourg.

Chiswick Mall★★. – Among the more outstanding 18/19C houses with bow windows and balconies overlooking the river and wisteria hazing the walls are **Morton House,** dating from 1730, of brick with red brick surrounds to the windows of its three storeys, **Strawberry House,** next door, 1730 also but 6 bays wide, 2 floors high with attic dormers, a wide central balcony supported on iron pillars and, at the centre, slender fluted pillars outlining the porch. **Walpole House,** begun in 16C, was increased in 17C so that it presents an irregular advanced brick face. In front are a fine iron gate and railings. A one time owner was Barbara Villiers, Duchess of Cleveland, towards the sunset of her days (d 1709). In 19C the house became a school with Thackeray among its pupils – the Miss Pinkerton's Academy of *Vanity Fair* it is said.

The **Bedford Park** estate at Turnham Green, a garden suburb of 2 to 3 storey houses, each with its own garden, was begun in 1877 and soon became identified with the aesthetic movement of which Ruskin and William Morris were leading exponents. The red brick Queen Anne style, with tile-hanging, rough-cast rendering and white woodwork, was set by Richard Norman Shaw who also designed the church, shop and inn.

The City, fortified by the Romans and with the perimeter rebuilt in the Middle Ages, retains a unity of place, although walls, ditches, gates and bars remain in name only; urban development beginning as early as 12C in suburbs just beyond the walls, increased by the Plague and the Great Fire, when some 300 000 left the inner city, and intensified in 19 and 20C, hems the City on all sides but does not blur its particularity. The buildings, relatively, have never been old: the fires for centuries were too frequent – in 7, 8C, in 1087 when St Paul's was burnt, and finally in 1666, too devastating. The Act for Rebuilding the City of London in 1667 stipulated that all future structures, houses included, should be of brick and thus reduce fire damage; the demands of commerce which occupied an ever greater area, called for repeated rebuilding to expand or, as a mark of prosperity, to be in the latest approved 19 or 20C style be it Victorian, Classical, 20 s modern... Finally fire again, in the form of bombs, cleared much of the ground once more and, with further demolition, provided space for tower office blocks.

Of the **Celtic fishing village,** established on the north bank where twin hills rose behind the gravel strand which provided the first ford and subsequently first bridging point across the river, nothing remains outside the Museum of London; of the Roman **Londinium,** a river crossing fortified after Boadicea and her hordes had sacked the City in 61AD and it had been rebuilt as a bridgehead and hub of the road system which led from the Kentish ports to all parts of the country including the more important capitals of Verulamium (St Albans) and Camulodunum (Colchester), there are stretches of wall and the Temple of Mithras.

William I, who received a separate submission by the citizens two months after the Battle of Hastings, built the Tower, his fellow Norman, Baynard's Castle (and another, Mountfichet), at either river extremity of the City wall, both fortified less against future invaders than as a symbol of strength should the citizens reconsider their submission! The spokesmen requested and the Conqueror granted the City a **Charter,** the first, whereby government, law and dues devolved directly upon the citizens themselves; under John, who in 1215 confirmed a second charter, government advanced towards the Corporation and Londoners were empowered to elect annually their own mayor (elsewhere a royal appointment) who had only to submit himself formally at Westminster for royal approval – "ridings" now known as the Lord Mayor's Show. The City thrived: it loaned or gave money to Edward III and Henry V for wars on the continent and apart from the risings of Wat Tyler in 1381 and Jack Cade in 1450, kept clear of strife, even the Wars of the Roses. Merchants, such as Whittington, and including the Hanseatics who had arrived by 1157, grew rich in every variety of trade particularly wool and cloth; they built great timber framed, gabled, mansions and some bought country estates. The craft and artisan guilds developed into livery companies with a powerful voice; the population teemed, increased by refugees especially Flemish, and later French, Huguenots (15-16C). Houses, tall and oversailing, lined the narrow streets.

In place of royal and ecclesiastical palaces there were monasteries with magnificent churches erected by the religious orders – the Dominicans who arrived in England in 1221 and constructed Blackfriars in 1276, the Franciscans (1224) whose Greyfriars Church was begun at Newgate in 1306, the Carmelites (1241) had a house off Fleet St and the Austin Friars (1253) by Moorgate; there were also priories: Rahere's with the attached medical school of St Bartholomew, St John's and Charterhouse. All were ripe for picking at the time of the **Dissolution** and Henry VIII plucked them all, seizing riches, destroying buildings, nominating himself as re-founder of the hospitals – St Bartholomew's and Bedlam – and all without souring his relations with the City from now on the home of the royal wardrobe. Finally St Paul's, one of the great Gothic cathedrals of Europe, was stripped of its holy statues and remaining riches under Edward VI.

Elizabeth's merchant adventurers were financed more often by the City than the queen but James I subsidised the New River scheme *(p 72)* which brought fresh water to the street standards. Charles I, always forcing loans, requiring gifts, ship money and tonnage, and applying restrictions to trade, worsened relations to such a degree that the five members the king went down to the Commons to search out in 1642 were given sanctuary in the City; under Cromwell the Jews, banished in 1292, returned in strength.

The City was by now peopled not only by merchants, bankers and craftsmen but had entered on the period of being the forum of those who write and print broadsheets and newspapers and talk, of Shakespeare, Donne, Ben Jonson, Dryden, Pepys, Evelyn, Addison and Steele, Swift, Dickens, of Wren, of Reynolds, of Samuel Johnson...

One fifth of the increasingly humanly diversified City within the walls remained standing on 6 September 1666 after the **Great Fire** had died down. Wren submitted a sketch plan for its rebuilding on 11 September and Evelyn on 13 September 1666. Neither materialised. **Wren** eventually rebuilt St Paul's but not as a focal point; the streets and courts, of which 400 had been destroyed, were soon lined by new brick houses and taverns; the prisons, numerous, insanitary, corrupt and cruel were rapidly rebuilt. Only in 19C were wide roads cut through to the bridges in an endeavour to ease the persistent traffic congestion.

Today the resident population numbers about 8 000 – half in the Barbican; the workforce nearer 4 million. Traditions are maintained alongside the latest practices – transactions are still agreed on the nod as well as contracted on a worldwide electronic network; there is an annual cutting of a red rose by the Watermen and Lightermen, the occasional presentation of a fan; the PM makes a major policy speech at the Lord Mayor's Banquet, visitors of state attend a banquet or ceremony in the City, the royal carriage halts at Temple Bar when the sovereign enters the City – gestures symbolising a unique tradition, jealously guarded.

NB: *the Square Mile being so compact and the interest being particularly by subject, sights have been grouped: St Paul's and the City Churches; the Corporation and Livery Companies; the Bank and exchanges; the markets; the main thoroughfare landmarks.*

When an ancient site is cleared for redevelopment, it is often made available for archaeological investigation before rebuilding begins. Such sites are often open to the public who may also be invited to assist in the dig.

■ ST PAUL'S CATHEDRAL★★★

Where its predecessors had perished, Wren's cathedral was preserved (on specific orders from Churchill) and became, for wartime Londoners, a talisman, as the dome and cross, which had soared above the smoke and flames of the raid of 29 December 1940 when the whole City and docks were set ablaze, remained inviolate and appeared serene each morning against the pale dawn sky.

HISTORY

Our St Paul's is probably the 4th or even the 5th in line on the site. The first, of which no trace remains, was founded in 604 AD; a second may have been built in 675-85 under the aegis of St Erkenwald, Bishop of London. It or its successor was burnt down by the Danes in 962, rebuilt and burnt again in the fire which devastated the City in 1087. The cathedral which next arose took until 1240 to construct being on a great scale with a nave of 12 bays, far flung transepts and a shallow, apsed chancel which was replaced in 1258-1314 by a longer decorated choir until finally the building measured 620ft from west to east. In 1221 the massive tower above the central crossing was embellished by the addition of a lead covered steeple which rose to 514ft. In 1561 this spire was struck by lightning and caught fire; despite the evidence of some contemporary engravings, it was never replaced and the whole building suffered from general neglect and even desecration: the west towers were used as prisons, relics and shrines had been

(After Vischer's engraving, Pitkin Pictorials)

St Paul's before the Great Fire.

looted, "the south aisle", wrote a Bishop of Durham of the time, was used "for popery and usury and the north for Simony, and the horse fair in the midst for all kinds of bargains, meetings, brawlings, murders, conspiracies and the font for ordinary payments of money".

Royal commissions under the first two Stuarts on the "decayed fabric" resulted in the refacing of the nave and west transept walls, repairs to the choir screen and in **Inigo Jones** erecting an outstanding Classical portico with columns 50ft high at the cathedral's west end. Neglect in the Civil War brought, in Carlyle's words, "horses stamping in the canons' stalls" and mean shops squatting in the portico. A new commission (1663), included among its members **Christopher Wren,** then 31 and untried as an architect though reputed as a geometer, astronomer, FRS. On 27 August 1666 his fellow commissioner, John Evelyn, noted in his diary "I went to St Paul's church with Dr Wren... to survey the general decays of that ancient and venerable church; ... we had a mind to build it with a noble cupola". Ten days later, after the Fire, he wrote: "St Paul's is now a sad ruin and that beautiful portico now rent in pieces...".

Wren's cathedral. – Within 6 days of the end of the Fire, Wren had submitted a plan for rebuilding the City; it was not accepted. For two years the authorities dallied with the idea, opposed by Wren, of patching up the cathedral fabric. Then in 1668, they invited him to submit designs. He produced the First Model, the Great Model, the Warrant Design; each was rejected by the church authorities so he resolved to submit no more plans but as Surveyor General to the King's Works (1669) to go ahead "as ordered by his Majesty". The foundation stone was laid without ceremony on 21 June 1675 and work proceeded until, after thirty-three years unceasing work, Wren saw his son set the final stone, the topmost in the lantern, in place – he was 75, the date 1708. Fifteen years later, in 1723, he was buried within its walls.

Figures. – The cost of the cathedral, on record as £736 752 3s 3 1/4 d was met, together with that of rebuilding the City Churches, by a tax levied on all sea coal imported into the Port of London. Wren was paid £200 a year during the cathedral's construction (the font cost £350 in 1727). The dimensions are: length overall 500ft; height to the summit of the cross 365ft; of the portico columns 40ft. St Paul by Francis Bird at the pediment apex is 12ft tall. The length of the nave is 180ft, the width, including the aisles, 121ft; width across the transepts 242ft; internal diameter of the dome110ft; height of the nave 92 1/2ft; to the Whispering Gallery 100ft; to the internal dome apex 218ft. The total area is approximately 78 000 sq ft.

When visiting St Paul's take time also to explore the precinct, to spot the steeples of the nearby City Churches. Return to visit the churches, organising yourself to be present at midday for a service, concert, debate... (programme from the City Information Centre, St Paul's Churchyard, EC4; Tel. 01-260 1456/7, 01-260 3456).

The CITY★★★

TOUR

Open 9am to 6pm. Dome and galleries (£1, children 50p), Crypt and Treasury (80p, children 40p) and Choir and Ambulatory (60p) 10am weekdays (11am Saturdays) to 4.15pm; closed Good Friday and Christmas Day. Guided tours 11, 11.30am, 2 and 2.30pm, except Sundays, £3.60, children £1.60. Access limited during services: weekdays 8am, 5pm, Saturdays 10am, Sundays 8, 10.30, 11.30am, 3.15pm. Subject to alteration for special services.

St Paul's from the south.

Exterior. – The **dome,** mounted on a balustraded drum, encircled by pillars and crowned above a stone lantern by a golden ball and cross, is not only the cathedral's dominant feature but also that of the London skyline – even today when office blocks rise all around.

The dome is, in fact, three structures *(see illustration):* the outer profile, a lead covered timber superstructure; an invisible inner brick cone which supports the weight of the lantern; and the inner brick dome with a 20ft diameter opening at the apex into the space beneath the lantern and which, as frescoed and circled by the Whispering Gallery, is the one seen from inside the church.

The drum, outside, is in the form of two tiers, the lower encircled by columns, punctuated 8 times (for structural reasons) by a decoratively niched radiating wall and crowned by a balustrade; the upper tier is recessed behind the balustrade in such a way as to afford a circular viewing gallery, the **Stone Gallery.** Unlike the dome of St Peter's, which so fascinated and influenced Wren, it is not a true hemisphere. The lantern, 21ft across, is also of restrained English Baroque with detached columns projecting on all four sides and a small cupola serving as plinth to the 6 1/2ft diameter golden ball.

The **west end** presents, at the top of two wide flights of steps, a two tier portico of coupled Corinthian and composite columns beneath a decorated pediment surmounted by the figure of St Paul. On either side rise the west towers, Wren's most Baroque spires, designed as the close foil to the dome.

The **north and south sides, and east end** are enclosed within a wall two storeys high with coupled pilasters against the rusticated stone, punctuated, at the lower level by rounded windows with segmental hoods, garlanded and cherub decorated beneath the cornice frieze. On the upper level the blind windows are designed as niches.

The **transepts,** which are shallow, end in semicircular, columned porticoes crowned by statues surmounting the triangular pediments. The upper level of the 111ft high wall, except at the east and transept ends, is an advanced screen – an enclosure of the structural buttressing, and is itself a support for the dome.

The overall design is majestic; each feature fits and adds to the effect – many only stand out, to the untutored eye, when caught by a change in the light or when the floodlights are on. Finally, and on no account to be missed, is the carving everywhere: statues, reliefs, figures by Caius Cibber, Francis Bird, garlands, swags, panels, cherub heads in the stone by Grinling Gibbons.

Interior. – The immediate impression is one of size, of almost luminescent stone all around and, in the far distance, of gold and mosaic.

Wren's church was without extraneous monuments. They were introduced in 1790 when the figures of four national benefactors (Joshua Reynolds, John Howard the penal reformer, Dr Johnson and Sir William Jones the orientalist) were placed by the dome piers; since then marble statuary has proliferated.

The nave. – Before advancing up the nave, note immediately abutting the aisles respectively to left and right the chapels of St Dunstan, and St Michael and St George each preceded by a 17/18C finely carved wooden screen rising to a crest incorporating broken pediments, coats of arms, vases. The square pillars dividing the nave and aisles are faced towards the centre with fluted, Corinthian pilasters which sweep up to the entablature, the wrought iron gallery railing, clerestory and garlanded saucer domes.

The Wellington monument, which occupies the entire space between two piers in the north aisle and ascends from a recumbent bronze effigy at the base to a full size equestrian statue of the duke at the apex, was the lifework of Alfred Stevens and completed only in 1912 long after the sculptor's death (1875). Holman Hunt's *The Light of the World* hangs in the south aisle.

Note the late 19C bronze gasoliers and in the pavement the Night Watch memorial stone (cathedral guardians 1939-45), the inscription commemorating the resting of Sir Winston Churchill's coffin in the cathedral during the state funeral service on 30 January 1965 and, beneath the dome, Wren's own epitaph in Latin: Reader, if you seek his monument, look around you.

The Dome. – *Times of opening: see above; £1. Entrance: south aisle transept: 530 steps.*

From the **Whispering Gallery** *(259 steps)* there is an impressive view of the concourse far below; there are also unusual perspectives to be seen of the choir, the arches, the clerestory and close views including that of the interior of the dome itself painted by **Thornhill.**

The **views**★★★ from the **Golden Gallery** at the top of the dome are better than from the Stone Gallery *(530 steps)* because it dominates most of the post-war tower blocks and one can walk round to see in all directions.

The crossing and transepts. – The open space beneath the dome is emphasised by the giant piers which surround it and mark the openings to the shallow transepts. That to the north serves as a baptistry and contains the dish shaped font carved in 1727 by Francis Bird, that to the south includes the exceptional portrait statue of **Nelson** by Flaxman and at the end the beautiful wooden doorcase of fluted columns enriched by garlands made up in 19C from a wood screen designed by Wren and carved by Grinling Gibbons.

Choir and Ambulatory. – *60p.* The marble high altar, covered by a massive post-war pillared baldachino, carved and gilded after drawings by Wren, fills the east end. Above, the gilding is reflected in gold and glass mosaics of the turn of the century, which also face the vaulting above the aisle (note the Christ in Majesty in the apsidal dome). In the foreground, warm in the light of red shaded candle lights, are the dark oak **choir stalls**, pillared beneath a crested canopy, the exquisite work of **Grinling Gibbons** and his craftsmen. Each stall differs in detail, in the flowers, leaves and fruits that make up wreaths and garlands, in the cherubs' expressions. Even the stall backs are carved forming a screen on the chancel aisles. The organ,

(By courtesy of Architectural Press)

St Paul's: dome cross section.

originally a late 17C Smith instrument, and the case, again by Gibbons, have been divided and now tower on either side of the choir opening.

The iron **railing**, originally the altar rail, the **gates** to the choir aisles, and the great gilded **screens** enclosing the sanctuary, are the work of **Jean Tijou,** wrought iron smith extraordinary. In the north aisle, before the Chapel of modern martyrs, a 14C Graduale, a 'Breeches' Bible (16C) and mementoes of thanksgiving services from Queen Anne to Elizabeth II are on display. The graceful sculpture of the Virgin and Child is by H. Moore (1984). In the south choir aisle, against the first outer west pillar, is the statue of **John Donne**, Dean of St Paul's 1621-31 and metaphysical poet, carved by Nicholas Stone. He stands on an urn in the up-ended coffin (which he kept in his house), wrapped in his shroud, crowned, but from his expression, much alive!

Crypt. – *Times of opening: p 48; 80p, children 40p. Entrance in south transept.*

At the east end, simply decorated with royal banners, is the OBE chapel. Grouped in bays formed by the massive piers which support the low groined and tunnel vaulting, are the tombs, memorials and busts of men of all the talents of the 18, 19 and 20C, British, Commonwealth or foreign who contributed to the national life; not all those commemorated are buried in the crypt:

- In the south aisle east of the staircase are John Rennie (2nd recess), Sir Max Beerbohm and Walter de la Mare (north and west faces of pillar) and Christopher Wren, beneath a plain black marble stone with above him the inscription: *Si monumentum requiris circumspice.* Others commemorated in this aisle, known as Artists' Corner, include George Dance the Younger, Blake, Novello, Lutyens, Landseer, Lawrence, Benjamin West, Leighton, Millais, Turner, Reynolds and Holman Hunt.
- In the north aisle are Sir Arthur Sullivan, Parry, William Boyce (on the floor), John Singer Sargent, beneath a relief by himself (choir face of dividing wall), Steer, Munnings, Constable, Sir Alexander Fleming and a bronze bust of Stafford Cripps by Epstein (1953).
- Down the steps in the Cornish porphyry sarcophagus is **Wellington.** Recently added in the chamber are memorials to ten of the great soldiers of World War II. Beyond, to the south, is the plaque to Florence Nightingale.

Below the dome, at the centre of a circle of Tuscan columns lies **Nelson** beneath a curving black marble sarcophagus (originally intended for Cardinal Wolsey and subsequently proposed but rejected for Henry VIII). Beneath the arches to the south are admirals Beatty, Jellico and Cunningham, and a bronze bust of W E Henley by Rodin (1903). Opposite on the north side are military figures, also T E Lawrence by Epstein. Only a handful of effigies were rescued from Old St Paul's in which were buried John of Gaunt, Thomas Linacre (c 1460-1524; founder of the Royal College of Physicians, teacher of Greek to Thomas More and Erasmus), Sir Philip Sidney, Sir Anthony van Dyck (modern plaque).

The **Treasury** *(north transept)* displays plate and vestments belonging to the Cathedral and on loan from parishes in the London Diocese.

At the west end are models showing the construction of the Cathedral and dome.

■ The CITY CHURCHES★★★

Rare men have designed cathedrals, as did Wren; none, at any time except Wren after the Great Fire, has been called on in a matter of years to draw plans for 51 parish churches and, as congregations collected additional sums, crown the west end of nearly every one with a tower or spire. Each church is different; every tower and steeple unique among its peers.

Before the Fire there had been 87 churches within the City walls. Eleven were unharmed and it was decided after uniting some of the parishes, which before the fire covered on average 3 1/2 acres each, to rebuild only 51 on former sites. By 1939 the construction of new roads in 19 and 20C had reduced the total to 43 churches of which 32 were by Wren; nearly all were damaged, several totally destroyed, during the war but the plans, although by their very nature not as elaborate or famous as those for the Cathedral, all existed and the churches were able to be reconstructed. There are now 39 City Churches in all, of which 11 are pre-Fire and 23 by Wren, and also the towers of 9 former churches, 6 by Wren.

Details of activities. – Twenty-four are still parish churches and 15 have become guild churches – some are both. *Most open throughout the week from 10am, some earlier, to about 5pm and conduct midday services, recitals, debates and counselling. For detailed information apply at the City Information Centre or at the churches themselves.*

Money for rebuilding the churches in 17C was granted under acts of parliament which increased the dues on coal entering the Port of London. By the time Wren was called upon to design the churches, and each parish made a separate request, houses were once more abutting all sides of the traditional site and the architect, therefore, ignored almost entirely all exterior walls and windows except those overlooking the street; the interest, therefore, lies in the spire, the entrance and the often irregular shape of the building. Inside note how a single side aisle is turned to advantage, unequal corners are made to appear right angled, an interior is converted into a lozenge shape, a clerestory or lunettes light a barrel roof, how pillars present a cross, within a square, how the domes at St Stephen Walbrook and St Mary Abchurch foretell St Paul's. From a regard of the interplay of columns and complementing pilasters – fluted, circu-

(National Portrait Gallery)

Christopher Wren.

lar, square, Corinthian or Ionic capitalled – look at the complementary cornice and decorated plaster vaulting. Examine in detail the superb 17C woodwork, much of it from Grinling Gibbons' workshop: the reredoses with gilded pelicans, the pulpits and sounding boards with garlanded cherubs. The churches, so individual and personal, would seem to epitomise the phrase "small is beautiful".

All Hallows-by-the-Tower (RZ)   7/8C, 17 and 20C
Open Mondays to Fridays, 9am to 6pm; weekends 10am to 6pm. Brass rubbing: 11am (12.30pm Sundays) to 5pm; average price: £1.75, time: 40 mins.

Tower and Spire: 17C square brick tower. The lantern, encircled by a balustrade and supporting a tapering green copper spire, was added after the war making it the only shaped spire to be added to a City Church since Wren. The tower is the one climbed by Pepys on 5 September 1666 when he "saw the saddest sight of desolation that I ever saw".

The church, that time, was saved by Sir William Penn, whose son William, founder of Pennsylvania, had been baptised there on 23 October 1644. Four churches have stood on the site: in late 7C, a chapel erected soon after its parent house, Barking Abbey; 12 and 14C churches and finally 20C rebuilding. Inside, the south wall of the tower is pierced by the only Anglo-Saxon arch (AD 675) still standing in the City; modern sculpture has been grouped in the south aisle whilst in the baptistry is an exquisite wooden **font cover**★★, attributed to Grinling Gibbons for whom, obviously, no cherub was anonymous. 18 exceptional **brasses**★ dating from 1389-1591 (of which 8 may be rubbed – *by appointment only*), wall tablets, sword rests, model ships in the Mariners' Chapel, the **Toc H** association chapel and lamp, give the church a distinctive atmosphere despite its inevitable "newness". In the undercroft are tessellated Roman pavement fragments, pottery, 11C Saxon stone crosses, memorials of Archbishop Laud, William Penn's baptism record and the marriage lines of John Quincy Adams (1794), Sixth President of the U.S.A. who was married here.

All Hallows London Wall (PX)   G. Dance jr: 1765-1767
Open Mondays to Fridays, 10am to 1pm and 2 to 5pm; enquire at 83 London Wall.

Tower: Portland stone rising by stages from a pedimented doorway to an urn quartered cornice, pilastered lantern cupola and final cross.

The interior, lit by semicircular clerestory windows, has a particularly splendid gold "snowflake" patterned barrel vault rising on fluted Ionic pilasters from a frieze, and a coffered apse in blue and gold. The nave houses the library of the Council for the Care of Churches.

St Andrew Holborn, Holborn Circus (KX)   Wren: 1686-1687, 1704
Tower: stout and square with angle buttresses; at the summit are an overhanging cornice and balustrade decorated at each angle with a great vase.

The City church escaped the Fire but was rebuilt nevertheless. Saxon, Norman and 15C churches all stood on the site; by 17C, however, the medieval church in which Henry Wriothesley, future Earl of Southampton and Shakespeare's patron, had been baptised with Henry VIII as godfather in 1545, had fallen into decay. Wren designed a long basilical building of stone with windows in two tiers and a crowning balustrade. (Note the stone of the Resurrection – outside, north wall, and figures of two charity schoolchildren above the entrance.)

The church was gutted by fire in 1941 but has been restored so that the interior is once more panelled as are the pillars which support the gallery and continue as Corinthian columns to the green and gold ceiling, and adorned with a stained glass lunette at the east end. At the west end, in a recess, is the tomb, delightful with its shy child, of **Thomas Coram** (d 1751), sea captain and parishioner, transferred here from the Foundling Hospital *(qv)* in 1961, together with the font (1804), the pulpit (1752) and the case and organ, presented to Coram by Handel in 1750.

St Andrew-by-the-Wardrobe, Queen Victoria St (LY)   Wren: 1685-1695
Tower: square red brick with irregular stone quoins and a crowning balustrade.

The church was known as St Andrew juxta Baynard Castle until the Great Wardrobe or royal storehouse, previously in the Tower, was erected on a site close by in 1361 *(plaque in Wardrobe Place)*. Church, Wardrobe, Castle and St Ann Blackfriars, were all destroyed in the Fire; only St Andrew was rebuilt. On 29/30 December 1940, fire again gutted the church leaving just the tower and outer walls. It was rebuilt from 1959-61. The galleried church has attractive vaulting and plaster work.

St Andrew Undershaft, Leadenhall St (RY)   *c* 1520
Open Mondays and Thursdays, 10.15 to 11.45am.

Tower: small and ancient, its square stone outline misshapen by a staircase turret; the top is 19C and crenellated, the base probably early 14C.

The present 16C church, the third on the site, is named after the maypole shaft *(p 68)* which stood before it until 1517 and, after being laid up, was finally burnt in 1549.

The nave, now bare of pews, is divided from the aisles by 5 slender shaft and hollow columns which support a plain glass clerestory. Flat wooden roofs cover the aisles and nave, the latter punctuated by 130 carved and gilded 16C oak bosses. The west window (originally at the east end) of Tudor and Stuart sovereigns, the Renatus Harris organ, the pulpit, the font, are late 16 and 17C; the altar rails of 1704 are by Tijou.

Among St Andrew's **monuments**★ are the Datchelor family *(qv)* memorial and, most famously, in a decorated alcove, the half-length ruffed figure carved in alabaster by Nicholas Stone of **John Stow,** 1525-1605, the antiquarian whose *Survey of London and Westminster,* published in 1598, remains a major source for every guide to London. The quill pen poised to "write something worth reading about" is renewed bi-annually by the Lord Mayor.

St Anne and St Agnes, Gresham St (MX)   Wren: 1676-1687
Open Mondays, Wednesdays, 10am to 6pm and for Lutheran Services: Estonian, Latvian.

Tower: small square stuccoed stone with, above, an even smaller square domed turret, flaunting a vane in the shape of the letter A.

Mentioned *c* 1200 and rebuilt to the ancient domed cross plan within a square by Wren after the Fire, St Anne's had to be rebuilt again after the war. The exterior is of rose-red brick with round headed windows under central pediments.

St Bartholomew the Great★★, West Smithfield (LV)   1123, 19C
Tower: brick, square, castellated with a small vaned turret.

St Bartholomew's was once a great, spacious church of which the present building was only the chancel. It was founded in 1123 by a onetime courtier, Rahere, following a pilgrimage to Rome: on land granted by Henry I he established both the hospital and an Augustinian priory of which he became the first prior. By 1143, when he died, the Norman chancel had been completed; by 1539 when Henry VIII dissolved the priory, the church was 280ft long, the west door being where the gateway on to Little Britain now stands. Henry left the hospital untouched: the priory, valued at £693 9s 10 1/2 d four years earlier, he sold, after first demolishing the church nave and ordaining that the truncated building be used only as a parish church. The monarch's attorney-general, Sir Richard Rich, paid him £1 064 11s 3d for the property which the family retained for 300 years. In that time the church fell into disrepair: the Lady Chapel was "squatted in", became a printers' workshop (where in 1724 Benjamin Franklin was employed) and later a fringe factory;

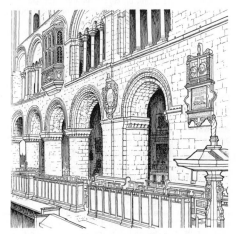

St Bartholomew the Great: the choir.

the north transept was turned into a forge – note the blackened walls, the remains of the cloister became a stable, thick layer of earth covered the church floor, limewash obscured the walls and murals, a brick receptacle, Purgatory, behind the altar, was filled with human bones...

Restoration, including the buying out of extraneous occupants, took from 1863-1910.

The building. – The gateway, a 13C arch and the original entrance to the nave, is surmounted by a late 16C half-timbered gatehouse (restored 1932). The path through the churchyard is at the level of the medieval church. The porch, west front and other exterior flint and stone refacing date from 1839 (restoration by Sir Aston Webb) and the **tower,** erected off-centre at the west end of the curtailed church, from 1628. The **choir**★ is Norman with circular arches on massive round piers and plainly scalloped capitals beneath a gallery of small, rounded arches in groups of 4 slender columns within a relieving arch affording spacious perspectives of arch within arch. The clerestory, which was rebuilt in late Perpendicular style in 1405, reveals no later added carving except an **oriel** filling one south gallery arch, inserted by Prior Bolton in 1520, stamped with his rebus – a bolt or arrow transfixing a tun or cask – and from which, behind the leaded lights, he could follow the service. The Lady Chapel completed in 1336 was rebuilt in 1897, except for the end north and south windows. 15C oak doors (by the west door) lead to the east walk of the old cloister (*c* 1405, rebuilt early this century).

The **monuments: Rahere,** the founder, lies on a 16C decorated tomb chest beneath a crested canopy, all fashioned some 350 years after his death. The **font,** used at Hogarth's baptism in 1697, dates from early 15C and as such is one of the oldest in the City.

St Bartholomew the Less (LX)   Pre fire: George Dance, 1789, 19C
Tower: 15C square with a domed corner turret (within hospital walls but visible from the market).

St Bartholomew's Hospital, on the same site since its foundation by Rahere in 1123 and caring nowadays for some 500 000 in and out patients a year in massive new blocks, has retained buildings from the collegiate style reconstruction by James Gibbs of 1730-66. The north wing includes the great staircase with the vast murals by **Hogarth** (1734) which leads to the Great Hall

The CITY★★★

(not open) hung with portraits by Holbein, Kneller, Lawrence, Reynolds, Millais... The gatehouse from West Smithfield erected in 1702, contains an 18C statue of Henry VIII who gave the hospital to the City of London in 1546 – having sequestered the monastery of which it had previously been a part!

The 12C hospital church appears on mid 17C maps as a substantial building with a stalwart tower; by 18C, however, it was in decay so that it was renewed first by George Dance the Younger, in 1789 and again, in 1823, by Philip Hardwick. Monuments, chiefly to hospital personnel, date from 20C back to 14C (vestry pavements).

St Benet's Welsh Church, (St Benet, Paul's Wharf) (LY)   Wren: 1677-1685
Open only by arrangement and for Sunday services at 11am and 3.30pm.

Tower: of dark red brick, defined squarely with white stone quoins, rises only two stages before being crowned by a small lead cupola, lantern and spire.

The church, at the time of the Great Fire, when it was already some 6 centuries old, stood directly behind Baynard Castle which fronted the river and which, like the church, was totally destroyed. The castle was not rebuilt and Wren designed a small brick church with a hipped roof, rounded windows with carved stone festoons and a general country, Dutch, air. The tower is at the northwest corner so that inside it divides the north and west galleries supported on panelled Corinthian columns which rise, clearcut, above the base of the galleries. Below all is of wood – note the west doorcase decked with cherubs and crowning royal arms, a balustered communion rail, ornate table and behind, a high pedimented reredos with surmounting urns.

St Botolph Aldersgate (MX)   Nathaniel Wright: 1788-1791
Open Mondays to Fridays, 11am to 3pm April to October; noon to 2pm November to March; closed week after Christmas.

Tower: small square and built of brick, topped by a cupola with a wooden turret and gilded vane.

The tower and oblong vessel with conventional rounded windows and clerestory are of dark red brown brick; this building was "improved" in 1829 by the addition of a pedimented east end in stucco. The interior is mainly Georgian with elaborate rosettes in high relief on the white plaster ceiling, coffered apses, galleries with two ward rooms where the children sat during the services, 19C glass and an east "window" transparency, a painting on glass by James Pierson (1788) of the *Agony in the Garden*. The inlaid pulpit stands on a carved palm tree. Wall monuments are a reminder that the present church is a 3rd rebuilding on the site by the gate in the City Wall; the position provides the natural dedication to the 7C Saxon saint, patron of travellers.

St Botolph Aldgate (SXY)   George Dance the Elder: 1741-1744
Tower and Steeple: a stone steeple on a four tier brick tower trimmed with stone quoins.

The site on the outer side of the gate through the City Wall and beside a bridge spanning the moat (Houndsditch), had been occupied by a church for 1 000 years or more when George Dance came to rebuild it in 18C. Dance's interior was transfigured in 1889 by J F Bentley when he redecorated the church, fronting the galleries with balusters, geometrically re-leading all but the east window, decorating the coved ceiling with a plasterwork design of shields and standing angels, leaves, garlands... The domed font cover, rails and inlaid pulpit are all 18C.

St Botolph without Bishopsgate (RX)   George Dance: 1725-1729
Tower and Steeple: a square brick tower unusually at the east end rises directly from the Bishopsgate pavement to support a balustrade, clock tower, turret, cupola and crowning urn.

The church was rebuilt in 1725-9 on a 13C site. The south front, overlooking the former burial ground, is of brick trimmed with stone. Inside giant Corinthian columns support the galleries and wide coved ceiling; a drum-shaped glass dome was added in 1821; the east window is Victorian and there are 19C box pews. The poet Keats was baptized in the existing font in 1795. The church hall at the west end was built to harmonise with the church in 1861 and restored after the war by the Worshipful Company of Fanmakers. 19C charity school children in Coade stone stand on either side of the doorway.

St Bride★, Fleet St (KY)   Wren: 1670-1684, 1701-1703
Open daily 9am to 5pm.

Steeple★★: the white, wedding cake spire rises by 4 open octagonal stages to a final open pedestal and tapering obelisk which terminates in a vane 226ft above the ground – Wren's tallest and most floating steeple. A baker made a fortune modelling wedding cakes after the spire when it was newly erected and inaugurated a lasting tradition. The baker's wife's silk dress is in the museum.

In 1940 Wren's church was gutted by fire leaving only the steeple and calcined outer walls standing. During rebuilding the crypt was opened; it had been used for burials from c 1720 until it was closed after the cholera plague of 1853, which killed 10 000 Londoners. Subsequent excavations have revealed a Roman ditch, walls, a pavement and the outlines of church buildings on the site dating to Saxon times at least. *(Museum in the crypt.)*

The exterior was restored by Godfrey Allen to Wren's design with tall rounded windows between pedimented doors surmounted by circular windows; above is a line of oval clerestory windows; at the east end a tripartite window beneath a pediment.

The interior has been re-arranged to enclose the nave, now set with collegiate-style pews, and to fill the east end with a massive 17C style reredos against a trompe-l'œil painting. Wren's design of a barrel vaulted nave and groined aisles has been retained. The decoration is 17C.

(After photo Pitkin Pictorials)

St Bride's steeple.

Associations. – St Bride's associations, however, rather than its architecture, are what make it unique to many. Becket was born close by; King John held a parliament in the church in 1210; Henry VIII lodged in Bridewell Palace which lay between the church and the river, when he received Charles V in 1522; high ranking churchmen, who chose to live outside the City Wall, built town houses in the neighbourhood (Salisbury Sq) and since the clergy were the largest literate group in the land it was only natural that when **Wyken de Worde** acquired his master's, Caxton's, press on the latter's death in 1491, he should remove it from Westminster to St Bride's and Fleet St. By Wyken's death in 1535 (he was buried in St Bride's), the parish boasted several printers. The church and the Street, with its taverns and coffeehouses, were frequented by Chaucer, Shakespeare, Milton, Lovelace, Evelyn, Pepys (born nearby and like all his family christened in the church), Dryden, Izaac Walton, Edmund Waller (poet), Aubrey, Ashmole, John Ogilby (mapmaker), Thomas Tompion (father of English clock and watchmaking), Addison; in 18C by Johnson and Boswell, Joshua Reynolds, Goldsmith, Garrick, Burke, Pope, Richardson (coffin in the crypt) and Hogarth; in 19C by Charles Lamb, Hazlitt, Wordsworth, Keats, Hood, Leigh Hunt, Dickens. Today new pew backs are labelled with the names of contemporaries for St Bride's remains the printers' church, the Cathedral of Fleet St.

St Clement Eastcheap (PY)   Wren: 1683-1687
Tower: unassuming brick with stone quoins and balustrade.

The medieval St Clement's was the first City church to burn in the Great Fire; it cost £4 362 3s 4 1/2d to rebuild to Wren's design (in which there is no right angled wall!) and the architect was presented on its completion by the satisfied parishioners with "one third of a hogshead of wine" costing £4 2s 0d. The **panelled interior★★** has finely carved 17C door and organ cases (Purcell played on the organ), above the pulpit a massive sounding board, garlanded, swagged and gay with adoring cherubs. The marble font and cover, carved bread shelves, Stuart arms, sword rest, are all contemporary. A wreath adorns the flat ceiling.

St Clement claims to be the church of the old *Oranges and Lemons* rhyme: its parish East Cheap dates from the time of the Saxon market on the City's eastern hill, its association with oranges from the Middle Ages, when Spanish barges tied up at London Bridge to sell their oranges on the stone steps – all within cry of the church.

St Dunstan-in-the-West, Fleet St (JY)   Shaw: 1831-1833
Open Mondays to Fridays 8.30am to 2.30pm and 3 to 6pm alternate weeks.

Tower: neo-Gothic, rising from an arched porch to an octagon of slender open bays, superimposed by a crown of tapering finials and crocketed pinnacles.

The 19C church was a rebuilding, slightly to the north on a site on which churches had stood since 1237; the 17C building narrowly escaped the Fire; the 19C was badly bombed in 1944. The exterior, apart from the tower, is chiefly remarkable for the additions which associate the church with Fleet St: the bust of **Lord Northcliffe** (1930), the public **clock,** made by Thomas Harrys in 1671 and for which he was paid £35, and its giant oak jacks; the **statues** from the 1586 Lud Gate: Queen Elizabeth, modelled during her lifetime (modern inscription) and originally on the gate's west face – purchased in 1786 for £15 10s and now in a pedimented niche over a doorway (to the right) in which stand statues of the mythical King Lud and his two sons (again of 1586 manufacture). Corbels at the main door show the visages of Tyndale (west) and John Donne (east), associated with St Dunstan's as were Izaac Walton (the *Compleat Angler* was printed in the churchyard) and the Hoares. John Shaw's church is octagonal with a high, star, vault; the altar, oriented to the north, is set in "choice panelling" – Flamboyant Flemish in style (17C).

Since 1960s, one bay has been closed by an ornate 19C Romanian screen from the Antim Monastery, Bucharest. *(The community hold weekly services.)* The chapel next to the pulpit is used by the Oriental churches; another, which contains a fine brass (1530), by the Old Catholic Churches in the Union of Utrecht.

St Edmund the King and Martyr, Lombard St (PY)   Wren: 1670-1679, 1706-1707
Closed holiday Mondays and week after Christmas.

Tower and Spire★: a distinctive black (lead covered) octagonal lantern and stout spire ending in a bulb and vane, rise from a square stone belfry. The corbelled parapet and inverted brackets at the tower base are decorated with flaming urns.

The façade, opposite Clement's Lane, is outlined by quoins and a central pediment.

The small oblong interior with squared apse and coved skylit ceiling, is remarkable for its woodwork: panelling and pierced galleries, carved pulpit with drops and swags, choir stalls, communion table with stout legs, font with semicircular rail, urns on reredos and doorcases...

St Ethelburga, Bishopsgate (RX)   15C and later
Open Mondays to Fridays 11am to 4pm.

Turret: a square belfry and vaned turret stand slightly back from the medieval ragstone and brick repaired west wall on Bishopsgate's east pavement.

The early 15C church (two cinquefoil piscinas in the south wall) escaped the Fire but was damaged in 1939-45 bombings. It has a nave, 4 bay arcade and south aisle, besides an organ loft and gallery (1629; rebuilt 1912), all within an overall dimension of 57ft. It is lit by a clerestory. The furnishings date from medieval to modern, the accounts back to 1569.

St Giles Cripplegate★, the Barbican (VM)   14, 16, 19 and 20C
Tower: dwarfed but in no way overpowered by the Barbican, St Giles' tower is built of stone below and brick above; corner pinnacles guard an open cupola merry-go-round shaped turret which sports a weathervane. (Peal of 12 bells; chiming clock.)

The latest rebuilding in St Giles' 900 year history came after bombs had destroyed the interior in 1940. Almost every century previously had seen similar if not comparable disasters, or enlargement, back to 1090 when a Norman church was first erected on the site outside the City Wall beside the postern gate on to the moor. A 15C arcade rising to a clerestory divides the nave and aisles. Memorials, after so many vicissitudes, are few, although associations recorded by signature in the registers are many: **John Milton** (buried in the chancel, 1674; bust by John Bacon, 1793 – south wall), **Martin Frobisher,** navigator (buried in south aisle 1594), **John Foxe,** author of the *Book of Martyrs* (buried 1587), **John Speed,** mapmaker (buried 1629 below his monument on the south wall), **Oliver Cromwell** (married 22 August 1620), **Sir Thomas More, Ben Jonson, Shakespeare** (at the baptism of his nephew), Edward Alleyn, Prince Rupert, Holman Hunt, Sir Ebenezer Howard (pioneer of garden cities). Fine sword rest, lectern and marble font. In the southeast corner of the chancel are a medieval sedilia and piscina.

The CITY★★★

St Helen Bishopsgate★, Gt St Helen's (RX)   12-17C

Tower: a small square 17C white belfry turret, lantern, ball and vane, rise sturdily from the double fronted stone church; outside are a patch of grass and plane trees.

The two low west doors, side by side, beneath embattled gables typify St Helen's architecture and history. It began as a small parish church which by 1150 extended in two equal rectangles from the present east wall to the south entrance (originally Norman arched). In early 13C a Benedictine nunnery was established in the church grounds and a conventual church built abutting St Helen's to the north; the nun's chapel was probably wider and considerably longer than the existing parish church which was then extended to give the double front. The arcade between the churches was rebuilt in the late 15C and the dividing screens were removed in 1538 when the nunnery was dissolved. In 1874 when St Martin Outwich was demolished, 18 major monuments and brasses were transferred.

Furnishings. – In the north wall is one of several 13C windows (NW), the **Night Staircase** of c 1500, built from the dormitory to the church for nuns attending night services, the **Processional Entrance,** originally 13C, and, at the east end, the **Nuns' Squint** (since 1525 arranged as a memorial). Note the canopied carved pulpit, the 17C doorcases and font, the grotesque choirstall armrests from 15C Nuns' Choir and the two sword rests, one very rare being made of wood (1665). In the south transept are two late 14C piscinas.

Monuments★★: by the Nuns' Choir is the black marble slabbed tomb chest of Sir Thomas Gresham (d 1579); adjoining that of Sir Julius Caesar Adelmare (d 1636), Privy Counsellor to James I with no effigy but a parchment and seal; within the railing, beneath the canopy is the marble effigy of Sir William Pickering, Elizabeth's Ambassador to Spain (d 1574) and opposite, Sir John Crosby (d 1475) and his first wife (d 1460), owner of the great City mansion, Crosby Hall *(qv)* and the 14C-15C monument to John de Oteswich and his wife. The **brasses,** 15-17C and rich in expression and costume detail, are in the transept and north aisle *(covered with carpets).*

Windows: there is 15C and 17C glass in the 3rd and 5th north windows and in the Holy Ghost Chapel. Shakespeare (north wall) was assessed for local rates at £5 6s 8d in 1597 but left the parish, according to the record, having paid off only the s and d!

St James Garlickhythe, Garlick Hill, Upper Thames St (MY)   Wren 1676-1683, 1713
Open Mondays to Fridays, 10am to 4pm; closed holiday Mondays.

Tower and Spire★: the tower, square, of stone ending in a balustrade, is quartered by pointed urns and crowned by the spire, added in 1713. This rises in a square 3 tier lantern, quartered by paired, advanced, columns, crowned on high by a vaned spirelet (cf St Michael Paternoster Royal).

Inside the tower, through the door decorated with a scallop shell, the emblem of St James of Compostella to whom the church is dedicated, two tablets summarise the later history of the church which dates back to 10/11C. "This church", the upper plaque states, "was consumed by the late dreadful conflagration AD 1666; the foundation thereof was laid AD 1676; it was rebuilt and opened AD 1682 and completely finished AD 1683"; the inscription below continues, "The church was damaged by enemy action in 1940 and 1941 ; the work of restoration was completed in 1963".

The church was built to an entirely symmetrical plan, on an isolated site, and christened "Wren's Lantern" owing to its many windows.

The woodwork is principally 17C: note the dowel peg for the preacher's wig. The marble font carved with cherubs' heads is late 17C. The ceiling is ornamented with gilded plaster work. **Sword rests★,** complete with unicorn supporters, recall six medieval lord mayors and others.

St Katharine Cree, Leadenhall St (RY)   1628-1631
Open Mondays to Fridays 9.30am to 4.30pm; closed at Easter and Christmas.

Tower: the ragstone corner tower, late 15C below 16C above, rises to a parapet and small white pillared turret.

The present church is thought to be the third on the site which marked the corner boundary of the precincts of the Augustinian Priory of Holy Trinity, Christchurch, founded by Matilda, Queen of Henry I, in 1108 and dissolved in 1539. Note the two tiers of windows in the stone wall on Leadenhall St, straight headed with centres raised to include 3 lights each. Inside the nave remains with giant Corinthian columns supporting decorated round arches beneath the clerestory. High up, above the plain reredos, a rose said to resemble in its tracery that in Old St Paul's and glazed with 17C glass, leads one's eye back along the ceiling where the ribs meet in central brightly coloured bosses, the badges of 17 City Companies. Note the early 17C alabaster font, 18C pulpit and altar table and the Throckmorton effigy (1571) in the Laud Chapel.

Since 1960 St Katharine has been the Guild Church for industry, commerce and finance.

St Lawrence Jewry, Gresham St (NX)   Wren: 1670-1687

Tower and Spire: stone, rising to a balustrade with corner obelisks which encloses a pedimented lantern set out of alignment with the base (which parallels the west wall) but in line with Gresham St. Above is a lead obelisk spire from which flies the original gridiron weathervane now also incorporating a replica of the incendiary bomb which caused the church's almost total destruction in 1940.

"St Lawrence, called in the Jury because of old time many Jews inhabited thereabout" was, according to Stow, a "fair and large" parish church. Built in 1196 and closely surrounded by houses, it perished completely in the Fire. Wren designed a building of modest outward appearance squaring up the interior by varying the thickness of the walls. The restored ceiling, coffered and decorated to Wren's original design with gilded plasterwork, emphasises the rectangular plan. The brilliant windows by Christopher Webb contrast with the plain and unassuming modern woodwork. More ornate are the organ case, modelled on 17C original, and the screen in the north aisle; the wrought iron gates, given by the Royal Marines, the Parachute Regiment and Airborne Forces, lead into the Commonwealth Chapel. This modern church by Cecil Brown, which became the church of the City Corporation in 1957, contains pews for the Lord Mayor (sword rest), sheriffs, aldermen, sword and mace bearers ; also Sir Thomas Beecham's piano *(Recitals 1 to 1.45pm: Mondays – piano, Tuesdays – organ).*

St Magnus the Martyr, Lower Thames St (PZ)   Wren: 1671-1687, 1706
    Open Tuesdays to Fridays, 10am to 4pm.

Tower★: the massive balustraded and urn decorated square block of stone supports an octagonal belfry, lead cupola, lantern and obelisk spire and, still higher, at 180ft, a golden vane. A 1709 clock projects over the churchyard.

From 1176 St Magnus stood a stone sentinel on an ancient Roman wharf at the foot of London Bridge. Wren rebuilt it on the same site. When, c 1760, the houses and shops which lined the bridge were removed, Wren's building was curtailed to leave the tower as a church porch astride the bridge's east footpath. Its postern situation continued until 1831 when Rennie's bridge was constructed 100ft upstream.

The interior, remodelled in late 18C, has a barrel vaulted nave, supported by fluted Ionic columns and punctuated by the deep recesses of the oval clerestory windows. Although much remains from 17C, inscriptions on the west gallery explain the decoration: the church was "repaired and beautified" in 1886 and 1924. Note the iron **sword rest★** dated 1708, 16-17C shrine (right of the altar), altar piece and rails, font (1683) and pulpit.

St Margaret Lothbury★ (NX)   Wren: 1686-1690, 1701
Tower and Spire★: from the square stone base (clock) topped by an iron railing, rise a lead covered cupola and slender obelisk spire balancing a gilded ball and vane.

While the derivations of Lothbury are speculative and various, the church's certain foundation dates back to the 12C. There were repeated rebuildings culminating in that by Wren in 1686-90. The unequal parallelogram inside is divided by Corinthian columns into a nave and chancel and shorter south aisle. The **woodwork★** especially attracts the eye: from a dark base of wall and column panelling and cut down box pews, rise in clear silhouette, a wonderful oak screen, exquisitely carved pulpit, massive sounding board, gay with dancing cherubs, and a reredos with balustered rails.

St Magnus: sword rest.

The **screen★**, made c 1689 for All Hallows, Upper Thames St, and one of only two *(p 57)* to Wren's design, is divided into 4 paired arcs by two strand balusters; at the centre are pierced pilasters and above three broken pediments, the central one supported by a great carved eagle and filled above with a royal coat of arms.

The chapel with a dividing screen made from the altar rails of St Olave Jewry, has a reredos also from St Olave. The **font★** is attributed to Grinling Gibbons. 18C sword rests and bust of Sir Peter le Maire (d 1631) by H. Le Sueur.

St Margaret Pattens, Eastcheap (PY)   Wren: 1684-1689 and 1698-1702
    Open Mondays to Fridays 8.30am to 3.30pm; closed during August and holidays.

Spire★: the lead covered, and therefore, black spire, a polygon which sharpens to a needle point at 199ft where the gilded vane balances, rises from a square stone tower: the only ornament is the pinnacled balustrade at the tower summit.

The site at the corner of Rood Lane was possibly already occupied by a wooden church in 1067. The church as redesigned by Wren, is a plain oblong with a flat ceiling and round clerestory windows. The **woodwork★** is outstanding: to the east, the reredos, 17C, gold lettered and framing a contemporary Italian painting, is carved with fruit, a peapod, flowers; in front, turned balusters support the communion rail; a high boxed beadle's pew and below, a low "punishment bench" with ferocious devil's head, choir stalls, a finely carved eagle lectern, pulpit with hour glass aloft for all to see the sermon's duration. On the north side, the Lady Chapel has a former doorcase as reredos and dowel pegs on which to hang wigs on hot days; also in the church are the only two canopied pews in London (the ceiling of the south pew, monogrammed CW 1686, is by tradition the one occupied by Christopher Wren), 18C monuments and font.

"Pattens" was added for distinction to the dedication and according to Stow was after the pattens or iron shod overshoes *(show case in south aisle)* sold in the abutting lane.

St Martin-within-Ludgate, Ludgate Hill (LY)   Wren: 1677-1687
    Open Mondays noon to 3.30pm, Tuesdays to Fridays, 10am to 4pm.

Tower and Spire★: from a lead covered cupola and lantern, ringed by a balcony, there rises a black needle spire, the perfect foil to the green cathedral dome.

The church by the medieval Lud Gate and with a west wall just inside the Roman perimeter, is said to have been built first by King Cadwalla in 7C; it was certainly rebuilt in 1439 and burnt down in the Fire. Wren cut off the hill frontage inside by means of stout pillars on which he rested a gallery and thick coffered arches. At ground floor level beneath the gallery the bays were filled with three doors with **cases★** richly carved by **Grinling Gibbons.** The remaining area is laid out as a square within a square by means of 4 inner columns on which rest the groined vault formed by the intersection of barrel vaulting above the nave, chancel and transepts. The woodwork is 17C. The churchwardens' double chair dating from 1690 is unique.

St Mary Abchurch★, Cannon St (NY)   Wren: 1681-1686
    Closed for restoration.

Tower and Spire★: red brick with stone quoins, surmounted by a cupola, lantern and slender spire of lead, all to the miniature scale of the church.

The Fire consumed "a fair church", last of a line dating back to 12C. The site was minute, some 80ft square, and Wren decided to cover the new church with a painted **dome★**. Approximately 40ft in diameter, it cannot be seen from outside and inside it rises from arches springing directly from the outer walls. There are no buttresses and only one interior column.

Tall carved pews line the north, south and west walls as originally. Receipts in the parish records show that many of the greatest craftsmen of the day worked on the furnishings: the font and stonework, the gilded copper pelican weathervane (removed as unsafe 1764), the pulpit with garlands and cherubs' heads, doorcases, font rails and cover, the lion and unicorn and royal arms. Authenticated by bills and a personal letter from **Grinling Gibbons** himself, is the **reredos★★**, massive in size, magnificent in detail and delicacy. Note the many rich monuments and urns.

St Mary Aldermary, Queen Victoria St (NY)   Wren: 1681-1682, 1701-1711
Open Tuesdays to Fridays, 11am to 3pm.

Tower: Gothic with corner buttresses, robust pinnacles and gilded finials.

St Mary is "the older Mary Church" – older that is than the Norman St Mary-le-Bow. After the Great Fire, a benefactor appeared offering £5 000 to rebuild the church as it had been; Wren, therefore, built a Gothic church – for £3 457!

Despite successive remodellings of the interior with its fan vaulting and central rosettes, there remain a Grinling Gibbons pulpit and rich west doorcase (with a peapod; from St Antholin *qv*), a 1682 font and, against the 3rd south pillar, an oak **sword rest** also of 1682, one only of 4 in wood to survive and uniquely carved with fruit and flowers by Grinling Gibbons.

St Mary-at-Hill★★, Eastcheap (PZ)   Wren: 1670-1676; John Savage: 1849
Closed for rebuilding after a fire in 1988.

Tower: stock brick of 1780, overlooking Lovat Lane; stucco east end with great Venetian window by Wren, and projecting clock on St Mary at Hill.

A church is first mentioned on the site in 1177. The Wren **plan★**, almost square, is divided into 3 × 3 bays beneath a shallow central dome, supported on free standing Corinthian columns; at each corner are plain square ceilings at cornice height.

St Mary's is known for its **woodwork★★** which dates from late 17C (font cover), early 18C (great oak reredos, communion table, altar rails) and 19C work by **William Gibbs Rogers** (organ gallery – musical trophies – pulpit, garlanded with fruit and flowers, massive sounding board, beautiful curved staircase, lectern and turned balustrade). Box pews add a Dickensian atmosphere, 6 gilded and enamelled wrought iron sword rests a touch of pageantry.

St Mary-le-Bow, Cheapside (MY)   Wren: 1670-1683, 20C
Open Mondays to Fridays, 7.30am to 6pm; closed holidays.

Tower and Steeple★★: the tower from which **Bow Bells** ring out advances into Cheapside supporting Wren's most famous spire (1671-80), in which he used examples of all five Classical orders and of the bow – a stone arch to a mason. The weather **vane**, a winged dragon 8ft 10ins long, was hoisted the 239ft to the top with an intrepid rope dancer riding on its back.

Completed in 1673 in Portland stone, the church was Wren's most expensive, costing over £8 000 and the steeple only slightly less. In May 1941 the church was bombed; only the tower and outer walls remained. The exterior was restored to Wren's design while the interior lay-out was re-designed by Laurence King who also restored the roof. The unique carved rood is a gift from the people of Germany, the bronze sculpture was given by the Norwegians in memory of those who died in the resistance. The stained glass is by John Hayward. The twin pulpits recall the famous lunch-time dialogues. Note the majestic organ and ornate doorway adorned with the royal arms.

The Norman **crypt**, built in 1087 with rough ragstone walls on the ruins of a Saxon church, contains the original columns with cushion capitals supporting the bows (arches) from which the church, takes its name. Also named after them is the Court of Arches, supreme judicial court of the Archbishop of Canterbury, which has met here since 12C.

In 1334 the **Great Bell of Bow** called people from bed at 5.45am and rang the curfew at 9pm; the practice continued for over 400 years ceasing only in 1874 and the sound came to define the limits of the City, giving rise to the saying that "a true Londoner, a Cockney, must be born within the sound of Bow Bells". According to legend it was these bells that chimed out "Turn again Whittington, Lord Mayor of London". Wren made room for a peal of 12 although only 8 were hung originally. During 1939-45 war the 12 bell chime was used as a recognition signal by the BBC and came to mean hope and freedom to millions all over the world thus deserving the title "the most famous peal in Christendom".

St Mary Woolnoth of the Nativity, Lombard St (NY)   Hawksmoor: 1716-1727
Closed holidays and week after Christmas.

Tower: rusticated stone below, Corinthian columned above, rising to twin turrets, linked and crowned by open balustrades.

The church, built in Saxon times possibly by someone called Wulfnoth, hence the name, was rebuilt in stone by William the Conqueror. A medieval parishioner was Sir Martin Bowes, Lord Mayor in 1545, who left his gilded helmet, gauntlets, spurs, sword, crest and banner and who, with his three wives, is buried beneath the altar. The site was always hemmed in; Hawksmoor, however, made his building arresting by the use of heavily rusticated stone and idiosyncratic by his flat tower. The small area inside he planned beneath a shallow dome as a square within a square with massive fluted Corinthian columns in threes marking each corner and supporting a heavily ornamented cornice and beam. There is an unusual canopy with twisted columns above the altar and a fine inlaid pulpit.

St Michael, Cornhill (PY)   Wren 1670-7; Hawksmoor 1718-1724; G G Scott 1857-1860
Open Mondays to Fridays 8am to 5.30pm; Sundays 10am to 12.30pm.

Tower: of stone rising by 4 stages to strongly stemmed, ornamented corner pinnacles between which stand slim miniature pinnacles, braceleted by a balustrade.

The Gothic style tower was designed at the end of Wren's life by Hawksmoor, when the old tower which had survived the Fire had become unsafe; the neo-Gothic doorway, framed by small marble columns, carved stone covings and tympanum, by Giles Gilbert Scott, as part of an 1857-60 remodelling. Inside, the vaulting on tall Tuscan columns is by Wren; the Venetian windows by Scott; the carved bench ends in the Wren tradition, pulpit and lectern by W Gibbs Rogers (19C); the font is 17C and the large wooden pelican 18C...

St Michael Paternoster Royal, Upper Thames St (NY)   Wren: 1686-1694, 1715-1717

Tower and Spire★: square of stone rising to a balustrade quartered by urns. The spire, added in 1715, takes the form of a three tier octagonal lantern, marked at each angle by an Ionic column and urn; on high is a vaned spirelet (cf St James Garlickhythe).

The "fair parish church", as Stow described it, "new built by Richard Whittington", in place of the earliest known building of the mid 13C, was destroyed by the Fire; in July 1944 history was repeated. The south wall with 6 rounded lights and a balustraded parapet is of stone, the east end of brick, stone trimmed. Above the door and windows are cherub's head keystones. The pulpit, reredos and lectern are 17C. The red, gold, green windows include (south-west corner) young Whittington with his cat. **Whittington,** who lived in an adjoining house, founded an almshouse, also adjoining, and on his death in 1423, was buried in the church. The last part of the name Paternoster Royal is from La Riole, a town near Bordeaux from which the wine long imported by local vintners came. The west end houses the offices of the Missions to Seamen.

St Nicholas Cole Abbey, Queen Victoria St (MY)   Wren: 1671-1681
Open at service times or by arrangement.

Tower and Spire★: from a small square stone base marked by corner urns, rises an octagonal lead spire, lifting finally to a **gilded three masted** ship weathervane.

St Nicholas' recorded history goes back to 1144 but even Stow "could never learn the cause of the name and therefore let it passe". The church was burned out in 1666 and again in 1941 so that it has had to be totally rebuilt. The stone exterior is pierced by tall rounded windows beneath corbelled hoods and circled by an open balustrade. The woodwork is 17C.

St Olave★, Hart St (RY)   15C

Tower: the square medieval ragstone lower stage with 18C brick sections above, is crowned with a lantern and weathervane. A round faced clock projects back over the nave.

Three parish churches have been built on this site: in wood (c 1050) and stone (c 1200; enlarged to present size c 1450). The church was restored in 1953 after severe bomb damage in 1941. Throughout associations have been kept alive: the dedication to St Olaf, who in 1013 helped Ethelred against the Danes remains vivid in the new Norwegian flag; a bust (19C) of Samuel Pepys appropriately blocks the former south doorway (inscription outside) which used to be the entrance to a gallery where Pepys had the Navy office pew.

The churchyard gateway on Seething Lane, decorated exclusively with skulls is dated 1658 – opposite is the site, now a garden, of the Navy office of Pepys' day (burned 1673).

The church porch, into which one descends, like the major part of the church, is 15C. The interior is divided into a nave and aisle of three bays by quatrefoil marble pillars, probably from a former, 13C, church; the clerestory and roof are post war, as is the glass, except for the late 19C heraldic panels which had been removed for cleaning in 1939. Furnishings have been presented: the **pulpit,** made reputedly in Grinling Gibbons' workshop for St Benet Gracechurch (Wren; demolished 1867); Jacobean altar rails; four 18C sword rests. The monuments, which incredibly, survived the fire, include tablets, brasses, effigies of highly coloured or natural stone: **Elisabeth Pepys** (17C bust in an oval niche – high on the sanctuary north wall), the 17C kneeling and brightly coloured Bayninge brothers (below); Sir James Deane (17C kneeling figure with 3 wives and children – all in colour; south wall over 15C vestry door); Sir Andrew Riccard, Chairman of East India and Turkey Companies (17C standing figure – north aisle).

The **crypt** (steps at west end) of two chambers with ribbed vaulting, is built over a well and is a survival of the early 13C church.

St Peter upon Cornhill (PY)   Wren: 1677-1687
Open 8am to 4pm; closed August, holiday Mondays and following Tuesdays.

Spire: visible only from the churchyard (south) and Gracechurch St (east): square brick tower crowned by small green copper dome and obelisk spire from which flies a vane in the form of a key (which measures 9ft and weighs 2 cwts).

The vessel exterior, again visible only from the south and east, is stuccoed with rounded and circular east windows surmounted by a pediment. Inside there is a geometrical interplay between the basilical ground plan divided by square pillars and the arcs of windows, tunnel vaulting, arches, underlined by a double plaster fillet, between nave and aisles and the outlines of the rood screen. The upper area is light and minimally decorated; the lower, to sill level, darkly panelled. The pews were cut down in 19C apart from two retained at full height for the church wardens (at the back). The oak **screen★,** one of two only in Wren's churches (p 55) and said to have been designed by the architect and his young daughter, has strong central pillars rising high to support a lion and unicorn; on the central arch are the arms of Charles II. Organ gallery, doorcases at the west end, sounding board with cherubs' heads, pulpit with domed panels and carved drops of fruit and leaves, are original. The font dates from 1681.

St Peter's upon Cornhill, one of the two hills upon which London was first built, claims to stand on the highest ground and to be the oldest church site in the City.

St Sepulchre–without–Newgate (Church of the Holy Sepulchre), Holborn Viaduct (LX)
          15C; Wren 1670-1677, 19C
Open Mondays to Fridays 9am to 4pm (3.30pm in winter); closed January.

Tower: 15C square stone surmounted by 4 top-heavy crocketed pinnacles.

An early foundation, the church which stands "Without Newgate" was renamed at the time of the Crusades after the Jerusalem church "without the city wall". The porch, with fan vaulting and carved bosses, and the tower, though restored externally, date from 1450. The interior is furnished with a contemporary pulpit, font and octagonal cover gay with cherubs' heads and at the entrance, the beautiful font cover rescued from Christchurch (qv) in 1940. The organ, built in 1670, reputed to have been played by Handel and Mendelssohn, and where Henry Wood at 14 officiated as assistant organist, has a superb case, including the monogram of Charles II. Mementoes comprise: a stone from the Church of the Holy Sepulchre in Jerusalem; sword rests; the hand bell rung outside condemned men's cells at midnight in the old Newgate Prison; a brass plate to Captain John Smith, sometime Governor of Virginia who died in 1631 and is buried in the church; colours of the Royal Fusiliers, City of London Regiment; in the north Musicians' Chapel, the ashes of Sir Henry Wood (1869-1944), windows, chairs, kneelers to British musicians.

The CITY★★★

St Stephen Walbrook★ (NY)   Wren: 1672-1677, 1717
*Open Mondays to Fridays, 10am to 5pm and Sunday mornings; closed Easter, Christmas
and holiday Mondays.*

Tower and Steeple★: both are square throughout – the tower of ragstone rising to a trim
balustrade; the later steeple of Portland stone through 8 stages all with the same outline, to two
balls and a vane. The characteristic dome, green, turreted and also vaned can be seen at the rear.

St Stephens' is the birthplace of The Samaritans, founded in 1953 to befriend the suicidal
and despairing: by 1984 182 branches in the British Isles and 101 in the rest of the world.

The dominant feature is Wren's **dome★** which may have served as a model for St Paul's
which it pre-dates. It is slightly off centre, since the ground plan is not quite square, and the
cupola rests on a ring of circular arches. The bays are delineated by free standing Corinthian
columns, grouped to produce unexpected perspectives within the typically enclosing panelling
and carved furnishings. Under the dome stands a monumental altar approached by two
communion steps, all carved from travertine by Henry Moore (1986).

St Vedast, Foster Lane (MX)   Wren: 1670-1673, 1697
Tower and Spire★: a square stone tower, then an overhanging entablature which is the dividing
line between the earlier construction and later fantasy, when Wren set a lantern on it with
advanced triple pilasters at the corners through 3 stages, below the ribbed stone spire
surmounted by a ball and vane.

The exterior, with a pre-Fire curving southwest wall which Wren retained when he rebuilt
the church for £1 853 15s 6d (the cheapest of all the City churches), is almost unnoticeable from
Foster Lane. (The street's name is a corruption of Vedast, 6C Bishop of Arras to whom the
church was dedicated in 13C.) The interior is entirely new. The floor has been marbled in black
and white; pews aligned collegiate style beneath the **ceiling★**, reinstalled to Wren's design with
a central wreath, cornice and end panels in moulded plasterwork, highlighted in gold and silver
against a white ground – St Vedast's is the Goldsmiths' Church. The wooden altarpiece and
the ornate octagonal pulpit are also of interest.

Towers and other places of Worship

St Alban, Wood Street (MX)   Wren: 1697-1698
Tower: Wren's pure Gothic tower with slim corner buttresses crowned by a balustrade and
crocketed pinnacles, rises like a white stone needle out of the sea of traffic.

All Hallows Staining (RY)
Tower: the 15C ragstone tower, battlemented but solitary since 1870 when its church of 1671
was demolished, is now dwarfed by overshadowing office blocks.

St Alphage, London Wall (NX)
Tower Base: 14C pointed stone arches in black flint walls, mark the west tower of the chapel of
Elsing Spital Priory dissolved by Henry VIII. (Revealed by 1940 bombs.)

St Augustine and St Faith, Watling St (MY)   Wren: 1680-1687
Tower and Spire: the square tower of newly hewn stone ends in a pierced parapet quartered by
obelisk pinnacles; above rise an almost black, tulip shaped, dome and lead spire – all rebuilt,
since the war, to Wren's original design.

The church was not reconstructed; instead new buildings were erected abutting the tower
to provide premises for St Paul's Cathedral Choir School.

Christ Church★, Newgate St (LX)   Wren: 1704
Tower: slender, square and of stone, the tower rises by stages marked by urns and alternately
solid and colonnaded, to a slim, decorated turret and vane.

Christ Church was founded by Henry VIII on the site occupied from 1225-1538 by the
Greyfriars monastery; close by was a second royal foundation, Christ's Hospital, the Bluecoat
School (1552-1902). The church, destroyed in the Fire, rebuilt by Wren in 1667-91 on sufficient
scale to accommodate the boys, is now a garden. The tower houses an architect's office. The
font cover, recued by a postman in 1940 is in St Sepulchre's.

St Dunstan-in-the East★★, St Dunstan's Hill, Lower Thames St (RZ)   Wren: 1702
Steeple: of Portland stone entirely. The spire is poised on flying buttresses with pinnacles
canting the 4 tier tower. A magnificent garden flourishes in the ruins.

St Martin Orgar, Martin Lane (PY)
Tower: 19C solitary square brick and stucco tower marks the site of a medieval church.

St Mary Aldermanbury, Aldermanbury/Love Lane corner (NX)   Wren: 1670
Site: the 12C site is now a garden, with only bases of the perimeter walls and pillars outlining the
bombed Wren church. The stones were numbered and sent to Fulton, USA where the church has
been rebuilt to the 17C plan.

St Mary Somerset, Upper Thames St (MY)   Wren: 1695
Tower: slim, square and white, the tower rises from its garden setting to a parapet, quartered
with square finials and obelisk pinnacles. Note the masks.

St Olave Jewry (NX)   Wren: 1670-1676
Tower: a two stage stone tower is topped by a beautiful **weathervane,** the three master fully
rigged from St Mildred Bread St (Wren: destroyed 1940).

City Temple, Holborn Viaduct (KX)
Tower: high, square and pillared, surmounted by a square lantern, lead dome and cross.

The history of the City Temple, the only English Free Church in the City, goes back to 1567
although occupation of the site on the viaduct dates only from 1874. The church is famous for its
preachers, among whom this century have been Dr Maude Royden, in 1917 the first woman to
step into a pulpit, and Dr Leslie Weatherhead. Wartime bombing gutted the sanctuary so that the
building now presents the contrast of a Victorian/Palladian exterior and modern interior.

Dutch Church, Austin Friars (PX)   Ansell and Bailey: 1955
Ring for admission: Mondays to Thursdays, 11am to 3pm; closed holiday Mondays.

Spire: slender lantern crowned by a spirelet and weathervane by John Skeeping.

The church received a direct hit in 1940 and has been entirely rebuilt to a modern design with a hall interior and brilliant windows beneath a shallow curved roof.

Founded in 1253, rebuilt in 14C, dissolved by Henry VIII; only the nave of the Augustinian monastery remained when in 1550 it was granted to refugees from the Low Countries.

Spanish and Portuguese Synagogue, Bevis Marks (RX). – *Open for services.*

The synagogue of 1701, successor to the one in Creechurch Lane *(plaque)* which was the first to be opened after the Jews had been invited to return by Cromwell in 1657, is known particularly for its rich appointments: the Ark, containing the hand-written Scrolls, the raised Tebah, surrounded by twisted balusters, the 7 brass chandeliers from Holland.

The City's only other synagogue, the Great Synagogue, Duke's Place, Aldgate, opened in 1722, rebuilt in 1790, was totally destroyed in an air raid.

Bevis Marks is a corruption of Buries Marks, an abbreviation for the mark or site of the 12C mansion of the abbots of Bury St Edmunds. In 16C the mansion was acquired by Thomas Heneage whose name is perpetuated in the nearby lane.

■ The CORPORATION OF LONDON

The **City** is governed by the Corporation of London, which acts through the Court of Common Council. The latter, numbering 25 Aldermen and 159 Councilmen, is presided over by the Lord Mayor and meets in Guildhall.

Guildhall* (NX). – *Open daily 10am to 5pm; closed 25 December and Sundays in winter.*

History. – "This Guildhall", Stow quoted in 1598 "was begun to be built new in the year 1411; ... the same was made of a little cottage, a large and great house... towards the charges whereof the (livery) companies gave large benevolences; also offences of men were pardoned for sums of money, extraordinary fees were raised, fines... during 7 years, with a continuation of 3 years more... Executors to Richard Whittington gave towards the paving of this great hall... with hard stone of Purbeck". All was complete by *c* 1440. The Great Fire left the outer walls and crypt standing. Rebuilding began immediately and in 1669 Pepys noted "I passed by Guildhall, which is almost finished".

In 1940 after 18 and 19C restorations and remodellings, history repeated itself. Reconstruction was once more completed in 1954 (west crypt: 1972; new west wing: 1974). In the course of recent building work excavations have revealed the site of a Roman amphitheatre, and traces of the medieval Jewish quarter and of the 15C Guildhall chapel.

The City was granted its first charter by William the Conqueror in 1067; the first **Mayor** was installed in a building, of which no trace remains, probably on the present site in 1193; for at least 850 years, therefore Guildhall has been the seat of civic government.

Richard Whittington. – Whittington was four times Lord Mayor; in 1397, 1397-8, 1406-7 and 1419-20; he died in 1423, a man in his early sixties. The 3rd son of a Gloucestershire squire, he came to London, entered the mercers' trade, married well and rose rapidly both in trade, from which he amassed a fortune, and in the Corporation where he progressed from ward member to Lord Mayor. He was not knighted though an important part of his contact with the crown seems to have been the provision of considerable loans; according to legend he gave a banquet for Henry V at which he burned bonds discharged for the king worth £60 000.

His great wealth continued after his death, as in his lifetime, to be devoted to the public cause: permanent buildings for Leadenhall Market, the construction of Greyfriars Library, half the cost of founding the Guildhall Library, repairs at Bart's, the foundation of a college (dissolved at the Reformation) and almshouses at St Michael Paternoster Royal, the rebuilding of Newgate Prison...

Such great personality, wealth, benefactions, were embroidered into legend until in 1605 licence was granted for performances of a play (now lost), *The History of Richard Whittington, of his lowe byrth, his great fortune;* when an engraver, Renold Elstrack, about the same time portrayed him in classic pose with his hand upon a skull, popular protest was so loud that the engraver altered the plate replacing the skull with a cat which may have given rise to the legend, although an alternative source is a coal barge, known as a *catte,* since Whittington traded in coal.

(National Portrait Gallery)

Richard Whittington.

Architecture. – Guildhall's facade, a mixture of Classical and Gothic motifs, extends across 9 bays, rises to 4 storeys and culminates, on the four buttresses which divide the face into equal parts, in large and peculiar pinnacles. Crowning the central area are the City arms with griffin supporters *(1)*. All this dates from the restoration of 1788-9 by **George Dance the Younger.** The **porch,** at the centre, however, is still covered by two bays of medieval tierceron vaulting.

---

(1) The City arms are composed of the Cross of St George, the sword of the patron saint, St Paul, on a shield supported by winged griffins, probably incorporated in 16C.

Inside the **hall** also is in part medieval: the walls date back to the 15C and the chamber in which today's banquets are held is the same in dimension (152 × 49 1/2ft) as that in which Lady Jane Grey and others were tried.

A cornice at clerestory level bears the arms of England, the City and the 12 Great Livery Companies whose banners hang in front *(p 61)*; below, the bays between the piers contain memorial statues, notably (north wall) a seated bronze of **Churchill** by Oscar Nemon; Nelson; Wellington; Pitt the Elder by John Bacon. East of the entrance porch in the south wall, behind where the lord mayor sits at banquets, is a canopied oak buffet on which are displayed the City sword and mace and plate; to the west beneath the only remaining 15C window are the Imperial Standards of Length (1878) with the Metric measures (1973) on the right.

Guarding the Musicians' Gallery are **Gog and Magog** – post-war replica giants, each 9ft 3ins tall, carved in limewood by David Evans after the figures set up in Guildhall in 1708, themselves descendants of 15 and 16C midsummer pageant figures who were said to have originated in a legendary conflict between ancient Britons and Trojans in 1 000 BC.

(After photograph, Pitkin Pictorials)

Gog and Magog.

Crypt. – *Guided tours only. Mondays to Fridays.* ☎ *01-606 3030.*

The crypt is divided into two: the western pre-15C part, beneath the earlier hall which collapsed in the Fire, was repaired with a barrel roof by Wren and has recently been restored so that it now has a vaulted ceiling once more resting on four pairs of stone columns. The eastern 15C part below the present Guildhall survived both 17 and 20C fires and is particularly notable for its size – it is the largest medieval crypt in London – and the 6 blue Purbeck marble clustered pillars which support the vaulting.

Library. – *Open Mondays to Saturdays 9.30am to 5pm. Newspaper and Exhibition Rooms closed on Saturdays, closed all public holidays. No ticket required (reference only).* The library, founded *c* 1423, despoiled in 16C, refounded in 1824, possesses a unique collection of maps, prints, drawings and mss on the history and development of the City and London.

Two other nationally famous libraries with extensive resources and information on their special subjects *(open Mondays to Fridays 9.30am to 5pm)* are: **City Business Library** (RY – 106 Fenchurch St) and **St Bride Printing Library** (KY – Bride Lane, Fleet St).

Clock Museum★. – *Open Mondays to Fridays, 9.30am to 5pm; closed public holidays.*

The 700 timepieces which make up the Museum of the Worshipful Company of Clockmakers range in size from long case (grandfather) clocks to minute watches, in date from 15 to 20C, in manufacture from all wood composition, in movement from perpetual motion (the ball rolls 2 522 miles a year) and in aesthetic appeal from a silver skull watch, said to have belonged to Mary Queen of Scots, to jewelled confections, enamelled, decorated, engraved, chased...

Mansion House★ (NY). – *Apply in writing for guided tours Tuesdays, Wednesdays, Thursdays at noon and 2pm; closed August, early September and public holidays.*

The house dates only from 1739-52 – previously lord mayors remained in their own residences during the years of their mayoralty.

George Dance the Elder, the architect selected by the Corporation, designed a Palladian style mansion in Portland stone, before which modest staircases on either side at the front lead to a raised portico of six giant Corinthian columns, surmounted by a triangular pediment.

The interior, designed as a suite of magnificent state rooms from the portico, leads to the dining or Egyptian Hall (named after an interior Vitruvius described as an Egyptian Hall and favoured by 18C Palladians but having nothing to do with Egypt). In the hall, giant Corinthian columns forming an ambulatory support the cornice on which the coved ceiling rests and the walled niches are filled with Victorian statuary on subjects taken from English literature from Chaucer to Byron. The Ball Room is on the second floor. The Lord Mayor is Chief Magistrate of the City and on the ground floor on the east side is a Court of Justice, with cells below, the only such appointments in a private residence in the kingdom.

Plate and insignia★★. – The Corporation plate, rich and varied, dates from 17C. The insignia includes much older pieces: the Lord Mayor's **chain of office,** *c* 1535 with later additions, suspends from a collar of SS gold links, knots and enamelled Tudor roses, a pendant known as the Diamond Jewel, an onyx, carved in 1802 with the City arms, set in diamonds; the **Pearl Sword,** 16C and according to tradition presented by Queen Elizabeth at the opening of the Royal Exchange in 1571; the 17C **Sword of State** and the 18C **Great Mace,** silver gilt and 5ft 3ins long.

Lord Mayor's Show★★. – The show is the lord mayor's progress to his swearing in before the Lord Chief Justice, an observance which dates back to the charter of 1215 which required that the mayor be presented to the monarch or his justices at the Palace of Westminster. The procession was, for centuries, partly by water – the mayor owned a civic barge in the 15C. In 1553 full pageantry became the order of the day with men parading their best liveries, trumpets sounding, masques and poems recited along the route. Today with the judges removed from Westminster, the oath is taken at the Royal Courts of Justice; the pageantry, after a decline in the 19C, has returned with floats and the new and old mayors progressing in the golden state and other horsedrawn coaches accompanied by outriders.

The Show on the second Saturday in November is followed on the Monday evening by the Lord Mayor's Banquet in Guildhall which by tradition (although not invariably) begins with turtle soup. The principal speakers are by invariable tradition the new Lord Mayor and the Prime Minister.

City Livery Company and Ancient City Guild Halls

There are 92 guilds of which 12 make up the so-called Greater Companies. Most are successors of medieval religious fraternities, craft or social guilds; some adopted uniforms and were thus styled livery companies. The Great Fire, local fires, changes of fortune, incendiary bombs, have reduced the number of halls to 25 including the Master Mariners, transferred to the frigate HMS *Wellington* (moored in the Thames off the Victoria Embankment). New guilds have been created by the modern professions.

The halls are not generally open to outsiders. Specials visits are arranged in summer by the City Information Centre – prior application essential.

Although in 1523 Henry VIII "commanded to have all money and plate belonging to any Hall or Crypt", many halls have collections or pieces dating back to 15C which they either managed to hide from the king or re-purchased.

MERCERS · GROCERS · DRAPERS · FISHMONGERS · GOLDSMITHS · SKINNERS

Mercers (NY). – *Ironmonger Lane*. 1958 rebuilding of earlier halls (1540, 1672-82) on the site of St Thomas of Acon Hospital. Major collection of plate dating from 15C.

Grocers (NY). – *Prince's St*. 1889-93. Elizabethan hall with 17C iron screen; courtroom with overmantel from late 17C hall; 16-20C plate; John Piper tapestries.

Drapers (PX). – *Throgmorton St*. 1868. Pillared and mirrored hall with full length portraits; silver from Elizabeth I to II.

Fishmongers (PZ). – *London Bridge*. 1831-4. Neo-Greek building in a unique position with windows overlooking the river which enhances the rich interior gold leaf decoration (restored post war). Late 17/18C and 20C plate; the **Annigoni** portrait of the **Queen** hangs in the drawing room.

Goldsmiths (MX). – *Foster Lane*. 1835. Exceptional plate in a lavish, baroque setting. The hall is also notable for its jewellery exhibitions.

Skinners (NY). – *Dowgate Hill*. Late 18C building, staircase and still aromatic sandalwood panelling of 1670; 18C plasterwork; hall 1850 with Frank Brangwyn decorations (1904-10); plate. Courtyard.

Merchant Taylors (PY). – *Threadneedle St*. Plate including a cloth yard with Henry VIII cypher.

Haberdashers (MX). – *Staining Lane*. Rebuilt 1956. Outstanding Elizabethan and 17C plate.

Salters (NV). – *4 Fore St*. The company owned a City hall from 1454-1941 and has occupied its present modern building since 1976.

Ironmongers (MX). – *Aldersgate St*. 1924 Gothic stone porch; the small building is now surrounded by the Museum of London. Early 16C funeral pall. Late 15/18 and 20C plate.

Vintners (MY). – *Upper Thames St*. 1671, restored 1948; very fine late 17C panelling in majestic hall; staircase with outstanding balusters; 15C tapestry, 16C funeral pall; plate includes a double "milkmaid" cup, the Glass Tun etc. The monarch, the Vintners, and the Dyers own the swans upon the Thames, the company swans being marked on the bill as cygnets at the annual swan upping.

Clothworkers (RY). – *Mincing Lane*. 1955-8. 17/18C plate.

MERCHANT TAILORS · HABERDASHERS · SALTERS · IRONMONGERS · VINTNERS · CLOTH WORKERS

Apothecaries (LY). – *Blackfriars Lane*. 1632, rebuilt *c* 1670; pillared lamp over the old monastic well in the courtyard; interior remarkable for 1671 oak panelling, stone jars (one of 1566), apothecary vessels; chandeliers; banners from former state barge.

Armourers and Brasiers (NX). – *Coleman St*. 1840; large collection of 17/18C plate.

Barber-Surgeons (MX). – *Monkwell Sq*. Inigo Jones hall destroyed in the war; rebuilt on adjoining site (bombing exposed Roman fort and bastion). Superb 16/17C plate.

Cutlers (LX). – *Warwick Lane*. 1886-7. Elephant shaped poor box; sets of 17/18C spoons.

Founders (NY). – *St Swithin's Lane*. 1877-8. 16/18C plate.

Innholders (NY). – *College St*. 1886. Plate includes remarkable salts and spoons.

Stationers (LY). – *Stationers' Hall Court, Ludgate Hill*. 1800, 1887; splendid carved screen and panelling of 1670; 1800 ceiling (re-erected).

Tallow Chandlers (NY). – *Dowgate Hill*. Rebuilt 1670-2; Italianised 1880. Courtyard; 17C seating in courtroom; 16/20C plate.

Watermen and Lightermen (PZ). – *St Mary at Hill*. (An ancient City Guild dating back to Tudor times.) 1780; small hall in a pilastered building.

On 20 June each year the guild pays a "fine" of one red rose to the Lord Mayor imposed on Lady Knollys in 1381 for building a bridge across Seething Lane without permission.

■ FINANCE

Wealth, resources, once visible in gold coin and bullion, now in the form of computer impulses on tape, quoted always it seems, in millions, existing as transactions, "futures", indexes... personal fortunes made or unmade as "confidence" rises or falls – though outside the common experience, the mystery – magic associated with the name of the City remains. The pervasive atmosphere of wealth is immediately recognisable in what has been for hundreds of years and remains a world centre of finance.

Bank of England (NY). – *Open by appointment; apply to Information Division.* The Bank, massive, blank and undistinguished was designed by Sir Herbert Baker and erected between 1924 and 1939. It is taller and larger than its immediate predecessor by Sir John Soane whose Bank building was his life's masterpiece. Of this only the outer walls remain. The large sculptures on the façade are by Sir Charles Wheeler. To the northeast stands the Tivoli corner, a circular pavilion inspired from the Temple of the Sibyl at Tivoli, crowned by a statue of Ariel. An annexe of the Bank, erected since the last war, with a concave façade on New Change at the east end of St Paul's, is notable only for its size.

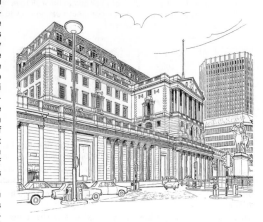

Bank of England.

The Bank, the concept of a Scot, William Paterson, was incorporated under royal charter in 1694 with a capital of £1 200 000 to finance, in the modern way by raising loans and not by royal extortion as heretofore, the continuation of the wars against Louis XIV. It acquired its nickname a century later during the Napoleonic wars: the crisis had forced the Bank to suspend cash payments – Sheridan referred in the House to the "elderly lady in the City of great credit and long standing", Gillray drew a caricature which he captioned "The Old Lady of Threadneedle Street in Danger". The Bank has since weathered other crises, become a bankers' bank and in 1946 was nationalised. It supervises the note issue and national debt and acts as the central reserve. The Governor is appointed by the Crown.

A museum *(entrance in Bartholomew Lane)* tells the 300 year old history of the Bank of England. *Open Mondays to Fridays 10am to 6pm, Saturdays and Sundays afternoons only.*

Royal Exchange★ (PY). – *Cornhill and Threadneedle St.* The exchange was "first built with brick at the sole charge of **Sir Thomas Gresham,** merchant, who laid the foundation 7 June 1566... On 27 January (1571) Queen Elizabeth came to view it and caused it to be proclaimed the Royal Exchange. But being consumed by the dreadful Fire in 1666 was rebuilt with Portland Stone by the City and Mercer's Company... King Charles II laying the first stone". This building, "esteemed the most beautiful, strong and stately of its kind in Europe" was designed by E. Jarman on the same courtyard plan; in 1838 it was again burned down and a third, larger, building constructed. The wide steps, monumental Corinthian portico and pediment with 10ft tall allegorical figures, provide an impressive entrance to an edifice once the very hub of the City. Around and on the outside walls are 19C portrait statues: in front, an equestrian bronze (lacking stirrups!) of **Wellington** (Chantrey); against the north wall, Whittington and Myddelton; at the rear, Gresham, whose emblem, a gilded bronze grasshopper, acts as a weathervane.

The central courtyard, lined by an arcade at ground and first floor levels, where merchant brokers congregated besides "walking the central square", became a market again in 1982 when the London International Financial Futures Exchange, for dealing in interest and exchange rates, was opened. The Visitors' Gallery *(open Mondays to Fridays 11.30am to 1.45pm; closed public holidays)* enables visitors to see the trading floor. Apply to LIFFE to see the interior walls decorated with historical murals (c 1900).

Stock Exchange★ (PX). – *8 Throgmorton St. Visitors' gallery and film (1/4 hr) theatre open Mondays to Fridays 9.45am to 3.45pm; closed public holidays. Apply in advance to the Public Information Unit.* ☎ *588 2355.* Trading in stocks and shares originated in 17C in this country, at first in the Royal Exchange and local coffeehouses. The first stock exchange, as such, was inaugurated in 1773 in Threadneedle St. In 1801 and 1971 ever larger buildings rose on the site.

From a gallery inside the sleekly functional stone and glass edifice surmounted by a 350ft tower, the visitor looks through plate glass on to the trading floor below. In 1986 a change in the legislation governing the Exchange brought about the abolition of the distinction between jobbers and brokers and the introduction of electronic dealing systems. Membership is no longer restricted to individuals but is open to outside institutions and to international share dealers. As transactions are carried out away from the Exchange the frenetic activity on the trading floor has been stilled and a new use for the hall is under consideration.

Baltic Exchange (RX). – *14 St Mary Axe. Guided tours for groups 11.30am and 12.30pm, Mondays to Fridays. Apply in advance to the Secretary.* The Victorian building houses the world's only shipping Exchange covering international chartering of ships and aircraft, worldwide fats, oil and oilseed markets and two futures markets in grain and potatoes.

London Metal Exchange. – *Plantation House.* The market for non-ferrous metals: copper, tin.

Lloyd's (RY). – *Leadenhall and Lime Sts.*

Until this century the biggest insurance corporation in the world possessed no premises of its own: Lloyd's Shipping Register opened in 1900, the first insurance offices in 1928.

History. – In 1691 **Edward Lloyd,** coffeehouse owner near the Tower, took over Pontaq's at 16 Lombard St (plaque on Coutts), a French owned eating house frequented with relish by Pepys, Evelyn, Wren, Dryden, Swift... Under Lloyd, the house, at the heart of the business world and surrounded by literally hundreds of competitors, became the meeting place of merchants, shippers, bankers, underwriters, agents and newsmen. He inaugurated the still current system of port agents to provide shipping intelligence. In 1734 began the publication of the daily, *Lloyd's List,* and in 1760 of the annual *Lloyd's Register.* Edward Lloyd had died in 1712 (plaque in St Mary Woolnoth) and in 1769 his successors split: New Lloyd's moved into 5 Pope's Head Alley (the Lombard St house closed in 1785).

Through the good offices of John Julius Angerstein and the Mercers' Co, in 1774 Lloyd's transferred to more spacious quarters "over the northwest corner of the Royal Exchange" where it remained until this century. In 1771 the association became formalised by the institution of a minute book; in 1871 it was incorporated by act of parliament. (Policies are subscribed by members or underwriters acting for a syndicate of which there are now about 360; the requirements for membership are minimum assets of £75 000 and to be able to lodge a deposit of at least £10 000. Some £6 000 million is placed annually in premiums.) The organisation, guarded by doormen, resplendent in red frock coats with black velvet collars and gilt buckled top hats, covers everything except "life" it is said.

On the site in Leadenhall St, once occupied by the East India Company to which Elizabeth I granted a charter in 1600, is a striking steel and glass building (1986) designed by R. Rogers. It features a central atrium rising to a 200ft high glass barrel vault and glass walled galleries, six towers and external lifts. An exhibition (4th floor) traces Lloyd's history and a viewing gallery enables visitors to observe the trading activities of the Underwriting Room and galleries. *Open Mondays to Fridays 10am to 4pm.* To renew with tradition the new building has a coffee shop where members can entertain and do business with their clients.

The offices east of Lime St, in neo-Classical style, were opened in 1957.

Among Lloyd's traditions are the Captains' Room, first so-called in the Exchange when Lloyd's took over the Refreshment Room and the catering and still the name of the members' exclusive dining room; Nelson mementoes; policies including that of 1680 at 4% on the *Golden Fleece* bound for Venice from Lisbon; the Underwriting Room; the daily publication, the *Shipping Index,* recording movements of some 20 000 vessels... and the striking of the **Lutine Bell** for an overdue vessel, once for a loss, twice for a safe arrival. The bell came from a captured French frigate, sunk off Holland in 1799 with gold and specie valued at nearly £1.5 million and insured by the house but partly salved in 1857-61.

(After photograph, Pitkin Pictorials)

The Lutine Bell.

Lloyd's Shipping Register (RY). – *71 Fenchurch St.* The building, columned, turreted and topped by a gilded ship vane, is decorated with *art nouveau* figures and friezes towards Lloyds Avenue. *Lloyd's Register,* gives details of ownership, tonnage etc.

Institute of London Underwriters (RY). – *49 Leadenhall St.* The institute founded in 1884, handles only marine and aviation insurance and reinsurance worldwide.

The City Markets. – Only two of the main markets are still to be found in the City.

Smithfield (LV). – *London Central Markets. Time to visit: early morning to noon.*

Smithfield was opened as a wholesale and retail dead meat, poultry and provision market only in 1868. Previously the stock had come in live, driven into the City through Islington: from 12C the summer Fair of St Bartholomew, from 1614 all the year round. After centuries of overcrowding on the site and chaos and congestion in the narrow streets, the livestock market was transferred in 1855 to the Caledonian Market, Islington. The buildings, erected in 1868 and since enlarged, are of red brick and stone with domed towers at either end; they extend over 8 acres, with 15 miles of rails capable of hanging 60 000 sides of beef. An underground railway depot *(car park)* originally linked the market to the national railway network.

Leadenhall Market (PY). – *Gracechurch St. Open all day.*

Leadenhall, a retail market selling poultry, meat, fish, fruit, cheese and specialising in game, is at its most spectacular at the start of the season when the shop fronts are hung with grouse, partridge, pheasant... and at Christmas. The area was a market in Roman times *(p 46)* and then a manor which Whittington purchased and converted, in part, once more into a market under the Corporation – hence Whittington Avenue and the market's name after the house's lead covered roof. It was burned down in the Fire, rebuilt and rebuilt again in 1881 in the present form.

The City Pubs – many are closed at the weekend.

There are now as many pubs as there once were churches in the City – namely some 200! Ye Olde Watling (MY), like so many, dates from before the Fire, was rebuilt in 1668 and again after a second baptism of fire, in 1947; the Square Rigger (PYZ), with decks aslant as though sailing a slight swell, has only recently been fitted out. Between the ancient and the modern, usually in a court or at the bend in an alley between main thoroughfares, are such 17 and 18C houses as Williamson's (MY) on the site of Sir John Falstaff's house and Ye Olde Dr Butler's Head (NX, reconstructed), named after King James' physician who established a number of taverns where a medicated ale was sold which the doctor claimed rejuvenated the imbiber! Among 19C pubs, all mahogany and cut glass mirrors, is the White Swan (KY) and, worth visiting for its Spy cartoons alone, the Punch Tavern (KY)... and then there are wine bars: El Vino's (JY)...

■ ADDITIONAL SIGHTS ON THE MAIN THOROUGHFARES

The City's network of alleys, courts, yards and steps – everyone's personal short cut often enlivened by an old tavern, newly planted with half a dozen trees, arranged with benches, a fountain, a statue, would take a volume to describe. Their history – and often the City's – is reflected in their names: Pope's Head Alley, Puddle Dock, Glasshouse Alley, Bate's Court, Panyer Alley, Wardrobe Terrace, Seacole Lane, French Ordinary, Ave Maria Lane, Paternoster Row, Amen Court, Turnagain Lane...

FLEET ST – ST PAUL'S (JKL/Y)

Fleet St, running east-west, is named after the River Fleet which flowed south from Hampstead and drained into the river at Blackfriars.The character of the famous 'Street of Ink' is changing as the major newspaper publishers move their offices east to Docklands.

Temple Bar. – The bar has been the City's western barrier since the Middle Ages and is still where the sovereign pauses to receive and return the Pearl Sword from the Lord Mayor on entering the City. The present memorial pillar with statues of Queen Victoria and the future Edward VII surmounted by the City griffin, dates from 1880. It replaced the "bars" which had developed from 13C posts and chains and at various times constituted a high, arched building, a prison (thrown down by Wat Tyler in 1381) and finally an arch of Portland stone designed by Wren in 1672 and used, in the days of public execution, as a spike for heads and quarters. It was dismantled in 1870 but plans to re-erect it in St Paul's Church Yard *(qv)* have been approved.

Child & Co. – *No 1.* One of the country's oldest banks (now Royal Bank of Scotland), originally "at the sign of the Marigold" also known as the Devil Tavern *(plaque)*.

Prince Henry's Room. – *No 17. Open 1.45 to 5pm (Saturdays 4pm); closed Sundays and public holidays.* The upstairs tavern room is Tudor panelled with an ornate strapwork, Jacobean ceiling with a centre decoration of Prince of Wales' feathers and the initials PH. It is now overfilled with Samuel Pepys mementoes.

Cock Tavern (Ye Olde Cocke Tavern). – 17C overmantel, panelled long bar and upstairs restaurant rooms; Dickens and Thackeray associations.

Fetter Lane. – At the north end are the Printer's Devil (pub, printing decoration) and the *Daily Mirror* building.

The courts. – To the north is a series of narrow alleys: Crane, Red Lion, Johnson's, St Dunstan's, Bolt, Three Kings, Hind, Wine Office, Cheshire and Peterborough.

Dr Johnson's House★ (KX). – *Gough Sq. Open daily May to September 11.00am to 5.30pm (October to April 5pm); closed Sundays and public holidays; £1.50, children, students, OAPs £1.* The typical late 17C house, where he lived between 1749 and 1759, was chosen by Johnson almost certainly for its long, well lit garret, where he worked with his secretaries to complete his *Dictionary* which was published in 1755. The small rooms on each floor contain 18C furniture, prints, mementoes and the first edition. The work completed, he moved to chambers in the Temple, in 1765 to no 7 Fleet St (known purely coincidentally as Johnson's Ct) and finally to Bolt Ct where he died in 1784.

Cheshire Cheese. – *Wine Office Court.* The pub in a house rebuilt in 1667, has Johnson associations. It includes a restaurant, small beamed rooms and coal fires on 3 floors.

No 143 is Gothic with a 19C statue of Mary Queen of Scots between the first floor windows.

Bouverie and Whitefriars Sts. – *Daily Mail* buildings.

Reuters and Press Association. – *No 85.* The building was designed by Lutyens in 1935.

No 135. – 1928 building in a ponderous mixture of styles, formerly occupied by the Daily Telegraph.

Shoe Lane. – Narrow winding lane.

Nos 121-8. – As much a landmark as when first built in 1931 for the Express newspaper group: black and clear glass panels set in chromium, with straight lines throughout except for the corner on Shoe Lane.

Ludgate Circus. – The circus which was built in 1875 on the site of the Fleet Bridge to Ludgate Hill, includes a plaque (northwest angle) to Edgar Wallace (1875-1932).

Ludgate Hill. – A plaque on the south abutment of the 19C railway states "In a house near the site was published in 1702 the *Daily Courant* first London daily newspaper". Above the bridge stood Lud Gate, demolished in 1760 – plaque on the wall of St Martin-within-Ludgate *(qv)*. It was the first curfew gate to be closed at night and was named after the legendary King Lud (66BC) said to have built the first gate on the site. Statues from the 1586 gate were removed to St Dunstan-in-the-West *(qv)*.

St Paul's Church Yard. – The statue within the circular railing is of Queen Anne, in whose reign the cathedral was completed.

Between the 19C offices on the south side is a narrow lane in which stands the Old **Deanery** built by Wren in 1672-3. The adjoining building on the corner of Carter Lane, built in 1873 as the Choir School and now a youth hostel, is decorated with sgraffito ornamentation in the spandrels and a terra cotta inscription from Gal IV, 13.

Further on is the single storey circular building of the **City Information Centre,** and a paved court (Old Change) and garden – setting for modern sculptures, *Icarus* by Michael Ayrton and *The Young Lovers* by George Ehrlich.

St Paul's Cross. – Paul's Cross (site marked on the pavement, north of the apse) which is known to have been in existence as a preaching cross in 1256, became the centre and symbol of free speech and so was removed by the Long Parliament in 1643. The monument in the garden with St Paul at the summit dates from 1910.

The Chapter House. – This perfectly proportioned red brick building with a crowning parapet and stone quoins marking the angles and centre, was built by Wren in 1710-14. Note the iron hand pump to the west erected by St Faith parishioners, 1819.

The sculpture at the centre of Paternoster Square is by Elizabeth Frink (1975).

The TEMPLE★★ (JY)

The Temple church dates back to 1185, when the order acquired the spacious site on the river bank in place of their first plot at the north end of Chancery Lane. The Templars were suppressed in 1312 and their property assigned to the Hospitallers who, in turn, were dispossessed by Henry VIII. The church reverted to the crown; the outlying property remained with the lawyers to whom it had previously been leased by the Hospitallers and to whom it was granted, together with the safekeeping of the church, by James I in 1608. The lawyers early formed themselves into the three Societies of the Inner (being within the City; emblem a Pegasus), the Middle (emblem a Pascal lamb) and the Outer Temple, but the latter, on the site of Essex Street, has long since disappeared.

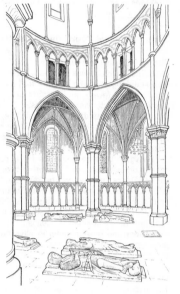

Temple Church.

Inner Temple. – The Tudor **Inner Temple Gateway** (between 16/17 Fleet St), gabled, half timbered, 3 storeys high, each advanced on the one below so that the tunnel arch and pilastered stone ground floor are in shadow, dates from 1610 (reconstructed 1906). It leads into the lane, past 19C buildings and the house where Dr Johnson *(qv)* lived from 1760 to 1765 to the church.

The Temple Church★★. – *Open daily 10am to 4pm except for services; closed August to September.*

The west doorway into the round church of 1160-85 is itself circular being Romanesque; the porch is rib vaulted and has a Perpendicular archway; the tower and clerestory are Romanesque – all dates from the period of transition. The exterior is of stone, the upper central tower is even crenellated; the later 13C hall plan chancel is alternately buttressed and pierced by tall pointed triple windows.

The round church is circled inside by an ambulatory, rib vaulted and walled by blind arcading with grotesque heads filling the spandrels between the pointed arcs. Six pillars of Purbeck marble, each of two stout, two slender, shafts heavily ringed midway, support curved Perpendicular arches; above is a Transitional triforium of rounded arcs bisected to form pointed arches which rest on slender, full capitalled columns; higher still are the round windowed clerestory and conical roof (dating from 1862 and restored to the same pattern after the war). On the stone floor are 10-13C effigies of knights – Templars and their illustrious supporters.

At the side is the door to the Penitential Cell of Templar times – a cubicle less than 5ft long. The chancel of 1220-40 is beautiful with slender shafted Purbeck columns dividing the nave and aisles and rising to form the ribs of the quadripartite vaulting. The dark oak reredos designed by Wren was carved by **William Emmett** in 1682 for £45. Note the heraldic floor brass with a Latin scroll winding between 29 shields (half-way down the nave), the 16 and 17C tombs at the west end.

To the northeast of the church stands the Master's House rebuilt in 17C style.

The Inner Temple Hall, Treasury and Library were all rebuilt after the war.

King's Bench Walk. – The northern of the two ranges, in the largest Temple court, dates from 1678 and is by **Wren** (no 1 rebuilt). The mellow red brick fronts are marked by attractive doorways while below the east gate are two houses of especial note, no 7 of 1685 and no 8 of 1782.

Middle Temple. – In **Pump Court** the cloisters (from Church Court) and the south side have been rebuilt (Edward Maufe); the north (except for 19C Farrar's Building) is late 17C.

Middle Temple Hall★. – *Not usually open – apply to the Head Porter. Entrance through the 19C corner tower in Fountain Court.* The great hall is Elizabethan and rich as only ancient oak timbers, panelling and fine carving can make an interior: the roof is a double hammerbeam, the finest of the period, 1574. The small panels in the high wainscot are bright with the arms of readers who instructed the medieval law students who not only ate but attended lectures and even slept in the 100 × 40ft hall. At the west end above the high table are royal portraits including Charles I (after van Dyck), Charles II (Kneller) and Queen Elizabeth who, according to tradition, watched the first performance of *Twelfth Night* (1602) in the company of the benchers in the hall. The heraldic glass, helmets and armour are also of interest.

When the spectacular 16C carved screen at the hall's east end was shattered by a bomb the biggest jigsaw in the world was begun as splintered pieces were dug out of the rubble and fitted into place; it took years to complete but finally the screen was able to be reinstalled. The roof, incredibly, remained unharmed.

Up the steps from Fountain Court is **New Court** with its Wren building of 1676.

Middle Temple Gateway and Lane. – The pedimented gateway with giant pilasters was erected only in 1684 although the lane is referred to as early as 1330 since it used to end in stairs on the river, affording a short cut by water to Westminster. Just inside the gate are two houses of 1693, their ground floors overshadowed by jutting timber–faced upper storeys with 17C windows.

HOLBORN – NEWGATE ST (JKL/X)

Holborn (See text and map pp 95 to 98).

Prudential Assurance Building. – The Pru, on the site of Furnival's Inn, is an all red building designed by Alfred Waterhouse at the turn of the century. Many gabled, lancet windowed, it extends symmetrically on either side of a central tower, capped by a pyramid roof.

The CITY★★★

Daily Mirror Building. – A 170ft high curtain wall of stone on the street, is topped by yet taller buildings of glass extending south between Fetter and New Fetter Lanes (1957-60).

Holborn Circus. – Prince Albert, mounted and with hat aloft, serves as a traffic island.

Holborn Viaduct. – It was built in 1863-9 to connect the City and West End – previously all traffic had to descend to the level of Farringdon St and climb up again. The bridge is an example of Victorian cast iron work: strongly constructed and ornate with uplifting statues and lions.

Fleet Lane. – The lane recalls the notorious Fleet Prison which dated back to the 12C, was rebuilt after the Fire and finally demolished only in 1846 (Mr Pickwick made a brief but not painful stay).

Central Criminal Court, the Old Bailey. – *The public are admitted when Courts are sitting, approximately 10am to 4.30pm with an adjournment for lunch.*

History. – This is the third Criminal Court on the site: the second was opened in 1774, the first in 1539. The 16C court was built because sickness and infestation, rife in the gaols, brought "much peril and danger" to the judges – they still carry posies from May to September, traditionally to ward off gaol fever – and because no halls were available in which trials could be held; the Common Council, therefore, passed a resolution "that a convenient place be made... upon the common ground of this City in the old bailey of London". The site was hard by New Gate, the gate in the wall twice built by the Romans, on the main road west, enlarged in the early Middle Ages and by 1180 a City gaol, with Ludgate, to relieve the always overfull Fleet Prison.

Newgate became notorious for appalling conditions, for cruelty and barbarism. It was several times rebuilt: in 1423 with a bequest from Richard Whittington, in 1783 to designs by George Dance junior; it was broken open by Wat Tyler in 1381, fired by Gordon Rioters in 1780. Public executions, transferred from Tyburn in 1783, took place outside the prison (the Magpie and Stump opposite did great business – demolished 1988) until abolished in 1868. The gate was demolished in 1777; the prison, by then used only for prisoners on trial, in 1902. The bell once rung outside the condemned cell is in St Sepulchre's.

Among the most famous to have been tried were **William Penn** and another in 1670 for preaching to an unlawful assembly in Gracechurch St; a tablet "commemorates the courage and endurance of the jury who refused to give a verdict against them though they were locked up without food for two nights and were fined for their verdict of "Not Guilty", from which developed the "Right of Juries to give their Verdict according to their convictions".

The building. – The Lady of Justice, a gold figure on a green copper dome, has been a dominant feature of the London skyline since she was placed on the then newly reconstructed Old Bailey in 1907. Cast in bronze, covered in gold leaf (regilded every 5 years and cleaned every August), holding scales and a 3ft 3in sword, she is 12ft tall and is neither blindfolded nor blind. The building is of Portland stone on a granite foundation, with a large entrance emphasised above the segmental pediment by figures of Truth, Justice and the Recording Angel. Inside all is marble – grand staircase, halls on two floors... and mural painting. The four original courts are large. After the war additional courts were required and an extension was added in 1972. Faced with Portland stone but otherwise bearing no relation whatsoever to Mountford's building, the annexe accommodates small, light panelled, modern, courts so that there are now 18 in all.

There are 60 cells; prisoners are brought daily from Brixton and Holloway – there is no gaol on the premises. No prisoner has escaped from an Old Bailey cell since 1907.

Giltspur St (to Bart's). – At the junction with Cock Lane stands the **Fat Boy,** a gilded oak figure said to mark where the Fire stopped. The site, then known as Pie Corner, gave rise to the saying that the Fire began in Pudding Lane and ended at Pie Corner.

General Post Office. – Plaques on the turn of the century building indicate the site of Greyfriars (f 1225) and Christ's Hospital which occupied the buildings from 1552-1902. Outside the main building stands the statue of Sir Rowland Hill, who in 1840 introduced the penny post – the uniform rate for a letter sent anywhere in the kingdom.

National Postal Museum. – *Open weekdays 9.30am to 4.30pm (4pm Fridays); closed at weekends and all public holidays; special facilities on application for society and school visits, research, etc. Souvenir shop.*

The museum, established in 1965, claims to house what is probably the most important and extensive collection of postage stamps in the world. The 250 000 stamps on display include the R M Philips **19C British Collection,** the Post Office collection of all stamps issued at home and overseas under British PO control since 1840 and stamp issues by members of the Universal Postal Union since 1878. A special feature is the story of the creation of the **penny black.**

Master Gunner. – Pub with Royal Artillery associations.

QUEEN VICTORIA ST – CANNON ST (LMN/Y)

Queen Victoria St is relatively modern having been cut through a maze of alleys and buildings only in 1867-71. It was the first City street to be lit by electricity.

Cannon St, in the Middle Ages Candelwriteystrete, the home of candle makers and wick chandlers, is now an area of vast offices at its west end where it was bombed, tailing off into late 19/20C constructions.

Printing House Sq. – Within ten years (1964-74) *The Times* constructed a new slate and glass building with the old square as forecourt and moved away to a still newer building in Gray's Inn Rd *(qv)*. In 1986 the paper moved again to Wapping *(qv)*.

Printing House Sq got its name after the Fire, when, on the site of the Norman, Mountfichet Castle and the later Blackfriars Playhouse, the King's Printer set up presses and began to publish acts, the King James Bible, proclamations and the *London Gazette* (1666 – as *Oxford Gazette* 1665). The name remained after the printer moved, in 1770, nearer to Fleet St. In 1784 John Walter purchased a house in the square and the following year began publication of the *Daily Universal Register,* altering its title on 1-1-88 to *The Times.*

The square's history is related in full on a plaque situated on what is now the Continental Bank House.

Telecom Technology Showcase. – *Baynard House, 135 Queen Victoria St. Open Mondays to Fridays 10am to 5pm; closed public holidays.*

The exhibits trace the development of telecommunications from the inventions of Bell, Edison and Marconi to the applications of modern technology: optical fibre transmission, microwave towers, satellites, electronic and digital systems.

In the forecourt of Baynard House is a tall pillar sculpted by R. Kindersley (1980).

Faraday Building. – 1932. International telephone headquarters.

College of Arms. – *The courtyard and Earl Marshal's Court only open Mondays to Fridays 10am to 4pm.* The college, overlooking a forecourt behind splendid wrought iron gates, dates from 1671-88 when it was rebuilt after the Fire. Unlike the churches nearby, St Benet's and St Paul's, it was not designed by Wren, but by Francis Sandford, Lancaster Herald of the time, and Morris Emmett, master bricklayer to the Office of Works. The mellow red brick building, formerly pedimented, now parapeted, has shallow return wings on either side of a full length terrace approached up shallow flights of steps at either end. The interior woodwork – staircases, panelling, pilastered and garlanded screen – is by William Emmett, contemporary of Grinling Gibbons.

Salvation Army HQ. – An imposing stone building (1963), well back from the south side of the road, the rear dropping down to the level of Upper Thames St.

Bracken House. – A large post-war building by Sir Albert Richardson, employing small red bricks and red sandstone in no marked architectural style.

Temple of Mithras. – The stone temple with a double course of red tiles, 60ft long, 20ft wide, was erected on the west bank of the Walbrook in 2C AD when Roman legions were stationed in the City. All traces had long since vanished and even the Walbrook had altered course and level by 1954 when excavations preceding the construction of Bucklersbury House revealed walls laid in the outline of a basilica divided into a narthex, nave and aisles separated by columns and a buttressed apse at the west end.

The head of the god Mithras in a Phrygian cap, those of Minerva and Serapis, Egyptian god of the Underworld with a corn measure on his head, and other statuary fragments and artefacts are now in the Museum of London. The temple itself, transposed to enable the office block to rise as planned, was then reconstructed in the forecourt.

The temple stood near the centre of the Roman city; to the south, on the Thames foreshore stood the governor's palace, to the northwest the basilica and forum which together occupied some 60 acres fronting what are now Cornhill and Leadenhall St and backing on to Fenchurch St.

Cannon St Station. – The mid-Victorian viaduct and the station, with its monumental towers adorned with gilded weathervanes crowning the train sheds high above the riverbank, stand on the site of two churches and the important medieval steelyard of the Hanseatic merchants.

London Stone. – *(Behind a grill in the wall of no 111, the Bank of China).* A limestone fragment, touchstone of the legend on the plaque which states "its origin and purpose are unknown".

Martin Lane. – South to St Martin Orgar Tower *(p 58)* and **Ye Olde Wine Shades** (1663). This double fronted pub with painted boards outside, has been left as much as possible like a 17C tavern with dark wooden booths inside. It claims to be the oldest wine house in London having originally been the bar attached to the Fishmongers' Hall. It took its name from its position in the shadow of the hall. The adjoining marble and glass buildings are in marked contrast.

UPPER AND LOWER THAMES STS (KLMNPR/YZ)

Probably in Roman times and certainly in the early Middle Ages Thames St ran along the line of the river wall; by the 17C it served as a through route from the Wardrobe to the Tower, crossing the furriers' and vintners' quarters, lined by 8 churches and providing rear access to castles and mansions, quays, warehouses and markets, whose main thoroughfare was the river. Earthworks, under and overpasses, warehouse clearance, widening, promise to transform it once more into a major road. The revitalisation of the riverside area is underway.

Unilever House. – 1931. The vast stone building, a rusticated ground floor, pillars, large sculptures and miles of corridors inside, stands on part of the site of **Bridewell Palace**, built by Henry VIII in 1522 as his residence during the visit of Charles V who elected to stay in Blackfriars Monastery on what was then the far bank of the Fleet. Edward VI gave the Bridewell to the City which converted it into an orphanage and after the Fire rebuilt it as a prison, soon notorious as one of London's most evil houses (demolished 1864). Blackfriars Monastery, dissolved in 1538, was abandoned until in 1576 a theatre was founded in the cloisters where a professional children's company would rehearse before performing at court. Twenty years later James Burbage converted another part of the monastery into the Blackfriars Theatre for the performance of Shakespeare's later plays and those of Beaumont and Fletcher. The theatre, demolished in 1655, is commemorated in Playhouse Yard.

The wedge-shaped Blackfriars pub (1896), with a jolly fat friar on the façade, is decorated inside with friezes of monks at work and play in a strange art nouveau style.

Mermaid Theatre. – *Puddle Dock.* In 1959 a disused warehouse opened as the Mermaid Theatre, the first theatre in the City for three centuries. In the late 1970s, when the Blackfriars underpass was constructed, the road system entirely re-designed and the tall, inconvenient 19C offices demolished, the old theatre closed. Some ten years later there appeared on the same site a £4-5 million construction in which offices formed a superstructure to the foyers, exhibition area, bars and, most importantly, the auditorium and modern stage of the new Mermaid Theatre.

The site itself is historic as that of **Baynard Castle**. In c 1100 a fort was built on the river bank, pendant to the Tower downstream, by one "Baynard that came with the Conqueror" according to Stow. When it burnt down in 1428 it was rebuilt by Duke Humphrey of Gloucester and was the scene in 1460 of Richard of Gloucester hearing the news that his plans to seize the crown were progressing (Richard III, 3 vii). Henry VII reconstructed it as a spacious palace and Lady Jane Grey heard there in 1553 that she was to be queen; it finally disappeared in the Fire of 1666.

Samuel Pepys. – *Brooks Wharf.* Pub with Pepys mementoes in a converted tea warehouse.

Queenhithe Dock. – An unremarkable inlet is all that remains of what was London's most important dock above London Bridge.

Billingsgate Market. – There was a market on the site from 1297 to 1982 when the fish market – established as a free fish market in 1699 – moved to new premises in the West India Docks on the Isle of Dogs. Excavations of the lorry park have enabled archaeologists to investigate evidence of a neighbouring Roman quay and Saxon harbour. The market building, designed in 1876 by Sir Howard Jones, with Britannia presiding over two dolphins on its decorative roof, is being developed as offices but the original features have been retained.

Custom House. – The house of rusticated stone and yellow stock brick, nearly 500ft wide, dates from 1813-17 with a central riverfront bay by Robert Smirke of 1825. Three storeys high, with five lanterns as sole decoration, it is the sixth to stand on this reach of the Thames.

A small museum describes the role of the Customs and Excise in dealing with smuggling, fraud and other illegal activities. The displays range from a custom seal from the reign of Edward I, tally sticks, the King's chest from the time of William III, 18C kid gloves found under floor boards in an old house in 1937 to modern equipment used in crime detection. *Open Mondays to Fridays 10am to 4pm.*

CHEAPSIDE - KING ST (MN/XY)

Cheapside, originally West Cheap, was from earliest times until the Fire a microcosm of life in the City. *Ceap* meant to barter in Anglo-Saxon and local street names (Milk St, Bread St, Honey Lane) indicate the commodities sold first on stalls, later in shops; in addition craft and tradesmen lived in the houses in tributary lanes and alleys – Stow tells how Bow Lane was previously Hosiers' Lane and before that occupied by shoemakers. In medieval Cheapside there were 3 churches of which only one was rebuilt, St Mary-le-Bow; facing Wood St was one of the crosses erected by Edward I to mark a halt in Queen Eleanor's funeral journey to the Abbey (1290; demolished 1643); there were also three communal fountains, of which the middle one was a place of public execution (Lesser Conduit at the west end, The Standard before St Mary-le-Bow and the Great Conduit, east of Ironmonger Lane). Mansion House stands on a site adjoining the Stocks Market (named after the nearby stocks), which sold meat and other provender but was especially famous for its herbs and fresh fruit. It flourished from 1282-1737, the stall rents being allocated to the maintenance of London Bridge.

Cheapside. – Wide and commercial as throughout its history, it opens out west of St Mary-le-Bow into a small garden at the centre of which stands a statue of Captain John Smith (1580-1631), a leading settler of Jamestown, Virginia. In the Middle Ages the street was the setting for many a tourney, the contests being watched from upper windows by householders and by royalty, the lord mayor and aldermen from a balcony in the tower of St Mary-le-Bow, and recalled by Wren at the time of the reconstruction after the Fire in a window. A tablet (west side of church) commemorates the poet Milton. **Bow Lane** on the east side of the church, narrow, winding, is still marked by old houses – Williamson's Tavern *(Groveland Ct)* is in a 17C house, once the Lord Mayor's residence (1666-1753), with a contemporary wrought-iron gate.

King St. – This leads north directly to Guildhall crossing Gresham St by St Lawrence Jewry. Further east along Gresham St the 1912 building at No 91 was formerly the premises of **Gresham College.** The college, under the will of Sir Thomas Gresham, was founded as a kind of free university in his mansion in Bishopsgate, Gresham House, which fronted on Old Broad St. The house was demolished in 1768, and the institution re-established in 1843 in a building on the present site. The lectures for graduate students are now held in new premises at the Barbican Centre under the auspices of the City University *(qv)*.

Poultry. – **Midland Bank,** by Lutyens (1924-39) with, high on the corners, a fat boy driving a goose to the Stocks Market (sculptor: Reid Dick).

EAST OF THE BANK: CORNHILL - LOMBARD ST (P/YZ)

From Mansion House there radiate: Prince's St (bordered entirely along one side by the Bank), Threadneedle St, Cornhill (named after a medieval cornmarket) and its continuation Leadenhall St, Lombard St and its continuation Fenchurch St, and finally King William St, constructed in 1829-35 as a direct route to the new London Bridge.

Freeman's Place. – Behind the Exchange with fountains at either end (south: bronze maiden beneath a pillared red granite canopy; north: mother and child by Georges Dalou, 1879) may be seen the seated figure of George Peabody (1869), the American philanthropist *(qv)*, founder of the trust to provide housing for the poor.

Jamaica Wine House. – The pub dates from 1652 when as the Pasqua Rosee Wine House, it was the first establishment licensed to sell coffee in London. Note the early percolator.

George and Vulture. – This pub, now Dickensian *(Pickwick Papers)* has been twice destroyed by fire in its 600 year old history. On the introduction of coffee in 1652 part of the then tavern became a chocolate, tea and coffeehouse. Nearby, George Yard is adorned with a fountain.

P & O Deck (RY). – Tall new buildings line an open court at the back of which stands St Helen Bishopsgate. The beaver weathervane in the background is on the former Hudson's Bay House *(no 52 Bishopsgate)*. To the west stands Crosby Sq, the original site of Crosby Hall *(qv)*. By Shaft Stairs is displayed a replica of the maypole associated with St Andrew Undershaft *(qv)*.

Lombard St, its name derived from the Lombard merchants of the late 13C and now synonymous with City banking, is lined with 19 and 20C buildings; association dignifies it; the gilt, the brightly painted bank signs, overhanging the pavement, distinguish it. Beginning with Lloyd's horse of 1677 (left), it continues with the 3 crowns of Coutts (right, no 15) the grasshopper, 1563, formerly Martins (now Banque Paribas), the crown and anchor of National Westminster (right), the anchor of Williams and Glyn's (left), now the Royal Bank of Scotland, Alexander's artichoke *(St Swithin's Lane)*, and at the end, a massive Barclays eagle in stone.

The Clearing House. – *No 10.* This institution has its origins in the 18C and grew out of the daily meeting in the streets of bank clerks, known as "clearers", to exchange and settle for cheques payable at their respective banks. From a post and one another's backs which they used as desks, the clearers migrated to a bay window, a room and finally a house, always in the same street. The first Clearing House was built on the site in 1833. The present building is post-war.

N M Rothschild and Sons Ltd (NY). – Rothschild's achieved its status in this country when in its first years, under its London branch founder, Nathan Mayer, it took over at low cost and renewed drafts issued by Wellington which the government was unable to meet; ultimately they were redeemed at par – NMR increased his fortune, the government appointed him chief negotiator of future Allied war loans! Confidence in victory and his own intelligence service again increased his wealth, it is said, on the occasion of Waterloo, fought throughout Sunday 18 June. On the Monday, when only rumour was circulating, Nathan bought – the market rose; he sold – it plunged; he bought again, making a fortune as his personal messenger arrived from the scene confirming victory – Wellington's despatches arrived by messenger on Wednesday, *The Times* report was published on Thursday (22nd).

The clean lined building is postwar; the lane remains old and narrow, and is often blocked from end to end with waiting Rolls, Bentleys, Jaguars...

Square Rigger. – Pub with square rigged ships of 17C and 18C as its theme.

Monument★. – *Open April to September, 9am to 6pm (Saturdays and Sundays, 2 to 6pm), October to March 9am to 4pm Mondays to Saturdays; closed 1 January, Good Friday, 25, 26 December; 311 steps; 50p, children 25 p.*

The fluted Doric column of Portland stone, surmounted by a square viewing platform and gilded, flaming urn, was erected in 1671-77 in commemoration of the Great Fire. The hollow column stands 202ft tall and 202ft from the baker's in Pudding Lane where the Fire began. The relief of Charles II before the City under reconstruction (on the west face of the pedestal) is by Caius Cibber. A later inscription blaming the papists for the Fire was finally effaced in 1831. The **view★** from the platform is now largely obscured by the towering office blocks which also mask the column at ground level. The monument does, however, remain a distinctive landmark from the river downstream.

The Monument: engraving of 1680.

ALDERSGATE ST, MOORGATE, BISHOPSGATE, ALDGATE (MNPRS/VXY)

Aldersgate St. – A Saxon named Aldred, is said to have built the gate... James I entered the capital through it and in celebration it was rebuilt in 1617 but demolished in 1761.

London Wall, more or less, follows the line of the Roman Wall east to Bishopsgate, Houndsditch the course of the old ditch outside the wall; inside it was paralleled by Camomile St, Bevis Marks and Duke's Place. All along London Wall are outcrops of excavated wall (Barbican, St Alphage, All Hallows, Sir John Cass College, the Tower), usually with a Roman base and upper area of medieval construction. The **London Wall Walk** *(1 3/4 miles, about 2 hours)* from the Tower to the Museum of London is well mapped out with 21 descriptive panels.

Museum of London★★. – *Open Tuesdays to Saturdays 10am (Sundays 2pm) to 6pm; closed Mondays, 1 January, 24, 25, 26 December; restaurant.*

The best of modern architectural style buildings has been designed by Powell and Moya for the new museum. Faced with white tiles below, linked by a bridge to a purple brick rotunda set like an advanced bastion in the sea of Aldersgate traffic, in traditional City fashion it takes advantage of the disadvantages of the site by making an interesting shape round the Ironmongers' Hall. By the main entrance, in Nettleton Court stands a memorial to the Methodist J. Wesley *(qv)*, a monumental bronze leaf.

Open galleries inside divide into bays according to time and theme as the story of London is traced from pre-history to the present by exhibits as various as the sculptures from the Roman Temple of Mithras, medieval pilgrim badges, the Cheapside Hoard of Jacobean jewellery, a diorama of the Great Fire, the doors from Newgate Goal, 19C shops and interiors, the Lord Mayor's Coach, souvenirs of the women's suffrage movement and the 1930s lifts from Selfridge's department store. The development of domestic life and public utility services – gas, drainage, the Underground – are illustrated as well as political and fashionable London.

Prior to the opening in 1992 of its Museum in Docklands which will be devoted to London's river and port activity, industrial life and traditional crafts, the Museum of London offers a preview of its collections which will form the basis of the new museum. *For information on guided tours of Docklands and of the museum in Docklands apply by phone: 01 515 1162.*

West Gate (MX). – *Open twice monthly, first Tuesday 10.30am to noon, third Friday 2.30 to 4.30pm.* This, the west gate of the Romans' north fort, including the outline of the guard turret, lies in a chamber off the west end of the underground carpark. *Entrance via Museum.*

Barbican★. – The Barbican project, for a residential neighbourhood, incorporating schools, shops, open spaces, a conference and arts centre, to be established in the City on the bombed sites of Cripplegate, was conceived in the aftermath of World War II; construction began in 1962. The first residential phase was completed in 1976 and the arts centre finally opened in 1982.

The rounded arch motif, used vertically in the arcades and on the roofline and horizontally round the stairwells, gives a sense of unity to the various elements – 40 storey tower blocks, crescents and mewses – linked by high and low level walkways and interspersed with gardens and sports areas. The Barbican centre – five of its ten storeys are below ground – contains a concert hall (permanent home of the London Symphony Orchestra), two theatres (London home of the Royal Shakespeare Company), three cinemas, a library, art gallery, sculpture court (on the roof of the concert hall), exhibition halls, meeting rooms and restaurants. The soaring theatre fly-tower is disguised by a roof-top conservatory, a green jungle of eucalyptus, ferns and cacti.

At the heart of this city within a city, beside the lake with its cascades and fountains, stand St Giles' church *(qv)*, founded in 1090, the only tangible link with the past and the Guildhall School of Music and Drama (1977) with its canted façade.

Royal Britain. – *Open 9am to 5.30pm; closed 25 December. £3.95, children, OAPs £2.50.*

The displays, using the latest audio-visual technology, highlight momentous events in a thousand years of British royal history: Edgar's coronation, the Wars of the Roses, Queen Victoria's Diamond Jubilee and the modern role of the monarchy.

Moorgate. – The gate giving access to Moorfields – the open common on which people practised archery, dried clothes *(plaque on site of Tenter St by Tenter House),* flew kites – was cut in the City wall in 1415; two and a half

The Barbican.

centuries later it was one of the main exits for thousands fleeing the Great Plague. It was demolished in 1760. The street overlooked by the City of London College, dates from the rebuilding of London Bridge in 1831.

Finsbury Circus. – Mid 19/20C buildings surround the only bowling green in the City.

Bishopsgate. – The street, one of the City's longest, was the principal road to East Anglia in Roman and medieval times. The gate, said to have been rebuilt slightly west of the Roman gate by Bishop Erkenwald in Saxon times, was renewed several times, once even by the Hanseatic merchants, before being demolished in 1760. Note the gilded mitres from the old Bishop's Gate on the walls of nos 105 and 108 *(first floor, Wormwood and Camomile St corners* – RX).

In the centre of Bishopsgate Churchyard stands an exotic one-roomed building, faced with glazed tiling, beneath a stained-glass onion dome; it was the entrance to an underground Turkish bath, built in 1895: the rosewood panelling and decorative wall tiles are of interest.

Liverpool St Stn. – The station *(redevelopment in progress)*, erected in 1875 on the first site of Bethlehem Hospital (founded 1247, removed 1676) is vast, an iron Gothic cathedral, romantic or filthy and impractical according to taste. Adjoining is the Great Eastern Hotel gabled and mullioned and close by is the Railway Tavern with steam locomotives as the decorative theme.

Broadgate. – A development scheme on a grand scale encompassing the railway station and comprising buildings designed in a variety of architectural styles, squares and open spaces enhanced by fountains and dramatic sculpture. Open air entertainment in the Arena.

Bishopsgate Institute. – This building with its arched entrance, mullioned windows, corner turrets and ornate decoration was designed by Charles Harrison Townsend (1894). It houses a library and a collection of prints and drawings of old London.

Aldgate. – The street, after the Anglo-Saxon – *aelgate,* meaning free or open to all, was before that a Roman gate to the road to Colchester (Whitechapel Rd). In 14C Chaucer leased the dwelling over the gate and in 16C Mary Tudor rode through it after being proclaimed queen. It was demolished in 1761. In the forecourt of the Wingate Centre is a bronze by K. McCarter (1980).

Aldgate Pump. – The proverbial pump is still extant.

Hoop and Grapes. – This pub is in a 17C brick house with a wooden bay.

CLAPHAM (Lambeth and Wandsworth)

Clapham village expanded into a fashionable residential area in the 17 and 18C as citizens moved out of London to avoid the plagues and the frequent City fires, notably the Great Fire which destroyed so many City merchants' houses. Around the common rose mansions and terraces for the prosperous, houses in designated streets for the more modest and, in the 19C, terrace houses and shops along the High St. The original inhabitants, others of low income and the very poor congregated round the railway, particularly Clapham Junction (known first as Battersea), built in 1845 and by the late 19C and still, Britain's busiest junction handling some 2 000 trains daily. The district remains densely populated, new housing estates replacing the old, the modern shopping areas and street markets as crowded, raucous and vigorous as ever.

Public transport began modestly enough in the early 18C with a single stage coach making the journey daily from Clapham village to Gracechurch St. A century later (1827) the service had expanded into "short stage" coaches travelling several times a day to the City, Westminster, Piccadilly Circus and Holborn. By 1839 there were horse drawn omnibuses operated by twelve rival companies. 1870 saw the tube (Clapham Common station), 1903 the first electric tram and 1912 the first motor omnibus. Gone were the days of highwaymen on the common (the last hold-up was in 1801), of roads being so poor that it took several hours to reach the capital: Clapham, the site of a Roman battle, a medieval village, "pretty suburb" in the words of William Thackeray, had become a part of the great metropolis.

Among Clapham's famous men are William Wilberforce (1759-1833); Lord Macaulay (1800-59) who grew up in a house on the Pavement; Thomas Hood (1799-1845) who went to school on North Side; Lytton Strachey (1880-1932) born at Stower House; Henry Cavendish (1731-1810), who retired to a house in the road now named after him; Cardinal Bourne (1861-1935), Archbishop of Westminster, born at Larkhall Rise and ordained at St Mary's, Clapham.

Northeast of Clapham Common

Holy Trinity. – The church at the corner of the common was erected in 1776 to replace the parish church which had fallen into ruin. The rectangular stone quoined building with two tiers of plain, round headed windows, was embellished, in keeping with growing local prosperity, by the addition of the giant columned portico and clock tower turret in 1872.

North side. – The long mellow brick terrace with an archway in the west end house dates from 1720. Many of the doorways, windows, iron gates and arches are original (nos 14, 16, 21). Clarence House is credited with being the home of Captain Cook (1728-79), Chase Lodge on the corner of The Chase, as the oldest house in Clapham.

No 29 opposite is a grand Georgian Mansion which was for years the home of Sir Charles Barry, architect of the Houses of Parliament (now Clapham Trinity Hospice).

Cedar and Thornton Terraces (flanking Cedars Rd) epitomise hybrid Victorian – French Renaissance revivalism: round and flat topped windows with coarse iron infillings, cornices, balconies, are crowned by high pavilion slate roofs coronetted with ironwork.

Old Town (northeast end of North Side) and its continuation, Rectory Grove which leads to St Paul's Church, include a few modest Georgian houses and short terraces: nos 39-43 is a group of mellow red brick with uniform windows and dormers but a separate segmented pediment over no 39 and a wider arc over the adjoining doors of nos 41 and 43; no 16 has an attractive doorway; no 4, proudly sporting two royal warrants, an unusual façade with a projecting upraised and pillared porch and two half moon windows. No 23, St Peter's Vicarage, has round headed ground floor windows and an early iron gateway with an overhead arch. No 52 Rectory Grove is unique in its Coade stone decoration including a false arch on the side wall.

St Paul's Church. – *To visit, apply at the Vicarage.* By 1232, and probably long before, there was a parish church by the name of Holy Trinity in Clapham; by 1774-6 it had fallen into ruin and had been superseded by the new Holy Trinity; in 1814 a plain Georgian brick building was erected in which there is an interesting group of monuments (southeast end):

1401: a brass plate records the death of an unknown man William Tableer.
1589: Francis Clarke, a small ruffed figure at prayer remains from a larger monument to his father, Bartholomew, who rebuilt the manorhouse (now vanished).
1647: a bronze plaque to William Glanville, Merchant of Exeter, describes how he "never got to London as he died of fever in Clapham", then a day's journey from the capital.
1689: Sir Richard Atkins in full armour, his wife and three children. Only the almost lifesize figures remain from the great tomb and even those were "lost" in an underground vault for nearly two centuries. The Atkins were lords of the manor from 1590.
1715: Richard Hewer, naval administrator and friend of Samuel Pepys who retired to Hewer's house in the Chase where he died in 1703.
1849: a tablet records the death of John Hatchard, who with a capital of £5 in his pocket founded the bookshop in Piccadilly in 1797.

The Polygon, Pavement and High St have been almost entirely rebuilt.

Crescent Grove. – *Off Clapham Common South Side.* Only the grove, a wide arc and terrace of identical tall stucco houses, remains entire of the extensive Clapham Park Estate laid out by **Thomas Cubitt** as a series of squares and crescents in the 1870s.

CLERKENWELL (Islington)

Map pp 5-8 (FG/V).

Clerkenwell recalls in name the medieval parish clerks who each year performed plays outside the City at a local wellhead (viewed through a window at 14-16 Farringdon Lane); Finsbury is named after the Fiennes family, the owners of the local manor (OE bury/burh/burg) who in 14C gave **Moorfields,** an unprofitable marsh, to the people of London as an open space – the first so designated. The outflow of artisans and cottage industry workers from the City, particularly after the Plague and Fire of 1665/66, caused poor quality housing and tenements to be erected up to the very walls of the Charterhouse, St John's Priory, Bethlem (on what is now City Rd) and other hospitals of which only Moorfields Eye Hospital, founded in 1805, is extant. Some open land remains: Finsbury Sq, Finsbury Circus, Bunhill and the HAC Fields; the crowded days of home industry in the early 19C are recalled by the Eagle Pub (Shepherdess Walk, City Rd) and the old rhyme: Half a pound of two penny rice, Half a pound of Treacle... Up and down the City Rd, In and out the Eagle, That's the way the money goes, Pop goes the Weasel.

■ THE PRIORIES

Charterhouse*. – At every stage of its history – 14C priory, Tudor mansion, 17C hospital and boys' school, 20C residence for aged Brothers – the buildings of the Charterhouse have been replaced or altered in a variety of materials and architectural styles.

Between 1535-1537 the prior and 15 monks of the 170 year old Charterhouse were executed for refusing to recognise Henry VIII as head of the church; he dissolved the community and removed treasure, timber, stone and glass for his own use. Within ten years, the house began a new life as a Tudor mansion under the Norths and then passed to the Norfolks whom Elizabeth visited several times before having her host, the 4th Duke of Norfolk, executed in 1572 for intriguing with Mary Queen of Scots. In 1611 the house was sold to **Thomas Sutton** for £13 000 and letters patent were issued for the founding of a hospital for 80 old men and 40 boys under the name of the Hospital of King James in Charterhouse. Sutton (d 1611) lies in an elaborate tomb by Nicholas Stone in the crypt under the chapel. In 1872, the school moved to Surrey.

The Building. – *Open April to July, Wednesdays only 2.30 to 4.15pm, £1.50.* ☎ 01 253 9503.

The 15C gateway, with its original massive gates, is built in flint and stone chequerwork like the precinct wall to the east. The superstructure and adjoining house, now the Master's lodging, are dated 1716. The graceful concave pyramidal roof opposite the gate covers the water conduit house of the monastery.

On the north side of Master's Court the Tudor **Great Hall,** with hammerbeam roof and 16C screen and gallery remains intact. The carved stone fireplace was added in 1614. The Elizabethan **Great Chamber,** hung with Flemish tapestries, has a painted and gilded late 16C plaster ceiling, an ornate painted chimney-piece and leaded lights. The ante-room opens on to a terrace built in 1571 by Norfolk above the west walk of the Great Cloister, in which a cell door and hatch have been discovered.

Charterhouse: Great Chamber.

In the tower, to which the belfry and cupola were added in 1614, is the treasury, vaulted in the Tudor period, with a squint looking down on the high altar of the original chapel where the tomb of the founder, Sir Walter Manny (d 1372), was discovered in 1947.

The present **chapel** was created in 1614 out of the monks' Chapter House with the addition of a north aisle and further enlarged to the north in 1824. The 17C screen, organ gallery, pew heads and pulpit are noteworthy.

St John's Gate. – *St John's Lane, off Clerkenwell Rd. Open Tuesdays, Fridays, museum 10am to 6pm (4pm Saturdays), closed Easter, public holidays and Christmas week; tours of the church and gatehouse, 11am and 2.30pm.*

The Grand Priory in the British Realm. – The Order, which developed from the First Crusade as a religious order to look after pilgrims visiting the Holy Land, became a military order during the 12C. It left the Holy Land on the fall of Acre in 1291, establishing itself first in Cyprus, then Rhodes (1310) and finally Malta (1530) where it became a sovereign power. Priories and commanderies were instituted in Europe, the **Grand Priory of England** being in Clerkenwell in 1144; to these were added the Templars' properties on their suppression in 1312. In 1540 Henry dissolved the Hospitallers and in 1546 issued a warrant *(in the museum)* for the buildings to be dismantled (Protector Somerset later took the stone for his house in the Strand) but the gate survived. St John's was re-established as a Protestant Order by Royal Charter in 1888.

The Gatehouse and Museum. – The 16C gatehouse, flanked by four storey towers, was the Priory's south entrance. Wide, vaulted, with the lamb of God, the arms of the order and of Prior Thomas Docwra, who built it, on the bosses, it contains the rooms which were occupied in the reigns of Elizabeth and James I by the Master of Revels, licenser of the plays of Shakespeare and Ben Jonson, and in the 18C by Edward Cave, publisher and printer of England's first literary periodical, *The Gentleman's Magazine* (1733-81), to which Dr. Johnson was a regular contributor. In the 20C Tudor style Chapter Hall, where the Maltese banners hang in the lantern, in the Council Chamber and the Library are displayed pharmacy jars from the hospitals in Rhodes and Malta, silver filigree work and a rare collection of beaten silver Maltese glove trays; fine inlay work in wood and marble, two magnificent Chinese tobacco jars and the illuminated Rhodes Missal on which the knights took their vows. A rare 16C spiral staircase with wooden treads leads to a room displaying insignia, portrait medals and the Order's own coinage issued in Rhodes and Malta. The museum illustrates the life of the Order with items from its hospitals, priories and commanderies. A new museum traces the history of the St John Ambulance Brigade from 1887: uniforms, medical instruments, first aid kits, medals...

St John's Church and Crypt. – The Grand Priory Church of St John, once extended further west into the square where setts in the road mark the site of the round nave. The 16 and 18C brick walls of the former choir are now hung with the chivalric banners of Commonwealth priories.

The crypt is 12C, the only original Priory building to survive. Beneath the low ribbed vaulting, against the north wall, lie the rich alabaster form of a Spanish grandee and the cadaverous effigy of the last Prior before the Dissolution.

■ ADDITIONAL SIGHTS

Clerkenwell Green. – The rallying point in 18C and 19C for work people protesting against the social and industrial injustices of the period is an appropriate site for the **Karl Marx Memorial Library,** an 18C house (no 37a). Cheerful pavement cafes strike a more affluent note.

Mount Pleasant. – The early 18C landmark, perhaps ironically named as it was the local rubbish dump, is now one of the main Post Office inland mail sorting offices and the centre of the Post Office railway. The line runs 70ft below ground from Paddington to Liverpool Street and Whitechapel, carrying the mail in automatically controlled trucks along 2ft gauge tracks.

New River Head. – *Thames Water Authority, Rosebery Av.* The neo-Georgian building contains a fireplace attributed to Grinling Gibbons and plaster ceilings *c* 1693.

History. – The New River undertaking originated in 1609 when **Sir Hugh Myddelton** (statue on Islington Green), a City goldsmith and jeweller, put up the capital to construct a canal from springs in Hertfordshire to the City. The winding channel some 40 miles long took 4 1/2 years to dig and might well have ruined Myddelton but for the personal financial support of James I. The New River Head was inaugurated in 1613 when water was carried down from Clerkenwell to the

City in wooden pipes. Individual subscribers were supplied with water on tap at 5s a quarter; the enterprise was a financial success and was sold for £5 million when taken over by the Metropolitan Water Board (1904-1974) which built its head office on the site of the New River Head so that the river is now only 24 miles long ending at Stoke Newington. The elegant terraces of **Myddelton Square** were built in the late 1700s on part of the New River Company's estate.

Sadler's Wells Theatre. – *Rosebery Av.* Music house at the centre of late 17C pleasure gardens and medicinal wells, mid 18C theatre, Shakespearean and classical drama centre under **Samuel Phelp** in the 1840s, music hall, derelict ruin: such was the site's history when **Lilian Baylis** took it over and had a completely new brick theatre erected in 1931. From 1934 the Wells specialised in opera and ballet to become the cradle of the future Royal Ballet and English National Opera, which in 1946 and 1968 respectively transferred to Covent Garden and the London Coliseum. The Wells itself now presents visiting opera and ballet companies. The theatre is named after a builder, Mr Sadler, whose workmen in 1683 rediscovered the medicinal wells.

City University. – *St John St.* Surrounded by the modern buildings of the University *(p 29)* is the original Northampton Institute (1894-6), designed by E. Mountford in an eclectic baroque style.

Companies House. – *55-71 City Rd. Open Monday to Friday 9.30am to 4pm; closed public holidays.* The Register of Companies, dating back 130 years was transferred to Cardiff in 1976. Annual returns and accounts for the last 3 years of 650 000 companies, changes of directors and registered office addresses dating back 7 years are available on microfilm.

Wesley's Chapel and House. – *47 City Road. The Chapel and House are open 10am to 4pm, closed 25, 26 December; house and museum £1.20; children, OAPs 60p.* Daily prayers in the Foundry Chapel. John Wesley, who is buried in the churchyard, laid the foundation stone of the chapel in 1777. The oblong building of stock brick with a shallow apse, is notable inside for the tribune supported on seven jasper columns, presented by overseas Methodists in replacement of the pine dockyard masts (now in the vestibule) originally given by George III, and the white and gold ceiling by Robert Adam. Wesley's mahogany pulpit, formerly a two decker, 15ft tall, stands at the centre. There is a Museum of Methodism in the crypt.

The preacher's house next door is rich in mementoes: his desk, study and conference chairs, clock, clothes, library, furniture and, in the minute prayer room, table desk and kneeler.

Bunhill Fields. – *City Road. To view the graves, apply for appointment to the Superintendent of Parks and Gardens:* ☎ *01-472 3584.*

Long before 1549 when the first wagon load of bones was delivered for burial from the overflowing charnel house in St Paul's Churchyard, the field had been given the name Bone Hill. From 1665, when the City Corporation acquired it, to its closure in 1852, 120 000 were buried there including many non-conformists since the ground was never consecrated. Among the tombs are those of: William Blake (1757-1827), John Bunyan (1628-88), Daniel Defoe (1661-1731), Susanna Wesley, mother of John and Charles (1669-1742)... In the adjoining Quaker yard is the grave of the founder of the Society of Friends, George Fox (1624-91).

Honourable Artillery Company HQ (Finsbury Barracks). – The buildings on the historic Artillery Fields, designated for archery practice in Tudor times, date from 1735 and 1857.

Whitbread Brewery. – *Chiswell Street.* On the south side is the original brewery building which includes the Great Porter Tun Room (1784) with its magnificent hammerbeam roof *(not open).* The grey shire horses used to pull the Lord Mayor's Coach (see Museum of London) and deliver beer in the City are a picturesque feature in the area and can be seen in the stables in Garrett Street. *Visit by appointment only 11am to 3pm;* ☎ *01-606 4455.*

COVENT GARDEN (Westminster)

Theatres are marked in blue on plan.

Covent Garden in ancient times. – Soho was a chase, named after the cry of the medieval hunt which often found in St Giles' Field; St Giles was a leper colony, established outside the town limits by Queen Matilda in 1117 (dissolved 16C); St Martin's was a church erected in the fields between Westminster and the City in early 13C and Covent Garden a 40 acre walled property belonging to the Benedictines of Westminster.

Henry's dissolution of the monastery at Westminster and confiscation of the garden was followed in 1552 by the first of the royal warrants which were to shape the area to its present form, give it its traditions and much of its character: Edward VI granted the land to the long serving Tudor diplomat and soldier, John Russell, later 1st Earl of Bedford. The 4th Earl, on payment of £2 000 – Charles I was ever impecunious – obtained a licence in 1631 to erect buildings "fit for the habitacions of Gentlemen and men of ability" subject only to the approval of the King's Surveyor, Inigo Jones. Charles II, a lover of the theatre (and also of actresses) granted two royal warrants in 1660 which resulted in the building of two Theatres Royal, Covent Garden and Drury Lane.

■ COVENT GARDEN TODAY

The Piazza and St Paul's*. – The 1631 license gave Inigo Jones the opportunity to design London's first square; he modelled it after those he had seen in Italy, with approach roads at the centre of the north and east sides, the same two sides being lined by three storey, terrace houses of brick, above a pavement colonnade of stone which provided a covered way to shops and coffeehouses. Only those to the west of Russell St remain (rebuilt). The south side was filled by the garden wall of the earl's new town house which fronted on the more fashionable Strand. (In 1700, when fashion departed, Bedford House was demolished and the area developed.) A church was planned for the west side but the Earl was unwilling to afford anything 'much better than a barn' so Jones, declaring he should have 'the handsomest barn in England', designed **St Paul's** with classical simplicity in red brick (the easterly stone facing is a later addition) beneath a pitched roof which affords wide eaves. Overlooking the square is the famous Tuscan portico in which on 9 May 1662 Pepys saw the first ever *Punch and Judy* show in England and in 20C Shaw set the opening scene of *Pygmalion.* The church, completed in 1633, has always been closely associated with actors, artists, musicians and craftsmen – a wreath of limewood, carved by Grinling Gibbons for St Paul's Cathedral, now decorates the west screen (beside the door).

Grinling Gibbons: limewood wreath.

The Market. – Originating with the monks before the Reformation and persisting throughout the development of the piazza, the market was regularised by Letters Patent in 1670 and reconstituted in 1830 when royal permission was granted for special buildings to be erected. By 20C the market filled the piazza, overflowing into the neighbouring streets. From midnight to noon the whole district was brilliant with flowers and fruit, crowded with vendors, porters and buyers, alive with open pubs and cafes and blocked solid with lorries. In November 1974, the market with its characteristic reek of old cabbage removed to Nine Elms.

The Central Market buildings, designed in 1832 by Charles Fowler, comprise three parallel ranges running west off a north-south colonnade and linked by glass canopies in 1872; the market regulations are still written up on the walls. In 1980 the buildings were refurbished and are now occupied by pubs, cafes, wine bars and restaurants together with shops dealing in food, fashion, gifts and perfumery. In the main avenue the Victorian cast-iron trading stands from the flower market are now hired out daily to craftsmen or gardeners selling their own products. On summer evenings people sit out on the steps at the west end listening to musicians playing under St. Paul's Porch.

Light Fantastic Gallery of Holography. – *48 South Row. 1st floor. Open 10am (Sundays 11am) to 6pm (Saturdays 7pm, Thursdays and Fridays 8pm). £1.25, children 75p.* There are over 200 holograms on display.

Holography is a process which with the aid of coherent light or laser beams, creates three-dimensional images known as holograms. Invented in 1947 by Dennis Gabor it experienced a rapid expansion with the invention of the laser beam. Among the many interesting exhibits are a series of disconcertingly lifelike portraits.

The Jubilee Market *(Antiques Mondays, General Goods Tuesdays to Fridays, Crafts Saturdays and Sundays)* is let out to stall holders. The Jubilee Hall (1904) nearby is a leisure centre.

London Transport Museum⋆. – *Open 10am to 6pm daily except 24, 25, 26 December; £2.40, children, students, OAPs £1.10.* Opened in 1980 in the old flower market, the Transport Museum covers 200 years of London transport services. Trams, trolleybuses, motor buses, railway engines and coaches occupy the central area, together with working demonstrations of underground signalling equipment and a driver's cab with controls which the visitor may operate. Round the walls, well illustrated with photos and posters, is a detailed history from the Hackney Carriage and the first horse bus to the Jubilee Line. There is a lecture theatre, research library, coffee bar and external shop selling memorabilia.

Theatre Museum. – *Open 11am to 7pm; closed Mondays and public holidays. £2.25, children £1.25.* Housed in the old flower market the Theatre Museum of the Victoria and Albert Museum *(qv)* opened in April 1987. On the ground floor a large mural, a golden angel blowing a horn, ornate theatre boxes and an old box office set the theatrical theme. Its rich collections relate to all aspects of the performing arts: opera, ballet, Edwardian melodrama, pantomimes, circus, toy theatre and plays, popular music, music hall and puppetry, and include designs, archives, portraits, drawings, photographs and a wealth of other material. A gallery houses a semi permanent display of the story of the performing arts. Two other galleries are devoted to temporary exhibitions. There are also a Paintings Gallery and a theatre for special events.

Theatre Royal, Drury Lane. – The present Georgian theatre is the fourth on the site, one of London's largest (2 283 seats) and beautiful inside with symmetrical staircases, rising beneath the domed entrance to a circular balcony.

Killigrew's company, known as the King's Servants, opened in 1663 in the first theatre which was frequently patronised by the monarch who met "pretty witty Nell" there in 1665. After being burnt down the theatre was replaced in 1674 by one designed by **Wren** which knew a golden age under **Garrick** (who was manager from 1747 to 1776 and lived at 27 Southampton St), the Kembles and Sarah Siddons and was replaced in 1794 by a third building which opened under **Sheridan's** management with his new play *The School for Scandal*. Fire again destroyed the theatre and the present house, to designs by **Wyatt,** was erected in 1812. Kean, Macready, Phelps, Irving, Ellen Terry, Forbes Robertson played there; Ivor Novello's dancing operettas filled the stage; *My Fair Lady* entranced more...

The **Baddeley Cake** is a Lane tradition even older than the ghost; it is provided from money left by an 18C actor, Robert Baddeley, and is cut on stage after the performance on Twelfth Night. The ghost emerges from the left circle wall (where a corpse and dagger were found bricked up in 19C) to cross the auditorium and disappear.

London Coliseum. – *St Martin's Lane.* The theatre was built in 1904 by Sir Oswald Stoll to rival Drury Lane. Retained marble pillars, terracotta front, electrically lit globe winking against the night sky, combined with an interior refurbishing, have transformed it since 1968 into the home of the former Sadler's Wells company, now the **English National Opera.**

Royal Opera House⋆. – Charles II's patent was eventually secured by John Rich whose earlier presentation in 1728 of John Gay's *The Beggar's Opera* "had the effect, as was ludicrously said, of making Gay rich and Rich gay" (Samuel Johnson). He leased a site, erected a playhouse and in December 1732 opened his Theatre Royal, Covent Garden, with Congreve's *Way of the World* which he followed with a revival of *The Beggar's Opera*. A second theatre, designed by Robert Smirke, after the first had burned down, opened in 1809 with a double bill lasting nearly 4 hours, presenting Kemble and Mrs Siddons in *Macbeth* plus a musical entertainment. The public not caring that rebuilding had cost £187 888 and convinced that price increases were due to exorbitant fees paid to foreign artists, drowned the stage in what came to be known as the OP or

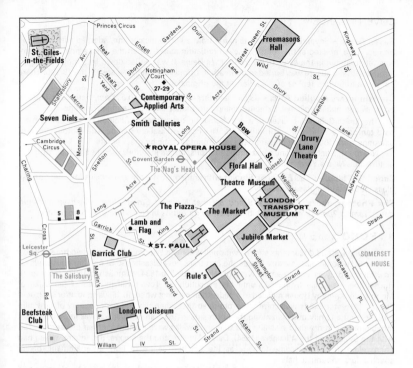

Ol Prices Riots. Two months later prices were reduced (pit: 3s 6d). After a second fire in 1856 the present house was built, with a first floor portico and Classical pediment, facing Bow St, thus leaving room to the south for E.M. Barry's green-painted glass and iron structure, known as the **Floral Hall** which was used for promenade concerts and balls. When the theatre fell into financial straits the hall was leased to the market in 1887 and for nearly 100 years served as an annexe to the fruit and vegetable, not the flower, market. Inside the theatre, decoration has always been white and gold with deep crimson and rose hangings; the blue dome is also a dominant feature. From the first there was a Crush Room.

Extensions to the west (in the 1858 style) have provided new dressing rooms and rehearsal facilities. A second phase of improvements is planned around the Floral Hall.

The Sadler's Wells Ballet transferred to the house in 1946 and in 1956 it was granted a charter by the Queen to become **The Royal Ballet.** The opera company received a royal charter in 1968. Around performers (and characters) such as Patti, Melba, Caruso, Thomas Beecham, Lotte Lehmann, Elisabeth Schumann, Gigli, Conchita Supervia, Tauber, Flagstad... golden memories abound, legends grow – Patti in 1895 as Violetta wore a white dress studded with 3 700 diamonds – and two Bow St detectives joined the guests in Act 3 of *La Traviata* (Flora's party); Queen Victoria decided that the bearing of Italian choristers appearing in *Fidelio* was unmilitary and that as "Our soldiers can do better than that" extras to swell processions should be provided from the Brigade of Guards. This practice continued until 1978.

The area's long standing theatrical association attracted builders of new theatres when the passage of the Theatre Regulation Act in 1843 broke the Covent Garden and Lane monopoly and some 40 new playhouses were licensed and erected in as many years.

■ ADDITIONAL SIGHTS

St Giles-in-the-Fields. – The church was rebuilt in 1734 by Flitcroft after the styles of Wren and James Gibbs; the steeple rising directly from the façade echoes St Martin-in-the-Fields.

Bow St. – "So called as running in the shape of Bent Bow" according to John Strype, the early 18C mapmaker. By the mid 18C, when **Henry Fielding,** novelist, dramatist and magistrate and his half brother, John, the **Blind Beak,** moved into a house on the site of the present police station, the street had become the haunt of footpads. At once the Fieldings began their crusade for penal and police reform which included the organisation in 1753 of the **Bow Street Runners.** The white lights outside the present station (1881), the only such in the country, were suggested by Queen Victoria who, visiting the opera, considered the customary blue lights very dreary.

Rule's. – *34-5 Maiden Lane.* Caricatures and prints recall the law, theatre and artists, in London's oldest restaurant and oyster bar, established in 1798 by Benjamin Rule and his sons, "who rush wildly about with dozens of oysters and pewters of stout".

Lamb and Flag. – *Rose St.* The tavern, the quarter's oldest, was known when it was built in 1623 as the Cooper's Arms and unofficially after 1679, when John Dryden on his way home to Long Acre was attacked outside, as the Bucket of Blood.

Clubs and Coffeehouses. – Two of the traditional clubs still flourish: the **Garrick** (1831) since 1864 in the house built for it in the new street which the club requested should be named after the actor (no 15); on the walls hang an unrivalled collection of theatrical portraits; the **Beefsteak** (9 Irving St), dating from 1876, and always a dining club drawn from the worlds of politics, the theatre and literature.

Of the 17 and 18C coffeehouses for which Covent Garden was as famous as the City, none remain: **Will's** at no 1 Bow St, frequented by "all the wits in town" according to Pepys, **Button's** in Russell St, the **Bedford,** the **Piazza...**

Royal Masonic Institution. – *Great Queen St.* The Masons occupy the greater part of the street which includes 18C houses (nos 27-29) and the **Freemasons Hall** (1927-33).

Seven Dials. – Seven Dials derives its name from a 40ft Doric column, adorned with a sundial on each face, erected at the centre of seven radiating streets when the area, a notorious slum, was rehabilitated in the early 1690s by Thomas Neale. It was pulled down by a mob in 1773 on a rumour that treasure was buried underneath it. Crime was rife in the area in the 18-19C. There are plans to build a replica of the pillar on the original site.

Contemporary Applied Arts. – *43 Earlham Street. Open 10am to 5.30pm; Saturdays 11am to 5pm; closed public holidays.* Exhibitions and information on crafts and applied arts.

The **Smith Galleries,** housed in a warehouse on the corner of Sheldon St and Earlham St, hold temporary exhibitions of modern art. The Postcard Gallery has on sale reproductions of paintings from 1500 to the present day and of photographs by great artists.

Nearby in Neal St are specialist shops (buttons, artists'materials) and health food stores in picturesque Neal's Yard.

Endell St Place. – *27-29 Endell St.* Studios with craftsmen at work and articles for sale: pottery, glass ware, stained glass, jewellery...

The Photographers' Gallery. – *5 and 8 Great Newport Street. Open Tuesdays to Saturdays,11am to 7pm.* Temporary exhibitions showing trends in contemporary photography.

■ **SOHO** *Map p 119*

Early maps and documents show a windmill where Gt Windmill St is now, two breweries on Brewer St, a bottle glass factory beside the cart track now Glasshouse St and big houses which now remain only as street names: Newport House (built *c* 1634, demolished 1682), Monmouth House, the residence from 1682 until his execution on Tower Hill in 1685 of the Duke of Monmouth, Karnaby House recalled in a pedestrian precinct where in 1960s shop after shop sold "gear". Leicester Fields was common ground, so that when the 2nd earl, nephew of Sir Philip Sidney, built a family mansion along the north side in 1631, an open space was left where local inhabitants could dry their washing and tree lined walks were planted for their pleasure. In 19C with the building of the **Alhambra** (1854), Daly's Theatre and the **Empire,** the square, which had been relaid in 1874, became famous as the dazzling centre of light entertainment, ballet, spectaculars and music hall.

Leicester Square is now a pedestrian precinct, almost entirely surrounded by cinemas and eating houses. A statue of **Charlie Chaplin** by John Doubleday (1980) stands in the south west corner. To the north is the Theatre Ticket Kiosk *(open 2.30 to 6.30pm)* where tickets for same day performances can be bought at half price. The square is to be redesigned.

By mid 19C, through piecemeal development, Soho included the worst slums in the capital with 300 people to each acre or 30 000 in all – today there is a residential population of 3 000 and a working population of 10 000. The building of Regent Street *(qv)* divided the West End from its disreputable neighbour and three new streets were built to penetrate the foetid tangle : **Charing Cross Road** (1880), **Shaftesbury Avenue** (1886) and Kingsway (1905).

Today Charing Cross Rd is known for its bookshops: Foyle's (no 119), Zwemmer's (nos 72, 80), Collet's (nos 52, 66, 131), Waterstone's (no 121) and smaller shops stacked with long out of print editions; Cecil Ct dates back to 1670 and is again becoming, as in the 18/19C, a bookseller's close. Goodwins Ct (off St Martin's Lane) is a narrow alley entirely lined by 18C bow windows of former shops. The southern end of Shaftesbury Avenue is known for its theatres.

The **Trocadero,** traditionally a place of entertainment, has been redeveloped behind its original façades to provide shops, restaurants and entertainment around an 80ft atrium.

The **Guinness World of Records** exhibition *(first floor)* presents the amazing facts featured in the Guinness Book of Records using the latest display techniques. *Open Monday to Saturday 10am to 10pm, closed 25 December; £3.80, children £2.40.*

The **London Experience** *(first floor)* offers an exciting audio-visual presentation of the colourful history of London. *Open daily 10am to 10pm; closed 25 December; performances every 40 mins, £2.25, children £1.75.*

The complex will be linked by a tunnel to the **London Pavilion** site which has been redeveloped along the same lines and to the renovated Piccadilly underground concourse. The building is crowned by 13 sculptures of Victorian maidens. The London Pavilion will include an exhibition devoted to the world of entertainment and popular music presented by Madame Tussaud's *(qv).*

People of all nations. – The indigenous Londoners of Soho have always been artisans, cottage industry workers, and, until planning regulations eliminated local factories, craftsmen in labour intensive factories. Refugees began to arrive in 17C, settling where their skills and labour would find a market: Greeks, fleeing the Ottoman Turks, Huguenots after the Revocation of the Edict of Nantes in 1685, refugees from the Revolution and 19C political changes, who established French restaurants and cafés – Wheeler's (19 Old Compton St) was founded by Napoleon III's chef – Swiss, Italians, Spaniards, and, most recently, Chinese from Hong Kong, Singapore and the docks who transformed Gerrard St into a Chinatown with exotic street furniture and who at the Chinese New Year (a moveable feast in January or February) celebrate in traditional fashion.

William Blake was born in Soho (1757), Hazlitt died there (1830); Edmund Burke, Sarah Siddons, Dryden, Sheraton lived there; Marx, Engels, Canaletto, Haydn lodged there; Mendelssohn and Chopin gave recitals at the 18C house in Meard St of Vincent Novello, father of Ivor and founder of the music publishers. J.L. Baird first demonstrated television in Frith St in 1926...

Churches and Charities

St. Anne's. – *Wardour Street.* There are plans to rebuild the church which was bombed in the war. The tower, now occupied by the Soho Society, was restored, together with the clock, in 1979. Beneath it are buried the ashes of Dorothy L. Sayers, Churchwarden, while Hazlitt and the legendary 18C Theodore, King of Corsica, lie in the churchyard.

Notre Dame de France. – *Leicester Place.* The church (RC), erected on the ashes of its mid 19C predecessor, is circular. Inside an Aubusson tapestry hangs above the altar, mosaics enrich the side altar, and outline paintings (1960) by **Jean Cocteau** adorn the walls.

Our Lady of the Assumption. – *Warwick St.* The plain church, originally the chapel of the Portuguese, was rebuilt in 1788 after the Gordon Riots with only a pediment as decoration.

House of St Barnabas. – *Greek St. Open Wednesdays 2.30 to 4.15pm. Thursdays 11am to 12.30pm. Closed Christmas and Easter*. The House of Charity, a temporary home for women in need, was built c 1750. The exterior is plain except for two obelisks at the entrance; the interior is one of the finest in Soho with beautiful plasterwork ceilings and walls; the crinoline staircase is unusual. The proportions of the small chapel, built in 1863 in 13C French Gothic, are unique.

Trade and Entertainment

Market: Berwick St market in all its colour and variety dates back to 1778, possibly 100 years earlier when the street began.

Media: Films from first features to commercial flashes are dreamt up, made, cut, etc. in Wardour St (once a furniture area), Soho Sq, Beak and Dean Sts.

Food shops, restaurants: the shops line Old Compton St, the restaurants – French, Italian and Greek – are in Romilly St, Dean St, Frith St and Greek St; Chinese in Wardour St and Gerrard St.

Discos, drinking clubs, casinos, cinemas, night clubs: add to the area's lively character.

Shops and workshops: there are timber merchants and silversmiths, tailors (tailoring remains the largest local cottage industry), violin makers (3 where there were once 40) and jazz and pop instrument shops, the last in Shaftesbury Avenue, Charing Cross Rd and Denmark St – **Tin Pan Alley.** The jazz club, **Ronnie Scott's,** is at 47 Frith St *(open 8.30pm to 3am)*.

Pubs: of the 60-70 in Soho, most date back to early 18C although, owing to industrious Victorian and mid 20C renovation, few look old. One is unique, the York Minster (49 Dean St) which for two generations has had a French host, father and son, and is known as the **French Pub.**

CRYSTAL PALACE PARK ★ (Bromley)

The **Crystal Palace,** an enormous cathedral-like structure in cast iron and glass, was designed by Joseph Paxton (1801-65), the Duke of Devonshire's gardener at Chatsworth, to house the Great Exhibition of 1851, conceived and organised by the Prince Consort and held in Hyde Park for six months. When the exhibition closed the Crystal Palace was taken down and re-erected on Sydenham Hill where it served as a place of public entertainment until destroyed by fire in 1936. Only the 290ft twin water towers by Brunel survived but were demolished five years later for fear that they would serve as landmarks to enemy bombers. Its successful new role led to imitations: Alexandra Palace in north London and Albert Palace *(demolished)* in Battersea.

South of the now empty terraces has arisen the **National Sports Centre** *(day membership obligatory 45p, children 30p)*, a modern complex built to Olympic standards.

The surrounding **park**★ contains a lake *(boating, summer concerts)*, a children's zoo *(open April to October: school holidays 11am to 6pm, term time 1.30 to 5.30pm)* and the endearing, brightly coloured monsters. A familiar modern landmark is the TV relay mast.

DULWICH ★ (Southwark)

King Edgar bestowed the manor of 'Dilwihs' to one of his thanes in 967 AD. It was then owned by Bermondsey Abbey until the Reformation and in 17C was acquired by Edward Alleyn *(see below)*.

Dulwich's glory lies in its trees. The houses reflect the transition from 17C manorial village to small country town where 18/19C city merchants and gentlemen chose to reside (a low triangular milestone on Red Post Hill *(north of rly station)* indicates that it is 4 1/2 miles to the Standard in Cornhill or the Treasury in Whitehall). Commuter trains and cars have transformed it into a south London suburb; yet it remains rural in character, the main street, known as Dulwich Village, dividing at the green where Alleyn built his school.

■ DULWICH COLLEGE

Edward Alleyn: man of the Theatre, founder of God's Gift. – Alleyn, born in 1566 the son of a City innkeeper, was by common consent one of the greatest actors of his day although Shakespeare disagreed and voiced his dislike in Hamlet's counsel to the Player King. His marriage in 1592 to the step-daughter of Philip Henslowe, theatrical businessman, leaser of plays, costumes, theatres, builder of the Rose Playhouse (1587), extended Alleyn's interests so that by 1605 he had virtually retired from the theatre and for £5 000 bought Dulwich manor. Having no heir, he established in 1613 a charity for "six poor men and six poor women and the education of twelfe poor children", which he named the Chapel and College of God's Gift (1619).

Old College and Chapel. – The buildings on the triangular site are entered through 18C iron gates surmounted by the Alleyn crest. Between the much altered two storeyed white building which still serves as almshouses, stands the central wing including the clock tower and door to the chapel where Alleyn is buried.

Dulwich Picture Gallery★. – *Open Tuesdays to Saturdays 10am to 1pm and 2 to 5pm; Sundays 2 to 5pm; closed Mondays and bank holidays; £1.50, students, OAPs 50p.*

History. – Dulwich Gallery, which opened in 1814, is the oldest public picture gallery in the country. Edward Alleyn bought pictures, as a man of substance, rather than a connoisseur – in 1618 he paid £2 for six royal portraits and later £2 13s 4d for a further eight crowned heads! His final collection of 39 pictures, including his own full length portrait, probably painted from a death mask, was later increased by 80 likenesses of contemporary authors and players: Michael Drayton, Richard Lovelace, Burbage, Nat Field (now mostly in the East Room).

In 1811, virtually a double legacy of 400 pictures necessitated the construction of a special gallery. This gift originated with a Frenchman, **Noel Joseph Desenfans,** unsuccessful language teacher, who changed his profession to become the richest picture dealer of his day. Among his patrons was King Stanislaus of Poland who commissioned a gallery but abdicated in 1795 before paying for the paintings which Desenfans incorporated in his own collection and left to his widow and his friend, **Sir Francis Bourgeois,** a Londoner of Swiss origin, Royal Academician, landscape painter and inspired collector. He chose Dulwich as the gallery site; Mrs. Desenfans contributed £6 000, suggested Soane as architect and presented the furniture still on display.

DULWICH★

The building. – Sir John Soane had a free hand in 1811 and three years later the gallery, much as it is today, was opened. The plain exterior belies the skilful inside plan: facing the central entrance, on the far side of two adjoining square galleries is the small domed mausoleum of the founders, Sir Francis Bourgeois, Noel Desenfans and his wife: symmetrically dependent on this central suite are oblong and final square galleries of subtly varied dimensions. The walls have been restored to their original red colour. The rooms are ingeniously lit by skylights.

The pictures. – **Aelbert Cuyp's** landscapes (gallery VI), three superb **Rembrandt's** including *The Girl at a Window* and *Titus* (XI), 17 and 18C landscapes and pastorals by **Poussin** (IV, XII), Claude (IV) Watteau and Lancret (XII); **Gainsborough** portraits of the Linley family (I), a **Reynolds** self portrait and portrait of *Mrs. Siddons* (I) are among the most memorable pictures in the collection. There are also paintings by van Dyck (II, III); Teniers the Younger (II); Raphaël, Tiepolo, Canaletto (VIII), Rubens (II, III, VIII) and peasant boys and *Flower Girl* by Murillo (V, III), Reni, Rosa, Lebrun, Guercino, Veronese (IV). Some of the paintings may be on loan to other galleries.

South via Dulwich Village and College Rd

Dulwich Village. – Pond House, Village Way, at the opening of the Village, is a three storey house with spanking white trims, a delicate balustrade edging the roof at the rear and a round headed door complemented by the curving lines of the porch, steps and balustrades.

Nos 60, 62 – **The Laurels, The Hollies** – date from 1767. In 18C the ironwork canopy on iron pillars over the pavement shaded the fare of the village butcher. Nos 93 and 95 – North and South Houses are of a later date. Nos 97-105 is an 18C terrace, the last two houses mid 1700s.

College Rd. – On the pair, nos 13 and 15 built *c* 1765, note the early Sun Insurance fireplate. The small house at no 31, Pickwick Cottage, is said to be where Dickens envisaged Mr. Pickwick's retiring. Bell Cottage *(no 23)* is a rare example of the once common small white weatherboarded local cottages; Bell House *(no 27)*, of brick by contrast, dates from 1767.

Dulwich College, now nearly 1 400 strong, is housed in buildings of 1866-70 designed by Charles Barry in Italian Renaissance style, complete with a stout campanile. Great crested iron gates mark the entrance on College Rd.

Pond Cottages (beyond the main road, Dulwich Common) is an 18C group overlooking the Mill Pond, several wholly or partly weatherboarded. The **Toll Gate** is the last in use in the London area: charges are 10p for a car, previously 6d and 10d for "a score of beasts"...

Kingswood House. – *Seeley Drive. Accessible from beyond the Toll Gate or Alleyn Park.*

The castellated house built of ragstone in 19C baronial style, was known, when the owner was the founder of the meat extract firm, as Bovril Castle! The Jacobean style interior now serves as a library and community centre.

■ EALING (Ealing)

Ealing Abbey, St Benedict's RC Church. – *Charlbury Grove.* The powerful medieval foundation which grew from the small number of Benedictines sent by Pope Gregory to England in the 6C, was dissolved in the 16C by Henry VIII. The re-established community has erected a new abbey, neo-Gothic in style and golden in colour (1897-1935).

Pitshanger Manor Museum. – *Mattock Lane. Open Tuesdays to Fridays, 10am to 5pm; closed 1 January, Easter and Christmas.*

The south wing and central range only remain of the house built by **George Dance junior** in 1770, and bought by **John Soane**, as a country villa in 1800. Soane retained the south wing containing an upper and a lower room, both of modest proportions with finely moulded plaster decorations and added, besides other rooms, an entrance of four colossal Ionic columns surmounted by standing figures before a high, ornamental screen. The hall, inside, lit by a raised lantern between tunnel vaults, is minute. Many features reappear in the house in Lincoln's Inn Fields *(qv)*. The interior has been restored and houses a display of Martinware.

St Mary's Parish Church. – The present heavy, dark brick construction of 1866 contains the tomb of John Maynard, successful lawyer to Stuart Kings, the Commonwealth, William and Mary, builder of Gunnersbury House and an expressive, late 15C brass to "Richard A'wnsh'm some tyme Mercer and Marchaunt of the stapyll (wool) of Calys and Kateryn his wyf" and their 3 sons and 6 daughters.

Gunnersbury Park. – In the park are two early 19C mansions acquired by the Rothschilds in 1835 and 1889 and now, in part, converted into a local history museum *(open March to October, Mondays to Fridays 1 to 5pm – weekends and bank holidays 2 to 6pm – November to February 1pm (weekends 2pm) to 4pm; closed 1 January, Good Friday, 24, 25, 26 December).*

The Katyn Memorial to massacred Polish officers, a polished black granite obelisk crowned with a gold eagle, was erected in 1976 in Kensington cemetery, south of the park.

■ FULHAM (Hammersmith)

Fulham, Parsons Green, Walham Green, all within a wide loop of the river were once separate riparian villages with the odd large mansion in its own grounds which ran down to the water's edge. Market gardens covered the fertile marshlands. The Bishop of London was the lord of the manor, a property of vast extent. Urbanisation came within a period of 50 years: in 1851 the population numbered 12 000; in 1901, 137 000.

The **Charing Cross Hospital** *(Fulham Palace Road)* an outstanding modern building – tall, capacious and clean lined, dates from 1973 when the hospital moved from the Strand.

Downstream from the bridgehead, **Hurlingham House**, an 18C mansion in its own wooded grounds is the last of the big houses which once lined the river bank. It is now a private club.

Fulham Pottery. – *210 New King's Road.* One bottle kiln *(not in use)* still stands tall on the site of a 7-9 kiln pottery established by John Dwight in 1671 and soon known for its stoneware and busts and statuettes in salt glazed earthenware.

All Saints Church. – Fulham parish church has been a landmark at this bridging point of the river since the 14C, its square Kentish stone tower a twin to Putney church on the far bank, although the vessel was rebuilt in Perpendicular style in 19C.

Inside there is a rich collection of monuments and brasses: note the tombstones in the chancel floor to William Rumbold standard bearer to Charles I in the Civil War and Thomas Carlos, whose coat of arms, an oak tree and three crowns, was granted to his father after he had hidden in the oak tree at Boscobel with Charles II after the Battle of Worcester, 1651. Fourteen Bishops of London are buried in the yew shaded churchyard.

Close to the church note the 19C Powell Almshouses with steep pitched roofs over a single storey, forming an L shaped building around a quiet garden.

Fulham Palace. – *Bishop's Avenue. Grounds only open.*

The palace, which was from the 7C to 1973 the official residence of the Bishops of London, retains the appearance of a modest Tudor manor. The gateway, a low 16C arch with massive beamed doors, leads through to the courtyard with a large well in the centre. The two storey red brick walls, except in the restored range to the right, are strongly patterned with a black diaper design. The remains of a nearby moat may date back to the Roman occupation.

Bishop's Park, beside the river, was originally part of the palace grounds and contains a walled botanical garden.

GREENWICH ★★★ (Greenwich)

Greenwich offers a variety of places to visit: the Royal Observatory where one can stand astride the meridian with a foot in either hemisphere, the wooded park sweeping downhill to the Queen's House, the Royal Naval College by the river and the National Maritime Museum with its mile and a half of galleries illustrating British seafaring down the ages.

Access. – *In summer go or return by river bus from Westminster and Charing Cross (allow 1 hour) or the Tower to Greenwich Pier. Trains (20 minutes) run from Charing Cross, Waterloo to Greenwich or Maze Hill (5 minutes' walk). Buses run from Trafalgar Sq (No 1) and from Euston via Waterloo (No 188). Or travel by the Docklands Light Railway to Island Gardens and via foot tunnel. Greenwich Tourist Information Office, Cutty Sark Gardens, SE10. ☎ : 01-858 6376. Open May to October, daily 10am to 6pm (5pm November to April).*

Bella Court. – Greenwich has been in the royal domain since King Alfred's time. It was Humphrey, Duke of Gloucester, brother of Henry V, who first enclosed the park and transformed the manor into a castle, which he named Bella Court; it was he also who built a fortified tower upon the hill from which to spy invaders approaching London up the Thames or along the Roman road from Dover. On Duke Humphrey's death in 1447, Henry VI's queen, Margaret of Anjou, annexed the castle, embellished it and renamed it **Placentia** or Pleasaunce.

Tudor Palace. – The Tudors preferred Greenwich to their other residences and Henry VIII, who was born there, magnified the castle into a vast palace adding towers and halls, a tiltyard and a royal armoury where craftsmen beat out and chased armour rivalling the suits from Italy and Germany and like them dramatically displayed at the Tower.

Henry also founded naval dockyards up and downstream at Deptford and Woolwich which he visited by sumptuous royal barge to inspect his growing fleet which by 1512 included the *Great Harry*, the first four-master to be launched in England. It set square sails on the fore and mainmasts, it had topsails on all four masts and top gallants on the first three. The docks were also accessible by a road skirting the wall which divided the extensive and quite magnificent royal gardens from the park. Overlooking the thoroughfare was a two storey gatehouse which, legend has it, Queen Elizabeth was approaching one day in 1581 when Walter Raleigh, seeing her about to step into the mire, threw down his cloak so that she might cross dryshod.

Palladian House and Pretty Palace. – Rich as the Tudor palace was, in 1615 James I commissioned **Inigo Jones** to build a house for his queen, Anne of Denmark, on the exact site of the gatehouse even to its straddling the Woolwich-Deptford road. Jones, at forty (b 1573) was known for his revolutionary stage settings; he proved equally inventive in his design for the Queen's House which was based on the principles of the Italian architect, Palladio (1508-80), and contained a "bridge room" over the road. Work stopped on Anne's death to be resumed only when Charles I offered the house to his queen, Henrietta Maria, whose name and the date, 1635, appear on the north front, and whose initials can be seen over the fireplace in the queen's bedroom "urnished, that it far surpassed all other of that kind in England".

English Mechanical Equinoxtial Dial *c* 1690.

The Tudor palace was despoiled during the Commonwealth, its collections sold and interior used as a barracks and prison; the Queen's House alone emerged relatively unscathed so that, at the Restoration, Henrietta Maria could return to live there from time to time until her death in 1669 (in France). Charles II disliked the derelict palace, found the Queen's House too small for his court and in 1665 commissioned instead a King's House from John Webb, a student of Inigo Jones. The result was what is now known as the King Charles Block with its giant pilasters in groups of four at either end and at the centre where they are crowned by a pediment. With the exception of the Observatory, however, all construction had to cease for lack of funds long before Charles' "pretty palace" was complete.

Royal Hospital to Royal Naval College. – Work at Greenwich was resumed in 1694 when William and Mary, who preferred Hampton Court as a royal residence, granted a charter for the foundation of a Royal Hospital for Seamen at Greenwich, on the lines of the Royal Military Hospital in Chelsea, and appointed Christopher Wren as Surveyor. Wren, as usual, submitted numerous plans, before proposing the one we know today which, at Queen Mary's insistence, retained the Queen's House and its 150ft wide river vista (only acquired at the demolition of the Tudor palace), incorporated the King Charles block and involved the construction of three additional symmetrical blocks, the King William (SW), Queen Mary (SE) and Queen Anne (NE, below which exists a crypt, sole remainder of the earlier palace; *not open*). To complete the scheme the vista was focused by twin advanced cupolas before the refectory and chapel and the course of the Thames modified and embanked – this was Wren's only major vista design to be realised. The project took more than half a century to complete and involved Vanbrugh, Hawksmoor, Colen Campbell, Ripley, "Athenian" Stuart... John Evelyn who, as he recorded in his diary, on 30 June 1696 "laid the first stone of the intended foundation at five o'clock in the evening... Mr. Flamsteed, the King's Astronomer Professor observing the punctual time by instruments", by June 1704 observed that the hospital had begun "to take in wounded and worn out seamen... the buildings now going on are very magnificent", but as treasurer he also noted that by 1703 the cost already amounted to £89 364 14s 8d (a list of donors in the entrance to the Painted Hall shows that the King gave £6 000, the Queen £1 000, Evelyn £2 000).

In 1873 the buildings were transformed into the Royal Naval College. The Queen's House, meanwhile, extended by colonnades and two wings in 1807 became first the Royal Hospital School and in 1937 the National Maritime Museum. Royal yachts still moor at Greenwich.

■ MAIN SIGHTS

The Park. – *Open daily sunrise to sunset.* Greenwich Park, palisaded in 1433 and surrounded by a wall in Stuart times, is the oldest enclosed royal domain. It extends for 180 acres in a great sweep of chestnut avenues and grass to a point 155ft above the river crowned by the Old Royal Observatory and the General Wolfe monument. Beyond the Roman Villa and Great Cross Avenue are a **flower garden**, before ancient cedars of Lebanon, a pond with wild fowl and a Wilderness with a small herd of fallow deer.

Royal Naval College★★. – *Open daily, except Thursdays, 2.30 to 5pm; closed Good Friday and 25 December.*
In 1873, when the Admiralty turned the Hospital into a centre of scientific instruction, steam and steel had just replaced wood and sail. Today it is a naval university offering courses such as defence and nuclear science to men and women of the NATO alliance.

Painted Hall★. – Wren's domed building, designed as a refectory and forming a pair with the chapel was completed in 1703. In 1805 it was the setting for Nelson's lying in state before his burial in St Paul's. The hall and upper hall were painted in exuberant Baroque by Sir James Thornhill: William and Mary, Anne, George I and his descendants, celebrate Britain's maritime power in a wealth of involved allegory. The artist portrayed the current monarch as he worked through each new reign (1708-27) and was paid £3 a sq yd for the ceilings, £1 for the walls.

The Chapel★. – The chapel by Wren was redecorated after a fire in 1779 by "Athenian" Stuart and William Newton as a Rococo interior in Wedgwood pastels. A delicate pattern of formal swags and panelled rosettes covers the upper walls and ceiling; corbels and beams are masked by a lacework of stucco. In contrast, blocking the apse, is *St Paul after the Shipwreck at Malta* by Benjamin West (1738-1820), who also designed the Coade stone medallions for the pulpit made from the top deck of a 3 decker.

National Maritime Museum★★. – *Open Monday to Saturday 10am to 6pm (5pm in winter), Sunday 2 to 6pm (5pm in winter); closed 1 January, Good Friday, May Day holiday, 24, 25, 26 December; combined ticket museum and Old Royal Observatory £2.20, OAPs, children £1.50. Restaurant, Bookshop, Library, Print Room, navigational maps and charts accessible for research by appointment only.*

Queen's House★★. – *Closed for restoration until 1990.* This elegant white house was the first Palladian villa to be built in England; such style, proportion, sophistication, were hitherto unknown. Inigo Jones matched the beauty of a horse-shoe shaped staircase leading to the terrace (which formerly included the main entrance overlooking the Tudor palace), a first floor loggia on the park *(south side)* and crowning stone balustrade, with an equally attractive interior.

West and East Wings. – The **Neptune Hall** *(mezzanine floor by the West entrance)* is a museum in itself with 1907 paddle tug *Reliant* with machinery running, 19C merchant shipping artefacts – wheels, figureheads – 1893 screw steam launch *Donola* and others. Adjoining is the **Barge House,** with the gold and scarlet painted Prince Frederick's barge and Queen Mary's graceful shallop.

In the **West Wing** the second floor is devoted to the early voyages of discovery, the creation of the Royal Navy from the Early Tudor fleet, artefacts from the Dutch wars and the role of the navy at the period of the Glorious Revolution of 1866. One room contains ships' models. Other galleries trace Britain's marine history from Captain Cook's exploration of the Pacific to Nelson's battles with the French, in contemporary paintings including many great portraits, highlighted by uniforms, logs, guns, maps and navigational instruments, models and a large collection of decorated chinaware. Other galleries cover shipbuilding in wood, iron and steel, navigation and maritime archaeology and conservation with a replica of the Ferriby boat.

The **East Wing** galleries house special exhibitions.

The Old Royal Observatory★. – *Same opening times as for the National Maritime Museum; combined ticket Observatory and museum £2.20, OAPs, children £1.50.*
In 1675 Charles II directed Sir Christopher Wren to "build a small observatory within our park at Greenwich, upon the highest ground, at or near the place where the castle stood" for "the finding out of the longitude of places for perfecting navigation and astronomy". Originally map and chart makers fixed the zero meridian where they chose: Greenwich, Paris, the Fortunate Islands... The British reading began to be generally adopted with the inauguration in 1767 of the annual publication, the *Nautical Almanack,* which in combination with the marine chronometer and sextant enabled navigators to find their longitude in relation to the Greenwich

meridian. Map and chart makers soon also began to base their calculations on Greenwich. The standardisation of the meridian came finally when the speeding up of communications (railways and the telegraph) produced anomalies and even legal disputes – the time lag between London and Plymouth was 16 minutes. By 1884, when the Meridian Conference was called in Washington, 75 % of the world's charts were based on the Greenwich meridian and it and GMT were agreed as the standard.

Flamsteed House. – As architect and a former astronomer, Wren designed in his own words, for John Flamsteed, first Astronomer Royal, a house of red brick with stone dressings, an upper balustrade and miniature canted cupolas "for the Observator's habitation and a little for pompe". Inside, beside the usual small 17C rooms, is the lofty **Octagon Room** beautifully proportioned and, according to John Evelyn, equipped already in the 17C, as now, "with the choicest instrument". Note the displays on the "history of the measurement of time" and the domestic quarters. Outside note the sundials *(south façade)* and the red time ball *(roof)* which was erected in 1833 to serve as a time check for navigation on the Thames: the ball rises to the top of the mast and drops at exactly 1300 hours GMT.

The Meridian Building. – This mid-18C addition of the same brick as Flamsteed House, was built to house the observatory's growing **collection★★** of telescopes of all sizes, and other instruments, many of which are still in their original positions. Note Airy's Transit Circle through which the meridian passes, the 28 in refracting telescope in the dome and outside, the brass meridian of zero longitude, the clocks showing world time, the 24 hour clock and British Standard Measures *(main gate)*.

Planetarium. – *South Building. Open Saturdays, May to August, lectures at 2.30 and 3.30pm; free.*
A variety of lectures on the moon and stars are given at different times.

Cutty Sark★★. – *Open 10am (Sundays from noon) to 6pm (5pm October to March); closed 25 December; £1.30, children 70p.*

Launched at Dumbarton in 1869 for the China tea trade, the *Cutty Sark* became famous as the fastest clipper afloat – her best day's run with all 32 000 sq ft or 1/4 acre of canvas fully spread was 363 miles. In her heyday she brought tea from China and later wool from Australia, chasing before the wind like the cutty sark or chemise of the witch, Nannie, in Robert Burns' poem, *Tam O'Shanter,* from which she took her name and witch figurehead. She was converted into a nautical training school in 1922 and transferred to dry dock at Greenwich in 1954. In her hold are papers, charts, mementoes and models, illustrating the history of the clipper trade and her own story in particular. In the lower hold is a lively collection of boldly coloured 19C figureheads.

Gipsy Moth IV. – *Open April to September daily 10am (Sundays, noon) to 6pm; 20p, children 10p.* The 11 ton, 53ft, ketch in which the late Sir Francis Chichester circumnavigated the world alone in 1966-67, stands nearby looking incredibly small.

(After photograph, Pitkin Pictorials)

The Cutty Sark.

Footway Tunnel. – *Open daily.* In the round domed building beside the river a lift and steps *(100)* lead down to a foot tunnel beneath the Thames *(10 mins)* to the Isle of Dogs for a fine **view★★** of Greenwich Palace, as painted by Canaletto in 1750 *(see Maritime Museum).*

■ THE TOWN

The tall parish church stands at the crossroads near the Antique Market *(all year Saturdays; May to September Sundays also)*, the theatre and shops selling antiques and maritime mementoes. Some facades and buildings date from the late 17C, 18 and early 19C.The **Dreadnought Seamen's Hospital,** *(King William Walk)* was designed in 1764 by James "Athenian" Stuart.

St Alfege's. – *Open April to October, Mondays to Fridays 11am to 3pm, Saturdays and Sundays 2 to 4pm; November to March, Thursdays to Sundays, 11am to 3pm; closed Tuesdays and holiday Mondays.* The somewhat gaunt church (1718) with an elegant Doric portico is by **Hawksmoor,** the superimposed tower by John James. Inside there are no pillars, although the span measures 65 by 90ft. The murals *(east end)* are by Thornhill and the carving by Grinling Gibbons. On the site where Alfege, Archbishop of Canterbury, suffered matyrdom at the hands of Danish invaders in 1012, churches were erected which witnessed Henry VII and his queen at worship, the baptism of Henry VIII, heard Thomas Tallis, the father of English church music, playing the organ for 40 years (console in SW corner) and saw his burial also that of General Wolfe, parishioner and Commander of the British Army at the capture of Quebec (d 1759). Two other parishioners were Lavinia Fenton, the original Polly Peachum in *The Beggar's Opera* and John Julius Angerstein. The registers *(visible by prior application ☎ 01-858 8387)*, which date back to 1615, vividly portray the large families, child mortality, the decimation of plague years and contrasting, usual, longevity.

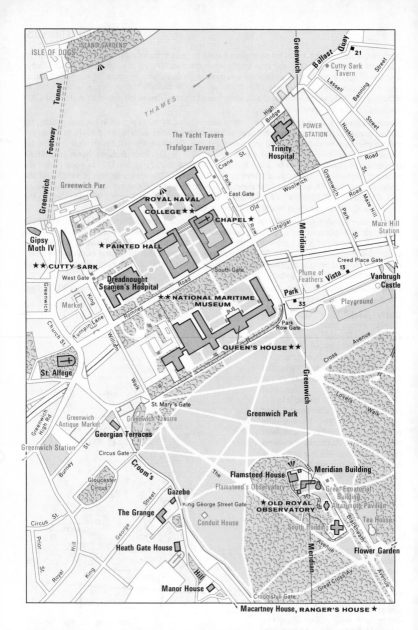

Macartney House, **RANGER'S HOUSE** ★

Croom's Hill. – Croom's Hill, already an established local throughfare in 15C, was taken as a natural western boundary, when the park was enclosed. The west, or right side of Croom's Hill, is lined all the way up by 17, 18, early 19C houses. The east side includes, at the bottom, the Greenwich Theatre, built in 1968 in the shell of a Victorian music hall, and a terrace of five humble 17C tenements (nos 3-11) with weatherboard backs. Opposite are **Georgian terraces** – the first the oldest, the second marked with a central bow and main doorway (C Day Lewis, Poet Laureate, lived in No 6 from 1968-72). Nos 10-12 will house a Fan Museum *(opening 1990)*. Further up, **The Grange**, an early 17C building with 18C additions, stands on a site recorded as having been given in 818 by a daughter of Alfred the Great to Ghent Abbey. The small square **gazebo** with a pyramid roof and carved plaster ceiling, beside the road, was built in 1672.

Heath Gate House is a relatively low brick mansion with large gabled dormers and pilasters on brackets supporting the upper floor. Built in the 1630s the house is a rare example of so early a domestic building with its exterior unaltered.

The **Manor House** of red brick, two storeys high, overlooking the heath, is typical of 1697, even to the hooded porch with a finely carved shell motif.

At the hilltop are houses built in 1674 on land filched from the royal domain by Andrew Snape, Serjeant Farrier to Charles II and, according to Evelyn, "a man full of projects". Snape's speculative building can be seen in the large, rambling **Macartney House** (now private flats) built of mellow brick and stone with a roof balustrade and tall rounded windows overlooking the garden, and the Ranger's House.

Ranger's House★. – *Open 10am to 5pm (4pm November to January); closed Good Friday, 24, 25 December.*

The mansion was originally a small brick villa with a stone balustrade lining the roof and steps leading up to an elegant stone frontispiece decorated with a mask. Rounded wings in pale yellow brick were added during the house's ownership by Philip, 4th Earl of Chesterfield (1694-1733), politician, diplomat and wit. The resultant south gallery, 75ft in length with a compartmented ceiling and three fine bow windows commands, its satisfied owner declared, "three different, and the finest prospects in the world" – the gardens are still as beautiful.

The **Suffolk Collection** of 53 paintings includes an outstanding series of full length family portraits by William Larkin (*fl* 1610-20) all in the finest clothes of the period, embroidered, slashed, jewelled, lace collared and ruffed. Daniel Mytens (1590-1647), Cornelius Johnson (1593-1661) and other fashionable painters were also patronised to record family traits. Note a 17C Lotto rug displayed over a table as in the paintings.

The panelled rooms on the first floor house the Dolmetsch collection of musical instruments: spinet (1709), lute, clavichord, flute etc. There are also some instruments including the green harpsichord (1896) on the ground floor. A view of Croom's Hill painted 150 years ago by T. Hofland is of particular interest.

East of the College

East of the College lie Park Row and the **Trafalgar Tavern** of 1837 where bars and dining rooms, named after the personalities and events of Nelson's time, overlook the river from cast iron balconies resembling the galleries of a man o'war. In the early 19C the tavern was the setting for the Liberal ministers' "whitebait dinners" and later was described in *Our Mutual Friend* by Dickens who used to meet there with Thackeray and Cruikshank.

In the old and narrow Crane Street, is **The Yacht Tavern,** at least a century older and also overlooking the Thames. High Bridge, beyond, is fronted by a small white, importantly gabled and crenellated charity building, the **Trinity Hospital** with the date 1616 on the gateway tower.

Ballast Quay. – The terrace of neat 17C, early Georgian houses (note the 1695 Morden *(qv)* estate marks), and **Cutty Sark Tavern,** rebuilt with a great bow window in 1804 on the site of earlier inns, ends in the four square Harbourmaster's Office (no 21) which for 50 years, until the 1890s, controlled colliers entering the Pool of London.

Park Row, Park Vista and Maze Hill lead up to Blackheath east of the park. In Park Vista are the early 18C plain two storey **Manor House** (no 13), the **Vicarage** (no 33) a rambling 18C house incorporating Tudor fragments, and the 18C public house, the Plume of Feathers.

Vanbrugh Castle. – The caricature of a medieval fortress, stands at the top of the hill, built and lived in by the architect and playwright himself, Sir John Vanbrugh, from 1717-26 while Surveyor to Greenwich Hospital. Gothick towers, turrets, high walls, crenellations and all – it preceded Strawberry Hill *(qv)* by some 30 years.

HAM HOUSE ★★

Open 11am to 5pm; closed Mondays (except holidays), 1 January, Good Friday, May Day holiday, 24, 25, 26 December: £2, children and OAPs £1p. NT.

Ham House was at its prime under **Elizabeth Dysart, Duchess of Lauderdale,** "a woman of great beauty but greater parts... a wonderful quickness of apprehension and an amazing vivacity in conversation... (who) had studied... mathematics and philosophy; but... was restless in her ambition, profuse in her expense and of a most ravenous covetousness; she was a violent friend, and a much more violent enemy". She lived in dangerous times – her father, William Murray first Earl of Dysart, had literally been youthful "whipping boy" for Prince Charles, future Charles I; Elizabeth, it was said, became for a time the Protector's mistress. Her first husband, Sir Lyonel Tollemache, founded the line who, as Earls of Dysart, remained owners of Ham House until modern times when it was presented to the National Trust; her second, the Earl, later Duke of Lauderdale, favourite of the Stuart restoration, was a learned, ambitious, vicious character. A double portrait, *Both ye Graces in one picture,* by Sir Peter Lely in the Round Gallery, presents them graphically – the toll of years is clearly evident in the duchess of whom there is an earlier portrait on the same wall.

The Lauderdales, according to their contemporaries, "lived at a vast rate". They enlarged the house, which had been built to the conventional Jacobean plan in 1610, and modified the front to give a continuous roof line with a horizontal emphasis. A family idiosyncrasy for inventories and hoarding furniture, paintings, hangings, and bills for structural and decorative alterations, has enabled the house to be returned to its 1678 appearance when it was described by John Evelyn as "furnished like a great prince's". The gardens have been relaid to the 17C plan.

Exterior. – The fabric is brick with stone dressings; the building, three storeys beneath a hipped roof with a five bay centre *(north side)* recessed between square bays and typical, canted Jacobean outer bays. The fine iron gates and piers date from 1671; previously the house had been approached by a tree-lined canal from the river to a watergate near the main door; the present forecourt, with the Coade stone figure of **Father Thames** by John Bacon, was laid out in 1800.

(By courtesy of the V & A)

Ham House from an engraving *c* 1730.

Interior. – Paintings, in this house, bring to life the period of Charles II, the Cavalier generals, the women at court – young, fair, delicately complexioned and far from innocent. Furniture, doors, doorcases, fireplaces and ceilings display the craftsmanship of the period – frequently Dutch for Dutch craftsmen were well established long before the accession of William III. The remarkable ceilings show the progress from geometrical type plasterwork to garlands and spandrels (compare the original, north and later, south rooms).

HAM HOUSE★★

Ground Floor. – The house has an impressive entrance in the Great Hall, increased above by the Round Gallery with a decorated plaster ceiling by Kinsman (1637). Lely portraits adorn the gallery and below, Kneller, Reynolds paintings of Dysarts of 17, 18C.

The most notable features of other rooms on the ground floor are the gilt leather wall hangings and 1679 cedar side tables in the Marble Dining Room (parquetry replaced the marble paving in 18C), the artificially grained and gilded panelling, fashionable in 1670s, the chimney furniture of silver, considered very ostentatious by contemporaries. In the Duchess's Bedchamber are damask hangings while in the Yellow Bedroom or Volury Room the bed (note the carved cherub feet) is hung with purple and yellow; in the White Closet are an oyster work veneered writing desk and picture of the south front of the house in 1683 *(fireplace)*. The altar cloth of "crimson velvet & gould & silver stuff" in the chapel is original.

The **Great Staircase** of 1637, built of oak round a square well and gilded, has a singularly beautiful balustrade of boldly carved trophies of arms.

Upper Floor. – Lady Maynard's suite contains 17C Flemish tapestries after Poussin below a wooden frieze and family portraits, the Museum Room, examples of the original vivid upholstery, an 18C toilet set, a prayer book of 1625 and ledgers and bills of the alterations to the house and the 1679 inventory which has enabled the rooms to be arranged as in Elizabeth Dysart's day, the Cabinet of Miniatures, a collection of miniatures by Hilliard, Oliver and Cooper. The North Drawing Room is sumptuous, epitomising the Lauderdale passion for luxury and display in a plaster frieze and rich ceiling (1637) above walls hung with English silk tapestries (woven by ex-Mortlake workers in Soho), carved and gilded wainscoting, doorcases and doors; furniture is carved, gilded and richly upholstered; the fireplace is exuberantly Baroque... Equally opulent is the Queen's Suite, rich with late 17C garlanded plaster ceilings, grained wainscoting and carved wood swags above the fireplaces; the furniture includes then fashionable Oriental screens, English japanned chairs, a small Chinese cabinet on a gilded stand and 18C tapestries. In the heavily ornate closet with painted ceiling and the original satin brocade hangings, note the carved "sleeping chayre".

HAMMERSMITH (Hammersmith)

The buildings of North Hammersmith are known not for architectural merit but for their function: **Wormwood Scrubs** *(Du Cane Rd),* stock brick and white stone buildings, profusely chimneyed, turreted and betowered, was constructed behind high walls by convicts from 1874-90 as the last prison to be built in London; **Hammersmith Hospital,** in close proximity, was built in 1904, the original buildings being in red brick and stone, and now stands enlarged by utilitarian annexes built for the expansion of specialised services and the Royal Postgraduate Medical School and Wolfson Institute. (Two other famous hospitals in the borough are Queen Charlotte's, Goldhawk Rd, and the Royal Masonic, Ravenscourt Park.)

In Wood Lane, just south of the Western Avenue/Westway flyover is the site of the **White City Stadium** (now offices) built for the 1908 Olympics. Within sight is the attractive **BBC Television Centre** *(Wood Lane).* The original block, which dates from the early 1960s, is in yellow-brown brick and glass in the form of an open horseshoe with sides of unequal length and affords an interplay of curve and straight wall, of mounting heights and varied texture.

Shepherd's Bush Common, overlooked by the old Shepherd's Bush Empire, now a BBC TV Theatre, tree fringed and an incredible 4 acres in extent, serves only as a traffic island at the juncture of Wood Lane, the Uxbridge Rd, the M41, Goldhawk Rd, Holland Pk Av.

St Paul's Girls' School, Brook Green (south side), of red brick and stone with a formal entrance, carvings and segmental pediments, by Gerald Horsley, dates from 1903-4 when the school was founded. The music wing of 1913 is named after the composer and onetime music master **Gustav Holst** *(St Paul's Suite for Strings).* Further towards Hammersmith Rd but still within the calm of the green, are terraces of modest late 18/19C houses. At the end of Shepherd's Bush Rd by the fire station is the **Hammersmith Palais,** opened in 1919 and still vibrating as London's favourite dance hall. The **Lyric Theatre,** King St, re-opened in 1979, is a reconstruction of the original auditorium, built in 1895, incorporated in a modern shopping centre.

Hammersmith Broadway is pounded by traffic going west to join the M 4 and the Great West Rd, south to Putney Bridge and east to Hyde Park Corner along Cromwell or Hammersmith Rds. This last is marked on its north side by the West London Hospital, the extensive offices of J Lyons and, at the road's union with Kensington High St, by **Olympia.** The hall's front was refaced in 1930 but the actual building dates from 1886 (which explains those staircases); the rear extension was added in 1936.

St Paul's, Hammersmith. – *Open weekdays 9.30am to 2.30pm, Sunday services 8.30, 11am and 5.30pm.*

The parish church stands halfway between the Broadway and the bridge, grand in size, pink stone in fabric, neo-Early English in style with a tall tower surmounted by high pinnacles. It dates from 1882 when it replaced a 17C chapel of ease which, although restored and enlarged in 1864 proved too small to accommodate the teeming population: 1801, 6 000; 1861, 25 000; 1881, 72 000; 1901, 112 000.

The furnishings include a 17C pulpit, carved with cherubs' heads and garlands, from the Wren church of All Hallows, Thames St, late 17C chairs (chancel), 17 and 18C monuments. Note the one erected by the church benefactor, Sir Nicolas Crispe before his death in 1665, to "that Glorious Martyr King Charles I of blessed Memory" in the form of a bronze bust (Le Sueur).

The **Riverside Studios,** *Crisp Road,* consisting of two theatres, art gallery, bookshop, restaurant and bar, opened in 1977 in a building which started life as an iron foundry at the turn of the century before being converted to film studios between the wars.

Two big houses once bordered the Hammersmith riverside, both downstream from the bridge: **Craven Cottage,** an 18C cottage *orné* with Egyptian style interiors, burnt down in 1888 and now perpetuated as the name of Fulham football ground *(Stevenage Rd)* and 17C **Brandenburgh House,** the residence of Queen Caroline of Brunswick when she attempted to claim the rights of consort on the accession of her husband as George IV (the house was demolished after her death in 1821).

Hammersmith Bridge to Chiswick Mall

Upstream the embankment has developed gradually since the early 18C, modest houses being built singly or in terrace groups, the characteristic feature, besides the clouds of sometimes centuries' old wisteria, a balcony from which to watch, in olden days, sailing barges making for the harbour and now, yachts racing, oarsmen at practice.

Lower Mall. – Pleasingly notable in Lower Mall are, among the 18/19C group, no 6 (Amateur Rowing Association) with a canopied balcony and a bow window on slender, blue painted iron supports above the entrance to the boathouse; no 10, Kent House, with symmetrical bay windows, medallion decorations after Adam on the yellow brickwork and contemporary, late 18C, ironwork; the Blue Anchor, the later, Victorian, Rutland, then, marking the lower end of Furnival Gardens, Westcott Lodge, two storeys beneath a plain brick coping, the front door the last of the six bays, with an Ionic pillared porch which forms a canopied balcony above. At the garden's upstream end are the pier and a plaque which indicates the site of the creek and "harbour where the village began".

Upper Mall. – The Upper Mall opens with the 1726 Sussex House, stone urns at the corners of the brick coping and segmentally pedimented doorway flanked by Doric pilasters. The **Dove** which has had a license for 400 years, although the present building only goes back a couple of centuries, was a coffeehouse in 18C – James Thomson is said to have written the words of *Rule Britannia* in the upstairs room. It also housed the Doves Press and Bindery from 1900.

In the next group, **Kelmscott House,** 3 storeys high, 5 bays wide, plain, with dormers behind the brick coping, dates from the 1780s. In the 19C it was lived in consecutively by George Macdonald poet and novelist (1867-77) and **William Morris** (until his death in 1896). Morris put a loom in his bedroom, held meetings in the stables, and in the studio drew the illustrations and designed the founts for the fine books he printed in the nearby no 14 and published under the imprint of the Kelmscott Press.

Frank Brangwyn, Morris' apprentice from 1882-4, moved to no 51 Temple Lodge, Queen Caroline St, nearby in 1899. Adjoining the house (now owned by the Christian Community) he built a lofty studio *(temporary exhibitions and recitals)* to accommodate the large canvases which brought him fame.

One of the largest on the Mall is early 19C **Rivercourt House** (now a school); former Linden House, now the London Corinthian Sailing Club, is a century earlier (much refurbished) – note the Ionic pillared doorways. (Before the clubhouse, looking like a glassed-in crow's nest above the riverside wall, is the race officer's box). Two pubs, the Old Ship Inn and the Black Lion, mark the end of the Mall, the latter set back from the river behind a garden with a brick arcade from an old riverside factory.

Hammersmith Terrace. – Nothing could be more urban than Hammersmith Terrace: 17 almost identical brick houses of 3 and 4 storeys built as a single block with the main façade towards the river – yet it dates from the mid 18C when all around were fields, market gardens, vineyards and famous strawberry fields. Householders have included Philippe de Loutherbourg (artist and scenic designer at Drury Lane in 18C, n° 13), Sir Emery Walker (antiquary and typographer, collaborator with Morris at the Kelmscott Press, no 7), and for more than 50 years, Sir Alan Herbert – APH – writer, lover and ardent protagonist of the Thames (1890-1971, nos 12-13).

Upstream is Chiswick Mall *(p 45)*; inland are St Peter's Sq with substantial 1830s houses of three storeys, bay windows and Ionic pillared porches, simultaneously planned dependent streets with smaller houses and cottages and St Peter's Church, a yellow stock brick landmark with pedimented portico and square clock tower on the Gt West Rd. It dates from 1829, the sculpture before it of a reclining woman by Karel Vogel, from 19₆59.

HAMPSTEAD – HIGHGATE ★ (Camden and Haringey)

Hampstead Heath was the common of Hampstead Manor in Charles II's reign, an area where laundresses laid out washing to bleach in 18C and since earliest times, a popular place of recreation (vast one day fairs; *Easter, Spring and Summer holiday Mondays*).

Hampstead Village developed from a rural area of a few substantial houses (Fenton), manors and farms and later into a fashionable 18C spa when the chalybeate springs were discovered in what has been ever since, Well Walk. It was 4 miles only from the centre of London and by the time enthusiasm for taking the waters had subsided, builders had begun the erection of houses and terraces, the development which continues to this day. Finally, in 1907 came the tube. Throughout its history this pleasant district has attracted writers, artists, architects, musicians, scientists.

The village, irregularly built on the side of a hill, has kept its original street pattern; main roads from the south and southeast meet and continue north; between is a network of lanes, groves, alleys, steps, courts, rises, places... At the foot of the hill lie Hampstead Ponds.

Swiss Cottage. – The chalet was built as the latest style in tavern design in 1840 and was so novel that it gave its name to the small locality beginning to develop between Hampstead and St John's Wood. Buses – it became a terminal in 1856 – then the tube (1868), brought transformation to a Victorian suburb now replaced by modern apartment blocks. The chalet, more brightly painted than a stage set, still exists (pub and restaurant) at the centre of an island site.

The attractive, irregular buildings of **Swiss Cottage Civic Centre** (*Avenue Rd,* by Swiss Cottage Stn) by **Sir Basil Spence** include a library and swimming pool, opened in 1964. A temporary building houses the Hampstead Theatre Club.

Freud Museum. – *20 Maresfield Gardens. Open Wednesdays to Sundays 1.2 to 5pm; £2; students OAPs £1.* The house where Sigmund Freud lived after his escape from Nazi persecution in Vienna in 1938 until his death in 1939 has been turned into a museum devoted to Freud's life and work and to the history and development of psychoanalysis. On the ground floor are his study and library with his famous couch and collection of books, pictures and antiquities, kept intact by his daughter Anna.

East of Heath Street and Hampstead High Street

Downshire Hill going east from the foot of Hampstead High Street has some good Regency houses. **St John's Church** marks the Keats Grove fork, white and upright with a small domed bell turret, Classical pediment, large name plaque and square portico, a chapel of ease dating from 1818. **Keats Grove** is lined by early 19C houses and cottages irregular in height, detached and terraced, bay windowed, balconied with canopies, many with flowered front gardens.

Keats House. – *Keats Grove. Open Mondays to Fridays 2 to 6pm (1 to 5pm November to March), Saturdays 10am to 5pm, Sundays and Bank holidays 2 to 5pm (closed bank holidays in winter). Guided tours by appointment only.* ☎ *01-435 2062.*

The small Regency house, known as Wentworth Place, was erected in 1815-16 as a semi-detached pair with a common garden by two friends with whom Keats and his brother, in lodgings in Well Walk, soon became acquainted. In 1818, Keats came to live with his friend Brown in the left hand house; shortly afterwards Mrs. Brawne and her children became tenants of the right hand house. He wrote poems, including the *Ode to a Nightingale,* in the garden; he journeyed; he became engaged to Fanny Brawne; he became ill; in September 1820 he left to winter in Italy and in February 1821 he died.

"His short life" in Edmund Blunden's words "was of unusual intensity; it insisted on being recorded in many ways". These records are now assembled, chiefly in the Chester Room added in 1838-9 when the two houses were united. The original rooms are furnished much as Keats and Fanny Brawne must have known them.

The **Keats Memorial Library** *(available to students by appointment only)* is in the local library next door.

Off Hampstead High Street on the east side in **Old Brewery Mews** the brewery building has been converted to offices overlooking a well, protected by a wrought-iron cage, and a row of modern town houses. **Flask Walk,** higher up, which begins as a pedestrian street with a Victorian pub and tea merchant, continues east past Gardnor House, built in 1736, with a full height rounded bow window at the rear, to New End Square.

Burgh House. – *Open Wednesdays to Sundays, noon (bank holidays 2pm) to 5pm; closed Mondays, Tuesdays, Good Friday and Christmas.* This dignified house, with its south facing terrace, was built, probably by Quakers, in 1703 when Hampstead was becoming popular as a spa. The local physician, Dr Wm Gibbons, lived there in the 1720s; the wrought-iron gates bear his initials. It takes its name from Revd Allatson Burgh, vicar of St Lawrence Jewry in the City, who was so unpopular his parishioners petitioned Queen Victoria to have him removed. A frequent visitor from 1934-37 was Rudyard Kipling whose daughter and son-in-law rented the house. The panelled rooms, still served by the original oak staircase, are now used for poetry and music recitals, exhibitions by local artists and the Hampstead Museum – one room is devoted to the artist, John Constable *(qv);* information on the history, architecture and natural history of Hampstead and the Heath is available from the bookstall; home-made food is served in the basement buttery *(open 11am to 5.30pm).*

It was at no 40 Well Walk that **John Constable** lived from 1826 to his death. Christchurch Hill with its Georgian cottages leads to the mid 19C Church with a soaring spire visible for miles.

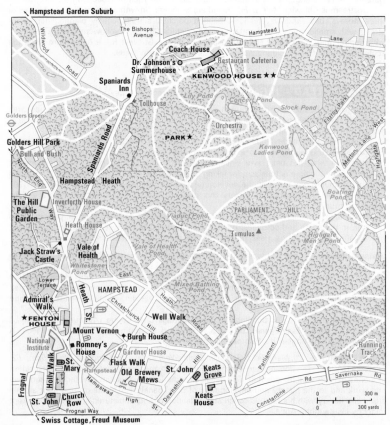

West of Heath Street and Hampstead High Street

Church Row. – The fine 1720 terrace of brown brick houses with red dressings, tall windows, straight hoods on carved brackets shading the Georgian doors, is separated from the uneven line on the north side by a file of tall trees planted down the centre of the wide road. The range along the north pavement, older, younger and more varied, includes cottages, a weatherboarded house with oversailing bay, full style town houses of 3 storeys with good ironwork...
St John's, the parish church at the row's end, obscured in summer by the trees, was built boldly on an ancient site in 1744-7 with a spire rising from a battlemented brick tower, banded in stone. The interior, with giant pillars supporting arches in the tunnel roof, galleries on three sides and box pews, was twice enlarged in 19C to accommodate Hampstead's rapidly growing population: 4 300 in 1801, 47 000 in 1881.

Frognal, to the west, once a manor, hence all the roads of the same name, presents some distinctive buildings: University College School, large and neo-Georgian with Edward VII in full regalia standing above the entrance door; Kate Greenaway's house (no 39) designed in 1885 by Norman Shaw in true children's story book appearance with rambling gables and balconies; and the Sun House (no 9 Frognal Way) by Maxwell Fry at his 1935 best, in stepped horizontals in glass and gleaming white.

Holly Walk. – The path north from the church, bordered by the 1810 cemetery extension crowded with funeral monuments, rises to the green and pink washed, three storey houses of Prospect Place (1814) and delightful cottages of Benham's Place (1813). Holly Place, 1816, is another short terrace flanking **St Mary's,** one of the earliest RC churches to be built in London, founded by the Abbé Morel, refugee from the Revolution who came to Hampstead in 1796. From the top of the hill a maze of steps and alleys leads down to Heath St.

Mount Vernon junction. – The triangular junction of Windmill Hill, Hampstead Grove and Holly Bush Hill, weighed down by the institutional late 19C National Institute for Medical Research, is redeemed by **Romney's House** (plaque), picturesquely built of brick and weatherboarding in 1797, and the tall 18C group: Volta, Bolton, Enfield and Windmill Hill, all of brown brick. The iron gateway of 1707 by Tijou at the end belongs to Fenton House.

Fenton House. – *Open April to October, Saturday to Wednesday, 11am to 6pm; March, weekends only, 2 to 6pm; £2, children £1, Mondays (except holiday Mondays) and Tuesdays £1.60, children 80p. NT.*

House★. – The red brick house, built in 1693, is Hampstead's finest besides being one of its earliest and largest. The east front, with a recessed porch, is less attractive than the south front of seven bays beneath a hipped roof with a central pediment.

In the original design a self-contained closet was attached to every room but the dividing walls in all but one have now been removed. The original main pine staircase, with its twisted balusters and wide handrail, has survived as well as some doorcases, panelling and chimney pieces. In 1793 the house was bought by a Riga merchant, Philip Fenton, after whom it is still named; in 1952 it was bequeathed to the National Trust.

Collection★★. – The furniture and pictures form a background to 18C porcelain – English, German and French – and the Benton-Fletcher collection of early **keyboard instruments,** some 18 in number ranging in date from 1540 to 1805, plus an early 17C Flemish harpsichord lent by HM the Queen Mother, an Arnold Dolmetsch clavichord of 1925 and some stringed instruments. (The instruments are for the most part kept in good playing order and are accessible to students. There are frequent concerts.) On the ground floor are harpsichords (1770 English, 1612 Flemish), the most important part of the English porcelain collection (Bristol, Plymouth, Chelsea, Bow, Worcester), some of the German figures, and an Oriental room (porcelain, lacquer pierglass, enamelled ware); on the landing Staffordshire figures and a Trubshaw grandmother clock. On the first floor are German figurines, teapots; Worcester apple green porcelain in satinwood cabinets, the most important piece of English porcelain in the collection, a Worcester pink-scale vase and cover probably decorated in London (Drawing Room), 17/18C Chinese blue and white porcelain, 18C English harpsichords, a 16C Italian and an early 18C English spinet, and a 17C virginal; on the top floor 18C square pianos, 17 and 18C harpsichords, 17 and 20C clavichords, and a 17C spinet and virginal. The 17C needlework pictures (Rockingham Room), the bird and flower pictures by the 18C artist Samuel Dixon (Porcelain Room) and the works of Sir William Nicholson (Dining Room) are noteworthy.

Admiral's Walk, to the north, leads to Admiral's House, built in the first half of 18C and given its nautical superstructure including, in his time, a couple of cannon with which to fire victory salutes, by the colourful Admiral Matthew Burton (1715-95) after whom the house, now resplendent in "tropical whites", is named. It was the home of Sir George Gilbert Scott from 1854-64 – he made no alteration. The adjoining Grove Lodge also white, probably older, was Galsworthy's home from 1918 until his death in 1933 where he wrote all but the first part of the *Forsyte Saga.* Lower Terrace, at the end of Admiral's Walk, is where Constable lived from 1821-5 before moving to Well Walk.

North of Hampstead village (Hampstead Heath)

Whitestone Pond. – The pond and the milestone (Holborn Bars 4 1/2 – in the bushes at the base of the aerial) from which it takes its name, are, at 437ft, on London's highest ground. The flagstaff is thought to stand on the site of an Armada beacon, the link with the signal south of the river on Shooter's Hill, Blackheath, visible on a clear day, and even more distinctly at night. (In 18/19C military and admiralty telegraphs stood on Telegraph Hill – west.)

Jack Straw's Castle. – The white weatherboarded inn, rebuilt in 1962-4, was first mentioned in local records in 1713. The name is thought to be derived from the possibility that supporters rallied on the spot before going to join Straw in Highbury and Wat Tyler in central London in the Peasants' Revolt of 1381. Standing on its own at the junction of the two roads, Heath House, a plain early 18C mansion of brown brick is chiefly remarkable for its commanding position and the visitors received by its 18/19C owner, the Quaker abolitionist, Samuel Hoare: William Wilberforce, Elizabeth Fry and the leading politicians of the day.

Vale of Health. – The Vale, a cluster of late 18, early 19C cottages, mid-Victorian and now a few modern houses and blocks, built in a dip in the heath and connected by a maze of narrow roads and paths, has at various times been the home of Leigh Hunt, the Harmsworth brothers, Rabindranath Tagore, D H Lawrence, Edgar Wallace, Compton Mackenzie. The origin of the Vale's name is unknown – until 1677 it was a marsh; the houses only began to be named from 1841.

To the west of North End Way stands Inverforth House, rebuilt in 1914 and now an annex to Manor House hospital. Its extensive but somewhat neglected pergola, sweet with wisteria, roses and trailing plants, now forms part of **The Hill Public Garden,** formally laid out on a steeply sloping site and framed by the natural beauty of the trees of the West Heath. Nearby on the northern edge of the West Heath lies **Golders Hill Park,** its landscaped lawns and shrubberies sweeping down to two ponds past bird and animal enclosures.

Bull and Bush. – The 1920s building with a modern inn sign, turn of the century paintings of Florrie Forde and a verse of the music hall song outside, reputedly stands on the site of a 17C farmhouse. In 18C it became for a brief time Hogarth's country retreat, then a tavern, patronised by Joshua Reynolds, Gainsborough, Constable, Romney...

Opposite is the gabled brick house (now a speech and drama college) where Anna Pavlova lived from 1921-1931. The Elder Pitt, Earl of Chatham, retired to a house, since demolished, at North End in 1767 (d 1788).

Hampstead Garden Suburb was conceived by Dame Henrietta Barnett, living in what is now Heath End House, as a scheme for rehousing London slum dwellers in the early 20C. Raymond Unwin, the principal architect, designed an irregular pattern of tree-lined streets and closes converging on a central square with its Institute and two churches (one Anglican and one Nonconformist) by Sir Edwin Lutyens. The houses are in varied architectural style.

Spaniards Inn and Tollhouse. – The inn and tollhouse have slowed traffic on Spaniards Road into single file since they were built in the early 18C. The small brick tollhouse stands on the site of an entrance to the Bishop of London's Park, the white painted brick and weatherboard pub on that of a house said to have been the residence of a 17C Spanish Ambassador. In 1780, the Gordon Rioters, having sacked Lord Mansfield's Bloomsbury town house, stopped to ask the way to Kenwood but were so plied with drink by the publican that they had not moved by the time the military arrived.

■ KENWOOD** (Iveagh Bequest)

Kenwood House★★. – *Open daily 10am to 6pm (4pm November to January, 5pm February to March and October); closed Good Friday, 24, 25 December; cafeteria.*

"A great 18C gentleman's country house with pictures such as an 18C collector might have assembled". – William Murray, younger son of a Scottish peer, acquired Kenwood, then a 50 year old brick house, in 1754, two years before he was appointed Lord Chief Justice and created **Earl of Mansfield.** He intended Kenwood as his country retreat, where he could relax and entertain, and in 1764 invited his fellow Scot, **Robert Adam,** to enlarge and embellish the house. The architect transformed it both outside and in and left so strong an imprint that all subsequent additions were in his style.

Kenwood was purchased by Lord Iveagh in 1925 and bequeathed to the nation in 1927. The house's contents, including much Adam furniture, had previously been sold and he filled it instead with the remarkable collection of pictures he had formed at the end of the 19C. Contemporary furniture as well as original pieces (Adam side-table and pedestals – 1775 – in the Parlour) are gradually being acquired to recreate an elegant 18C setting.

Exterior. – The pedimented portico with giant fluted columns, frieze and medallion was Adam's typical contribution to the north front; on the south front, from which there is a splendid view down to the lake *(concerts in summer),* Adam raised the central block to three floors (decorating the upper floors in his own style with pilasters and stucco), refaced the existing Orangery and designed the Library to the east to balance the façade.

Dr Johnson's Summerhouse *(north-west of the house).* – The summerhouse was provided by Henry and Hester Thrale for their guest at Streatham Place where he was a constant visitor from 1766-1782. It was rescued and re-erected on the present site in 1962.

Interior. – Of the rooms on either side of the hall, the most remarkable are the Music and Dining Rooms (cornice and doorcase related in motif to the preceding enriched columns and entablatures), the Adam Library and Orangery.

The Adam Library★★. – The "room for receiving company" as Adam described it, is richly decorated with Adam motifs and painted in blue and old rose, picked out in white and gold. The oblong room, beneath a curved ceiling, leads into two apsidal ends, each lined with bookcases and screened off by a horizontal beam supported on fluted Corinthian columns. Arched recesses, fitted with triple mirrors, flank the fireplace and reflect the three tall windows opposite.

The paintings★★. – A Rembrandt, *Self-portrait in Old Age,* the lusty *Man with a Cane* by Frans Hals, the ringletted young girl *Guitar Player* by Vermeer, and works by Bol, Rubens, Cuyp and Crome hang in the Dining Room. Van de Velde seascapes and a Turner, *The Iveagh Seapiece* are found in the Parlour; the Vestibule is mostly hung with Angelica Kauffmann. Portraits by the English school people other rooms: beautiful Gainsborough women, including *Mary, Lady Howe* in pink silk with that special flat hat, *Lady Hamilton* by Romney and children, sentimental, patient, delighted, by Raeburn *(Sir George Sinclair),* Reynolds *(The Brummell Children, The Children of J.J. Angerstein)* and Lawrence *(Miss Murray).* Gainsboroughs of unusual character hang in the Breakfast Room and Orangery: *Going to Market, Two Shepherd Boys with Dogs Fighting* and the dramatic *Hounds coursing a Fox;* the portrait of *J.J. Merlin* in the Music Room is also noteworthy. A portrait of special interest is that by John Jackson of the *Earl of Mansfield, Lord Chief Justice,* creator of Kenwood.

In the **Coach House** is the 19C family coach capable of carrying 15 people.

In 18C fashionable society flocked to the pleasure gardens at Ranelagh with its rotunda, Vauxhall, Cupers (South Bank), Spring (Admiralty Arch) and Marylebone, where patrons could wander under the trees or take tea and bread and butter in pleasant arbours. On special occasions there were fireworks and illuminations, dancing, concerts and entertainments. The Cremorne Gardens opened later in 1843 as the others became less exclusive and fell from favour.

Some of the gardens developed round mineral springs where the less wealthy, who could not afford to go to Bath, could take the waters in rural surroundings. Sadler's Wells, which offered dancing, pantomimes and rope dancing, accompanied by cold meat and wine, Hampstead and Islington were among the most popular. Less sophisticated and cheaper were the tea gardens at Highbury Barn, Hornsey and Greenwich where bowls and skittles were played.

■ HIGHGATE

Highgate Village developed from 16/17C when one or two decided it was the place to build their country seats; in 17C came rich merchants with their mansions; in 18C the prosperous... The mid and later 20C has continued the tradition. Nevertheless Highgate remains a village in character, centred on Pond Square and the High Street.

Small houses and cottages line three sides of the irregularly shaped Pond Square, from which the ponds disappeared in the 1860s.

South Grove. – Along the south side of **Pond Sq** are the early 18C Church House (no 10), the Highgate Literary and Scientific Society at no 11 and Moreton House (no 14) a brick mansion of 1715. **Rock House** (no 6) opposite, with overhanging wooden bay windows is 18C and, on the far side of Bacon's Lane, **Old Hall**, late 17C, plain brick with a parapet and at the back a great bow window, topped by a pierced white balustrade. **Bacon's Lane** recalls that the philosopher was a frequent guest and died at Arundel House on the site of which Old Hall now stands. **The Flask** (1721) on Highgate West Hill corner is a period country pub. The tapering octagonal spire belongs to St Michael's, built in 1830 and overlooking Highgate Cemetery.

The Grove. – This wide, tree planted, road branching off to the north, presents, behind open railings, late 17/early 18C terrace housing at its satisfying best; rose brick in colour, of dignified height, with segment headed windows and individual variations. The poet and critic S.T. Coleridge, lived at No 3 from 1823 till his death in 1834 and is buried in St Michael's.

Highgate Cemetery. – *Swain's Lane.* The cemetery is in two parts : the **Western** *(open 10am to 4pm daily and guided tours on the hour)* opened in 1838, contains some remarkable 19C monumental masonry and the tombs of Michael Faraday (1791-1867), the Rossettis, Charles Cruft (first dog show 1886).

The **Eastern** *(open Monday to Saturday 9am to 3pm, Sunday 2 to 4pm)* is still in use. Here lie buried Karl Marx (d 1883: bust by Laurence Bradshaw 1956), George Eliot (1819-80), William Foyle (1885-1963), William Friese-Greene (1855-1921).

Highgate High Street. – The street is lined by small, local shops and pubs with houses above, mostly early 19C on the north and some 18C on the south side. The **Gate House Tavern** stands on the site of a 1386 gate house to the Bishop of London's park (18C house at the rear); no 46, with a small paned bay window, dates from 1729; no 23 opposite, Englefield House with straight-headed windows and modillion frieze and nos 17, 19 and 21 are all early 18C.

Highgate Hill. – Just inside **Waterlow Park** stands **Lauderdale House,** 16C in origin but remodelled in the 18C in small country house style. This is the house about which the tale is told that in 1676, Nell Gwynn not yet successful in obtaining titled recognition for her princely 6 year old son, dangled him out of a window before his father threatening to drop him, whereupon Charles called out "Save the Earl of Burford" (the future Duke of St Albans). It is now used as a cultural and educational centre.

Opposite, high above the road, is The Bank, a row of brick houses: nos 110, 108 and 106, Ireton and Lyndale Houses are early 18C, no 104 Cromwell House (so called for uncertain reasons since 1833) of now mellow red brick with a solid parapet is 16C and has an octagonal, cupolaed, turret of 1638.

Whittington Hospital has grown out of the original 'Leper spytell' of 1473. The **Whittington Stone** (1821) – a marble cat sitting on a stone – marks the spot where according to tradition Dick Whittington *(qv)* heard Bow bells telling him to "turn again".

The tree lined **North Road** begins with the 19C red brick buildings of Highgate School (f 1565; now 700 strong) on the right and opposite a late Georgian terrace, nos 1-11, followed by individual houses of the same period (nos 15, 17 – plaque to A E Housman – 19) and at 47, 49 another early Georgian group. Beyond stand the clean lined buildings Highpoint One and Two designed by Lubetkin and Tecton in 1936 and 1938; the first has two Erechtheon caryatids supporting the porch; one facing front, but the other — fed up perhaps? – at the half turn!

HAMPTON COURT ★★★ (Richmond on Thames)

Open early March to September, daily 9.30am to 6pm; October to early March 9.30am to 4.30pm; Palace and park closed 1 January, 23 to 26 December. Admission to all areas £3.40, children £1.70, OAPs £2.50.

The three builder patrons. – Wolsey purchased the manor site at Hampton from the Knights of St John of Jerusalem in 1514: Henry VIII purloined it in 1530.

It was the age of the *Field of the Cloth of Gold* (1520 – painting in the Cartoon Gallery), of splendour and display, of unbridled ambition and meteoric careers. Thomas Wolsey, the son of an Ipswich butcher, appointed to a chaplaincy in the household of Henry Tudor while still in his early thirties, rose, under Henry VIII, to be Archbishop of York (1514), Lord Chancellor (1515), Cardinal (1515), Papal Legate (1518). Celebrating his position and wealth were his houses in and around London: Whitehall, Hampton Court and Moor Park (Herts).

Wolsey chose Hampton for its "extraordinary salubrity" attested by eminent English physicians and doctors from Padua. Spring water was brought from Coombe Hill three miles away passing under the Thames in leaden pipes. The palace was well supplied with waterclosets and great brick sewers draining into the Thames which lasted until 1871. The estate, which Wolsey enclosed, comprised some 1 800 acres.

Construction of Hampton Court in 1515 proceeded apace. The plan was the accustomed Tudor one of consecutive courts with surrounding buildings: Base Court, Clock Court, Carpenter's Court, hall, chapel. It measured 300 × 550ft overall and contained some 1000 rooms of which 280 were kept prepared for guests. The residence was richly furnished throughout with panelled and tapestry hung walls, painted and gilded ceilings and was peopled by the cardinal's personal household

Hampton Court: east front.

of 500. Wolsey's wealth, it was said, exceeded the king's; his mansion outshone the royal palaces. His power in the kingdom approached the absolute until after 15 years, he fell, disgraced, and within months had died (1530).

Sumptuous as Hampton Court was, **Henry VIII** enlarged and rebuilt much of it. He added wings on either side of the central gateway, a moat and drawbridge; he constructed the Great Hall, the Great Watching Chamber, the annexes around the Kitchen Court including the Haunted Gallery, the Fountain Court, the tennis court wing, the south front overlooking the Pond Garden. He built a tiltyard (where the restaurant and walled gardens are now) and planted a flower garden, kitchen garden and two orchards. It was one of the most splendid royal palaces in the kingdom.

Edward VI, who had been born and christened (1537) at Hampton Court, his two sisters and the early Stuarts resided at the palace when the season was fine or the plague rife in London.

Unlike other royal residences it was reserved for Cromwell and so preserved with its contents – notably the wood carvings and paintings. Charles II returned to initiate the modern garden layout but the palace, through the next 140 years, remained virtually unaltered and uncared for.

To **William** and **Mary,** the third and last of the palace's true builder patrons, Hampton Court offered delight and a splendid potential which they immediately began to realise through Wren and Talman and an unrivalled team of artist-master-craftsmen – Grinling Gibbons, Jean Tijou, Antonio Verrio, Morris Emmett, C G Cibber, the king's Dutch architect, Daniel Marot, and the great gardeners, George London and Henry Wise. The sovereigns intended to make Hampton Court their main residence outside London.

Wren began work in 1689 and, after schemes to demolish the 200 year old Tudor palace had been discarded, designed and rebuilt the east front entirely, and the south front to enclose between the façades, the State Apartments – two suites each including a guardroom, presence and audience chambers, drawing room, state bedroom and closet or dressing room and known respectively as the King's Side (overlooking the Privy Garden to the south) and the Queens' Side (overlooking the Fountain Garden to the east). The smaller informal royal apartments on the **Fountain Court*** he also rebuilt anew but left the Base Court much as it was only adding the colonnade and a new south range to the Clock Court.

To achieve such massive works, the crenellations, irregularities and forest of turrets of Henry's castle palace (still to be seen in an anonymous painter's view of *Hampton Court from the Thames*), were swept away and replaced by the classic Renaissance style of the 17C, executed in brick with stone centrepieces, enrichments and surrounds to the long ranges of tall, circular, square windows which emphasise the horizontal lines of the building, crowned by a seemingly infinite balustrade.

Queen Anne's contribution was to have Wren design and Grinling Gibbons decorate a small **Banqueting House** (frescoes and ceiling paintings, carving) *(open mid-March to mid-October)* overlooking the river and start the decoration and furnishing of the State Apartments, only finally completed under George II, the last monarch to reside at the palace. It was in his reign that William Kent decorated the Cumberland Suite, with typical 18C plasterwork. In 1771-3 the Great Gatehouse was rebuilt; two storeys being lopped off in the process.

In 1838 Queen Victoria opened the magnificent State Apartments, gardens and Bushy Park to the public.

■ THE PALACE★★★

State Apartments. – The map and key on page 92 are numbered in the sequence in which the apartments are visited – as courtiers would have approached the monarch in the king's rooms, in the reverse order in the queen's. Additional royal apartments may occasionally be opened. Galleries 3-10 and the Cartoon Gallery (30) are not available for viewing due to extensive fire damage in 1986 to the south range of Fountain Court.

The State Rooms are of especial interest as it is possible to trace the evolution of architectural and decorative styles from the Tudor period. Grinling Gibbons' carvings in cornices, friezes, doorcases, overmantels provide a superb finish to the king's state rooms, Cartoon and Queen's galleries and chapel especially. The royal collection of paintings dates back to Tudor and Stuart times with Henry VIII and Charles I as the major patrons.

King's Staircase (1). – Allegorical scenes painted by **Verrio** c 1700 and stylised wrought-iron balustrade by Tijou.

King's Guard Chamber (2). – The walls above the panelling are lined with over 3 000 **arms** arranged by John Harris, William III's gunsmith. A door to the right gives access to the Wolsey Rooms (**47**).

First Presence Chamber (3). – William III's canopied chair of state. Picture of *William III* by Kneller (1701) in its original position, *The Marquis of Hamilton* by Mytens. Oak door-cases and limewood garlands by Gibbons.

Second Presence Chamber (4). – This smaller room sometimes served as dining-room. Note the pier-glasses and the portrait of *Christian IV of Denmark.*

Audience Chamber (5). – View of the Privy Garden. State canopy and 17C chair; original pier-glasses. Carvings. Portrait of *Elizabeth of Bohemia* by Honthorst.

King's Drawing Room (6). – Elaborate frame to *Isabella of Austria* (F. Pourbus), headed by a crown of fruit and flowers and descending in drops including garlands, putti, birds; Tintoretto *The Nine Muses, A Knight of Malta,* Veronese *Marriage of St Catherine.*

William III's State Bedroom (7). – Ceiling painting by Verrio; tapestries from the 16C Abraham series (also **14, 43**). Limewood frieze and overmantel.

King's Dressing Room (8). – Ceiling depicting *Mars in the Lap of Venus* by Verrio. Paintings by Carracci and Giorgione.

From the adjoining Writing Closet (**9**) a door gave access to a private staircase linking the king's suite with his private quarters on the ground floor. A mirror above the chimney-piece reflects the whole perspective of the preceding rooms. The paintings include A. del Sarto's *Holy Family*, Parmigianino's *Portrait of a Boy* and *Minerva* and Pontormo's *Virgin and Child*. Next is Queen Mary's Closet (**10**) which leads into the Queen's Suite.

Queen's Gallery (11). – Carvings by Gibbons and a marble chimney-piece by John Nost depicting the *Triumph of Venus*. The Brussels tapestries illustrating the history of Alexander the Great were woven to Gobelin designs by Le Brun (1662). Note the china pagodas and vases.

Queen's Bedroom (12). – Ceiling by Sir J. Thornhill (1715); medallions of George I, the Prince and Princess of Wales. State bed, chair and stools (1715-16) in crimson damask. Portrait of *Queen Ann as a Child* by Lely.

Queen's Drawing Room (13). – Wall and ceiling paintings by Verrio (1703-05) commissioned by Queen Anne: the *Queen as Justice* (ceiling), the *Queen receiving homage* (west wall), *Prince George of Denmark as Lord Admiral* (north wall), *Cupid drawn by sea-horses* (south wall). From the central window there is a splendid **view**★ of the Great Fountain Garden.

Queen's Audience Chamber (14). – 16C tapestries illustrating the Story of Abraham. Canopied Chair of State. Portraits of the *Duke and Duchess of Brunswick* and *Anne of Denmark.*

Public Dining Room (15). – Decorated by Sir J. Vanbrugh c 1716-18 for the future George II and Queen Caroline. Cornice and royal arms carved by Gibbons. Painting of *Augusta, Princess of Wales with her family* by G. Knapton.

Prince of Wales's Suite (16-17-18). – These rooms were used by the future George II and his son. In the **Presence Chamber** are paintings by Carracci *Il Silenzio*, S. Ricci *the Holy Family, The Magdalen anointing Christ's Feet*. In the **Drawing Room** hang a tapestry *(removed for conservation)* from a set woven at Mortlake in 17C from Raphaël's cartoons of the Acts of the Apostles and a portrait of *Charles I, Henrietta Maria and Jeffrey Hudson* by Mytens. View of Lady Mornington's garden named after the Duke of Wellington's mother. The **Prince of Wales's Bedroom** contains a bed with a painted dome and delicate embroidery designed by Robert Adam for Queen Charlotte c 1775-6.

The **lobby (19)** – note the bird's eye view of the palace and gardens c 1700 – opens on to the **Prince of Wales's Staircase (20).** The designs of the Mortlake tapestry depicting a naval battle are attributed to W. van de Velde. The balcony and wrought iron festoons are by Tijou.

The **Anteroom (21)** connects the **Public Dining Room** *(above)* and the **Queen's Presence** and **Guard Chambers** *(p 92)* and gives access to the **Queen's Private Chapel (22)** and **Bathing Closet (23).** Next comes the **Private Dining Room (24)** ornamented with works by the Italians Pellegrini and Fetti. A second **closet (25)** opened into the **Queen's Private Chamber (26)** adorned with paintings by Mytens, Ruysdaël, Breughel, de Hooch and van de Velde.

The **King's Private Dressing Room (27)** contains a small early 18C bed; **George II's Private Chamber (28)** is notable for its 1730 flock wall paper and is adorned by Philippe de Champaigne's *Cardinal Richelieu*. A small **lobby (29)** gives access to the Cartoon Gallery.

Cartoon Gallery (30). – Designed by Wren (1699) to display seven of the ten tapestry cartoons designed by Raphaël (1515), purchased by Charles I in 1623. The cartoons on the lives of St Peter and St Paul are now in the V & A *(p 160)*, their place being taken by tapestries woven later after the cartoons. G. Gibbons carved the four doorcases and the very long drops framing the tapestry over the fireplace which cost £25 the pair. The panel below the mantel shelf is by J. Nost. This room contains historical paintings of Henry VIII's reign: *Field of the Cloth of Gold, The Journey to France (1520)* and *Family Group of Henry VIII* and his children including a posthumous portrait of Jane Seymour. An **anteroom (31)** gives on to the Communication Gallery.

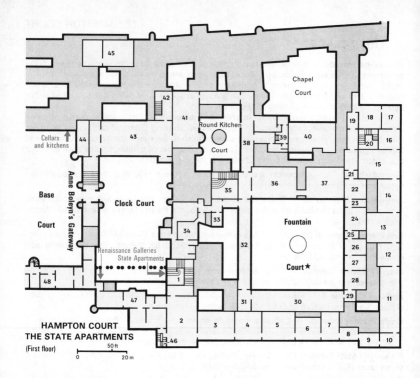

HAMPTON COURT
THE STATE APARTMENTS
(First floor)

50ft
0   20 m

Communication Gallery (32). – This gallery (west of Fountain Court) linking the King and Queen's State apartments, originally housed Mantegna's cartoons now in the **Orangery** *(p 93)* and now displays the famous *Windsor Beauties* of Charles II's court by Lely *(temporarily in Cumberland Suite)*.

Wolsey's Closet (33). – This room contains the cardinal's original furnishings: linenfold panelling (restored); painted wall panels; frieze with Tudor badges, mermaids and Wolsey's motto as running motif; ceiling of timber with plaster and lead mouldings, a chequerwork of Tudor roses, Prince of Wales' feathers, Renaissance ornament, all coloured and gilded.

Cumberland Suite (34). – Built by William Kent (1732) for George II's third son. Note the elaborate plasterwork and chimney pieces, and paintings depicting historical events in the life of Henry V.

Queen's Staircase (35). – Beautiful wrought-iron balustrade by Tijou. The walls and ceiling were decorated by Kent (1735); on the west wall is an allegorical painting by Honthorst (1628) depicting Charles I and Henrietta Maria as Jupiter and Juno. This was the ceremonial access to the Queen's State Apartments.

Queen's Guard Chamber (36). – The *Hampton Court Beauties* (Queen Mary's Court) by Kneller hang in this room which contains a monumental chimney piece carved by G. Gibbons.

Queen's Presence Chamber (37). – Decorated with an elaborate plaster ceiling by Vanbrugh, Gibbons carvings and a bed and furniture made for Queen Anne (1714).

Haunted Gallery (38). – This gallery so called because it is said to be haunted by the ghost of Catherine Howard, looks on to the Round Kitchen Court. The Flemish tapestries are probably from Queen Elizabeth's collection. Paintings by Ribera *Duns Scotus* and Mytens *Charles I*.

Holyday Closets (39). – A door to the right leads to the **Royal Pew** and adjoining closets where the king and queen attended services according to 16C custom. It was redecorated by Wren in 1711 and the ceiling was painted by Thornhill.

Chapel Royal (40). – Built by Wolsey but lavishly transformed by Henry VIII when the fan vaulted wooden ceiling was erected and gilded pendants added. The reredos between Wren's Corinthian pillars and segmental pediment, a wreath of cherubim above drops on either side of a framed oval, is by Gibbons.

Great Watching Chamber (41). – Built in 1535-36 at the entrance to the Tudor State Rooms (destroyed) with an elaborately panelled ceiling set with coloured bosses displaying Tudor and (Jane) Seymour devices between ribs which curve down to form pendants. The 16C Flemish tapestries depicting the Vices and Virtues were possibly purchased by Wolsey in 1522; three others illustrate scenes from Petrarch's Triumphs.

Horn Room (42). – The serving place for the upper end of the hall.

Great Hall (43). – 106 × 40 × 60ft high. The hall was built in 5 years (1531-36) with Henry VIII so impatient to see it finished that men even worked by candlelight. The magnificent hammerbeam roof is enriched with mouldings, tracery, carving and pendants relieved with gilding and colours. Its walls are hung with 16C Flemish tapestries made by van Orley to illustrate the *Story of Abraham*. At the far end is the Minstrels' Gallery with steps to the right leading to the Great Kitchen and a staircase to the left giving access from Anne Boleyn's Gateway. A doorway in the centre leads to a **servery (44)**.

Wolsey Rooms (47). – *Access from the Guard Chamber (2)*. These rooms probably used by guests not by the cardinal, are ornamented by 16C linenfold and later, plain panelling and an elaborate ceiling decorated with Wolsey's badges. The scriptural hangings are 17C north Italian needlework. The paintings include portraits of Henry VII, Elizabeth of York, Henry VIII and Jane Seymour after Holbein, Anne Boleyn, Mary I, Charles V, *Charles I and Henrietta Maria* by Mytens, a *Triptych of the Adoration of the Magi* and a *Coronation of the Virgin*.

Renaissance Picture Gallery (48). – *Access by stairs southwest of Clock Court.* The gallery displays in rotation 16 and 17C paintings from the Royal Collection including masterpieces of the Italian, German and Flemish schools: Correggio *(St Catherine, Holy Family)*, L. Lotto *(A Bearded Man)*, Parmigianino, Tintoretto, L. Cranach *(Judgment oof Paris)*, Holbein... etc.

Features of the exterior and auxiliary buildings

Trophy gates: built as the main gates in George II's reign with lion and unicorn supporters.

Moat and Bridge: constructed by Henry VIII; the moat was filled in, the bridge buried by Charles II; in 1910 the work was excavated and the bridge found to be complete apart from the parapet which was renewed and fronted by the King's Beasts.

Stone animals on the battlements: the weasels date from the construction by Henry VIII of wings with characteristic 16C diapered brickword, flanking Wolsey's gatehouse.

Henry VIII's arms: the royal arms appear in a (renewed) panel beneath the central oriel in the Great Gatehouse; also on Anne Boleyn's Gateway (Base Court side).

Terracotta roundels: the medallions of Roman emperors on the turrets and three other pairs inside were bought by Wolsey for Hampton Court in 1521. They were originally painted and gilded and cost £6 6s each.

Anne Boleyn's Gateway: so-called because the king embellished it during the queen's brief reign; bell turret, 18C; Base Court side, Elizabeth's badges, initials, date 1566; Clock Court side, Wolsey's arms in terracotta (restored) and cardinal's hat.

The Astronomical Clock: the clock in what was the main Court of Wolsey's house, was only brought to the palace (from St James's) in the 19C. It was made for Henry VIII in 1540 by Nicholas Oursian and on the 8ft dial are indicated the hour, month, date, signs of the zodiac, year and phase of the moon. It ante-dates the publication of the theories of Copernicus and Galileo and the sun, therefore, revolves round the earth.

Chimney Stacks: the brick stacks are a delightful example of Tudor fantasy.

Kitchens and Cellars *(access-Base Court):* The King's Beer Cellar beneath the Great Hall (note the wooden piers supporting the floor above, the stone pier beneath the hearth) and the New Wine Cellar, beneath the Great Watching Chamber, stored the home brewed ale and imported wine for the royal household of 500.

Tudor Tennis Court *(access: the Broad Walk, open mid-March to mid-October):* built by Henry VIII and still played on regularly. The windows are 18C.

East Front entablature: Caius Cibber carved the entablature (1694-6) combining the William and Mary cipher with crown, sceptres, trumpets... He also carved many of the palace's finest window and arcade ornaments (Fountain Court round window surrounds).

ER 1568: on the bay window stonework overlooking the Knot Garden (south front); the lead cupola and octagonal turret date back to the 16C.

Lower Orangery: the plain building by Wren now houses the Mantegna Cartoons *(10p)* (c 1431-1506): *Cartoons of the Triumph of Caesar.* 9 giant paintings of a triumphal procession, ending with the portrait of an ashen, withered, Caesar, high on his chariot. The Cartoons, possibly the earliest pictures on canvas to survive, were bought by Charles I in early 17C.

The Upper Orangery housed William III's orange trees during the winter season.

Royal Mews Museum (A, *map p 94) (access: Barrack Block, West Front; open April to September; 50p)* Royal carriages and harness, a landrover and miniature cars given to the Queen, Prince Charles and younger members of the family together with a French charabanc are displayed.

■ THE GARDENS***
Open 7am until dusk or 9pm in summer; 4pm in winter.

The gardens bear the imprint of the men who created them; the Tudor, Stuart, Orange monarchs, the designers and the great gardeners. In the 50 acres surrounding the palace, features have been levelled, schemes abandoned; fashion has translated 17 and 18C box edged *parterres* into lawns or woodland and growth transformed man-size yew obelisks into 30ft green-black cones; new species have been introduced; the herbaceous border along the Broad Walk laid...

Wolsey planted a walled flower garden in the area between the river and the forward south front. Under Henry VIII and the Tudors, this became the formal **Pond Garden** and **Knot Garden,** the last a velvety conceit of interlaced ribands of dwarf box or thyme with infillings of flowers, replanted this century within its walled Elizabethan site. A gazebo crowned mound erected by Henry VIII by the river with a spiral approach, flanked by gaudily painted King's Beasts, was levelled in 1700, the beasts being preserved to stand in the court before the main entrance, the soil used to construct the raised Queen Mary's Bower and Queen's Terrace on either side of the **Privy Garden.** Henry's tiltyards and five observation towers have also vanished, transformed into walled, old fashioned rose gardens, overlooked by one remaining tower (adjoining the restaurant) – roses cost 4 pence for 100 roses in Tudor times.

Charles I had a tributary of the Colne River diverted to Bushy Park to form the 9 mile Longford River; enclosed 10 miles as a deer park and commissioned Francisco Fenelli to sculpt the Diana Fountain, originally for the Privy Garden.

Charles II had the Long Water canal excavated and lime trees planted in the vast semicircle and three radiating avenues which still provide a "set piece" from the palace. The giant goosefoot *(patte d'oie)* with the canal as the central claw extending from the palace front to the horizon was very much in the style of contemporary garden design in France under Le Nôtre.

William III was a "Delighter" in gardening; Mary "particularly skill'd in Exoticks", for which she sent botanists to Virginia and the Canary Islands.

William determined to have a fountain garden. The long Water was curtailed to its present 3/4 mile and **Great Fountain Garden** laid out in the 10 acres between the semicircle of limes and the palace east front. 13 fountains played in a formal scrollwork setting of dwarf box hedges (a Dutch fashion), obelisk shaped yews and globes of white holly. Under Queen Anne, eight fountains at the circumference were removed, the box hedge arabesques replaced by grass and gravel; in Queen Caroline's time the fountains were reduced to the present singleton. The yews in the 19C grew as they willed and only in the 20C have they been gradually trimmed making room for brilliant flower beds and revealing spectacular vistas from the palace front.

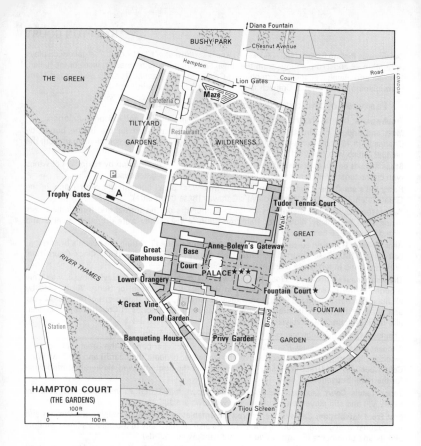

HAMPTON COURT
(THE GARDENS)
100 ft
0   100 m

Tijou designed the ironwork gates to the NE and SE lime avenues across the side arms of the Long Water, the Lion Gates and the unique 12 panel **screen** at the river end of the Privy Gardens – allusive with Scottish, English, Irish and Welsh emblems, and delicate as black lace.

The **Broad Walk** was planned by Wren and Queen Caroline to separate the Privy and Fountain Gardens. The border is now a permanent ribbon of colour throughout the seasons.

To the north of the palace, where Henry VIII had his orchard, William laid out a Wilderness – espaliers, clipped yews, hollies and box hedges – and included within its 9 acres a circular **maze**, replaced in 1714 by the present triangular version *(open March to October, 10am to 5pm; closed November to February; 35p)*. The formal layout has been replaced by natural woodland.

From the same period, the turn of the 17/18C, and the only memorial to Wren's grand design for a new north front, is the **Chestnut Avenue** in **Bushy Park.** To view the chestnuts in flower – 274 of them planted 42ft apart, extending over a mile and bordered on either side by 4 files of limes – remains a mid-May event to this day. Beyond the fountain, west of the avenue is a "new" – 20 year old! – 100 acre **Woodland Garden** where, on either side of the stream, patrolled by waterfowl and a black swan, beneath the trees, are rhododendrons and azaleas of every hue.

Under George III, Capability Brown planted in 1768 the **Great Vine**★, an incredible plant with a girth of 78 inches and an annual crop of 500-600 bunches of grapes *(on sale late August/early September)*. The massive wistaria, near the Vine House, dates from 1840.

■ HAMPTON COURT GREEN

At the palace gates are houses built for those associated with the court, particularly in the late 17 and 18C. Extending back from the early 19C hotel on the bridge road and receding in date are: Palace Gate House, The Green, **Old Court House,** the home of Sir Christopher Wren from 1706-23, Court Cottage, the 18C bow windowed **Faraday House** where Michael Faraday lived in retirement from 1858-67, and Cardinal House. Back from the road are the Old Office House with a hipped roof and the small square, white weatherboarded, **King's Store Cottage** (George III plaque). Beyond is the long brick range of the Tudor **Royal Mews,** built round a courtyard.

HARROW (Harrow)

The village of Harrow-on-the-Hill clings to the steep slopes below the parish church with a fine view of north west London on all sides.

St Mary's Church. – *Open 8am to 5pm, Sundays 7am to 8pm.* Little remains of the original building, begun by Lanfranc and consecrated by St Anselm in 1094. Two other famous visitors were Thomas-à-Becket and Cranmer. As Rector of Harrow Thomas Wolsey entertained Henry VIII at Headstone Manor (16C tithebarn).

Inside the church, there are interesting brasses, a 12C font and an early 18C pulpit. In the churchyard, where Byron's daughter Allegra lies buried, is the Peachey tomb where Byron used to sit; it was restored by his publisher John Murray with a marble tablet engraved with four lines from his poem "Written beneath an Elm in Harrow churchyard".

Harrow School. – *Guided tours by arrangement in term time.* ☎ 01-422 2303. Founded in 1571 by John Lyon *(monument in church),* the well known public school occupies a group of high quality 19C buildings including the Old School of 1611 which was twinned in 1818-20 by C. R. Cockerell.

The Chapel in flint and stone and the Vaughan Library in polychromatic red brick are by G. G. Scott. Also represented are Decimus Burton (Headmaster's house), Charles Hayward (boarding houses, labs, sanatorium and gymnasium) and William Burges who designed the New Speech Room (1874-7) in a D shape.

Famous former pupils include Byron, Robert Peel, Lord Palmerston, R. B. Sheridan who lived at the Grove in 1780s piling up debts, Anthony Trollope a miserable day boy who walked from his home nearby which later inspired his novel *Orley Farm,* Lord Shaftesbury, John Galsworthy, Sir Winston Churchill and Nehru.

The Old Speech Room Gallery with its many treasures is open to the public most afternoons. *Enquiries to the Custodian* ☎ *01-422 2196 Ext 225.*

■ ADDITIONAL SIGHTS

Headstone Manor. – *Headstone Lane, Pinner View.* A 14C manorhouse surrounded by a moat.

Tithe Barn. – The barn – 150ft long and 30ft wide – built *c* 1534 by Thomas Cranmer, Archbishop of Canterbury and surrendered to Henry VIII in 1545, has been beautifully restored and is now used as a museum and heritage centre.

Grim's Dyke. – *Old Redding, Harrow Weald.* The earthwork, a rampart and a ditch some 5 miles long, is probably of Saxon origin. It gave its name to a mansion (now the Mansion House Hotel) designed in Tudor style by Norman Shaw in 1875, where the composer W.S. Gilbert lived from 1890 to 1911. The Music Room is graced by the original 15ft high pink alabaster fireplace.

HOLBORN ★ (Camden)

Holborn, meeting place in the Middle Ages of roads from the north to the City, to Oxford and the west; site of the Bishop of Ely's palace – in Richard, Duke of Gloster's mind when he requested: "My lord of Ely, when I was last in Holborn, I saw good strawberries in your garden there, I do beseech you send for some of them" (R III; 3 iv). There were also manors and a market at the crossroads, open fields on which beasts grazed, archery was practised, duels were fought and washing laid out to dry. Today the manors are transformed into Lincoln's Inn and Gray's Inn –two of the four Inns of Court – the chapel and site of the episcopal precinct remain in name, the fields are less in extent but still open, the produce market is a world diamond centre...

Lincoln's Inn Fields. – By 1650 a developer, who had purchased the common fields to the west of Lincoln's Inn twenty years before, had surrounded them on three sides with houses. Of that period, one, **Lindsey House** remains, probably designed by Inigo Jones (since divided, nos 59-60, west side). The brickwork was originally all exposed, giving greater emphasis to the segmental pediment, the accented window and giant, wreathed, pilasters. 18C houses in the square include the Palladian style nos 57-8 dating from 1730, no 66, **Powis House** of 1777 with a pediment marking the centre window. On the north side nos 1-2 are early 18C, 5-9 Georgian, and no 15 with an Ionic columned doorway, frieze and pediment, mid-century.

The square's south side is occupied by official buildings: the neo-Jacobean Land Registry, neo-Georgian Nuffield College of Surgical Sciences (1956-8), 19-20C Royal College of Surgeons, housing the **Hunterian Museum** *(open daily 10am to 5pm; non-medical visitors must apply in writing to the Curator),* and the six storey, 1960s, Imperial Cancer Research Fund.

The Old Curiosity Shop. – *Portsmouth St, south-west corner of square.* The half timbered, little house on the corner is said to date back to the late 1500s and so be one of the oldest in London.

Sir John Soane's Museum★. – *13 Lincoln's Inn Fields. Open Tuesdays to Saturdays 10am to 5pm; closed 1 January, Good Friday, holiday Mondays, 24, 25, 26 December.*

In 1833 Soane obtained a private Act of Parliament to ensure the perpetuation of the Museum after his death. A stipulation was that nothing should be altered in any way, hence, house and collections are of interest not only in their own right but as an insight into his mind and those of other collectors of the period.

Born in 1753 (d 1837), the son of a country builder, Soane made his way through his talent: he worked under George Dance Junior and Henry Holland; he won prizes and a travelling scholarship to Italy (1777-80) while at the Royal Academy where, in later years, he was Professor of Architecture. He held the important office of Surveyor to the Bank of England (1788-1833) for which he executed the most original designs ever made for a bank. He acquired as his town house, no 12 Lincoln's Inn Fields in 1792, no 13 in 1805 as his museum and in 1824, built no 14.

Interior. – The rooms are small, passages narrow, the stairs not "grand" (note the wedge shape of the stairs in no 13 following the line of the house site), but recessed and angled mirrors, rooflights and windows on inner courts, ceilings slightly arched and decorated with only a narrow border or, as in the breakfast room of no 12, painted to resemble an arbour, give an illusion of space and perspective. Fragments, casts and models are displayed high and low throughout the galleries, while below ground are the Crypt, the Gothic Monk's Parlour and the Sepulchral Chamber containing the intricately incised sarcophagus of Seti I (*c* 1392 BC), celebrated on its acquisition in 1824 by Soane with a three day reception. On the first floor, past the Shakespeare recess on the stairs, in the drawing rooms and former offices are models, prints and architectural drawings (8 000 by Robert and James Adam, 12 000 by Soane), rare books and a collection of Napoleonic medals. The south drawing-room contains original furniture and a painting by Turner hanging in its original position opposite the fireplace.

The ground floor with dining table and chairs, desk, leather chairs, the domed breakfast room, the portrait of Soane at 75 by Lawrence, is highly evocative. His collection of pictures, mostly assembled on folding planes in the picture room, includes original drawings by Piranesi and 12 of Hogarth's minutely observed paintings (from which the engravings were made) of the *Election* and the *Rake's Progress.* Elsewhere are paintings by Canaletto, Reynolds and Turner.

Lincoln's Inn★★. – *Open at restricted periods, apply at porter's lodge (not Saturdays). Guided tours of the Old Hall, New Hall and Chapel mid-March to mid-September weekdays 9.30 to 11.30am; £2.* The site belonged to the Dominicans, until 1276 when they went to Blackfriars, and then to the Earl of Lincoln who built himself a large, walled mansion which he bequeathed as a residential college, or inn, for young lawyers.

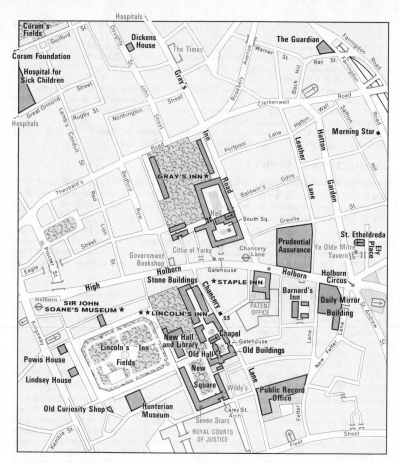

The buildings. – The buildings, mainly of brick with some stone decoration, date from the late 15C. The self-contained collegiate plan of intercommunicating courts is entered through a main gateway and the surroundings enhanced by beautiful gardens with an ornate Gothic toolshed.

The **gatehouse** on Chancery Lane, built of brick with square corner towers and a four centred arch filled with the original massive oak doors, dates from 1518. Above the arch are the arms of Henry VIII, the Earl of Lincoln and Sir Thomas Lovell.

Once through the arch, the gabled buildings immediately south of the court, known as the **Old Buildings,** are all Tudor redone in 1609 and all of brick. The **Chapel** *(open weekdays 12.30 to 2.30pm; closed 1 January, Easter, holiday Mondays, 25, 26 December)* on an open undercroft, was rebuilt in 1619-23 and is stone faced with later 19C pinnacles and additions to the west end. John Donne laid the first foundation stone and preached at the consecration. The windows illustrate with arms and names men who have been benchers and treasurers since the Middle Ages: Thomas More, Thomas Cromwell, Pitt, Walpole, Newman, Canning, Disraeli, Gladstone, Asquith...

The **Old Hall,** with paired bay windows at either end, dates from 1490. Inside modern linenfold panelling complements an early 17C oak screen, which is notable especially for the busts carved on the end pilasters; the painting *St Paul before Felix* (1748) is by Hogarth.

Towards Lincoln's Inn Fields is **New Square,** built in 1680 with identical four storey ranges with broken pediments above the doors and incorporating in the south range an archway to Carey St, wide and ornate with differing pediments on either side.

The **Stone Buildings** date from 1775-80. The **New Hall** and **Library** are mid 19C of red brick, diapered in the Tudor manner.

Chancery Lane. – The lane which takes its name from the grant of land by Henry III to his Lord Chancellor, Bishop of Chichester in 1227 (hence Rolls Passage, Bishop's Ct etc) is now commercial as well as legal. At the lane's top end are the Patent Office *(25 Southampton Bldgs)* and the **London Silver Vaults** *(no 53, Chancery House; open for business Mondays to Fridays, 9am to 5.30pm, Saturdays to 12.30pm)* where in some forty rooms, each entered through a strongroom door, there is a gleaming array of Georgian, Victorian and more modern silverware.

The Public Record Office Museum. – *Open Mondays to Saturdays (except public holidays) 10am to 5pm.* On display in the corridor are old chests including the Million Bank with multiple locks; in the museum are *Domesday Book,* and a wide selection of documents (charters, accounts, maps, seals, reports, registers, government papers...) illustrating major themes of British history. Periodic temporary exhibitions.

Several traces of the medieval Rolls Chapel (built 1232 for converted Jews, transferred to the Master of the Rolls in 1377 and demolished in 1896) are conserved in the present 19C neo-Gothic structure which was built to house the Public Record Office, established in 1838. Medieval and early modern records are housed here for the purposes of original research. Modern records from *c* 1780 are at the office at Kew. *(Admission to both by ticket only).*

Gray's Inn★. – It dates from the 14C in its foundation, from the 16C in its buildings, many of which, however, have had to be renewed since the war. The main entrance is from High Holborn through the **Gatehouse** of 1688, distinguished, above the wide arch, by a bay window flanked by niches; Dryden's publisher kept a bookshop in the house for many years in the late 17C.

South Square, just inside, which, except for no 1 of 1685, has been entirely rebuilt, has at its centre an elegant bronze statue of **Sir Francis Bacon** *(p 28),* the Inn's most illustrious member. The gardens *(open May to September Mondays to Fridays, noon to 2.30pm)* delighted in by Pepys and Joseph Addison, were considered by many, besides Charles Lamb, to be "the best gardens of the Inns of Court". The very fine wrought iron garden gateway is early 18C.

The hall, which was burnt out, has been rebuilt in its 16C style with stepped gables at either end and late Perpendicular tracery. Interior panelling sets off the late 16C screen which was saved from the fire and which is said to have been made from the timbers of a wrecked galleon of the Spanish Armada and presented to the Inn by Queen Elizabeth I.

Staple Inn*. – *Holborn.* Lying just inside the limits of the City, Staple Inn was one of the Inns of Chancery, where law students passed their first year of studies. Originally the home of wool merchants, it became a dependant of Gray's Inn and now houses the Institute of Actuaries.

For the row of half timbered houses to have survived on such a site since 1586-96, when they were built, seems incredible – true they have been restored (19C) and the backs rebuilt (1937) but the character remains and gives an idea of the pre-Fire City. The west house of 2 gables, is the taller with two floors overhanging; the east range has 5 gables each marked by an oriel and again two floors overhanging. An arched entrance at the centre leads to the Inn surrounding a central courtyard at the rear. The east and west red brick ranges were erected in 1731-4 and 1757-9. Much of the rest has had to be rebuilt, including parts of the hall which dates from 1581 and possesses an original hammerbeam roof.

The nearby **Barnard's Inn,** also an Inn of Chancery, was rebuilt in the 19C and is now entirely commercial. The Great Hall has 16C linen-fold panelling and heraldic stained glass.

Prudential Assurance and **Daily Mirror** buildings. – *Pages 65, 66.*

St Etheldreda's (RC), Ely Place and Hatton Garden. – The church has had a chequered history. It was erected in 1291 as a chapel to the Bishop of Ely's town house (St Etheldreda was the founder of Ely Cathedral). In the 14C John of Gaunt resided in the mansion from the time the Savoy Palace was burnt down in 1381 until his death in 1399, converting it the while into a minor palace, visited over the years by many monarchs.

At the Reformation, the property passed to Protestants and in 1576, when it extended over an area bounded today by Holborn, **Leather Lane** *(daily market),* Hatton Wall and Saffron Hill, at Queen Elizabeth's command, to **Sir Christopher Hatton,** her "dancing chancellor" for a yearly rent of ten pounds, a red rose and ten loads of hay. Hatton, whose portion included the famous garden, built a fine house and made such improvements that when he died in 1591 he was in debt to the crown for £40 000. The third Christopher Hatton followed Charles II into exile, selling the property to builders who erected slum tenements.

Ely House and St Etheldreda's, under Protestant jurisdiction since the Reformation, deteriorated, except from 1620-24 when leased by the Spanish Ambassador as his residence. By early 17C the crypt had become "a public cellar to sell drink in"; the Commonwealth made Ely Place a prison, the 75ft hall, all that remained of the house, and the church, a military hospital (1643). The precinct escaped the Fire but a century later was purchased, through the crown, by a Mr Cole who demolished the hall, built the pleasant four storey brick terrace with pilastered straight hooded doorways, which still lines the east side of Ely Place and, while retaining the church for his tenants, stripped it of such medieval furnishings as remained. The church's vicissitudes continued until finally in 1873 Ely Place again came up for auction and the church became the first pre-Reformation shrine in the country to be restored to the Roman Catholics.

St Etheldreda's. – Such age, so eventful a history and finally repeated bombing, have left little but the outer walls and undercroft of the 13C building. New stained glass windows depict the five English martyrs beneath Tyburn gallows and on the aisles the arms of the pre-Reformation bishops of Ely – note the 4 cardinals' hats. Against the east wall is a carved medieval wood reliquary. The **crypt** has 8ft thick bare masonry walls, modern abstract single colour windows, blackened medieval roof timbers, a floor of London paving stones. The six supporting roof columns were placed down the chamber's centre in 19C.

Early history is recalled in the name of the Mitre Tavern in Ely Court, a narrow alley leading west into Hatton Garden.

Hatton Garden. – The Garden, built up in the 1680s, is today the centre of diamond merchants and jewellery craftsmen. Halfway down are the London Diamond Club *(no 87, west side),* a white stucco house 6 bays wide with a triangular, pedimented door and, on the opposite side, a former church *(no 43),* attributed to Wren and built in 1666 by Lord Hatton. In 1696 it became a Charity School and figures of 17C charity schoolchildren still flank the pedimented doorway.

Gray's Inn Rd. – The commercial road north to King's Cross is marked at its top end by three hospitals – the Eastman Dental (no 256), the Royal National Throat, Nose and Ear and the Royal Free. The last is in a Classical style building of 1842 with additional wings on either side of 1855 and 1876, built originally as the Light Horse Volunteer Barracks.

The former Times building (1974) is strongly horizontal in line from the ribbon windows which bound it. In 1985 the paper moved to new premises in Wapping *(qv).*

National newspapers in the area are the **Morning Star** at 75 Farringdon Rd in a plain building of concrete and brick by E. Goldfinger (1949) and **The Guardian** at 119 Farringdon Rd.

Dickens House. – *48 Doughty St. Open Mondays to Saturdays 10am to 5pm; closed Sundays, holiday Mondays, 1 January, Easter and 24 to 31 December; £1.50.* **Charles Dickens** and his family lived in the late 18C house for nearly three years, from April 1837 – December 1839. During this stay, he completed *Pickwick Papers,* wrote *Oliver Twist* and *Nicholas Nickleby* besides articles, essays, sketches and letters. The house which contains portraits and mementoes, is particularly interesting for the letters and manuscripts, the early small paperback parts in which the novels were first issued, the prompt copies he used for his public readings and the original illustrations to his works. The drawing-room is decorated as in Dickens' time.

Coram's Fields. – *Guildford St.* A children's park *(adults admitted only if accompanied by a child)* extends over part of the area once occupied by the hospital buildings.

In his sixties, **Thomas Coram,** a successful sea captain, trader and founder-trustee of the Colony of Georgia, was so distressed on his visits to London by the plight of abandoned infants and small children, that he determined to better their lot. Campaigns, petitions to George II, determination, won a charter of incorporation in 1739 and wide support from the rich, the noble and the prominent, money to purchase 56 acres of Lambs Conduit Fields – 20 for buildings and playing fields, the remainder to provide revenue for the hospital by development.

By Coram's death at the age of 83 in 1751, the hospital was soundly established; hundreds of children had been saved. The patronage of artists, begun by Hogarth at the foundation, had already provided outstanding paintings and would continue with gifts and donations by the least and the greatest such as Handel.

In 1926 the hospital was sold and subsequently demolished. The children were moved to new buildings in Berkhampsted; in 1954 these in turn were sold and a policy of fostering inaugurated for the 2-300 children in the foundation's care. Meanwhile the Governors had bought back the site of the present museum building and adjoining Coram Children's Centre. (Coram's tomb is in St Andrew's, Holborn.)

Thomas Coram Foundation for Children. – *40 Brunswick Sq. NW of Coram's Fields. Open Mondays to Fridays 9.30am to 4pm; advisable to check, ☎ : 01-278 2424; closed public holidays; 50p.*

The 1937 neo-Georgian building with a bronze of Thomas Coram after Hogarth before it, incorporates notably the 18C hospital oak staircase (note the cartouches) around an open well, in which stands a jaunty peasant boy, hand on hip, and the Courtroom exactly rebuilt with dark red walls setting off the moulded ceiling and plaster enrichments, the mantelpiece with a relief of Charity Children given by Rysbrack, the oval mirror and the 8 contemporary views of London hospitals (Charterhouse by Gainsborough). The display cases contain coins and tokens left by destitute mothers with their children, rare letters and autographs.

Of particular interest are the full length portrait of *Thomas Coram* painted in 1740 by Hogarth, the Roubiliac bust of *Handel* (both on landing), the *March of the Guards to Finchley*, 1750 by Hogarth (lobby), the portrait of *Weber*. In the picture gallery hang part of the Raphaël cartoon of the *Massacre of the Innocents,* the surprising *Worthies of Great Britain* by Northcote, the full length governors' portraits by Ramsay, Benjamin Wilson, Thomas Hudson, Joshua Reynolds and Millais. In cases round the room are a Georgian silver gilt communion service, pewter porringers, Hogarth's punchbowl of blue and white Lambeth-delft, Handel's fair copy of *Messiah* and other mss, the keyboard of the organ he presented and the 1739 royal charter.

Hospital for Sick Children. – *Gt Ormond St.* Within 20 years of Coram's foundation the Hospital for Sick Children was being erected close by. Today within a small radius there are the Homeopathic and Italian Hospitals (both 19C foundations) and the National Hospital for Nervous Diseases on the site of another 19C children's hospital. Ancillary research institutes, clinics, nurses' homes, now line the streets but the primary association with children remains through the work of the almost entirely rebuilt and vastly extended Gt Ormond St hospital.

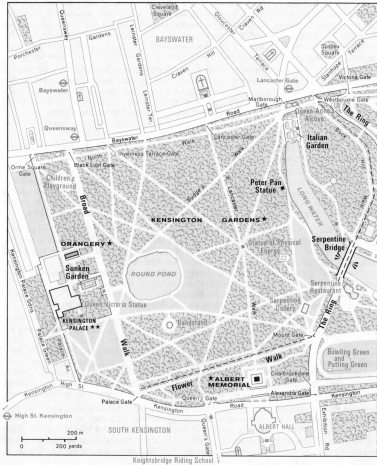

Place of relaxation, free speech, fashion: since 16C, of military manœuvres and encampments, and still of parades and royal salutes; a place, since 1800, for burying pet dogs; more recently for boating, swimming and cracking the ice on Christmas morning for a dip in the **Serpentine** (Lido, 1930). A place for listening to the band, sitting out the interval in a "prom" concert, for watching birds – over 90 species have been recorded in the park and **Hudson Bird Sanctuary,** marked by the Jacob Epstein sculpture **Rima** (1925).

The acres were once, in Saxon times, part of the Manor of Eia which, until "resumed by the King" in 1536, belonged to Westminster Abbey. Henry VIII enclosed the area and having stocked it with deer kept it as a royal chase. In 1637 it was opened as a public park and the crowds came to watch horse-racing and other sports only to be debarred when it was sold by the Commonwealth to a private buyer who, to Pepys' indignation, charged for admission. At the Restoration the contract of sale was cancelled and the park again became public although access was restricted, since it was surrounded by a high wall, replaced by railings only in 1825.

The activities of those who frequented and made use of the park were even more diverse in 18 and 19C than now: the last formal royal hunt was held in 1768; pits were dug along the east and north boundaries to supply clay for bricks to build the new houses of St Marylebone and Mayfair; gunpowder magazines and arms depots were sited in isolated parts; there was a large reservoir on the eastern boundary; soldiers were executed against the wall in the northeast corner; at the same time it was a fashionable carriage and riding promenade – first round the road known as the Tour and then **the Ring** (originally a small inner circle) or along the Row **(Rotten Row).** It was a convenient place for duels and a common spot for footpads (Horace Walpole wrote to all his friends about being robbed in the park in 1749).

Speakers' Corner is a relatively modern feature of the park; not until 1872 did the government recognise the need for a place of public assembly and unfettered discussion.

Marble Arch, a triumphal arch of Italian marble with three closely patterned iron gates but lacking a crowning quadriga or statue *(see p 176)* was designed by **John Nash** in 1828 as the royal entrance to Buckingham Palace. The construction of the palace's east front made the arch superfluous and it was rebuilt in 1851 where **Tyburn gallows** had stood until 1783 when hangings were removed to Newgate. The gallows, first a tree, then a gibbet, was finally replaced by an iron triangle for multiple executions. From the Tower or Newgate the condemned were drawn through the streets on hurdles to be hanged (and sometimes drawn and quartered too) before the great crowds who gathered to hear the last words, see the spectacle and enjoy the side shows. Popular victims were toasted in gin or beer as they passed. A stone in the park railings in the Bayswater Road marks the site.

The south end of the park was transformed in 1825-8 by the erection of a triple arched **screen,** crowned by a sculptured frieze, and a **triumphal arch** surmounted by a colossal equestrian statue of Wellington. Arch and screen, both designed by Decimus Burton, were intended as a royal progress from the palace to the park. In 1883 however the arch was moved to its present

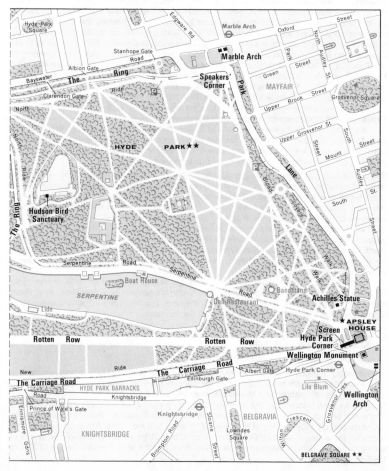

position, the statue transferred to Aldershot and replaced by a quadriga (1912). A new **statue** of the duke mounted on Copenhagen by Boehm (1834-90), guarded by a Grenadier, a Royal Highlander, a Welsh Fusilier and an Inniskilling Dragoon, cast from captured guns, was placed before the entrance to Apsley House. Other monuments at Hyde Park Corner are *David leaning on Goliath's sword* (1925; Derwent Wood), the memorial of the Machine Gun Corps and the Royal Artillery War Memorial in front of the old St George's Hospital building.

Inside the park is the 18ft, so-called, **Achilles** statue by Richard Westmacott cast from captured cannon and incidentally after an antique horse tamer on the Quirinal Hill, Rome and no god and said to have embarrassed the women who presented it to Wellington by its nakedness. Opposite is Byron meditating on a rock, in his own words "a worst bust".

Kensington Gardens★. – The gardens, originally 20 acres and extended finally to 275, were at their prime under Queen Mary, Queen Anne and Queen Caroline, consort of George II and the Royal Gardeners, Henry Wise (portrait in the palace) and his successor in 1728, Charles Bridgman. The original style of geometric and formal wildernesses was transformed in 18C when an octagonal basin, the **Round Pond,** was constructed facing the State Apartments of Kensington Palace *(qv)*. With the pond as focal point, borders were planted around it with flowers and small trees and avenues radiating north and southeast and due east to the New River, the Serpentine and the Long Water terminating in the Italian Garden and Queen Anne's Alcove. Other features of the period which persist are the **Broad Walk,** recently re-planted, and the **Orangery**★ with a massive stone centrepiece by Hawksmoor (1705). Later additions are the Edwardian **sunken garden** in which pleached limes surround brilliant flower beds and a long canal, the statue of **Peter Pan** (1912) to the west and the **Arch** by H. Moore (1979) to the east by the Long Water and the **Flower Walk** north of the Albert Memorial *(qv)*.

The **Serpentine Gallery** holds temporary exhibitions of modern art *(details: see the press)*.

The two parks meet where the Long Water and Serpentine are spanned by the **bridge** designed by John Rennie in 1826-8.

The most wondrous single event to have taken place in the park was, of course, the Great Exhibition of 1851 in the Crystal Palace *(qv)* after which it resumed its role defined a century before by the Elder Pitt as one of "the lungs of London".

IMPERIAL WAR MUSEUM ★ (Lambeth Rd, Southwark) ⎯⎯⎯⎯⎯⎯⎯

Open daily 10am to 6pm; closed 1 January, Good Friday, May Day holiday, 24, 25, 26 December; £2, children £1, free on Fridays. Reference departments: Art, Documents, Printed Books, Film, Photographs, Sound Records, open by appointment Monday to Friday 10am to 5pm.

The museum covers all aspects of warfare, military and civil, allied and enemy, involving Britain and the Commonwealth since 1914 *(see also pp 43, 80 and 131)*.

History. – The museum of what Churchill termed the Age of Violence stands on the site of a 19C madhouse. It was founded in 1917, opened in 1920 at the Crystal Palace, transferred in 1924 to South Kensington and in 1936 to the present building. This, to which the dome and great columned portico were added by Sydney Smirke in 1846, originally comprised the present 900ft wide central area and extensive patients' wings since it was designed in 1812-15 to serve as the new Bethlem Royal Hospital or Bedlam, as it was known, which dated back to the founding of the Priory of St Mary of Bethlehem in Bishopsgate in 1247. In 1547 this had been seized by Henry VIII but then handed over to the City Corporation as a hospital for lunatics. It was transferred in 1676 to Moorfields where the inmates afforded a public spectacle. A century and a half later came the move to Southwark and in 1930 the final remove to Beckenham.

A major redevelopment scheme provides for new galleries with the addition of a glass barrel roof and new buildings at the back of the museum.

The white obelisk milestone, originally at St George's Circus, commemorates Brass Crosby, Lord Mayor of London in 1771 who refused to convict a printer for publishing parliamentary debates. The authorities thereupon imprisoned the mayor in the Tower but he was freed by the populace and press reporting of Commons' proceedings was inaugurated.

The exhibits. – The museum in no sense glorifies war but honours those who served. A wide range of weapons and equipment is on display: armoured fighting vehicles, field guns and small arms, together with models, decorations, uniforms, posters, photographs and paintings. Among the more notable exhibits are a Mark V Tank, "Ole Bill" (most famous of the London "B" type buses which carried troops to the Western Front in the First World War); a Spitfire; the VC and GC Room. Historic documents include Montgomery's "receipt", as Churchill termed it, the typewritten sheet of foolscap which was the Instrument of Surrender of German armed forces in North-west Europe signed, complete with the corrected date, 4 May 1945. There are numerous mementoes of famous men and women – many unknown until all too often a final act of bravery or skill brought posthumous award.

Paintings and sculptures from the museum's permanent collection of 10 000 works of art reflect particularly the individual's lot in war: Orpen, Augustus John, Nevinson, Paul Nash, Kennington, Piper, Moore, Stanley Spencer, Sutherland, Topolski, painted food queues, people sleeping in tube shelters, the wounded, service life, boredom...

ISLINGTON (Islington) ⎯⎯⎯⎯⎯⎯⎯⎯⎯⎯⎯⎯⎯⎯⎯⎯⎯⎯⎯

For south of the Angel see Clerkenwell.

Islington, "a pleasantly seated country town" (John Strype, 1643-1737) became a suburb in 17C when the better off came there while the poor, numbering some 300 000, erected shacks and tenements on Finsbury and Moorfields when all fled the City after the Plague and the Fire. Islington became fashionable: tea gardens were set up around the wells (Clerkenwell, Sadler's Wells etc); taverns flagged the old well trodden roads from the north – following the course for centuries and until the coming of the railways, farmers and herdsmen drove cattle, sheep and swine south, resting them in fields and pens around the village, which became known as one of London's dairies. (Finally the beasts were driven down St John St to Smithfield, or, in 19/20C, to the Caledonian Market.)

In 19C, **Cruikshank,** who lived in Highbury Terrace, was commenting graphically in *London going out of Town* or the *March of Bricks and Mortar* on the new builder developers, including Thomas Cubitt, who were laying out squares and terraces and ever meaner streets soon to be inhabited by workers in the new light industries invading the neighbourhood (pop 1801 – 10 000; 1881 – 283 000; 1901 – 335 000). By this century Islington, and the Angel in particular, had become a synonym for slums, grime and grinding poverty, hilarious, raucous cockney kids, rough pubs, the Cally Market, the gas-lit glories of Collins Music Hall.

Since the war restoration and repainting have returned terraces and squares to their precise, well-groomed lines; slums have been largely replaced by 4 to 8 storey blocks of brick, reminder of the locality's past as a major London brickfield.

Islington and Highbury

The Angel. – Five main thoroughfares converge on the ancient crossroads. The Angel Inn which stood on the corner gave its name to the area. New office buildings signal the revival of the area.

Duncan Terrace, Colebrooke Row. – The brick, or brick and stucco three floor houses with shallow first floor iron balconies, built in long uninterrupted terraces (apart from postwar rebuilding in Colebrooke Row) date from 1761.

Charlton Place, a crescent and diameter complete, of 3 storey houses with rounded doorways and ground floor windows, leads off, left, to Camden Passage.

Camden Passage. – *Upper Street.* The quaint old alley is lined with small shops, arcades, restaurants, two Victorian pubs, and the newly built "Georgian Village". It is a major antiques centre with shops opening in surrounding streets. The small specialist shops can be searched for antique furniture, *art nouveau* ornaments in china and opalescent glass, Sèvres porcelain, heavy plate cameras, silverware, military mementoes. Markets days: antiques *(Wednesdays and Saturdays),* books *(Thursdays).*

The Little Angel Marionette Theatre. – *Dagmar Passage. Open weekends and school holidays; for details* ☎ *01-226 1787.*

A former temperance hall, north of St Mary's church, has since 1961 been a flourishing theatre devoted to puppetry. Marionettes, rod and shadow puppets, costumes and settings for the productions are made in the adjacent workshop.

Islington Green. – The shaded triangular green is pinpointed at its centre by a statue of Sir Hugh Myddelton *(qv).* A plaque marks the site (north side) where from 1862 until the middle of this century Collins Music Hall was boisterous with song.

Business Design Centre. – *Between Upper St and Liverpool Rd.* It is housed in the old **Royal Agricultural Hall** built in 1861-2 with a domed iron and glass roof and a grand entrance arch flanked by towers with pavilion roofs, and used in turn for cattle shows, military tournaments, revivalist meetings, bullfighting (1888) and Cruft's Dog Show (1891-1939). After many years of dereliction it has now been restored to its former glory.

Canonbury. – Canonbury is crossed by a network of streets and squares lined by early 19C terraced houses of which **Canonbury Square★,** since it is complete and beautifully proportioned, is the prime example. Minor connecting roads, such as Canonbury Grove with small country cottages overlooking a New River backwater *(towpath walks),* and others, like Alwynne Rd in which later 19C villas and semi-detached houses stand in the shade of tall plane trees, add to the atmosphere. Also in Canonbury is that north London landmark the Tower.

Canonbury Tower. – *(Now leased by a repertory drama company).* A square dark red brick tower 60ft high is all that remains of the manor rebuilt in 1509 on land owned in 13C by St John's priory. In 1570 Canonbury was acquired for £2 000 as his country residence by Sir John Spencer, Lord Mayor and owner of Crosby House in Bishopsgate who largely rebuilt his out-of-town house. Buildings which now abut the tower date from the 18/19C. Of the five late 18C houses overlooking Canonbury Place, the most imposing is the pedimented two storey **Canonbury House,** with a central door framed by slender Ionic Pillars.

Highbury Place. – By 19C Highbury had fallen into the hands of undistinguished developers except for Highbury Place, 1774-9, Highbury Terrace, 1789, Highbury Crescent, 1830s, where detached and semi-detached villas had been erected for the more opulent.

Holloway

The villages of Lower and Upper Holloway merged in 19C. The high street, Holloway Rd, continued north to what, since 1813, has been known as the **Archway** after the viaduct designed by John Nash to span the road (A1) cut 80ft below through the hill. Nash's bridge endured until 1897 when it was replaced by Alexander Binnie's metal construction.

Pentonville Prison. – *(East side).* The prison (1840), hemmed in by neighbouring flats, fronts the main thoroughfare. Most famous of those executed in Pentonville are Dr Crippen (1910) and Roger Casement (1916).

Caledonian Market Tower. – The tower, on the site of the 18C Copenhagen Tea Garden and Tavern, remains a landmark although the general meat market closed down in 1939 and the wholesale in 1963. White, Italianate, it rises to a square loggia with a pointed roof. The farmers, drovers, butchers who thronged the market, the banks, post office, shops and offices, the vast sheds, the 10 000 head of cattle and 8-10 000 sheep and pigs that weekly from 1876-1939 arrived, driven along the two main roads or transported by rail, have all vanished to be replaced by a still life of undulating lawns, overlooked by the low red brick ranges of borough apartment blocks and the new hall of residence of the N London Polytechnic. The only other reminder of the "Cally" are the distinctive 18/19C square brick Lamb, Lion and White Horse pubs, which marked 3 of the 4 corners of the 70 acre site.

Holloway Prison. – *Parkhurst Rd.* Holloway, erected in 1849, a women's prison since 1903, ceased to be the famous north London landmark in 1978 when the Warwick Castle towers gave place to an unobtrusive complex of high walled terra cotta brick buildings.

Michael Sobell Sports Centre. – *Hornsey Rd (junction with Tollington/Isledon Rd) open daily 9am to 10.30pm; Sundays 10am to 9.30pm; admission 25p or by membership.*

Circular, massively built of ribbed rough cast and brown tinted glass, the centre which opened in November 1973, is used weekly by 6 000 schoolchildren, 9 000 adults to practise cricket, judo, badminton, weight-lifting, play squash, snooker... to skate – the glass and lighting transforming the figures on the ice into a silent, Lowry-like scene.

The sports centre was launched with £1 100 000 from Sir Michael Sobell for the building, equipped from a further £1 000 000 from the Variety Club of Great Britain and designed free by Richard Seifert.

KENNINGTON (Lambeth)

Map pp 5-8 (F/YZ).

Kennington and Vauxhall were transformed from a rural hinterland of marshes, manorial estates, market gardens and even vineyards, into a prosperous and, finally, densely populated inner London area by the construction of Westminster Bridge in 1750. Until that time communication with the capital had remained by cross-river wherry as it had been in 1339 in the days of the Black Prince when he was granted the manor of Kennington and Vauxhall by his father Edward III. The Prince, whose way to the river is still marked by Black Prince Rd, built a splendid palace, it is said, although nothing remains, Henry VIII having pulled it down in 1531 (plaque on Edinburgh House, 160 Kennington Lane).

James I vested the manor in the royal heir as Duke of Cornwall and so it remains to this day. By the time Prinny was traversing the manor on visits to his new Pavilion in Brighton (1815), the paved Kennington Rd provided easy access to the capital for those who preferred to live outside and, coinciding with the increased commercialisation of the riverside, tempted others to move inland. Kennington Rd, Kennington Park Rd, Kennington Lane and a network of streets which gradually grew up between them, were bordered first by Georgian houses and terraces (Kennington Rd: nos 104, 121 (1770), 150, Kennington Park Rd: no 180), later by Victorian houses and bay windowed cottages.

Vauxhall Gardens. – The gardens, on a site north of Harleyford Rd, were greatly favoured by Evelyn and Pepys who frequently "took water to Fox-hall, to the **Spring Garden** and there walked an hour with great pleasure". In the 18C the garden of flowers, arbours, shaded walks, light refreshments and simple pleasures was modernised and provided music, sophisticated meals and pastimes, including nightly firework displays. But as the crowds thickened, knavery increased; the gardens became notorious and in the 19C they closed.

Lambeth Palace. – *Guided tours for groups on application to the Bursar.*

The primate, requiring a seat close, but not too close, to the crown, in 12C obtained a parcel of land on the far side of the river from Westminster, then accessible by wherry and public horseferry. Lambeth House, as it was first called, was commenced in the early 13C. Despite 19C additions and alterations, the mellow red brick palace, with its high, crenellated wall, 1490 gateway, 1434-35 Lollards' Tower, remains medieval in appearance. Especially notable inside are the hammerbeam roofed Great Hall, Library and Guard Room.

The Tradescant Trust. – *Open March to mid-December, Monday to Friday, 11am to 3pm; Sundays 10.30am to 5pm; other times by appointment; shop and brass-rubbing.*

The Museum of Garden History, incorporating a centre for lectures and exhibitions, was founded by the Tradescant Trust (1977) in the redundant church of St Mary-at-Lambeth. The two John Tradescants, father and son, who are buried in the churchyard next to Admiral Bligh of the Bounty (also memorial inside the church), who lived at 100 Lambeth Road, were gardeners to the first Lord Salisbury and Charles I. They planted the first physic garden in 1628 at their house in Lambeth where they also exhibited a collection of "all things strange and rare" which later formed the nucleus of the Ashmolean Museum in Oxford. A 17C garden, with a knot garden as the centrepiece, has been created in the churchyard using plants which the Tradescants grew in their Lambeth garden and other plants of the period.

Lawrence Lee designed the window depicting Adam and Eve and the Tradescants.

The Oval. – The ground was a market garden when acquired in 1845 as a cricket ground by the newly formed Surrey County Cricket Club. At the east end are iron gates erected in memory of Sir Jack Hobbs (d 1963); to the north the gasometers. Seen from the air, the ground stands out as the unequivocal landmark of south London.

Kennington Park. – Halfway along the road frontage, as the inscription in gold letters announces, is a "Model house for families erected by HRH Prince Albert", a prototype workman's cottage commissioned by the Prince for the 1851 Exhibition. After centuries as common grazing and popular meeting ground – some 200 000 Chartists had gathered there intending to march on Westminster – the park was enclosed in 1852.

Streets and squares. – Vauxhall Bridge traffic flows into Bridgefoot, also known as Vauxhall Cross, and now increased to six main roads, one, Nine Elms Lane, leading to the New Covent Garden Market (transferred from central London in 1974). From the Albert Embankment (1866-9), Black Prince Rd leads to **Lambeth Walk** (east side), grass verged and overlooked by new flats, far removed from the aged housing and cockney gusto of the war time song, and Woodstock Court (west) a model, two storey precinct constructed around a fountained court (1930). The north end of Kennington Road is notable for a long terrace (nos 121-143) dating from 1770s. Charlie Chaplin lived at no 287 *(plaque).* Kennington Park Rd has a very long, late 18C, terrace down its east side (91-165), appealing as a unit and for its fanlights (no 125). On its west side (beside the City and Guilds of London Art School) is the large, late Georgian, **Cleaver Sq.** In Kennington Lane (next to the NAAFI, nos 225-229) is an early 19C terrace beneath a central pediment, with apple green doors against white frames and window sashes. To the north in Courtenay Sq with its spring flowering trees the two storey 1837-9 brick houses are delightfully transformed by white painted, summer-house shaped, canopies supported on ironwork trellis pillars before each modest front door.

The village of Kensington was for centuries manorial, with a few large houses at the centre of fields. It increased slowly from small houses lining the main road to squares and tributary streets as estates and separate parcels of land were sold. Among the famous mansions were Nottingham House later Kensington Palace, Campden House, Notting Hill House later Aubrey House, Holland Park House and, on the site of the Albert Hall, Gore House, the home of William Wilberforce until 1823 and for 12 years from 1836 the residence of "the gorgeous" Lady Blessington whose circle included poets, novelists, artists, journalists, French exiles: Wellington, Brougham, Landseer, Tom Moore, Bulwer Lytton, Thackeray, Dickens, Louis Napoleon...

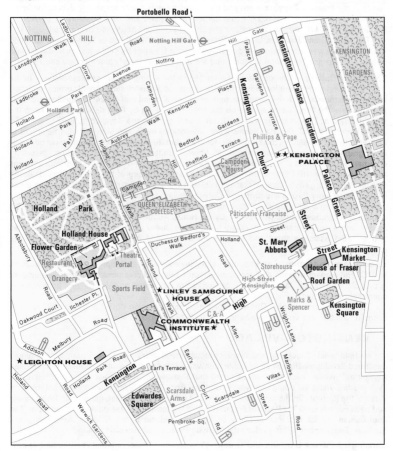

■ KENSINGTON PALACE★★

Entrance: NE corner. Open 9am (1pm Sundays) to 5pm; closed 1 January, Good Friday, 24, 25, 26 December; £2.60; children £1.30, OAPs £1.70.

"The house is very noble, tho not greate, the Gardens about it very delicious". – Since its purchase in 1689 by William III, Kensington Palace has passed through three phases: under the House of Orange it was the monarch's private residence with **Wren** as principal architect; under the early Hanoverians it was designated as a royal palace with **William Kent** in charge of alterations; since 1760 it has been a residence for members of the royal family.

"Kensington is ready" wrote Queen Mary to her husband, William, in July 1690 and, disliking Whitehall, she moved in. The house was not to be free of builders and carpenters until 1702 when it had grown from an early 17C Jacobean house, rebuilt in 1661, to a rambling mansion around three courts. Throughout Wren kept to a style befitting a modest house – it was known as Kensington House in 17 and 18C – in red brick beneath slate roofs.

Decoration was limited to the finely carved William and Mary monogram in the hood above the entrance to the Queen's Staircase and the royal arms on the pediment of the turreted clock tower. When Hawksmoor, working for Wren in 1695-6, designed the south front, the only embellishment was a central attic screen topped by Portland stone vases. Subsequent external modifications were of a minor character: a Georgian doorway acceding to the Queen's Staircase, a portico on the west front.

The **State Apartments** are approached up the Queen's Staircase designed by Wren (1691).

The Queen's Apartments: Gallery, Closet, Dining and Drawing Rooms, Bedroom. – The 84ft gallery is rich in carving, with cornice and doorheads by **William Emmett** and sumptuous surrounds to the gilt Vauxhall mirrors above the fireplace in the gallery by Grinling Gibbons in 1691. Portraits in the rooms are personal: *Peter the Great* in armour by Kneller in commemoration of his visit in 1698, *William III* as king and Prince of Orange, *Queen Mary* by Wissing, *Anne Hyde* by Lely and in the adjoining closet where the final quarrel (1710) took place between "Mrs Freeman" and "Mrs Morley", *Queen Anne* and *William, Duke of Gloucester* by Kneller. In the Dining Room there is a painting of Katherine Elliott who was James II's nurse; in the Drawing Room Kneller painted *Queen Anne* in profile and the first Royal Gardener, *Henry Wise*. The furniture includes an 18C mahogany cabinet (gallery), a late 17C inlaid cabinet, 17-18C Oriental porcelain and a fine Thomas Tompion barometer of c 1695, one of many possessed by William III who was a chronic asthmatic (drawing room). In the bedroom are a state bed of James II and an ornate, mid 17C, writing cabinet with Boulle mounts, marquetry and semi-precious stone inlays.

Privy and Presence Chambers, King's Staircase and Gallery. – The lofty rooms designed by Colen Campbell in 1718-20 for George I, bear William Kent's strong decorative imprint. The **Privy Chamber,** above busts of distinguished 17-18C scientists and David Garrick, blue and white Oriental porcelain and Mortlake tapestries of the months, has an allegorical ceiling of George I as Mars; the **Presence Chamber,** a red and blue on white ceiling with arabesque decoration in the Pompeian manner by Kent in 1724 (the earliest in England and later popularised by Adam). Remaining from 17C are the cornice and the Grinling Gibbons pearwood overmantel.

The **King's Grand Staircase,** built by Wren in 1689, was altered first in 1692-3 when the Tijou iron balustrade was incorporated and again in 1696 for George I by Kent who covered walls and ceiling with *trompe l'œil* paintings including a dome and gallery of contemporary courtiers.

The King's Gallery. – The gallery was intended as the setting for the greatest pictures in the royal collection and decoration was, therefore, limited to an elaborately carved cornice, enriched window surrounds and the practical and ornamental wind-dial (1624) connected from its position over the fireplace to a vane on the roof. The ceiling by Kent depicts scenes from the story of Ulysses. The gallery is hung with 17C paintings from the Royal collection.

Although the 19C **Victorian Rooms** were redecorated by Queen Mary, all else belonged to and epitomises Queen Victoria and her family – furniture, wallpaper, ornaments, portraits, photographs, toys and dollshouse, dried flowers under glass domes, beading, tasseling, commemorative china... The **Council Chamber** at the far end of the east front, contains mementoes of the 1851 Exhibition, including the famous picture of the opening crowds in the Crystal Palace, a garish jewel casket with inlaid portraits of the royal family and a massive carved Indian ivory throne and footstool. Only the ceiling of arabesques, figures and medallions remains of Kent's Baroque decoration in the **King's Drawing Room.**The musical clock (1730) depicts four famous figures (Alexander, Cyrus, Ninos, Augustus). In the **Cupola Room,** high and square with a vault patterned in blue and gold, where Queen Victoria was baptised, are trophies and gilded Classical statues and busts divided by fluted pilasters and a colossal marble chimneypiece.

Court Dress Collection. – An imaginative display traces the evolution of court dress from 18 to 20C. The elegant dresses and accessories, court suits and ceremonial uniforms resplendent with gold and silver, lace and embroidery, worn at levées and courts are presented in contemporary settings.

The Red Saloon in which Queen Victoria held her Accession Privy Council in 1837 and the room in which she is said to have been born in 1819 are also on view.

■ KENSINGTON VILLAGE

In 1846 when Thackeray and his daughters moved into a house in Young St, the eldest described **Kensington High St** as "a noble highway, skirted by beautiful old houses with scrolled iron gates", while Thackeray himself noted that there were "omnibuses every two minutes". Within a few years the population was to multiply from 70 to 120 000; shops spread along both sides of the High St. On the south side of the road is **Kensington Market,** gaudy with fashions old and new. Further west **The House of Fraser** offers all the facilities of a large department store. The **Roof Garden** (no 99, entrance in Derry St; lift) was laid out in the 1930s in three sections – Spanish, Tudor and a water garden; the fountain is fed by an Artesian well.

Kensington Palace Gardens and Green. – The private avenue, guarded at either end, is now almost exclusively the preserve of ambassadorial residences and embassies of which the most remarkable is the modern Czechoslovakian complex at the north end. The original houses were built in mid 19C when the palace kitchen gardens were sold for development. More or less Italianate in style their opulence earned the avenue the sobriquet, Millionaires' Row.

Kensington Church St. – The modern blocks of flats and the individual houses, large and small, built on the Campden House estate at the top of the hill, give way to specialist shops – clothes, ornaments, antiques and books – at the southern end, where the street winds east skirting a cluster of narrow lanes and footpaths around the church school which is adorned with a boy and girl in 18C costume over the door. On the corner with the High Street an unusual vaulted cloister leads to the parish church of **St Mary Abbots,** built in 19C Early English style, with a towering spire 278ft high, although the dedication goes back to 11C.

Kensington Sq. – The square, one of the oldest in London with houses dating from 17-19C, is as varied in design as the people who have lived in it: Sir Hubert Parry (no 17), John Stuart Mill (no 18), Mrs Patrick Campbell (no 33). The two oldest houses are nos 11 and 12 in the southeast corner; a cartouche over the door mentions previous owners: the Duchess Mazarin (Henrietta Mancini, niece of the Cardinal) 1692-8, Archbishop Herring 1737 and Talleyrand 1792-4.

Holland House and Park. – Open 7.30am to dusk. Dutch Garden floodlit until midnight. The restored east wing and George VI Hostel by Sir Hugh Casson serve as a youth hostel; open-air theatre performances (June to August, ☎ 01-602 7344) are held in the courtyard before the ruined house (bombed 1940). The gate piers were carved by Nicholas Stone in 1629. A restaurant occupies part of the 17C stable block converted to a conservatory in the early 19C; the ice house is used for exhibitions. The woodland has been re-established and the gardens replanted after long neglect.

It is 100-200 years since the house was in its heyday and approaching 400 since Sir Walter Cope, City merchant and courtier, built the first large house in the scattered village of Kensington. The mansion, characterised by Dutch gables, and known until 1624 as Cope's Castle, was lavishly furnished, equipped with a library and soon became a place of entertainment for king and court. Advanced wings on either side of the central range, were added by Cope's daughter whose husband, in 1624, for soldierly and other services was created Earl Holland. The tradition of hospitality was maintained in the 2nd earl's time and extended when his widow married **Joseph Addison.** In mid 18C the politician, Henry Fox, bought Holland House and was himself created Baron Holland. He was rich, a spendthrift and corrupt; he knew everyone, entertained lavishly and fathered, as his second son, **Charles James Fox,** who continued to frequent the house when it passed to his nephew, 3rd Baron Holland, politician, writer, literary patron and the last great host of Holland House. Among those who dined and visited frequently were the Prince Regent, Sheridan, Wilberforce, Canning, William Lamb the future Lord Melbourne, Byron, Thomas Moore, Talleyrand, Louis Napoleon, Macaulay (whose own house, Holly Lodge, stood on the site now occupied by Queen Elizabeth College), William IV, and almost the last visitor, Prince Albert – little wonder that Sydney Smith in a bread and butter letter to his hostess had once written "I do not believe all Europe can produce as much knowledge, wit and worth as passes in and out of your door".

Commonwealth Institute★. – *Kensington High St. Open daily 10am to 5.30pm; Sundays 2 to 5pm; closed 1 January, 24, 25, 26 December. Restaurant, library and resource centre (appt desirable); Education Centre: lunch room, activities room (advance booking); bookshop.*

The striking building lying back from the main road, with its 4 peaked, green copper roof, on glass curtain walls, was opened by the Queen in 1962. Sixty-nine years earlier her great, great, grand-mother, Queen Victoria, had performed a similar ceremony in a Renaissance style building equally

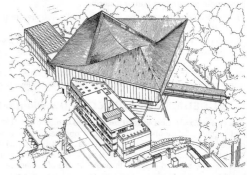

(After photograph by Aerofilms)

Commonwealth Institute.

outstanding in its time, the Imperial Institute, of which only the Queen's Tower remains *(p 108).* Inside, wide circular galleries on three levels present a colourful view of the Commonwealth (60 member countries) with the aid of backdrops such as the Snowy Mountains and artefacts from Nigerian house posts to a Manx cross, a model of the Brunei Saifuddin Mosque in its water village, a festival dragon from Hong Kong... Audio-visual presentations and special exhibitions.

Leighton House★. – *12 Holland Park Rd. Open weekdays 11am to 5pm; closed Sundays, and bank holidays.* Lord Leighton (1830-96) Victorian painter supreme, "high priest of the cult of eclectic beauty" as he has been described, remains most originally reflected in the house which he built for himself in 1866. In it the High Victorian art of the domestic rooms contrasts with ceramic tiles from the Middle East and others in brilliant blues by **William de Morgan** on the hall and stairs and even more exotically in his creation of an **Arab Hall.** This has a mosaic floor around a cool fountain and, on the walls, sets of 13, 16 and 17C tiles from Rhodes, Damascus and Cairo, tiles bearing inscriptions from the Koran, flowers and birds, brought back from their travels by Leighton himself and his friends, including Sir Richard Burton.

Linley Sambourne House★. – *18 Stafford Terrace. Open March to October, Wednesdays 10am to 4pm, Sundays, 2 to 5pm; groups by appointment ☎ 01-994 1019 on other days; £2.*

Edward Linley Sambourne, a leading Punch cartoonist and book illustrator, moved into this later Victorian town house on its completion in 1874. The original wall decoration by William Morris and the furniture, listed in an inventory dated 1877, have survived largely unaltered. Cartoons by Sambourne and his contemporaries line the stairs; pictures occupy every inch of spare wall space in the crowded rooms. The fan *(principal bedroom)* signed by Millais, Frith, Alma-Tadema and Watts testifies to the family's artistic connections; the back bedroom typifies Edwardian bachelordom. The stained glass panels were designed by Sambourne. Note the enclosed window boxes like mini greenhouses, the aquarium on the landing, the ventilators incorporated in the ceiling roses, the bell pulls and speaking tubes complete with whistles.

At the west end of Kensington is Earl's Terrace, a uniform brick range of large houses of 1800-10 and, just behind, **Edwardes Sq** with west and east ranges of more modest 3 storey houses built between 1811-20 as a single undertaking – even to the balcony, garden and square ironwork. In contrast, in the square's southeast corner stands a robust Victorian pub, the Scarsdale Arms, "established in 1837 ». Just south again is Pembroke Sq with Georgian ranges on three sides, matching iron balconies and, again, a pub in the southeast corner.

■ ADDITIONAL SIGHTS

Institut Français. – The institute buildings, although in *art nouveau* style, date only from 1938. It is a cultural and educational centre founded in 1910.

The number of students enrolled in the Institut and the nearby Lycée respectively is 1 250 and 2 250 of whom many are English. The French community in London now numbers 35 000.

Baden-Powell House. – The house built in 1961, signalled outside by a bareheaded statue of B-P, is the headquaters of the Scout movement and a hostel for visiting scouts. There is a memorial exhibition to the founder inside *(open 9am to 6pm).*

Ismaili Centre. – This distinctive modern building faced in grey-blue marble and adorned with slim windows, designed by the Casson-Conder Partnership, serves as a religious and cultural Ismaili centre. The Zamana Gallery holds temporary exhibitions devoted to the art and culture of developing countries.

Michelin House. – The 1910 building, the headquarters of the Michelin Tyre PLC until 1985, is a genuine example of the *art nouveau* style. The decoration is grandiose, the theme on the tiled front being the initial M and tyres which appear in the patterning and, three dimensionally, as supports to the gable containing the upper area of the colossal central window. On the sides and within is a **frieze** in which each panel illustrates a turn of the century motor car rally – note the strokes to indicate speed!

Royal Marsden and Brompton Chest Hospitals. – The Royal Marsden Hospital was built in 1859, the Brompton in 1844-54. Attached to the second is the Cardiothoracic Institute and to the first the Institute of Cancer Research (including the Chester Beatty Research Institute), both part of London University.

South of the **Old Brompton Rd** graceful **Pelham Crescent** (mid 19C) is probably by Basevi, while the fine white-stuccoed houses in **The Boltons,** laid out in a mandorla crescent, are by Cubitt. In between are Onslow Gardens, a typical mid 19C development of tall cream stuccoed houses with advanced pillared porches, and 19C artisan cottages in Elm Place and its immediate vicinity, still surrounded by small gardens brilliant with flowers throughout the summer. The Tudor style architecture of **Queen's Elm Square** reflects the tradition that Elizabeth I sheltered here under an elm tree during a storm.

Brompton Cemetery. – The vast necropolis, founded in the mid 19C, contains hundreds of neo-Gothic, Egyptian, Baroque style, tombs.

Portobello Rd. – *Notting Hill Gate. Market: all day Saturdays.*

The winding road, once a cart-track through the fields from the Notting Hill turnpike, comes unhurriedly to life on Saturdays as people arrive to search the shop tables and stalls between the Chepstow Villas crossroads and Elgin Crescent. Victoriana and later silver and chinaware, a stamp stall, small items, provide the interest; the motley crowd creates the atmosphere.

■ MUSEUMS and COLLEGES (Kensington)

The Great Exhibition Inheritance. – The exhibition of 1851, the first in the international field and initially bitterly and often spitefully opposed in parliament, was conceived, planned and opened in less than two years so steadfast was Prince Albert. Joseph Paxton's glasshouse or **Crystal Palace,** covered 19 acres in Hyde Park. It was tall enough to enclose the giant elms on the site, capable of rapid erection through the use of prefabricated unit parts and was beautiful to boot! It was apparently the problem posed by sparrows roosting in the elm trees which caused Wellington's celebrated retort: "Try sparrow hawks, M'am". Inside were the products of 13 937 exhibitors demonstrating man's inventiveness and 19C British achievement in particular. It was an exhibition which excited everyone: Queen Victoria, Wellington and some 6 039 195 others and it made a net profit of just under £200 000. The Crystal Palace was dismantled and re-erected at Sydenham (burnt down 1936); the financial profit Prince Albert proposed should be

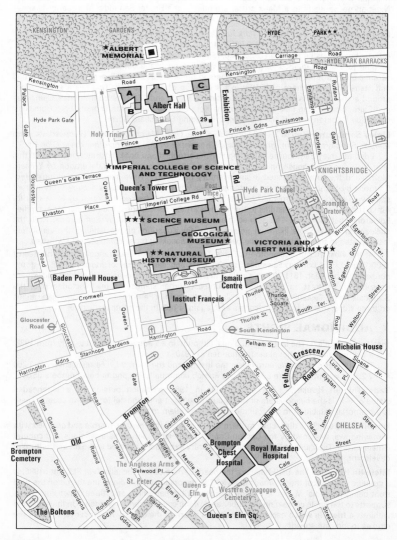

spent in establishing a great educational centre in south Kensington by buying land on which have become established the world famous museums and colleges to be found there today. In the event 86 acres were bought and there began a sequence of construction.

1856:	William Cubitt erects a utilitarian glass and iron building – the "Brompton Boilers" – in Cromwell Rd to house former 1851 exhibits and various art collections.
1861-1863:	Commemorative Exhibition statue erected (now sited behind Albert Hall).
1861:	Prince Albert dies; the Albert Memorial (1864-72) erected. 1876 unveiled.
1862:	International Exhibition held on site now occupied by Natural History Museum.
1867-1871:	Albert Hall built on site of Gore House as national memorial to Prince Consort.
1867-1871:	Huxley Building erected, Exhibition Road (originally as the Science Schools).
1873-1880:	Natural History Museum.
1875:	National School of Music later (1883) Royal College of Music founded in building, since 1903 the Royal College of Organists.
1881-1884:	City and Guilds College; rebuilt 1962 as Imperial College extensions.
1883:	Royal College of Music (transferred from previous building).
1887-1893:	Imperial Institute. Buildings demolished 1957-65, save for existing central tower, to assist expansion of Imperial College.
1899-1909:	Victoria and Albert Museum.
1909-1913:	Royal School of Mines (now part of Imperial College).
1914:	Science Museum.
1933-1935:	Geological Museum.
1960-1964:	Royal College of Art beside Albert Hall, first stage of a development to centralise College buildings scattered in south Kensington.

Albert Memorial★. – Proverbial as the epitome of mid-Victorian taste and sentiment, the memorial which stands at the summit of 4 wide flights of granite steps, was designed by Sir George Gilbert Scott as a neo-Gothic spire of 175ft and, as such, ornamented with mosaics, pinnacles and a cross. A 14ft bronze figure of the Prince Consort sits at the centre surrounded by allegorical statues of four continents and a frieze of 169 named portrait figures of architects, artists, composers, poets.

Albert Hall. – The round hall was designed by Capt Fowke, a Royal Engineer. Nearly 1/4 mile in circumference, built of red brick with a shallow glass and iron dome, it is the foil in shape and ornament to the memorial since its only decoration is an upper frieze of figures illustrating the Arts and Sciences. Reunions, pop and jazz sessions, exhibitions, boxing, political meetings, conferences and concerts, particularly the eight week summer series of **Promenade Concerts,** fill the hall with up to 7 000 people at a time.

Royal College of Art (A). – The Darwin Building, designed by Cadbury-Brown, with eight floors of studios and workshops is built of purple brown brick, dark concrete and glass. It dates from 1961 and, uniquely in such a district, is without applied adornment.

Royal College of Organists (B). – The small building, 4 floors tall, 3 bays wide, designed by another RE, Lt H H Cole, in 1875, is almost obscured by its ornate decoration

The Albert Memorial.

(F W Moody) of chocolate brown panels patterned in cream, a frieze of putti carrying musical instruments, garlands incorporating the VR monogram around the door.

Royal Geographical Society (f 1830) (C). – Against the outer wall are statues of Shackleton and Livingstone. The many gabled brick house was designed in 1874 by Norman Shaw. The map room *(open for research only Mondays to Fridays 10am to 5pm)* contains 30 000 old and historic maps besides the largest modern private collection in Europe.

British Library National Sound Archive. – *29 Exhibition Road. Open Mondays to Fridays 9.30am to 4.30pm (9pm Thursdays).* The Queen Anne style building (1878) was designed by J.-J. Stevenson. The collection includes three quarters of a million discs and more than 45 000 hours of tape recordings: music, oral history, sound effects and documentary material, spoken literature and drama, language and dialect. It is principaly a research centre but a permanent exhibition exploring the history of records and recordings is open to the public.

Royal College of Music (D). – The college is an architect's building of 1893, as opposed to an RE's; Sir Arthur Blumfield designed in dark red brick and grey slate, stepped and decorated gables between pavilion roofed towers and finally quartered his construction with pepper pot turrets after the French style. Inside are the **Department of Portraits** and the highly prized **Museum of Instruments,** including the Donaldson, Tagore, Hipkins and Ridley Collections, Handel spinet and Haydn clavichord. *Open in term on Mondays and Wednesdays, 11am to 4.30pm; £1.*

Imperial College of Science and Technology★. – The schools which go to make up Imperial College extend from either side of the Royal College of Music in Prince Consort Rd south to the Science Museum, apart from the small enclaves occupied by Holy Trinity Church (1909 replacement of a chapel of 1609 itself a rebuilding of the chapel of a former leper hospital), the Edwardian Post Office Building and the Underground exit. With the exception of the neo-

KENSINGTON★★

Georgian 1909-13 **Royal School of Mines** (**E**) of stone with an apsed entrance flanked by giant sculptures, the buildings date from the mid'50s. They are vast but homogeneous in proportion and human in scale, clean lined, in single, right-angled and hollow square ranges, surrounding interconnected quadrangles. From one of the quadrangles, guarded at its foot by a pair of lions, rises the old **Queen's Tower**, 280ft high, brick and stone below, green copper and gold turreted at the summit, last relic of Colcutt's Imperial Institute (1887-93), erected following the Colonial Exhibition of 1886; history has been imaginatively preserved in the midst of the present. *Open June to August; £1.50.*

Down Exhibition Rd on the east side is the Mormons' Hyde Park Chapel (1960) with a needle spire of gilded bricks.

Geological Museum★. – *Exhibition Rd. Open daily 10am (Sundays 1pm) to 6pm; closed 1 January, Good Friday, May Day holiday, 24, 25, 26 December; combined ticket with Natural History Museum £2, children, OAPs £1. Library daily 10am to 4pm; closed weekends.*

The museum developed as a result of the Geological Survey of Great Britain of 1835 when specimens were accumulated which in 1935, the centenary of the Survey, were established in the present building, now part of the Institute of Geological Studies. There are four displays on the ground floor – the Story of the Earth (exhibiting a piece of moonrock), Britain before Man, British Fossils *(mezzanine)* and Treasures of the Earth. Each is complete in itself and a good introduction to the upper floors where *(first floor)* the detailed geology of England, Wales and Scotland and Britain's offshore oil and gas exploration and exploitation are illustrated in bays, using rock specimens, maps, relief models, photographs, dioramas, and audiovisual displays, and *(second floor)* metalliferous ores and useful non-metallic minerals (including borax and salt) are displayed, together with building stone, marble *(note the entrance arch)* and exhibits of coal and oil. The world-famous gemstone collection occupies the central area of the ground floor: diamonds, rubies, sapphires, garnets, emeralds.

Science Museum★★★. – *Exhibition Rd. Open daily 10am (Sundays 11am) to 6pm; closed 1 January, Good Friday, 24, 25, 26 December. £2, children OAPs £1. Library open daily (except Sundays and holiday weekends) 10am to 5.30pm.*

Where to begin? – This factory-laboratory of man's continuing invention extends over 7 acres; there are innumerable working models, handles to pull, buttons to push. The Wellcome Galleries on the History of Medicine opened on the fourth and fifth floors in early 1980s.

FLOOR	SUBJECTS	NAMED OBJECTS
Ground floor	Introduction (mezzanine); motive and mechanical power (water wheels, hydraulic turbines); steam boilers, turbines; hot air, gas, oil and electric power	Pelton wheel: Watt beam pumping and rotative engines; Trevithick engine and boiler; Mill engine (1903); Lenoir, Akroyd, Stuart, Diesel engines.
	Space exploration: rockets	Apollo 10 capsule, Phobos probe, Mir space station, panorama of surface of Venus. Foucault pendulum (model).
	Transport (road and rail): roads, bridges, tunnels; fire engines	1888 Benz, 1734 fire engine, Puffing Billy (1813), Rocket (1829).
Lower ground	Children's gallery; firemaking, locks, 19C domestic appliances	Byrant & May firemaking appliances, Temple of Vesta fire machine, dioramas on transport and lighting; kitchen and bathroom (1880).
1st floor	Telecommunications; iron and steel; glass; plastics; agriculture; gas manufacture, distribution; meteorology; time measurement – clocks; map-making, surveying; food and nutrition (new gallery) Activity centre	Mascot 2000, Marconi beam transmitter; open hearth furnace; drilling rig; milking parlour; barographs, anemometers; Wells Cathedral clock; Ramsden's theodolite, Roman groma.
2nd floor	Printing, paper, typewriting Lighting Weighing and measuring Chemistry; cells, molecules and life; petroleum; nuclear physics and nuclear power; mathematics and computers; navigation (at sea and in the air); marine engineering, ships, docks, diving	Presses, 18C printing shop. Lacemaker's condenser. Standards bearing royal ciphers. Ramsden's balance, 16C assayer's laboratory; DNA model, X-Rays; oil refinery; Cockcroft and Walton's apparatus, cyclotron, Chicago pile I, million volt impulse generator, power reactors; computer terminal; gyro compasses, radars; ships' models, turbines, London's dock; aqualung chamber.
3rd floor	Magnetism and electricity; heat and temperature; optics; geophysics and oceanography; protective clothing; aeronautics	Kater's pendulum; holography, lighthouse optics; infra-red detectors, vacuum flask; Radio station GB2SM; balloons, Wright brothers' plane, Spitfires, Hurricanes, VI, Concorde engine.
	Photography (1835-1976), cinematography	Inventions of Niepce, Daguerre, Fox Talbot. Muybridge, Marey, le Prince, Edison.
4th Floor	Glimpses of Medical History – individual scenes illustrating the experience of being a patient in earlier centuries.	Neolithic trepanning; 14C human dissection; the orlop deck of a warship at Trafalgar; an iron lung.
5th Floor	Science and the Art of Medecine – the Wellcome medical collection together with later additions traces the development of Western medecine from Mespotamia and Egypt, through Greece and Rome, via Islam, to Western Europe and North America; ethnographic exhibits from non-literate societies, India and the Far East.	Amulets and votive offerings, 17C Chinese acupuncture figure, blood-letting bowls, drug jars, leper's rattle, 17C pomanders, dental and surgical instruments, 19C strait-jacket, pacemakers.

If massive beams pumping up and down, pulses and radio waves, printing machinery, mean nothing, select a subject and look at it as you would in an encyclopaedia: time (1st floor), public transport (ground floor), planes (3rd floor), polyhydra (2nd floor) or, mesmerised by Foucault's pendulum (ground floor) stand and stare, literally, at the earth's turning.

Natural History Museum★★. – *Cromwell Rd. Open daily 10am (Sundays 1pm) to 6pm; closed 1 January, Good Friday, May Day Holiday, 24, 25, 26 December; combined ticket with Geological Museum £2, children £1; Mondays to Fridays 4.30 to 6pm and Saturdays, Sundays and bank holidays 5 to 6 pm free.*

History and the building. – The museum has accumulated about 40 million specimens; the collections continue to grow by some 350 000 specimens a year of which 250 000 are insects. Such increase would not have surprised **Hans Sloane** whose own collection, begun with plant specimens from Jamaica soon outgrew his house, the house next door, the accommodation at Chelsea Manor. The BM, founded in 1753 as a result of his bequest, trebled in size almost immediately and continued to expand so that by 1860, despite new wings and annexes, the galeries were chaotic and quantities of objects were unable to be shown. It was therefore decided to move natural history, the nucleus of Sloane's original collection, to an available site in Kensington; the new museum opened to the public in 1880. The building (apart from a recent departmental annexe) expresses the solemn reverence and sense of mission in public education of the 19C; Alfred Waterhouse, the architect, took as his model 11/12C Rhineland Romanesque cathedral architecture, producing a vast symmetrical building, 675ft from end pavilion to end pavilion with central twin towers 190ft high above a rounded, recessed entrance, ornate with decorated covings and pillars. The fabric is buff and pale slate-blue terracotta blocks; the decoration includes lifelike mouldings of animals, birds, fishes.

The collections. – Skeleton dinosaurs, huge and horned, in the central and north halls announce immediately that despite the cathedral door, this is the Natural History Museum. There is a fascinating exhibition on the relationship between birds and dinosaurs.

The extensive ground floor galleries *(west)* are devoted to a systematic display of birds, classified by groups, showing variety of size, adaptation and plumage; British birds set in their habitat with recordings of their songs; insects (including butterflies); marine invertebrates leading to the exhibition on **Discovering Mammals** with its huge suspended skeletons, jaw bones and reconstructions establishing the relationship between mammals and their environment; the **Human Biology Hall** with modern displays skilfully dissembling the complexity of the subject. The eastern galleries exhibit fossils from bacteria to dinosaurs and a modern section on **Ecology**.

On the first floor, the west gallery, devoted to mammals, leads to a display on the **Origin of Species** terminating in the African mammals section; the eastern gallery showing **Man's Place in Evolution** leads to the gallery on minerals, rocks, gemstones and meteorites. Outside the British Natural History gallery *(top floor)* is a cross section of a 1300 year old sequoia.

In 1938, Baron Rothschild bequeathed the **Tring Zoological Museum** (Herts) to the nation, where mammals, insects and the major bird collections are now housed.

Victoria and Albert Museum★★★. – *Page 160.*

KEW ★★★ (Richmond upon Thames)

■ **THE ROYAL BOTANIC GARDENS★★★**

Open daily from 9.30am (except Christmas and New Year's Days) to between 4pm in midwinter, 8pm in midsummer; museums open at 9.30am (closed additionally Good Friday, 24, 26 December), houses at 10am, close at the latest at 4.30pm weekdays, 5.30pm Sundays. Admission: £1, children 50p.

There are a refreshment pavilion (Pagoda area), tea bar (Orangery – river direction), drinking fountains, numerous toilets. Invalid chairs are available for hire, apply in advance.

Kew Gardens are pure pleasure. Colour and the architecture of the trees, singly – the weeping willow, the stone pine – or in groups, delight at all seasons. The layman will spot common-place flowers and shrubs and gaze on delicate exotics, gardeners check their knowledge against the labels for this 300 acre garden is the superb offshoot of laboratories engaged in the identification of plants and plant material from all parts of the world and in economic botany. The curatorship of the biggest herbarium in the world, a wood museum, a botanical library of more than 100 000 volumes and the training (3 year course) of student gardeners are also within the establishment's province.

The botanical theme of the gardens, as opposed to the purely visual, began under Princess Augusta who was personally responsible for the inauguration of a botanic garden south of the Orangery and the enlargement of the gardens from seven to more than 100 acres. On moving into the White House *(see below)*, Prince Frederick had employed William Kent not only to rebuild the house but to landscape the garden. On the prince's death in 1751, the Dowager Princess of Wales, guided by the Earl of Bute, a considerable botanist if no politician, appointed William Aiton as head gardener (1759-93) and William Chambers as architect (1760). Under Aiton, a Scot who had worked at the Chelsea Physic Garden, his son who succeeded him (1793-1841), and Sir Joseph Banks (d 1820), voyager, distinguished botanist, naturalist, biologist, and finally director, plants began to be especially collected from all parts of the world for research and cultivation. By 1789, 5 500 species were growing in the gardens.

In 1772 on the death of Princess Augusta, George III combined the Kew and Richmond Lodge gardens and had them landscaped by "Capability" Brown. The Palace, Orangery, Queen's Cottage, Pagoda remain as colophon to the royal epoch.

The Gardens. – Major plantings and flowering seasons are indicated on the map overleaf, colour keyed to draw your attention to flowers in areas possibly not previously explored. Many fine specimens of trees some over 200 years old, have been uprooted in the storm of October 1987 but most of the damage has been repaired.

Plant Houses. – *For opening times see above. The Tropical Waterlily House opens in summer only.*

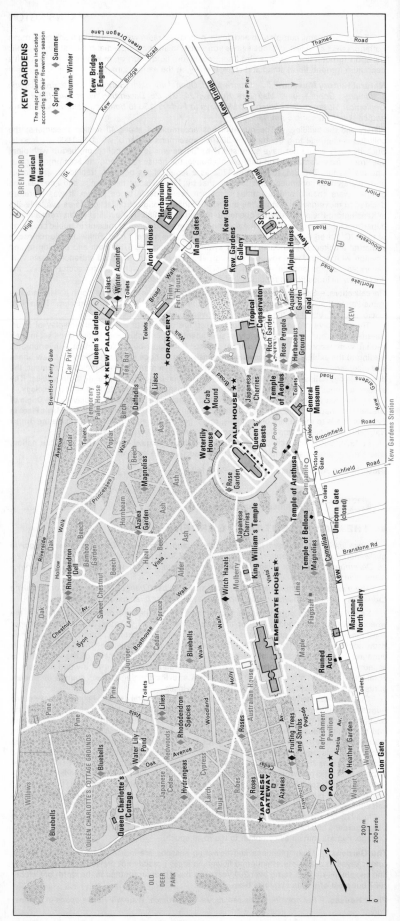

110

The Palm House★★. – *Closed for repairs. Plants exhibited in temporary greenhouse near the tea bar.* The house was designed by **Decimus Burton** and the engineer, Richard Turner, as a purely functional building – it measures 362ft in length, is 33ft high in the wings and 62ft at the centre. It is constructed entirely of iron and glass, has curved roofs throughout, took four years to erect (1844-1848). Inside are tropical plants both useful (coffee, cocoa) and ornamental.

Outside *(west)* is a semi-circular rose garden; the pond *(east)* is watched over by the Queen's Beasts (stone replicas of those designed by James Woodward to stand outside Westminster Abbey at the coronation in 1953).

Temperate House★. – The house, again by Burton, but 20 years later and including crested ridges, octagons, wings, ornamentation, epitomises Victorian conservatory construction. Inside note the camellias, rain forest and dragon trees.

Alpine House. – Beneath a glass pyramid, built in 1981, from which rainwater drains into the surrounding moat, is a rock landscape including a refrigerated bed.

Other specialist houses (Aroid, Fern, Tropical Waterlily and Australian) present creepers from rain-forests, cacti, gourds and wattles, mimosas and eucalyptus.

Princess of Wales Tropical Conservatory. – In this modern steel and glass diamond-shaped structure are recreated ten different tropical habitats ranging from mangrove swamp to desert. Also of interest are a Mohave desert diorama and displays of ferns, orchids, carnivorous and stone plants (Lithops).

Marianne North Gallery. – In a building (1882) specially designed by her architect friend, James Ferguson, are exhibited paintings by Miss North of plants, insects and general scenes from the many countries she visited between 1871 and 1884.

KEW: A ROYAL RESIDENCE

Early mansions. – Once upon a time there was a palace at Richmond which included in its domain the Old Deer Park, guarded by a keeper's lodge; this (on the site occupied since 1769 by Kew Observatory) was rebuilt and in 1721, sold to the future George II and his consort, Queen Caroline who laid out around the renamed **Richmond Lodge,** elaborate gardens in which she included typical 18C ornamental statues and follies.

In 1730, Frederick, Prince of Wales, although on unfriendly terms with George II leased a house only a mile away. The residence, the **White House,** "an old timber house" built in the late 17C, was redeemed in the diarist Evelyn's eyes only by the "garden (which) has the choicest fruit of any plantation in England". Frederick and Augusta rebuilt the house (known also as Kew House) on a site now marked by a sundial, in which the princess remained after Frederick's death in 1751, devoting herself particularly to the garden.

King George III (1760-1820) and Queen Charlotte found with an increasing family – they had 15 children – that Richmond Lodge was too small, and on Princess Augusta's death in 1772 moved into the White House. This also rapidly proved too small and, in 1773, the **Dutch House** was leased for the young Prince of Wales (the future George IV) and his brother as well as other houses on Kew Green. Not satisfied, however, George III commissioned **James Wyatt** to design a new "Gothic" enterprise to be sited on the riverbank. The **Castellated Palace,** as it was known, was never completed, but like the White House was demolished, leaving alone of all the cousin-hood of royal residences, just the Dutch House or Kew Palace, which was occupied, until her death in 1818, by Queen Charlotte. In 1899 it was opened as a museum.

Kew Palace★★ (or Dutch House). – *Open April to September daily 11am to 5.30pm; 80p, children 40p.*

The dark red brick building immediately recognisable by its Dutch attic gables and notable for the richness and variety of the brick laying, cutting and moulding, was built by Samuel Fortrey, a London Merchant of Dutch parentage, who commemorated his house's construction in a monogram and the date 1631 over the front door.

At the rear is the **Queen's Garden,** a formal design of pleached alleys of laburnum and hornbeam, *parterres,* a gebezo and including plants popular in 17C.

Interior. – The interior is that of a small country house of George III's time. Downstairs the rooms are all panelled: the King's Dining Room in white 18C style, the Breakfast Room in early 17C style and the Library Ante-Room in re-set 16C linenfold. Upstairs, apart from the white and gold Queen's Drawing Room, formally set out with lyreback chairs for a musical evening, the rooms are wallpapered with new paper printed from the delightful original blocks and intimate with family portraits by Gainsborough and Zoffany. In the king's rooms note the embossed terracotta paper in the Anteroom and in the bedroom a russet red paper patterned in dark green with matching hangings. Downstairs in the Pages' Waiting Room, is an exhibition of minor royal possessions – silver filigree rattles, alphabet counters, snuff boxes, lists of Prince Frederick's gambling debts, the queen's code of bell pulls...

Other buildings and monuments. – Under Princess Augusta, William Chambers set about constructing typical 18C garden follies: temples, a ruined arch, an **Orangery★** (1761) and a **Pagoda★** (1761), a garden ornament *(not open)* 163ft and ten storeys high, still the climax to a long vista.

(After photograph, Pitkin Pictorials)

The Pagoda.

The Queen's Cottage. – *Open April to September weekends and holiday Mondays, 11am to 5.30pm; 40p, children 20p.* Two storeyed beneath a thatched roof, typical of "rustic" buildings of the period (1772) but designed, in this case, purely as a picnic house by Queen Charlotte, the cottage is furnished including tea for two upstairs.

The **Main Gates** are by Decimus Burton (1848 – the lion and unicorn on the original gate are now above gates in Kew Rd). The **General Museum** by the pond, dates from 1857-8, when it replaced the original Museum of Economic Botany, the first in the world in 1847. The **Japanese Gateway**★ was imported for the Anglo-Japanese Exhibition of 1912.

■ KEW VILLAGE

Kew Bridge. – Three span stone bridge *(p 150)*.

St Anne's. – The west end is adorned by a triangular pediment and peristyle and crowned by a bell-turret. The nave and chancel were constructed of brick in 1710-14 on the site of a 16C chapel once frequented by Tudor and Stuart courtiers. In 1770 the church was lengthened, a north aisle built on and books and furnishings were presented by George III, who in 1805 added the royal gallery (note the fine Queen Anne arms and hatchments). In the churchyard lie Gainsborough (d 1788) and Zoffany (d 1810).

Kew Green. – The most attractive houses on the green are those on either side of the main gates to the gardens. Dominating the north, river, side are Kew Herbarium (collection of 5 million dried plants and library – *open only to specialists*), a three storey Georgian house and extensive annexe, followed by an irregular line of 18/19C houses of brick with canted bays, canopied balconies, rounded doors and windows in arched recesses... (nos 61-83). On the far side of the gates backing on to the gardens, are a line of onetime royal "cottages", including, at no 37, Cambridge Cottage, now the Wood Museum and Kew Gardens Gallery *(enter from inside the gardens)*.

Kew Bridge Engines and Water Supply Museum. – *Entrance off Green Dragon Rd. Open 11am to 5pm; closed Christmas week; £1 (£1.70 weekends and holidays), children, OAPs 50p (80p weekends and holidays).* There are six large engines regularly in steam *(weekends)* in this museum of water which demonstrates the development of James Watt's basic idea through over a century of improved efficiency and increasing scale: the Boulton and Watt (1820), the 90″ (1846), the Easton and Amos (1863), the Dancers End (1867), the Maudslay (1938) and the Hathorn Davey Triple (1910) which is in steam all day whereas the other five work on shifts. Awaiting restoration are the Bull (1856-7) and the 100″ (1869) which together with the 90″ pumped 6 1/2 and 10 million gallons daily. A variety of smaller steam engines, traction engines and steam lorries, a narrow gauge railway, a forge, machine shop and a collection of relics connected with London's water supply complete the display.

Buildings in 19C were, for the most part, erected round the engines with no provision for bringing in replacement parts so confident were our forefathers that their engines would last indefinitely. Exteriors were functional, the interiors dominated by giant columns, slender pillars and staircases enabling one to climb to cylinder and beam levels. The standpipe tower outside is a local landmark nearly 200ft high.

Musical Museum. – *368 High St, Brentford (150 yds from Kew Bridge). Open April to October, Saturdays, Sundays 2 to 5pm; £1.50.* Inside an acoustically rewarding neo-Gothic church (19C) is a collection of some 200 mechanical reproducers of music – pianolas, organs, a wurlitzer...

KING'S CROSS (Camden)

King's Cross, St Pancras and Euston Stations are each as near the centre as was permitted when they were constructed respectively as the Gt Northern terminus (1852), the Midland (1864) and the London and North Western (1837). Today the front of Lewis Cubitt's **King's Cross,** apart from the clock tower (clock from 1851 Exhibition) is largely masked by an advanced single storey hall providing covered access to the platforms at the rear; **St Pancras** remains as Sir George Gilbert Scott designed it, a combination of medieval Gothic in brick with Italian terracotta. **Euston** is modern (1968), clean lined, with exposed plain black piers supporting glass panels with the interior recessed west of the centre to provide a colonnade. A statue of Robert Stephenson, chief engineer of the London Birmingham line (1838) stands in the forecourt.

Many trade unions have their headquarters in the area, conveniently close to the stations for members arriving from the Midlands or the North. The new building of the British Library is under construction in Somerstown.

Old St Pancras Church. – This 13C church is the only survival of the medieval village of St Pancras. There remains one 13C lancet window and two funerary monuments including that of the 17C miniaturist Samuel Cooper.

Among the monuments in the churchyard is Sir John Soane's *(qv)* canopied memorial.

Camley Street Natural Park. – Overlooked by the Victorian gas-holders at King's Cross, a wild life haven has been created in a 2 acre park on the banks of the Regent's Canal including ponds, a marsh and reed beds with the aim of attracting insects, butterflies, birds and wild fowl.

KNIGHTSBRIDGE – BELGRAVIA ★★ (Westminster)

Knightsbridge. – This present synonym for elegant living with luxury stores and larger shops lining the main road, and antique and rare shops tucked away behind, was until *c* 1800 an unkempt village beside a stone bridge across the Westbourne River (where Albert Gate is now). It was outside London and, as such, a place for spitals, cattle markets and slaughterhouses, taverns, footpads and highway robbers, pleasure gardens frequented by Pepys and his friends; it was a highway crowded with travellers from the west and men and carts bringing in produce to the central markets. Only in later 18/early 19C did houses and shops begin to line the road in solid terraces: in 1813 Benjamin Harvey opened a linen draper's and in 1849 **Harrod** took over a small grocer's which by 1901-5 had prospered and enabled him to rebuild, in terracotta brick crowned by towers and cupolas, to today's familiar outline. Inside, in addition to the general joy of the items for sale, the food halls remain a prime example of *art nouveau* wall tile decoration. The other major local building in brick is the **Hyde Park barracks,** dark red, angular, with a tower block, designed by Sir Basil Spence in 1970-1. When the twin houses on either side of Albert Gate were built in 1852 for a railway baron called Hudson, they were the tallest in London; the **French Embassy** now occupies the east side.

The triangle between the main highway and the road to Brompton village developed as a residential area in true Georgian fashion round a series of squares which present an interesting progression: **Trevor Sq** 1818, **Brompton** 1826, **Montpelier** 1837. The houses have trim stucco ground floors and basements with brick upper storeys, neat windows and doors and slender balconies. Interlacing the squares are small streets, mews, closes, alleys, lined by one-up one-down cottages, colour-washed and transformed, the handkerchief sized front gardens (Rutland St) ablaze with flowers. By contrast **Ennismore Gardens** to the west, although only slightly later in date, is mid-Victorian, all stucco ranges with pillared square porches. **All Saints,** 19C Early English in style, is now a Russian Orthodox Church. Built from 1826-29, Holy Trinity with its large garden and fashionable associations is now half-hidden by **Brompton Oratory** *(Open daily 6.30am to 8pm (6pm holiday Mondays)).* It was designed by Herbert Gribble in Italian baroque, with a dome and lantern above a wide and lofty nave, flanked by side chapels and classical statues of the saints. Cardinal Manning preached at the official opening in 1884; a monument to Cardinal Newman stands in the forecourt.

Between **Brompton Road** and **Sloane Street** there grew up a fringe of small streets such as **Yeoman's Row** (1768) and **Beauchamp Place,** lined by modest brick terraces – the shops in the latter now as various as their appearance: reject china, oriental porcelain, handmade shoes, silver, antiques, restaurants, rare maps... Almost simultaneously, in 1773, Sloane St was developed, followed by the land to the west which came to be known as Hans Town. In the late 19C the area, together with Cadogan Place and Sloane Gdns, to the south, was rebuilt to Victorian taste in unfading red brick *(p 26).* Sloane St too has been rebuilt but piecemeal.

The most distinguished modern buildings in the area are the **Danish Embassy** 1976-7 by Ove Arup in Sloane St and in Pont St **St Columba's** of 1950-55 by Edward Maufe, perfectly sited with its green cupolaed, square stone tower in the street's axis.

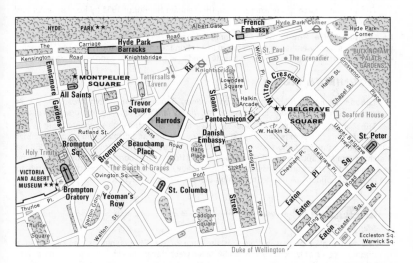

Belgravia. – Most remarkable of all was the development of the area east of Sloane St: within 6 years, 1821-27, the land, which was part of the Grosvenor estate, developed from the Five Fields and market gardens, bordered along Upper Grosvenor Place by houses and stables and St George's Hospital (f 1733; rebuilt in Classical style in 1829 and vacated 1977), into the well defined plan of **Wilton Crescent, Belgrave Sq, Eaton Pl** (Chopin's first London recital was given at no 99) and **Eaton Sq.** Impetus for such a development came from George IV's decision to transform the Queen's House, formerly Buckingham House, into Buckingham Palace *(qv).* Belgravia, built on soil brought from the newly excavated St Katharine Dock, is **Cubitt** territory.

Belgrave Sq✶✶. – **George Basevi** was the architect. The square of 10 acres has twinned, but not identical, sides with Corinthian centres and ends, urns and balustrades, statue decorated attic screens, pillared porches, all in white stucco; a uniform 3 storeys, cornice and floor above. The ironwork matches that enclosing the garden in which a bay has been cut at the southeast corner for a bronze statue of Simon Bolivar. The end of each range is carefully designed; three corners are canted allowing two roads to enter with a house between, facing on to the square.

Basevi also probably designed and Cubitt built the adjoining squares and streets extending far into Pimlico with Eccleston (formerly New) and Warwick Sqs, Upper Belgrave St, Belgrave Place, Eaton Sq, Chester Sq, echoing the same theme for, apart from a few streets of older houses, Belgravia, 150 acres in extent, is constructed to the basic terrace design of Basevi, varied by the addition of combinations of a restricted number of related forms of ornament to afford, overall, a strong family resemblance.

St Peter's. – The church was erected in 1827 as part of the project but off-centre because of the King's Rd thoroughfare and therefore lost effect. The design is classical but the interior is Victorian. The church was extensively damaged by fire in 1988.

Wilton Crescent. – The diameter and inner perimeter are lined by stucco terraces *(p 25* – the outer ring rebuilt); the 17C brick terraces of Wilton Place predate by a century St Paul's church which was erected in Perpendicular style in 1843 on the site of a guards' barracks, still recalled in local street and pub names. Between the crescent and Lowndes Sq (a different estate separately developed and largely rebuilt this century), are a maze of small streets, overlooked by colour washed cottages, new small houses, towering apartments and garden precincts. In Motcomb St stands the **Pantechnicon,** built in 1830 with an august Doric columned front; on either side and in W Halkin St and Halkin Arcade are small shops where through the windows one sees prints, modern watches, pottery from Mexico, carpets, antiques and customers sitting in leisurely consideration.

LEWISHAM (Lewisham)

December 1836 saw the opening of the first railway, the Deptford-London Bridge line on which 20 000 people travelled in the first week. Already the villages of Lewisham, Lee, Lee Green, Catford and New Cross were being urbanised; in the next century the population was to multiply fifty fold to 250 000.

Parish Church of St Mary's. – *High St.* The sturdy building of Kentish ragstone with an imposing portico and a low square tower, ornamented at the crest, which dates from 1775, stands on an ancient site. A board inside lists early incumbents, Richard of 1267, or his undated predecessor, Yeonomy of Ghent. On the opposite corner in Ladywell Rd is the late 17C vicarage, with a pedimented doorway and modillioned eaves.

Pentland House and Manor House. – *Old Road, Lee High Rd.* Next to 18C, white stucco, Pentland House stands the timelessly elegant Manor House, built in 1788 of brick and from 1797-1810 the residence of the banker, Sir Francis Baring (now a public library).

Note further along the High Rd, on the opposite side, the mid 19C Merchant Taylors' Almshouses and Boone Chapel (Wren, 1683).

Church of the Resurrection (RC). – *Kirkdale, Upper Sydenham.* The low fortress building of yellow brick is lancet windowed and buttressed (D A Reid: 1973-4). Surmounting the plain wooden door is a bronze and lead relief of Our Lord showing his wounds as the shroud drops away (Stephen Sykes).

The circular Church of the Annunciation (Beckenham Hill Rd) of 1964 by Roy Lancaster has an interesting thorn crowned roof.

St Antholin Spire, Roundhill. – *Dartmouth Rd, Forest Hill.* The slender stone spire by Wren with dragon's head weathervane, purchased in 1874 on the church's demolition by a City master printer to adorn his estate, now stands beside a cedar, at the centre of a modern housing estate.

■ HORNIMAN MUSEUM★

London Rd, Forest Hill. Open: 10.30am to 6pm; Sundays 2pm to 6pm; closed 24, 25, 26 December; refreshment room. Education centre, library (anthropology and zoology); aquarium.

Tribal masks, Buddhas, lutes and bagpipes line your path, until suddenly there is the walrus... for this museum is one of great variety, re-arranged and displayed in modern manner but continuing the enquiring tradition of its founder, Frederick John Horniman (1835-1906), tea merchant and MP. Successful private views decided Horniman to construct a museum which he had designed by Harrison Townsend (1901) in *art nouveau* style and then presented "as a gift, to the people of London". A mosaic by Anning Bell decorates the façade.

The MALL ★★ (Westminster)

Map p 133.

The Mall's alignment was traced at the time of the Stuarts but its completion as a thoroughfare dates only from 1910 when **Sir Aston Webb** transformed it into a processional way from the palace to Whitehall with monuments to Queen Victoria at either end; George V was the first monarch to ride along it to his coronation.

Admiralty Arch. – The massive curved arch, with a sovereign's gateway at the centre, is named after the adjoining admiralty buildings on the south side; the red brick extension is 19C and the pebble and flint Citadel on the edge of the park served as the operational centre for Churchill, the cabinet and chiefs of staff from 1939 to 1945.

The Arch replaced the first LCC office which stood on the site of the 17C **Spring Gardens** frequented by Pepys, now reduced to a court with modern statuary *(north side)*.

Carlton House Terrace★, Carlton Gardens. – Carlton House, built of brick in 1709, purchased by Frederick, Prince of Wales in 1732 and refaced in stone, was finally in 1772 taken over by the Prince Regent, who with Henry Holland and at a cost of £800 000 transformed it into what was briefly the country's most gorgeous mansion. The king, however, was by then tired of the house and it was demolished (1829) and the government commissioned **Nash,** who had just completed the Regent's Park scheme, to design a similar terrace surround for St James's Park. In the event only the two terraces on the north side were constructed.

Seen from the Mall, the white façades, each 31 bays wide with central pediments and angle pavilions, giant Corinthian columns and balconies, appear even more majestic as they stand upraised on squat, white painted, fluted, cast iron columns. The entrances are on the north side, porched, flanked by Tuscan or Ionic pillars, paired in some cases, beneath continuous balconies; the end houses are advanced to complete the composition. Among those now occupying the houses in the terrace are The Terrace Club at no 16, the National Portrait Gallery (annexe-archives and library) at nos 14-15, the Institute of Contemporary Arts at Nash House (no 12), the **Royal Society** at no 6, the Turf Club at no 5; no 1 was once the residence of Curzon.

On the site of Carlton House between the two terraces at the top of the steps down to the Mall is the Grand Old Duke of York who, according to the nursery rhyme, marched 10 000 men to the top of the hill then marched them down again and whose 124ft pink granite column was just high enough, according to his contemporaries, to place him out of reach of his creditors!

At the west end is **Carlton Gardens** where four grand houses surround a small grass plot shaded by plane trees: Kitchener lived at n° 2 and Palmerston at no 4 which was demolished and rebuilt Classically in grey stone in 1933. From 1940-45 it was the headquarters of the Free French Forces and is distinguished by a tablet inscribed with General de Gaulle's famous call to arms to the French people broadcast on 18 June 1940.

A slim bronze statue of George VI by William McMillan stands at the top of the steps down to the Mall.

Marlborough House. – *Pall Mall. Closed for tours during renovations.* ☎ 01-930 9249. Commonwealth Centre.

While John Churchill, **Duke of Marlborough,** was winning the final victories in the seemingly endless War of the Spanish Succession (Blenheim 1704, Ramillies 1706, Oudenaarde 1708) and the duchess was appointed one of the Ladies of the Bedchamber to Queen Anne and supervising the construction by Vanbrugh of Blenheim Palace (1705-24), Wren, in two years (1709-1711), designed and completed Marlborough House. It was of red brick with straight headed windows and slightly advanced wings at either end on the garden front. The mansion was altered in 1771 by William Chambers and enlarged in the 19C by James Pennethorne to include additional storeys, a balustrade, the Prince of Wales' feathers and the deep front porch. The house eventually passed to the crown and is now used as a Commonwealth Centre providing offices for the Commonwealth Foundation and some departments of the Commonwealth Secretariat.

The interior decorations include vast mural paintings by Louis Laguerre, godson of King Louis XIV of France, celebrating Marlborough's victories. The ceiling paintings, created originally for the Queen's House, Greenwich, by Gentileschi, are in the Blenheim Saloon.

Against the wall in Marlborough Road is a large *art nouveau* bronze fountain group in memory of Queen Alexandra (1926) and on the corner overlooking the Mall, a life-like relief by Reid-Dick of Queen Mary.

Queen's Chapel*. – *Marlborough Road. No access until renovations at Marlborough House are completed.* ☎ 01-930 9249. *The services of the Chapel Royal (see St James's Palace below) are held here from Easter to the last Sunday in July.*

The chapel was intended for the Infanta Maria of Spain but was completed for Charles I's eventual queen, Henrietta Maria, in 1625 by **Inigo Jones.** It was the first church in England to be designed completely outside the Perpendicular Gothic tradition. As a Roman Catholic foundation it was at first served by a friary of Capuchins and originally formed part of the palace; the road separating it from Friary Court dates from 1809.

The pedimented exterior of rendered cement with Portland stone dressings has three principal windows at the west end, of which the central one is arched above the unobtrusive, straight headed, door; at the east end is a broad Venetian window. The curved white coffered ceiling, framed by a richly detailed cornice, is picked out in gold above the chancel. The greyish-green walls are the original colour, the royal and other galleries, lower panelling, stalls and lectern are mid 17C; the organ loft by Grinling Gibbons. The beauty of the small edifice lies in its perfect proportions (it is a double cube) and the simplicity of the interior decoration.

St James's Palace **. – *Pall Mall. The Chapel Royal is open for services on Sunday (8.30, 11.15am) and Saints' days (12.30pm) from the first Sunday in October to Good Friday.*

Henry VIII's "goodly manor" became in 1532 a crenellated, turreted palace entered through the **Gate House** at the bottom of St James's, even then a regular thoroughfare. The original and early palace buildings, considerably more extensive before the fire of 1809 which destroyed the east wing, are of the traditional 16C Tudor red brick with a diaper pattern and stone trim along the line of crenellations. With later additions they now surround only four courts, the Colour, Friary, Ambassadors' and Engine.

St James's was the last royal palace to be built as such in the capital and became the chief residence after Whitehall had been burned down in 1698. Although no longer the sovereign's residence it remains the statutory seat – proclamations are made from the balcony on Friary Court, ambassadors are accredited to the Court of St James.

The **Chapel Royal** with its so-called Holbein ceiling is lit by a huge Tudor Gothic window visible from the exterior to the right of the gateway. The choir is famous for its long tradition since the medieval period and the choristers wear scarlet and gold state coats at services. The interior of the palace bears the imprint of successive architects and designers – Wren, Grinling Gibbons, Hawksmoor, Kent and William Morris. The splendid State Apartments *(open only for special functions),* are hung with full length portraits of Stuart and Hanoverian monarchs.

Many kings and queens have been born or died in the palace. Charles I spent his last night there, in the guardroom, before walking across the park to the Banqueting House and his execution on 30 January 1649.

It is a romantic building with gateway towers standing out against the sky and at dusk when the quiet courts are lit by crowned wall standards.

Clarence House. – The distinctive white stucco home of Queen Elizabeth, the Queen Mother, was built in 1825 by John Nash for the Duke of Clarence, the future William IV.

(After photograph, Parke and Roche, France)

St James's Palace.

115

The MALL★★

Lancaster House★. – *Stable Yard*. The mansion, designed by Benjamin Wyatt in 1825 for the Duke of York, who died in 1827, was for years in the 19C the town house of the Marquesses of Stafford and the Dukes of Sutherland when it became the setting for balls and soirees. Inside the Corinthian porticoed, square edifice of mellow Bath stone, is an opulent magnificence of mixed Baroque decoration – not for nothing did Queen Victoria on a visit declare to her hostess "I have come from my house to your palace". Beneath the coved and painted ceilings, the vast pictures, the gilding and chandeliers of the state apartments, a great marble staircase by Charles Barry divides and turns and turns again to enter the Grand Gallery, enriched with a painted ceiling by the Italian, Guercino, and four great decorated mirrors, and most impressive when thronged by people at an evening reception.

Queen Victoria Memorial. – The white marble statue, completed in 1910, with a gilded bronze victory at the summit and a seated figure of the queen facing east, was designed by Sir Aston Webb as the climax of his processional way but its disproportionate height (82ft) entailed alterations to Buckingham Palace *(qv)*.

■ **ST JAMES'S PARK**★★

London's oldest royal park. – Henry VIII was the inaugurator of London's royal parks and this, the oldest, goes back to 1532 when Henry exchanged the building occupied by a community founded before the Conquest as a "spittle for mayden lepers" for land in Suffolk. After demolishing the hospital, according to Stow, the king "built there a goodly manor, annexing thereunto a park, closed about with a wall of brick now called St James's Park, serving indifferently to the said manor and to the manor or palace of White Hall".

In Tudor times the park was stocked with deer. James I, a lover of wild life established a menagerie of animals and exotic birds. Charles II aligned aviaries along what came to be called Birdcage Walk, added the acres now known as **Green Park** (1667) and walked regularly, in the early morning, up a path which came to be known as Constitution Hill. Strongly influenced by the formal gardens of Le Nôtre which he had seen during his exile in France, the king had the park laid out according to the standard goosefoot *(patte d'oie)* design. The marshy ponds were systematised into a west-east canal from the west end of which extended two avenues – one along the line of the Mall towards the houses of Charing village.

In 19C when Nash was commissioned to design a project for the park's improvement, in addition to the terraces *(p 114)*, he landscaped the park itself after Repton, planting trees and shrubs and transforming the long water into a lake with islands (on which the duck and wildfowl originally on the "decoy" have flourished ever since). He also replaced the high surrounding wall by iron railings. The 18C ornamental gates on the south side of Piccadilly, by Robert Bakewell of Derby, originally belonged to Devonshire House which stood opposite the Ritz.

The park is known today for its brilliant flower borders and for the pelicans and wildfowl on the lake. From the bridge there are views of Buckingham Palace and Whitehall.

MAYFAIR ★ (Westminster) _____

Mayfair is named after the annual cattle and general fair which was held in May but became so unruly and the neighbourhood so notorious that it was officially closed in 1706. In 1735 the architect, Edward Shepherd took a 999 year lease on the site and opened a food market for the sale of fish, fowl, herbs and vegetables. Around the square and dependant streets he erected small houses, a practice renewed by his heirs so creating Shepherd Market. Development elsewhere arose as a rich overspill from the City.

Piccadilly★★. – *(North side from Hyde Park Corner; for south side see St James's p 134)*
The street is called after the house of a tailor from Somerset who made a fortune manufacturing the frilled lace borders, or pickadills, fashionable Elizabethans attached to their ruffs and cuffs. He bought a plot adjoining Great Windmill St and built upon it an imposing family mansion, Pickadill Hall.

The street's north side is still lined at the west end by late Georgian houses occupied by a diminishing number of clubs and notably at no 94 by the **Naval and Military** or In and Out Club, as it is known after the piers at the entrance (f 1862). The modest town house of 1756-60, two storeys high, with a Venetian window beneath a central pediment, was formerly the residence of George III's son, the Duke of Cambridge (1829-50), and from 1854-65 of Lord Palmerston.

Burlington House★. – In 1664 the 1st Earl of Burlington bought a plot on which to build a town house near courtly St James's; the 3rd earl, an architect in his own right, with **Colen Campbell** in 1715-6, remodelled and refaced the house in the Palladian style. In the 19C the house was twice remodelled, the second time in 1867-73 to its present neo-Italian Renaissance appearance.

Inside, the modifications were equally drastic as the house was converted to the use of the **Royal Academy** (f 1768) with a central grand staircase and exhibition galleries (changing exhibitions). The academy's treasures include splendid pictures by members (Reynolds, Gainsborough, Turner...), 18C furniture, Queen Victoria's paintbox, **Michelangelo's** unfinished marble tondo, *Madonna and Child*.

At the centre of the courtyard is a bronze statue of Sir Joshua Reynolds (1723-92), first PRA; in the ranges on either side are the libraries and rooms of learned societies.

The back of the building was remodelled in 1869 in ornate Italian style with towers, an upper portico of giant columns and a colossal porch, and suitably decorated with more than 20 magisterial statues. On completion the building became for many years the head-quarters of London University and is now the Museum of Mankind.

Museum of Mankind★. – *6 Burlington Gardens. Open daily 10am to 5pm, Sundays 2.30 to 6pm; closed 1 January, May Day holiday, 24-26 December.*

Directed by the Ethnography Department of the BM, the Museum presents regularly changing exhibitions illustrating both ancient and contemporary non-Western societies and cultures; its collections are drawn from the indigenous peoples of Africa, Australia and the Pacific Islands, North and South America and from certain parts of Asia and Europe.

The **Burlington Arcade**★★ along the west side of Burlington House, is delectable with embroidered waistcoats and jewellery, tobacco, pipes and cigars, cashmere scarves and camelhair pullovers, ivory and jade, behind bright shopfronts. It was built in 1819 and is patrolled by beadles; the gates are closed at night and on Sundays.

Albany is named after Frederick, Duke of York and Albany, he of the column, second son of George III. The prince was compelled on account of his debts to sell the 18C house, designed by **Sir William Chambers,** to a builder who converted it into chambers or the bachelor apartments which remain, increased in number, to this day. The building, as altered by **Henry Holland** in 1804, is in the shape of an H, the rear a stuccoed court on Vigo St enclosed by two lodges between neighbouring 18C houses. The front, with a forecourt on Piccadilly, is of brick with a central pediment, and porch. Distinction has always come to Albany through its residents, today as in 19C when they included Gladstone, Macaulay, Byron...

(After photograph, Parke and Roche, France)

Burlington Arcade.

Park Lane. – The Lane is now studded with hotels where it was previously graced by the town residences of local estate owners: Grosvenor House, in 1930, replaced the early 19C mansion of the Duke of Westminster; the Dorchester also in 1930, the mid 19C Dorchester House; the London Hilton replaces a short terrace; the Londonderry stands on the site of Londonderry House of 1765 and the Inn on the Park and Intercontinental (Hamilton Place) on the site of the Earl of Northbrook's residence.

Oxford St. – The road to Oxford, to Uxbridge, Tyburn Rd, are the names under which the street appears on old maps. By mid 18C it was almost entirely built up on the south side and the Harley estate had been laid out around Cavendish Sq. A turnpike just before the junction with Park Lane marked the western boundary of what soon became London's prime shopping street.

Gordon Selfridge confirmed the street's status when he erected his vast and imposing shop in 1908: windows below displayed wares in a new way; colossal Ionic columns soared up through three floors to be crowned by an attic and balustrade; a canopy protected the entrance.

Mayfair's three squares. – The squares were laid out in the first half of 18C: Hanover c 1715, Grosvenor in 1725, Berkeley from 1737. Little survives except the plane trees now overlooked from three sides of Berkeley and four sides of the others, by phalanxes of 20C office blocks with only the exceptional 18C or 19C house between.

Hanover Sq. – St George's *(open 9am to 3pm – Mondays to Fridays)* was constructed in 1721-4 as part of the quarter's development. It remains in address, a feature of the square, the free standing portico projecting across the street pavement and west tower with a lantern after St James' Garlickhythe, producing a distinctive landmark to the south. Inside all is white with the detail picked out in gold... and on the pavement, waiting for who knows who (since no one seems sure where they came from) two cast iron game dogs.

The London Diamond Centre. – *Hanover Street. Guided tours 9.30am to 5.30pm (1.30pm Saturdays); closed Sundays and 1 January and Christmas; 3/4 hr; £3.45.*

Behind automatic doors with combination locks is a glittering exhibition showing the mining, cutting, shaping, faceting, polishing and setting of diamonds, together with a display of precious and semi-precious stones which are for sale at manufacturer's prices.

Berkeley Sq. – The plane trees, dating from 1789, are all that remains of Berkeley Wood. The 1740s houses were built after Berkeley House, erected in 1664 overlooking Piccadilly, had given way in 1733 to Devonshire House which, in turn, was demolished this century (Berkeley St crossing the old site is dominated at no 45 by the headquarters offices of Thomas Cook). Nos 45-46 in the square, stone faced with balustraded balconies and pediments at the first floor windows are 18C (Clive of India lived at no 45) as are those on the far side of no 47 (rebuilt 1891). The brick and stucco house of 4 floors, at no 50, is occupied by Maggs, the antiquarians who display in beautifully proportioned rooms, equally attractive books, maps and autographs. Note the ironwork in first floor balconies and lamp holders at the steps to each house, complete with torch snuffers. No 52, on the corner, has a front also on **Charles St** where 18C houses continue, some less grand than in the square and some refaced or remodelled in the 19C as in the case of no 37 where three houses have been combined as premises for the English Speaking Union. The street ends in a confusion of backs and fronts and finally a small 19/20C pub in a cobbled yard.

Bourdon House, 2 Davies St at the square's northwest corner (now Mallett's antique dealers), was built in 1723-5 as a manorhouse amidst fields and orchards. It is a small square, brick house of two storeys with a third added above the cornice, pedimented to the south above a pedimented doorway, with a second door on the street. Fine 18C interior.

Grosvenor Sq. – The 18C square comprising 6 acres, one of London's largest, might be said to have been as effectively redesigned in the 20C as it was in the 18C – even the garden, originally circular with a central statue of George I, is now square with a memorial to Franklin Roosevelt on the north side and a monument to the RAF American squadrons. The first American resident

117

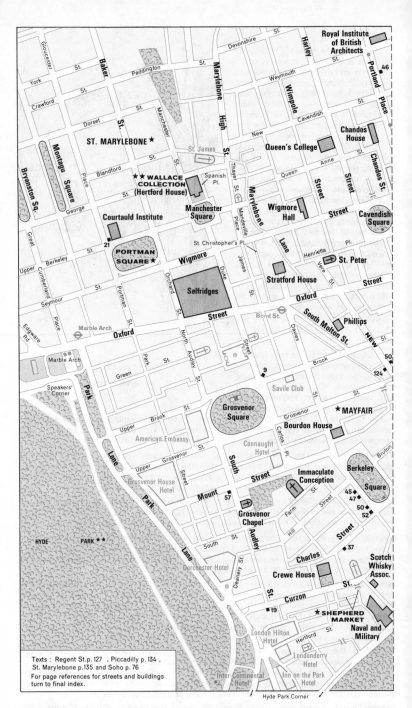

(at no 9) was **John Adams,** the first Minister to Britain and later President. Today the neo-Georgian buildings to north, east and south are almost all US State Department offices while the entire west side, since 1961, has been filled with the embassy designed by **Eero Saarinen.**

The streets of Mayfair. – Other than in the residential streets with their occasional Georgian houses, attention in Mayfair concentrates on the shop windows.

Bond Street★. – Old and New Bond Sts which existed as a lane in Tudor times are named after Sir Thomas Bond, treasurer to Henrietta Maria, who gave £20 000 to the impecunious Duke of Albemarle, demolished his mansion and began to build what are now Old Bond St, Dover, Stafford and Albemarle Sts completed by the construction in 1720 of New Bond St. Early residents included Nelson and Emma Hamilton, Byron, Boswell, Beau Brummell... as well as tailors, haberdashers, chemists. Today's shops and even the Antique Centre (124 New Bond St) specialise in the unique, the luxurious: handmade chocolates, leatherwork, stationery, perfumery, cigars, porcelain, jewellery, photographic equipment, watches, furniture, pictures...

In the street are **Chappell's** (50 New Bond Street), **Sotheby's** (no 35) who began in 1744 as book auctioneers, produced a turnover of £826 in the first year and are now the biggest firm of art auctioneers in the world, their notable rivals, **Phillips'** (7 Blenheim St, New Bond St), whose first big sale was on 9 February 1798, when they auctioned Marie Antoinette's pictures. No 143 retains an early 19C shop front and interior. Also famous are **Partridge** (no 144), **Asprey's** (165), **Marlborough Fine Art Galleries** (39 Old Bond St), **Agnew's** (no 43) and **Sac Frères** (no 45) who deal in amber. Antique dealers have overflowed into Brook St, site also of the Savile Club (69-71).

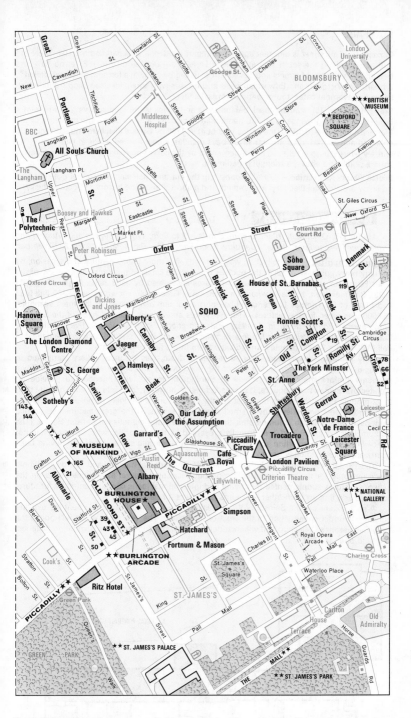

South Molton St has become a pedestrian precinct with pavement cafés, small restaurants, a shop smelling of and selling coffee, a clockmaker...

Albemarle St is lined by some 18C houses such as no 7, no 21 occupied by the Royal Institution (f 1799; **Michael Faraday Laboratory** – *open: Tuesdays, Thursdays 1 to 4pm; 40p)* and no 50 by the veteran publisher, John Murray.

Savile Row retains its tailors and a laboratory for the restoration of works of art.

Mount St has a more leisurely air; it leads from the northwest corner of Berkeley Sq past the Connaught (that epitome of late 19C luxury hotel building) to the park and is lined by tall, irregularly gabled terrocotta brick houses of 1888, 1893... Below window after window displays choice objects: antique furniture, Lalique glass, porcelain, pictures, Oriental screens... On one corner is a butcher, his shop faced inside with turn of the century tiles. During the Civil War the parliamentarians raised defensive earthworks here; hence the name and the topography.

The Church of the Immaculate Conception. – *Farm St*. The church of the Jesuit community, built in 1844-9, has a notable high altar, meticulously designed by Pugin.

South Audley St. – Halfway along the street is the **Grosvenor Chapel** of 1739 with a distinctive, Tuscan portico, square quoined tower and octagonal turret. Its garden was part of Berkeley Wood before serving as the burial ground for St George's *(p 117).*

Purdeys, gun and riflemakers, established in 1881 would hardly be noticeable at no 57, were it not for the richly coloured royal coat of arms above the door.

MAYFAIR★

Curzon St. – This street is different again, being part residential and part commercial. There are 18C houses along the south side at the Park Lane end – Disraeli died in 1881 at no 19 – and behind them a maze of streets and paved courts linked by archways forming **Shepherd Market★**, a quarter of Victorian and Edwardian pubs and houses with small, inserted shop fronts which serve as pavement cafés, tourist antique (brass) shops...

Crewe House (no 15), standing back behind trees and lawns is the only surviving example of a type familiar in engravings as an 18C gentleman's London mansion. Sometime residence of the Marquess of Crewe (d 1945), the house was built in 1730 by **Edward Shepherd** and subsequently enlarged and altered to its present seven bays with large bow fronted wings at either end. The entirely white stucco is relieved and ornamented by the curves of Venetian windows, a pillared, square porch and above, a triangular pediment.

Scotch Whisky Association. – *17 Half Moon St.* In the entrance hall stands a copper pot still. Also on show are a model distillery, implements and a short film on the history of Scotch whisky.

NATIONAL GALLERY ★★★ (Trafalgar Sq)

Map p 175. Open daily 10am to 6pm, Sundays 2 to 6pm; Wednesdays in July, August and September 10am to 8pm; closed 1 January, Good Friday, May Day holiday, 24, 25, 26 December.

Origin and habitat. – The collection was founded, after more than a century of discussion, by parliamentary purchase in 1824; the nucleus was not the spoils of monarchy as so many of the older European collections were, but 38 pictures assembled by **John Julius Angerstein** (1735-1823), City merchant, banker, owner of a mansion in Greenwich, a town house at 100 Pall Mall and friend of Sir Thomas Lawrence whose portrait of him can be seen in the main vestibule. £57 000 was given for the pictures – Titian's *Venus and Adonis,* Rubens' *Rape of the Sabines,* Rembrandt's *Woman taken in Adultery* and *Adoration of the Shepherds,* five paintings by Claude, Hogarth's *Marriage à la Mode* series and Reynolds' *Lord Heathfield* – which remained in Pall Mall, where 24 000 people came to view them in the first seven months.

Only in 1838, fifteen years after Angerstein's death, was the new gallery completed in Trafalgar Sq. This building, on the site of the Royal Mews and at first shared with the Royal Academy (before the latter's removal to Burlington House), was intended to provide an architectural climax to the square; it succeeded better, however, in its internal arrangement than in its monumentality of which the most spectacular feature in the long, disproportionately low and subdivided front relieved by a small dome and turrets, is the great pedimented portico composed of Corinthian columns after those of the recently demolished Carlton House. (The Carlton House columns had been frugally preserved by the authorities who, however, had not noticed their friable condition so that no economy was effected since, the design having been approved, more solid ones had to be made!)

The 1973-5 extension is the fifth to William Wilkins' original building and affords additional space not only for the permanent collection but occasional special exhibitions based on the gallery's pictures supplemented by private and international loans complemented by furniture, sculpture and fine art from other museums *(see press for details).*

A sixth extension, the Sainsbury Wing, designed by R. Venturi to complement the existing building, is under construction to the west of the gallery. The new wing which will house the Early Renaissance Collection and will include an auditorium and temporary exhibition galleries, is due to open in 1991.

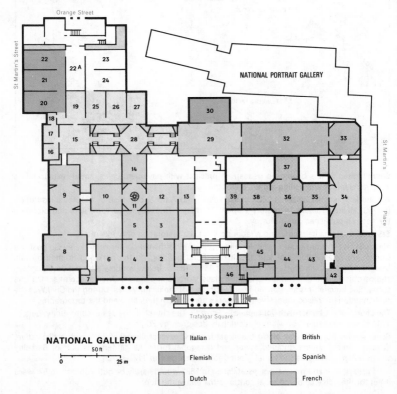

NATIONAL GALLERY

50 ft
0   25 m

Italian   Flemish   Dutch   British   Spanish   French

There are now more than 2 000 paintings in the collection; they represent the jewels in the public domain from early to High Renaissance Italian paintings, early Netherlandish, German, Flemish, Dutch, French, Spanish pictures and the masterpieces of the English 18C. (The fuller representation of British painting, particularly the more modern, and of 20C work of all schools, including sculpture, is in the Tate Gallery.)

The arrangement. – Italian paintings occupy the west galleries and continue broadly in chronological sequence round to 18C, north of the central publications room; the early German, early Netherlandish, Flemish and Dutch schools lie to the northwest, French collections north and south of the east wing, with British art in between and Spanish schools in the farthest east galleries. Some galleries may be closed for refurbishment and reorganisation.

GALLERY	SCHOOL AND DATE		ARTISTS (and some famous titles, but not necessarily the only work on view)
1 and 3	Early Italian	13/14C	Wilton Diptych; Duccio; Giotto (Pentecost); Gaddi; Veneziano.
2	Florence	15C	Uccello (St. George and the Dragon, The Battle of San Romano); Pisanello (Vision of St. Eustace); Fra Angelico; L. Monaco; Sassetta.
4-6	Italian	15C	Masaccio; Lippi; Piero della Francesca (The Baptism of Christ); Botticelli.
7		15C	Leonardo da Vinci cartoon (Virgin and Child).
8	Florentine and Roman	16C	Leonardo (Madonna of the Rocks); Michelangelo (Entombment); Andrea del Sarto; Raphäel (Pope Julius II, Ansidei Madonna); Pontormo; S. del Piombo.
9	Venetian	16C	Titian (Noli me tangere, Bacchus and Ariadne, Death of Actaeon, Vendramin Family); Tintoretto; Veronese; Giorgone.
10	Venetian and Paduan	15C	Bellini (The Madonna, The Doge, St. Dominic); Antonello da Messina; Mantegna; Cima (The Incredulity of St Thomas).
14	Italian	16C	Moretto, Lotto (A Lady as Lucrezia), Romanino, Savoldo, Moroni; Correggio (Ecce Homo, The Madonna of the Basket); Parmigianino (The Vision of St Jerome).
29		17C	Caravaggio (Supper at Emmaus, Boy Bitten by a Lizard); Carracci (The Dead Christ Mourned); Guido Reni (Adoration of the Shepherds); Guercino; Rosa.
34		18C	Canaletto (Venice, Regatta on the Grand Canal); Tiepolo (Allegory with Venus and Time); Guardi; Longhi; Solimena; Battoni.
15-19	Dutch	17C	Frans Hals (Young Man holding a skull, Family Group in a Landscape); sea and landscapes by Cuyp, de Cappelle, van de Velde, van Ruisdael, van Goyen; Interiors and domestic scenes by J. Steen.
25-28	Dutch	17C	Vermeer (Young Woman standing at a Virginal); Rembrandt (Hendrickje Stoffels, A woman bathing, Jacob Trip, Old Man in an armchair, 2 self-portraits, Saskia, Belshazzar's Feast); Pieter de Hoogh; N. Maes; Avercamp; Elsheimer; Hobbema (The Harlem Lock); Landscapes by Cuyp; van de Velde.
20-22 30	Flemish	17C	Van Dyck (Charles I on horseback and the beautiful courtly, double portrait, Lady Elizabeth Thimbleby and Dorothy, Viscountess Andover, the Earl of Pembroke and his family, Lords John and Bernard Stuart); Rubens (The Judgement of Paris, Samson and Delilah, View of Het Steen, Le Chapeau de Paille, the Nativity, the Brazen Serpent); Teniers the Younger, Jordaens.
22 a 23-24	Early German and Netherlandish	15/16C	Bruegel (Adoration of the Kings); Dürer (The Painter's father); Baldung-Grien (The Trinity, Portrait of a Man); Cranach (Cupid complaining to Venus), Holbein (The Ambassadors, Christina of Denmark); Jan van Eyck (Marriage of Giovanni Arnolfini and Giovanna Cenami); Rogier van der Weyden (Portrait of a Lady); Mabuse (Christus, Adam and Eve), Bosch; G. David; Memling.
35-39	British	17/18C	Hogarth (Marriage à la Mode series, Shrimp Girl); Reynolds (Anne, Countess of Albemarle, Lord Heathfield); Gainsborough (Mr and Mrs Andrews, The Morning Walk, The Painter's Daughters, The Watering Place); Constable (The Haywain, The Cornfield, Salisbury Cathedral, Weymouth Bay); Turner (The Fighting Téméraire, Calais Pier, Rain, Steam and Speed); Stubbs (The Melbourne and Milbanke families); Zoffany (Mrs Oswald); Lawrence (Queen Charlotte); Reynolds (Portraits).
41-42	Spanish	16/17/18C	Velazquez (The Rokeby Venus, St John on Patmos); El Greco (Christ driving the Traders from the Temple); Murillo (Self-portrait, The Two Trinities); Zurbaran; Goya (Duke of Wellington, Doña Isabel de Porcel).
32	French	17C	Poussin (Landscape, Bacchanalian Revell); Claude (Hagar and the Angel, The Enchanted Castle); Philippe de Champaigne (Cardinal Richelieu, full length and triple profile); Le Nain (Adoration of the Shepherds).
33		18C	Watteau (The Scale of Love), Chardin, Boucher, Lancret, Nattier, Fragonard, Greuze, de la Tour, David (Jacobus Blauw).
40		19C	Puvis de Chavannes, Delaroche, Moreau, Fantin-Latour.
43		19C	Ingres, Delacroix, Corot, Daumier, Géricault, Millet (The Winnower), Courbet.
44		19C	Manet (La Servante de Bocks); Monet (Beach at Trouville, La Gare St Lazare); Renoir (La Première Sortie); Toulouse-Lautrec; Degas (After the Bath); Pissarro (Box Hill, Upper Norwood, The Thames below Westminster, Montmartre at Night).
45		19C	Seurat (Bathers, Asnières); Cézanne (Les Grandes Baigneuses, Self-portrait); Van Gogh (Sunflowers); Gauguin; Bonnard; Picasso; Klimt; Redon.
46		19C	Monet (Water lilies, Irises); Renoir (Dancers); Vuillard (Lunch at Villeneuve-sur-Yonne).

Lower Floor: supplementary galleries – Early Italian, Historical Collection, Early Netherlandish and German, Dutch; Flemish, Italian; French; Italian; Spanish.

NATIONAL PORTRAIT GALLERY ★★

Map p 175. Open Mondays to Fridays 10am to 5pm, Saturdays to 6pm, Sundays 2 to 6pm; closed 1 January, Good Friday, May Day holiday, 24, 25, 26 December. Archives and Library in Carlton Gardens (p 114).

Chronologically the arrangement begins at the top *(lift)* with pre-Tudor sovereigns and ends three floors down with 20C.

The gallery is heaven on earth! Inside the Victorian-Italian-Renaissance building is everyone English one has read about or read: Tudor monarchs to 20C poets, men of science, politics, letters, music, the stage, diarists, architects, people in the social whirl... The act of foundation of 1856 states that paintings shall be collected for their subject but, portraiture having been a major *genre* since Holbein was court painter to Henry VIII, there are works by (or copies after) the greatest British and visiting artists including van Dyck, Mytens, Honthorst, Lely, Kneller, Gainsborough, Reynolds, Romney, Zoffany, Lawrence, Sargent, Orpen, Rothenstein, John, Gunn, the miniaturists Samuel Cooper, Nicholas Hilliard and Isaac Oliver, sculptors Roubiliac and Epstein and caricaturists and etchers Landseer, Max Beerbohm, Phil May, Spy, Low...

Top Floor: The Tudors to the Regency. – Dominating the scene are the royal portraits: Henry VII, Henry VIII (Holbein), Queen Elizabeth in youth, her coronation year and majestic old age, the Stuarts, George IV (Lawrence). Grouped by association are their contemporaries: Thomas More and family, Wolsey; Mary Queen of Scots; court favourites, Essex, Leicester, Raleigh, Buckingham; Purcell; Shakespeare – the best authenticated portrait – Ben Jonson, Marvell, Donne, Milton, Dryden, Swift, Pope, Addison and Steele, Johnson and Boswell (both by Reynolds); Pepys, Evelyn; Wren, Vanbrugh, Hawksmoor, Caius Cibber; Oliver Cromwell and the generals of both sides; the Cabal, the Kit-Cat Club; there are Fanny Burney in her stylish hat, self-portraits by Reynolds and Gainsborough, Garrick by Gainsborough, Sterne by Reynolds...

Mezzanine Floor: Middle Ages: effigies of kings and Geoffrey Chaucer.

First Floor: The Victorians and Edwardians. – There is a statue of unabashed sentimentality of the young Victoria and Albert. There are politicians in abundance, Melbourne, Gladstone, Disraeli, many in caricature; there are the reformers, explorers and generals; Darwin and T H Huxley; Barry and Pugin, the Scotts; Gilbert and Sullivan; Tennyson, the Brownings, Dickens, George Eliot, the Brontë sisters (by Branwell); Ellen Terry; Ruskin; the Pre-Raphaelites; Oscar Wilde, Aubrey Beardsley, Whistler, Steer, Sickert, George Moore, Max Beerbohm...

Mezzanine floor: Portraits of the Royal Family.

Ground Floor: Drawings, sculpture, photographs of 20C famous men and women: poets, writers, artists, politicians, scientists, actors etc... A gallery is devoted to new acquisitions.

NEWHAM (Newham)

Five miles to the east of the City, an industrialised area, which fell into decline when the Royal Docks closed in 1983, is experiencing extensive revitalization with major improvements to the infrastructure under the aegis of the LDDC.

London City Airport. – A modern airport situated on a strip between the Albert and George V Docks opened in 1987 as the world's first STOLport (short take-off and landing airport) bringing the City within easy access of several European capitals.

North Woolwich Old Railway Station Museum. – *Pier Head, North Woolwich. Open Mondays to Fridays 10am to 5pm, Sundays 2 to 5pm. Access by British Rail from Stratford to North Woolwich.* The Italianate style building (1847) has been converted into a museum featuring historical displays on the Great Eastern Railway and locomotives standing at the station platform.

Nearby are the Royal Victoria Gardens, formerly the North Woolwich Gardens where dances were held. Views of the Thames Barrier and the Woolwich Ferry *(qv)*.

OSTERLEY PARK ★★ (Hounslow)

Open Tuesdays to Sundays, Easter and holiday Mondays 11am to 5pm; closed 1 January, Good Friday, May Day holiday, 25, 26 December; car park; restaurant; £2, children £1 NT.

Osterley is the place to see **Robert Adam** interior decoration at its most complete – room after room is as he designed it: ceilings, walls, doorcases, doors, handles, carpets, mirrors and furniture – especially chairs standing in the exact positions for which they were designed. Osterley is also the place to look at trees: in the avenue of mixed species, four files wide leading to the house, shading the lawns...

The country seat of two City gentlemen. – **Sir Thomas Gresham** bought Osterley Manor in 1562 and immediately began to build a country house adjoining the old manorhouse, a late 15C Tudor brick building surrounding three sides of a courtyard. When Gresham's mansion was complete, Queen Elizabeth honoured her financier and merchant adventurer by a visit to the "house beseeming a prince" (1576), which on his death in 1579, passed to his stepson Sir William Read, husband of Lady Mary of Boston Manor (*see opposite*).

Osterley Park : rear staircase.

In 1711 the mansion was purchased by another City grandee **Francis Child,** clothier's son from Wiltshire, who came to seek his fortune in London in the 1650s, had found it, been knighted, elected Lord Mayor (1698) and become banker to Charles II, Nell Gwynn, Pepys, John Churchill, future Duke of Marlborough, King William and Queen Mary... He had started as a goldsmith's apprentice; moved to a second house where he married the owner's daughter, inherited the family fortune and business which he transformed to suit the times. Money – gold – was accumulating rapidly through increased trade in Tudor and Stuart times but was easily stolen; merchants, after finding that even deposits in the Tower were vulnerable – Charles I seized £130 000 from the vaults in 1640! – placed their bullion with goldsmiths usually for a fixed time; the smiths with Francis Child as a forerunner began to lend the cash out at interest and became the City's first bankers. Child's Bank (now Royal Bank of Scotland) "at the sign of the Marigold" – the building had been a tavern and there were no street numbers – can still be seen at No 1 Fleet St.

The old banker, never lived there himself; it was his grandchild, namesake and heir who, in 1756, began the transformation which was to continue for more than twenty years by which time the house was owned by Francis Child's great niece, Sarah Sophia who in 1804 married the future 5th Earl of Jersey; the 9th Earl presented Osterley to the nation in 1949.

Exterior. – The square form with corner towers of Sir Thomas Gresham's house remains, though enlarged and encased by new bricks and stone quoins in 18C by the first of the two architects employed on the transformation. Sir William Chambers in addition reduced the courtyard to provide a hall and continuous passage round the house and completed the Gallery and Breakfast Room before being superseded in 1761 by the now more fashionable, Robert Adam. The latter made two contributions to the exterior, the grand portico at the front and, at the rear, a horseshoe staircase with delicate wrought iron and brasswork (1770).

Interior. – By 1773 Horace Walpole, visiting from nearby Strawberry Hill, wrote: "The old house is so improved and enriched that all the Percies and Seymours of Sion must die of envy... There is a hall, library, breakfast room, eating room, all *chefs d'œuvre* of Adam, a gallery 130ft long, a drawing room worthy of Eve before the Fall".

The **Hall** is wide with apses at either end, a ceiling compartmented and filled with floral scrolls and a black and white marble pavement. Trophies on grey panels fill the spaces between pilasters, Classical statues flank the curved fireplaces. Apart from the statues, Adam personally designed every item, even to the door handles, such was his attention to detail.

Chambers, it is believed, designed the **Gallery** which runs the length of the house. Marble chimney pieces, Classical doorcases and the lighter Rococo style white frieze on an ochre ground are set off by green walls, as in the 18C hung with paintings. The portraits at either end are by S. Ricci, the views of Osterley in the late 18C after the water colourist, Anthony Devis. The laquerwork is 18C Chinese, the furniture thought to be by Adam and the pier-glasses and girandoles, garlanded, supported by nonchalant mermaids, are the Scotsman in his lightest vein.

The **Eating Room** is an all Adam room: motifs from the ceiling decoration of vines and ivy leaves reappear over the doors; wall panels, sideboard flanked by pedestalled urns, side tables of Italian mosaic, beautiful swagged, oval pier-glasses and a set of superb lyre back chairs of carved mahogany (18C custom required that the chairs be set formally, against the wall, when not in use and that gate-leg tables be brought in for dining).

The staircase, with Adam designed iron balustrade, decorative panels and cornice and three beautiful lamps and the north passage lead to the **Library.** In this room it is the furniture which is outstanding: there are lyre back armchairs, a pedestal desk veneered with harewood (stained sycamore) and inlaid with motifs matched in the side tables, all made in about 1775 by John Linnell, leading cabinet maker of his day, probably to his own designs under Adam's supervision. The ceiling decoration is in very low relief.

The **Breakfast Room** is decorated in an amazing lemon yellow with strong blue ornament. The ceiling is by Chambers; tables and pier-glasses, however, were designed by Adam and the lyre back mahogany armchairs probably by Linnell.

Retrace your steps and walk up the stairs to the **Yellow Taffeta Bedchamber** which is adorned with painted taffeta curtains and bed hangings and ornate gilded mirrors. The bed surmounted by cupped acorns was designed by Adam (1779). Next are the dressing-rooms and bedchamber designed by Chambers for Mr and Mrs Child. Few of the original furnishings survive: a 17C ebony cabinet and a lacquer dressing-table and cabinet of the same period. The 18C Chinese porcelain also belonged to the family. The white chimmeypiece with acanthus leaf decoration and the gilt mirror contrast with the bright blue walls of the end room.

Return to the gallery and make for the **Drawing Room,** rich with gilding and ornament, which has a ceiling studded with flower filled patterae framing a panache of ostrich feathers. Pale pinks and greens, gold and red reappear in cornice and carpet (made at Moorfields) and in the doorcases from which, in turn, motifs are taken for the fireplace and as part of the inlaid design and ormolu decoration of the two harewood veneered commodes. The serpentine sofas and chairs are after the early French neo-Classical style. French pier glasses and perfume burners.

In the **Tapestry Room,** the Adam motifs for ceiling and fireplace fade into insignificance beside the richness of the Gobelins' tapestries woven for the room, signed and dated by (Jacques) Neilson, 1775, an artist of Scots origin in charge of the works in Paris from 1751-88. On a rich crimson ground, framed in gold, is the Boucher series, *The Loves of the Gods,* and between are flower filled urns, garlands, cupids at play... Chairs and sofa are in the same style.

The **State Bed** chamber is in cool greens. Note the Child crest of an eagle with an adder in its beak on the eight poster valance, and the gilded chairs, upholstered in green velvet, oval backs supported on reclining sphinxes – one of Adam's most graceful designs (1777). The chimney glass, surmounted by the Child crest, is declared in the house inventory of 1782 to have been the "first plate made in England". The walls were originally covered in green velvet.

The interest of the **Dressing Room,** which forestalled a fashion for the Antique, lies in Adam's application of what he took to be Etruscan decorative themes, in fact Greek, to an 18C interior: even the chairs are made to conform in colour and patterning, though not in shape, to the theme.

The Demonstration Room is hung with plans and drawings of house and garden by Adam and others. The kitchens *(left of the east front)* are being reconstructed.

The **Stable Block** *(restaurant),* north of the house, with its mellow Tudor brickwork may have been part of the earlier manor house. Backing on to the kitchen garden (north west) is Adam's semi-circular garden house (c 1780) facing a Doric Temple of Pan.

OSTERLEY PARK★★

Boston Manor. – *Brentford. Open grounds only daily; house late May to October, Saturdays only 2 to 4.30pm.* The red brick house was begun in 1623 by Lady Mary Read who had acquired the property by settlement from Sir Thomas Gresham through marriage to his stepson; the magnificent moulded plaster ceiling in the State Room is dated 1623; the staircase with its *trompe l'œil* balustrade is also original. In 1670 James Clitherow bought the property for £5 136 17s 4d, adding the bold entablature, window architraves and garden door, and landscaping the grounds with cedars and a lake.

PADDINGTON (Westminster)
Map pp 5-8 (B/VX).

Paddington still numbered fewer than 2 000 souls in 1800; by 1900 it exceeded 125 000. Within the century it had become a canal junction and a railway terminal; bus services – horse drawn – had been inaugurated, also the metropolitan and district underground railway.

The Canal. – The completion of the Uxbridge to Brentford section of the Grand Junction Canal in 1795 provided a reliable waterway between London and the industrial Midlands; in the same year work began under a Cornishman, William Praed, on the construction of a canal from Uxbridge to Paddington. This, by 1801, was in use transporting produce from the market town and passengers in vast numbers on outings (half-a-crown to Uxbridge); between 1812 and 1820 Paddington was linked to the Thames at Limehouse by the Regent's Canal *(qv)*.

Paddington Station. – The GWR and the station were the undertaking, in 1850, of **Isambard Kingdom Brunel.** The station radiated 19C confidence beneath an extensive wrought iron and glass roof mounted on cast iron pillars; there were four platforms approached by ten tracks. The accompanying hotel (1850-2), by Hardwick the Younger, was French Renaissance and Baroque inspired, decorated with allegorical sculpture.

The underground. – The railway, the Metropolitan, was the first section to be constructed of what is now the London Transport Underground. The line, which ran from Praed St to Farringdon by way of King's Cross was opened on 10 January 1863 and within five years had been extended to South Kensington and Westminster and, in the east, to Moorgate. The carriages were open trucks and although the smoke and dirt going through the tunnels was asphyxiating, over 9 million passengers travelled on the new line in the first year.

The bus service. – Omnibuses were introduced to London from Paris on 4 July 1829 by the coachbuilder, George Shillibeer. He brought over a "handsome machine", as the papers called it, drawn by 3 horses abreast and with a capacity of 16-18. Long and short stage coaches were not licensed to take up or set down passengers "on the stones", in other words the pavements of central London, so Shillibeer discreetly ran his first omnibuses outside the central limits, from Paddington Green to the Bank by way of the New, now Marylebone, Road.

The development. – In 1827, after the gallows at Tyburn had been removed, development of the area between the Bayswater and Edgware Rds was undertaken and 150 years later has been renewed, maintaining the original layout of squares, crescents and terraces.

The London Toy and Model Museum. – *23 Craven Hill. Open Tuesday to Saturday, 10am to 5.30pm; Sundays and holidays 11am to 5.30pm; shop, reference library and refreshments; £2.20, OAPs, and students £1.20, children 80p.*

In two listed Victorian houses, just north of Kensington Gardens, is a growing exhibition of toys and models, which comprises one of the finest collections on public display. Nine rooms, devoted to working model trains, Basset-Lowke, Meccano and Dinky toys, tin toys, teddy bears, toy animals, dolls and dolls' houses, and a toy fort complete with military models, evoke childish delight or reverent nostalgia. A rare children's roundabout and model railway operate in the garden *(occasional locomotive trials on 0, 1" and 2 1/2" gauge)*. There is a boating pond and an activity area for small children.

PUTNEY (Wandsworth)

Putney's transformation was precipitated by the arrival of the railway in mid 19C. Evolution previously had been gradual, from settlement beside the ford to substantial village where Oliver Cromwell held a council of war round the communion table in St Mary's in 1647. Even the erection of a wooden toll bridge in 1729 – the first above London Bridge – had little effect. In the wake of the railway came builders... The early association with the river remains – rowing clubs still line the Surrey bank, oarsmen practise in midstream; the **Boat Race** over the four and a half mile course to Mortlake is rowed each spring as it has been ever since 1845.

St Mary's Parish Church. – The church at the approach to the bridge *(p 150)* was burnt out in 1973 and reopened after restoration in 1982. The 14C chantry chapel and 15C tower were preserved when the church was rebuilt in 1836.

Putney High St, Putney Hill. – The bustling High St with, halfway along a Tudor style, gargoyle decorated pub, the Old Spotted Horse, still includes tall 19C house-fronts.

At the start of Putney Hill, near the crossroads, are to left and right, no 11, The Pines, a monstrous tall grey attached Victorian House where **Swinburne** lived and no 28A, a pink washed Georgian villa with a firemark set like a beauty patch on its pale wall.

Lower Richmond Road. – Near the bridgefoot, low lying between the Lower Richmond Road and the river bank road which serves the club boat houses, is 18C **Winchester House,** dwarfed by the surrounding buildings.

Lower Richmond Road itself winds upriver past a straggling line of village and antique shops and small Victorian houses, punctuated by pubs of varying vintage: the White Lion, a flamboyant Victorian pub (1887) flaunting two caryatids like a ship's figurehead opposite the church, the Duke's Head, late Georgian overlooking the river and, just before the common, the Georgian French Revolution and the 19C gabled Spencer Arms. On the Lower Common is All Saints Church (1874), notable for its Burne-Jones windows *(open only during services)*.

The proposal. – It was a superb plan: the government wanted something done with Marylebone Fields (enclosed by Henry VIII, divided under the Commonwealth into manor farms of which the leases reverted to the crown in 1811) and they required direct access from north central London to Westminster. **Nash** proposed a tree landscaped park with a serpentine lake bounded by a road along which, on all except the north side left open for the view of Primrose Hill and the heights of Hampstead and Highgate, there would be terrace palaces, divisible into three bay town houses for the noble and fashionable. Within the park would be a circus, ringed by houses facing both in and outwards and, surmounting the upraised centre, a valhalla; elsewhere would be a *guinguette* or summer pavilion for the Prince of Wales, approached along a wide avenue (the Broad Walk) in the axis of Portland Place, numerous villas half-hidden in the trees and, as central feature, the proposed Regent's Canal; in sum, the park would become the most exquisite garden suburb.

The approach was to be up Robert Adam's Portland Place, a most successful speculation begun by the brothers in 1774 as a private road lined by substantial mansions and closed at the bottom by Foley House, whose owner insisted on an uninterrupted view which dictated the 125ft width. To link the place and park and traverse the psychological barrier of the New Road (Marylebone Rd), would be a circus with, at the centre, St Marylebone Church (not then built). Nash hoped to extend Portland Place, which he greatly admired, due south across Oxford St and Piccadilly by means of circuses and so arrive in the axis of Carlton House. From Oxford Circus south the street was to be lined with shops and houses behind a continuous colonnade which would provide shelter below for shoppers and fashionable promenaders and balconies to the houses above; under the street was to be a much needed new sewer system for central London.

The realisation. – In essence the plan survived – considering that it was subject to government commissions and the hazards of land purchase; the *guinguette*, all but seven of the villas and the would-be double Bath Crescent disappeared although an Inner Circle was laid out as a botanic garden, now transformed into **Queen Mary's Gardens**; the approach from Portland Place was modified to the open armed Park Crescent and Park Sq; the extension of Portland Place being out of line, was given a pivoted turn by the construction of the circular porch of All Souls, and the angle at the south beautifully swept round by means of the Quadrant. The plan took eight years to achieve, from 1817-25; New St, as it was called at first, was a fashionable and glittering success – it was the age of Beau Brummell; the houses along the park were taken; the Prince, by now George IV, had unfortunately tired of Carlton House but it remained the focal climax until 1829 when it was demolished and replaced by Waterloo Place *(qv)* and Carlton House Terrace *(qv)*. Nash personally probably only designed a few of the **terraces★★**, houses and shops, but he set the style and different architects, among them Decimus Burton, in accordance with the practice of the day, drew up plans which were formally submitted to Nash to ensure homogeneity before being executed. The common theme was the use of giant columns, generally Ionic or Corinthian to emphasise the centre and ends of the long façades which, in addition, were usually advanced and sometimes pedimented or given an attic screen decorated with statuary. Columns, of a different order, forming an arcade or framing doors or ground floor windows, balustrades and continuous first floor balconies of iron or stucco, united the long fronts into single compositions.

Round the park★★

The terraces, named after the titles of some of George III's 15 children, and other principal buildings are described in order starting from Park Crescent and circling the park clockwise, with a detour south from Winfield House to the Inner Circle and open-air theatre returning north via the Broad Walk and the Zoo *(qv)*.

Park Crescent (1821): paired Ionic columns in a continuous porch, and a balustrade and balcony emphasise the classical curve. The Doric lodges once flanked iron gates closing off the crescent and the square from the main road.

Park Sq, East and West (1823-4): single Ionic columns.

Ulster Terrace (1824): the idiosyncracy appears in two closely positioned pairs of bay windows at either end.

York Terrace (1821; west end now named **Nottingham Terrace**): 360yds long or nearly half the width of the park, the terrace comprises two symmetrical blocks, York Gate in the axis of St Marylebone Church *(qv)* and some detached houses. The sequence of column orders is giant Corinthian in the mansions at either end, Ionic above Doric colonnades in the pedimented main blocks and Ionic in the houses at York Gate.

Cornwall Terrace (1822): the 187yd front, marked at either end and the centre by Corinthian columns, is divided into a number of receding planes. Note through the trees the modest 18C brick houses and old pub on the far side of Baker St/Park Rd, also the lodge with rounded windows and pitched slate roof.

Clarence Terrace (1823): heavily accented Corinthian centre and angles above an Ionic arcade.

Sussex Place (1822; **London Graduate School of Business Studies**): the most surprising, finialled, slim, octagonal cupolas, in pairs, crown the ends and frame the pedimented centre of the curved terrace; below the domes are canted bays and, between, a continuous line of Corinthian columns (the far side from the park was rebuilt in a modern buttressed style in brick in 1972).

Royal College of Obstetricians and Gynaecologists (1960): the 4 storey brick building has a stone wing at right angles encompassing the low recessed entrance and over it, the hall.

Hanover Terrace (1822-3): pediments coloured bright blue as a background to plasterwork and serving as pedestals for statuary silhouetted against the sky, mark the terrace. Hanover Gate has a small, octagonal lodge with heavy inverted corbel decoration and niches with statues beneath a pitched slate roof and central octagonal chimney.

The Mosque (1977): the 140ft minaret, white with a small gold coloured dome and finial crescent, is a delicate addition to the skyline. The mosque itself has a pale grey façade, pierced by tall, four centred, arched windows of five lights each and blind arcades supporting a drum, crowned by a

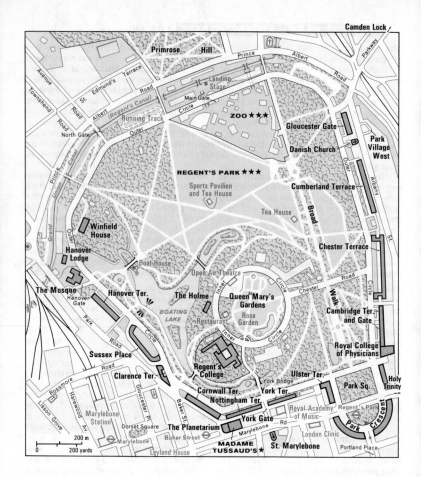

huge, gold coloured copper dome. To the rear are the extensive new buildings of the Islamic Cultural Centre. It stands on the site of one of Nash's villas (Albany Cottage) and was designed by Sir Frederick Gibberd.

Hanover Lodge, with a large modern brick addition, and **The Holme** are two of the 18C villas. **Regent's College,** formerly Bedford College (f 1849 in Bedford Sq and now merged with Royal Holloway College) is itself on the site of South Villa and St John's Lodge, rebuilt and enlarged this century in red brick.

Winfield House: the neo-Georgian house of 1936, now the residence of the US ambassador, is on the site of St Dunstan's Lodge where the organisation for blinded exservicemen was founded in 1915. The lodge was designed by Decimus Burton in 1825 for the 3rd Marquess of Hertford (qv) who, it is said, used it as a harem.

Down Albany St is **Park Village West,** the most attractive of the two dependent streets to the terraces. The small houses and modest terraces are in Nash's country cottage style, although not designed by him.

Gloucester Gate (1827): angle pediments with plasterwork against red painted tympana and surmounting statues, mark the main terrace.

Danish Church. – The neo-Gothic church in stock brick dates from 1829 when it was built for the St Katharine Royal Hospital Community (qv). In 1950 the church was taken over by the Danish community whose own building in Limehouse had been bombed. Inside are a coffered ceiling, below the windows shields of English queens from Eleanor to Mary, and beside the modern fittings, John the Baptist and Moses, two of the four figures carved in wood by the 17C Danish sculptor **Caius Cibber** for Limehouse. Outside to the right is a replica of the Jelling Stone.

Cumberland Terrace (1826): the Ionic pillars of the 267yd long façade recur in the intervening arches. Britannia, the arts and science are represented in the central pediment behind squat vases.

Cumberland Terrace.

Chester Terrace (1825): the longest unbroken façade (313yds) has Corinthian columns rising from ground level to emphasise the ends, centre and mid points between; at either end triumphal, named, arches lead to the access road to the rear.

Cambridge Terrace (1825): The terrace and neighbouring buildings have been restored.

Cambridge Gate (1875): the totally Victorian, stone faced block with pavilion roofs, stands on the site of the Coliseum, a large circular building with a portico and glazed roof used for exhibitions and panoramas (or dioramas).

Royal College of Physicians. – The tesserae faced building, extending squarely forward to afford a recessed entrance encased in glass, contrasts with a long polygonal construction of black brick to one side covering a hall. It was designed by Denys Lasdun in 1964.

Regent's Canal. – *Towpath open 9am to dusk.* The proposed canal, linking Paddington *(qv)* to the Thames, was incorporated by John Nash in his plans for Regent's Park, skirting the northern boundary, although he had originally intended a more southerly route. It runs for eight miles from Little Venice in Paddington to Limehouse in the docks, passing through Maida Tunnel, where the boat crews legged their barges along, lying on their backs and pushing against the tunnel roof with their feet, under Macclesfield Bridge, known as 'Blow Up' Bridge, owing to the explosion of a cargo of gunpowder and petroleum in 1874, between the animal houses of London Zoo, past former wharves and stabling for the horses which towed the barges, and through Islington Tunnel. A flight of 12 locks carries the canal down 86ft to the Thames.

  Little Venice at the western end is an attractive triangle of water, overlooked by Georgian houses, modern flats and the Canal Office (formerly a toll house). In summer the London Waterbus Company (☎ *01-482 2550*) operate a daily waterbus service from Little Venice (Delamere Terrace, W2) to the Zoo and Camden Lock *(April to September, daily 10, 11am, noon, 1, 2, 3, 4, 5pm).* In winter there is a weekend service only from Little Venice *(10.30am, noon, 1.30, 3pm)* and from Camden Lock *(11.15am, 12.45, 2.15, 2.45pm).* Trips: one way £2, children, OAPs £1.10; Rtn £2.60 and £1.50; trips including zoo admission from Little Venice, £5.75, children, OAPs £3.45; from Camden Lock, £3.90, children, OAPs £2.35. Traditional narrow boats ply between Little Venice and Camden Lock *(Jason's Trip, opposite 60 Blomfield Rd,* ☎ *01-286 3428):* Easter weekend at 10.30am, 12.30, 2.30, 4.30pm, April, May, September 12.30, 2.30pm, June, July, August 10.30am, 12.30, 2.30, 4.30, 1-5 October 12.30pm; £2.95, children £1.50; time: 1 1/2 hours Rtn); (Jenny Wren trips 250 Camden High St, ☎ 01-485 4433): March to October, daily 11.30am, 2, 3.30pm; £2.10, children £1.10; book in advance).

  Camden Lock, once a timber wharf with stabling and hay lofts, is now a lively crafts centre – with weekend antique and homecraft markets, restaurants and a dance hall. The Regent's Canal Information Centre presents historical displays relating to the canal development. The futuristic TV-AM building designed by T. Farrell is a notable new feature in the area.

  The Round House *(north in Chalk Farm Road)*, built as an engine shed by Robert Stephenson in 1847 to house 22 goods locomotives, became an arts centre in 1964.

Down the street★ *(Map pp 118-119)*

Portland Place. – In 18C the street, closed by gates to the north, overlooked by Foley House at the south end and houses by Robert and James Adam along either side, was a fashionable promenade. Foley House was replaced in 1864 by the high Victorian, pavilion roofed, Langham Hotel. The Adam brothers' houses, except no 46, have long since disappeared. In 1934 the **Royal Institute of British Architects** celebrated their centenary by erecting a tall stone corner building (no 66) adorned on the façade and on the pillars, with reliefs. Statues of Lord Lister, who lived in Park Crescent and Quintin Hogg, founder of the Regent St Polytechnic in 1882, stand at either end; Broadcasting House, designed by the architect G. Val Myer in 1931, marks the turn.

All Souls. – *Langham Place.* The fluted, candle-snuffer, spire set on a ring of columns mounted at the centre of a circular portico of tall Ionic pillars, gives All Souls a unique silhouette. Nash constructed this, his only important church, in 1822-4 as the pivot around which his triumphal way was to proceed south and so designed it to be the same from whatever angle it was viewed. The fabric is Bath stone; inside is a traditional, galleried hall church. In 1976 the floor was raised 18ins and an undercroft excavated revealing the unusual inverted arches of Nash's foundations. The BBC morning service usually comes live from All Souls.

Regent St★. – The street, which in 18C included chapels, a theatre and large and small façades, was related by the colonnades designed by Nash to run from Oxford Circus to Carlton House. Named the New Street, it was so successful that it brought about its own architectural downfall; the shops beneath the colonnades and round the sweep of the **Quadrant** had no room to expand beyond the small ground floor showrooms, so that from the turn of the century the Classical style fronts began to be demolished and replaced by the large, dignified buildings of today with plate glass windows and upper sales floors. The only colonnaded section, and that rebuilt, is beneath the London County Fire Office at the south end.

All Souls Church.

Among the places and shops of note are the **Polytechnic** (west side, no 309), Boosey and Hawkes (295); at Oxford Circus, Peter Robinson; southwards Dickins and Jones, Liberty's *(see below)*, **Jaeger, Hamleys** toyshop, **Garrard's,** the Crown Jewellers responsible for the royal regalia, Aquascutum, the Café Royal *(see below)*, and Austin Reed opposite; in Lower Regent St is Lillywhite's (sports equipment).

Liberty's. – The shop, founded by the son of a draper, Arthur Liberty, in 1875 on a borrowed £1 500, was soon dignified by the name of an emporium and associated with the Aesthetic Movement. From the first it was known for its silks and within three years was producing its own materials after old Indian prints; the riches are even more varied today: silks, lawns, wall papers, oriental carpets and bronzes, bamboo, china and glass, furniture, leather, jade and modern jewellery, scarves... The **Tudor Building** (1922-24), in Gt. Marlborough Street, was designed by Edwin T. and Stanley Hall and built from oak and teak timbers taken from the Royal Navy's last two sailing ships. Inside there are galleries on three floors around a central light well.

Café Royal. – The "café", now a multifloored restaurant with a hall where the National Sporting Club meets, a Masonic Temple and banqueting rooms, began as a tiny eating house opened in 1863 in Glasshouse St by a Burgundian and his wife. Daniel Nichols, as he anglicised his name, built up a reputation for good wine and good food, prospered and moved to the fashionable site in the Quadrant. In France the Second Empire was at its height; in Regent St the Café Royal adopted a new name and as house emblem a crowned N wreathed in laurel leaves! In 1890s the café became the meeting place of writers and artists – Oscar Wilde, Lord Alfred Douglas, Aubrey Beardsley, Whistler, George Moore, Max Beerbohm, Augustus John, Orpen...

Piccadilly Circus. – The circus, for which there have been innumerable plans since the war, was adorned with **Eros** – officially the Angel of Christian Charity – a memorial fountain to the philanthropist, Lord Shaftesbury, in 1892. The fountain has been moved to a site in front of the Criterion Theatre *(see below)* under the scheme for the redevelopment of the area.

The south front is occupied by the Criterion, a Victorian building with pavilion roofs now divided but originally in 1870s a hotel and restaurant with a marble hall beneath a mosaic ceiling *(Criterion Brasserie)*. Incorporated in the block and actually on the site of the 17C St James's market, is the Criterion Theatre (1874), largely underground and one of the first to be lit by electricity. The foyer is lined with decorative tiles.

RICHMOND ★★ (Richmond upon Thames)

Richmond, possessing what has been called the most beautiful urban green in England, grew to importance between 12 and 17C as a royal seat and, after the Restoration, as the residential area of members of the court – Windsor, Hampton Court and Kew are easily accessible. In the courtiers' wake followed diplomats, politicians, professional men, dames and their schools, and with the coming of the railway in 1840, prosperous Victorian commuters.

On the east side of the main road are reminders of the growing village in the parish Church of St Mary Magdalene with its 16C square flint and stone tower, early brasses and monuments (Edmund Kean), 18C houses (Ormond and Halford Rds), 19C cottages (Waterloo Place), the Vineyard dating back in name to 16/17C when local vines were famous, and the rebuilt almshouses of 17C foundation – Queen Elizabeth's, Bishop Duppa's and Michel's. In Paradise Rd stands Hogarth House built in 1748, where Leonard and Virginia Woolf who lived there from 1915 to 1924, founded the Hogarth Press.

Around the Green

Richmond Green★★. – The Green, overlooked by the Old Palace, scene of Tudor jousting and, since the mid 17C, of cricket, lies back from the bustle and traffic of the main road, George St.

Along the east, Greenside, are 17 and 18C houses with the ornate red brick 19C Richmond Theatre overlooking Little Green at the far end, and at the south end a series of narrow lanes, running into the high street, overlooked by the small front windows of jewellers, antique shops, pubs... At the corner there is a widening into a paved court, lined by the last of the enfilade of 18C houses and by two pubs, rebuilt on ancient sites, the Princes' Head and the Cricketers. Abutting is a group of six, two storey brick houses with straight hooded doorways, built between 1692-1700 by John Powell (who lived himself in no 32 which he also built) and known as **Old Palace Terrace.**

Continuing round are **Oak House, Old Palace Place** and **Old Friars.** The first two date back to 1700 and the third to 1687 (date on a rainwater head); Old Friars, so named as it stands on part of the site of a monastery founded by Henry VII in 1500, was extended to the right in the 18C to include a concert room for the holding of "music mornings and evenings".

Maids of Honour Row★★. – The famous row dates from 1724 when the future George II gave directions for "erecting a new building near his seat at Richmond to serve as lodgings for the Maids of Honour attending the Princess of Wales". There are four houses in all, each three storeys high with five bays apiece, pilastered, with friezed door cases, and small gardens behind 18C wrought iron gates and railings. The brick is mellow; the proportions are perfect.

Richmond Palace: royal residence through six reigns. – Henry VII, parsimonious where his son was prodigal, nevertheless, after a disastrous fire, "rebuilded (the palace) again sumptuously and costly and changed the name of Shene and called it Richmond because his father and he were Earls of Rychmonde" (in Yorkshire). This palace, the third on the site, was to be the last. The first residence, a manor house, erected in the 12C, was extended and embellished by Edward III, who died in it in 1377, was favoured by Richard II, his grandson while his queen, Anne of Bohemia was alive but demolished at her death in 1394; a new palace, the second, was begun by Henry V but completed only forty years after his death in the reign of Edward IV who gave it with the royal manor of Shene to his queen, Elizabeth Woodville, from whom it was confiscated by Henry VII. In 1499 it burned to the ground.

The new Tudor palace conformed to standard design: service buildings of red brick, preserved today in the gateway, enclosed an outer or Base Court, from which a second gateway led to an inner or Middle Court, lined along one side by a Great Hall of stone with a lead roof.

The Privy Lodging, which included the state rooms, surrounded another court. Domed towers and turrets crowned the construction which covered ten acres, and was by far the most splendid in the Kingdom. Henry VII died in his palace; Henry VIII and Catherine of Aragon frequented it; Queen Elizabeth held court in it, particularly in springtime, and died there; Prince Henry, James I's son, resided there and added an art gallery to house the extensive collection of royal paintings, increased after the prince's death (in the palace) by the future Charles I who also resided there notably during the plague of 1625. At the king's execution the palace was stripped and the contents, including the pictures, were sold. By the 18C little remained and private houses – the Old Palace, Gatehouse, Wardrobe, Trumpeters – were constructed out of the ruins on the site.

The Old Palace and the Gatehouse. – On the south side are two houses, the first castellated, bay windowed and with a central doorway, incorporating Tudor materials, notably brickwork, from Henry VII's palace, the second the original outer gateway of the palace (note the restored arms of Henry VII over the arch).

The Wardrobe (in Old Palace Yard *i.e.* the Base Court of the Tudor Palace). – Note the blue diapered Tudor walls incorporated in the early 18C building, also the 18C ironwork.

Trumpeters' House★. – *Old Palace Yard.* The main front of this house converted *c* 1701 from the Middle Gate of Richmond Palace, overlooks the garden and can be seen through the trees from the riverside path. The giant pedimented portico of paired columns was formerly guarded by stone statues, after which the house is still named. For a brief period in 1848-9 it was occupied by Metternich.

Richmond Riverside

Old Palace Lane, lined by modest, wistaria covered, 19C houses and cottages, leads from the southwest corner of the green to the river.

Asgill House★. – The house which stands at the end of the lane overlooking the river from a site once within the palace walls, was built *c* 1760 as a weekend and summer residence for the City banker and sometime Lord Mayor, Sir Charles Asgill. In pale golden stone with strong horizontal lines and a central bay advanced and canted for the full three storeys, it was one of the last of its type to be built overlooking the Thames.

The river path continues past the Trumpeters' House and beneath **Richmond Bridge★★** *(qv)*, which in 1777 replaced the horse ferry (note the milestone-obelisk at the town end), to re-emerge as the riverside promenade below Terrace Gardens (between Petersham Rd and Richmond Hill).

West of the bridge rises a new complex of offices, shops and restaurants built in Classical style by Q. Terry (1988) to harmonise with the surroundings.

Richmond Hill. – The **view★★** gets ever better as one climbs the steep road lined by balconied terraces and it has been immortalised by many artists including Turner and Reynolds.

The **Wick** and **Wick House,** both on the west side of the road and both enjoying the view across the bend in the river towards Marble Hill, were built in 1775 and 1772, the latter by Sir William Chambers for Sir Joshua Reynolds.

At the top, overlooking the park stands Ancaster House, a brick mansion with big bow windows, built in 1722 to designs principally by Robert Adam. The house is now attached to the Star and Garter Home opposite, which stands on the site of an inn famous in 18-19C and opened in 1924. (The British Legion poppy factory is at the Richmond end of Petersham Rd.)

The park gates which mark the hilltop are dated 1700 and are attributed to Capability Brown.

Richmond Park★★. – The countryside had been a royal chase for centuries when Charles I enclosed 2 470 acres as a park in 1637. It is the largest of the royal parks and is known today for its **wildlife** which includes badgers and herds of red and fallow deer, its majestic **oak trees** and the **spring flowers** (rhododendrons) of the Isabella Plantation.

On a fine day there is a **panorama★★★** from the top of the Henry VIII mound (said to have been raised to allow the king to survey the field) which extends from Windsor Castle to the dome of St Paul's.

Among the houses in the park are Pembroke Lodge *(cafeteria),* a rambling late 17/18C house at the centre of colourful walled and woodland gardens, Thatched House Lodge, the home of Princess Alexandra, and White Lodge, built by George II in 1727 as a hunting lodge and since 1955 the junior section of the Royal Ballet School.

ROEHAMPTON (Wandsworth – Richmond upon Thames) _____

The railway has never come to Roehampton and so its transformation to a residential suburb from a Surrey village, ringed by Georgian family mansions, came about only this century through the combustion engine – Roehampton Lane, so long a winding country road, is now a 4 lane highway. The different periods are marked by modern blocks of flats and houses grouped in long terraces following the contours of the slopes on the east side of Roehampton Lane and the Georgian mansions almost all shaded by magnificent cedars of Lebanon, and now occupied by educational establishments, which continue to give the district its special character.

High St. – Still with a few small 19C houses with shops on the ground floor (note the ironmonger, 1885, in a tall weatherboarded corner house) and containing within its ambit three pubs: the Angel, rebuilt this century on a traditional site, the 18C brick Montague Arms, and at the junction with Roehampton Lane, the rambling white weatherboarded 17-18C, King's Head.

The 200ft spire, to the south, is the dominant feature of **Holy Trinity Parish Church,** built of Corsham stone in 1898.

Manresa House. – *Battersea College of Education, Holybourne Ave.* The Classically plain 4 storey brick house with a slate roof was built in 1750 by Sir William Chambers for Lord Bessborough.

Downshire House. – *Garnett College, Roehampton Lane.* The two storey, square, parapeted house of red brick dates from 1770. Note the garden and contemporary Cedar Cottages.

ROEHAMPTON

Queen Mary's Hospital. – (1915) *Richmond, Twickenham and Roehampton Health Authority.* The hospital, behind tall iron gates, occupies **Roehampton House,** a wide, parapeted brick mansion of seven bays, four storeys high, built by Thomas Archer in 1712 and extended in 1910 by Lutyens with curving arcades on either side of the forecourt to new wings and pavilions. Adjoining are the Roehampton Artificial Limb Fitting Centre and related factories.

Mount Clare. – *Minstead Gdns.* The white, Palladian style house of 1772, with twin curving staircases and a balustraded portico added in 1780, is superbly sited on the crest of a hill. It is now overtopped by a great cedar planted in 1773 by Capability Brown.

The Froebel Institute occupies **Grove House** *(corner of Roehampton and Clarence Lanes)* – a low white stone and stucco mansion of nine bays built by James Wyatt in 1777 to which an Italian wing was added in 1850, **Ibstock Place** *(Clarence Lane)* – an early 18C mellow brick house with dormers in the tiled roof and an attractively irregular front, and **Templeton** *(Priory Lane)* – a tall, late Georgian, plain brick house with a rear terrace extending the width of the house and overlooking a garden enclosed at one end by yew hedges and shaded by two massive cedars.

Two strange houses mark Roehampton's north end: a deeply thatched white cottage of irregular shape (by Rosslyn Park RFC, at the Roehampton – Rocks Lanes, Upper Richmond Rd junction) and the Coach House (no 1 Fitzgerald Av, Upper Richmond Rd West), a 19C Gothick folly with disordered gables, pepperpot roof turrets, phoney Latin plaque, wall sundial – an Arthur Rackham illustration in a suburban street!

■ MORTLAKE

Mortlake, now known for its brewery and as the finishing point of the Boat Race, by contrast with Roehampton was reputed as early as 16C for its salt glaze pottery and in 17C for its **tapestry works.** Examples of the hangings, prized for the fineness of the weaving and elaborate borders, may be seen in the V & A, at Hatfield House, Hampton Court, Kensington Palace and in the House of Lords (arms of Charles II).

St Mary the Virgin Church. – *Open Tuesdays to Thursdays 9.30am to 12.30pm.*
The church was largely rebuilt in 19/20C except for the 17C brick vestry with its corner door shaded by a square hood on carved corbels and west tower where a 17C superstructure stands on foundations laid by order of Henry VIII. (A collection of salt glaze pottery may be seen on application.)

Sir Richard Burton's tomb. – *St Mary Magdalen churchyard, North Worple Way.* Sir Richard's widow had a Bedouin tent in stone erected as his memorial on the explorer's grave in 1890.

The north, river, side of Mortlake High St is bordered by short ranges of old cottages and several 18C houses: nos 115 Acacia House, 117 Afon House with an off centre door and unusual, peaked, roof, the L-shaped, brick, 119 and, most notably, **no 123,** a splendid two storey house of dull red brick built *c* 1720 and subsequently extended. The pedimented porch on Tuscan columns is repeated at the top of a short flight of steps at the back where it overlooks the garden and river; chandeliers alight inside *(not open)* add a romantic note. The house, then known as the Limes, was where Turner stayed when painting his Mortlake Terrace pictures, *Early Morning* and *Summer Evening.*

ROTHERHITHE (Southwark)

Rotherhithe. – The village served as a mooring to Olaf in 1013 when he supported King Ethelred against the invading Danes, as a Tudor dockyard in the reign of Henry VIII and as a berth to which the *Mayflower* returned after her historic voyage in 1621. The 19C warehouses are being converted – some into flats, the Hope Suffrance Wharf into a community centre with various crafts and industries: pottery, glass-blowing, book-binding, graphic design.

The Angel Inn. – An 18C, partly weatherboarded, inn painted white, overlooking the river.

Mayflower Inn. – *117 Rotherhithe St.* The inn, which dates back in part to the 16C, contains *Mayflower* and later 17C mementoes. It claims an ancient licence to sell British postage stamps and has permission also to sell American stamps.

St Mary's Church. – The present St Mary's on a 1 000 year old site dates from 1715. The brick building with a stone trim is crowned by an octagonal obelisk spire, collared by thin columns (rebuilt 1861), which is visible from the river. Inside, a wooden framed barrel roof stands on four massive pillars which are, in fact, plaster encased tree trunks, carpentered as would be a mast. The communion table and two Bishop's chairs are of wood from the *Temeraire;* the altarpiece includes rich garlands by **Grinling Gibbons,** "signed" with open pea-pods. The church flies the White Ensign so numerous are its Royal Navy associations. The captain of the *Mayflower* is buried in the churchyard.

Opposite the church is an 18C Charity School, 3-storeyed, 3-bayed, with coloured figures of a contemporary schoolboy and girl above the door. Next stands the Watch House (1821) matched by the Engine House (façade only); between them is the churchyard with the Old Mortuary on the south side.

Thames Tunnel Museum. – *Open first Sunday each month 11am to 4pm.* The first and most famous of the river tunnels was constructed by Marc Brunel from 1824-43 during which time it caved in twice, caused sickness and death among the labourers, was abandoned and finally, on completion, celebrated by an underground banquet and the award of a knighthood to the engineer. Since 1865 it has carried the Metropolitan underground line. Its history is set out in the old pump house near the tunnel shaft.

On the waterfront opposite is a nautical **Knot Garden** (rather dilapidated) composed of large scale hitches and bends in sculptured rope. Further east the natural flora and fauna of London are being reestablished in the 2 1/2 acre **Lavender Pond Ecological Park,** formerly part of the Surrey Docks. The area is being redeveloped for residential, business and leisure use and is served by the Thames Line Riverbus.

Scandinavian seamen's mission churches. – St Olave Kirk (1926), the Norwegian mission, stands at the entrance to the Rotherhithe Tunnel, the hospital and the rebuilt, attractively spare Swedish Church (1966) in Lower Rd. The 1957 Finnish Mission (Albion Road) with a spectacular belfry, has an interior east wall of stone, dark and running as a sea swell.

Deptford. – The riverside village became important under Henry VIII as a yard building ships later numbered among the fleet which defeated the Armada (1588). It was also at Deptford that Queen Elizabeth boarded the *Golden Hind* in 1581 to dub Francis Drake knight for his circumnavigation of the globe and where Christopher Marlowe was stabbed to death in a tavern brawl (1593). In 17C John Evelyn, who kept a journal as keenly observed if not as gay as Pepys', had a house there, Sayes Court where he cultivated a fine garden and which briefly, in 1698, and to his regret since he was a bad tenant, he leased to Peter the Great while the latter learnt the art of shipbuilding in the yards.

St Paul's. – *East of Deptford High St.* The church of 1712-30 by Thomas Archer has a lofty semicircular stone portico supporting an impressive steeple; inside, great columns with gilded Corinthian capitals uphold a richly sculpted plaster ceiling above an extensive gallery. Nearby, in Albury St, some 18C houses with elaborately carved doorcases have been preserved.

St Nicholas'. – *Corner of Deptford Green and Stowage Lane.* St Nicholas stands on a site occupied by Deptford parish churches since Saxon times. Of particular interest in the post-war reconstructed interior are the extended reredos by St Nicholas' 17C parishioner, **Grinling Gibbons**, with swags of leaves, flowers and fruit, a peapod, the ciphers and coat of arms of William and Mary. There is also a weird carved relief, an early work by Grinling Gibbons, known as the *Valley of Dry Bones*. The Jacobean pulpit is supported on a cherub believed to have been a ship's figurehead.

The laurel wreathed skulls on the gate posts originally dominated crossed bones and since so many privateers sailed from Deptford, it is claimed that the carvings inspired the traditional skull and crossbones flag. More honourably, the church so steeped in naval history has the privilege of flying the White Ensign.

Bermondsey. – *(Map pp 5-8, HY).* The square on the site of the ancient Bermondsey Abbey has been the setting since 1950 of the revived **Caledonian Market** *(Fridays 7am to noon).* The biggest flea market in London displays silverware, copper, Victorian jewellery, small furniture, telescopes and ships' compasses, china dolls' heads, books, bronzes... The area bounded by Abbey St, Tower Bridge Rd and Grange Rd is being excavated for remains of the Cluniac monastery.

St Mary Magdalen. – *Apply at the Rectory.* Adjoining is the parish church founded in 1290, rebuilt in 1691 and twice restored in the 19C. It retains 12C carved capitals (from Bermondsey Abbey, once on the same site), 17C woodwork, boards inscribed with 18C charity donations, three hatchments vividly painted with armorial bearings and tombstones in the aisle pavements giving a sad insight into 18C infant mortality.

ROYAL AIR FORCE MUSEUM ★★ (Grahame Park Way, Hendon)

Open daily 10am to 6pm; closed 1 January, 24, 25, 26 December. £3, OAPs, children £1.50. Restaurant; car park (Colindale underground: 1/2 mile).

On the historic site of Old Hendon Airfield, where Grahame-White established his flying school before World War I, two 1915 hangars behind a modern façade are devoted to the history of aviation and of the RAF.

The **Aircraft Hall** *(ground floor)* presents in chronological order a unique collection of aircraft from a Bleriot Monoplane and the Sopwith Camel to the Lightning Mach 2. In the centre (a modern structure linking the two 1915 hangars) is the Camm collection of 11 aircraft including a P 1127, prototype of the Harrier jump jet.

The **historical galleries** *(first and ground floors, starting upstairs)* recount the story of early experiments as illustrated by components, mock-ups and trophies, including two British Empire Michelin Trophies awarded to the British pilot flying the greatest distance in a British plane: Moore-Brabazon won No 1 in 1910 for a distance of 19 miles.

British Empire Michelin Trophy no 1.

Other exhibits such as Von Richthofen's flying helmet, escaping equipment and the ejector seat, lead via a gallery of VC and GC winners to an audio-visual section on the latest developments.

Bomber Command Hall. – Also in the same complex is the massive Bomber Command Hall with its striking display of famous bomber aircaft including the Lancaster, Wellington, B17 Flying Fortress, Mosquito and Vulcan.

Battle of Britain Hall. – German bombers and fighters line up in impressive dark array – Ju 87s, 88s, a Heinkel 111, Messerschmitts – against the minute Spitfires and Hurricanes which won the day. Here also is the Signature Board from the pub at Brasted, near Biggin Hill, recalling many of the famous Battle of Britain pilots.

A central feature of the exhibition is a replica of the No. 11 Group Operations Room at RAF Uxbridge. Equipment, uniforms, medals, documents, relics, works of art and other memorabilia are included in the permanent memorial to the men, women and machines involved in the great air battle of 1940.

*For hotels and restaurants in London use the **Michelin Red Pocket Guide – Greater London.***

St James's was the gift of Charles II at the Restoration to his loyal courtier, Henry Jermyn, later Earl of St Albans, who speedily developed the empty fields into an elegant suburb for members of the re-established court.

The founder of the West End, as he has since been described, laid out his estate around a square from which roads led from the centre of each side (not, as became the custom from the corners): to the east was a large market bordered by the Haymarket, to the north, Jermyn St, the local shopping street and, in the axis of Duke of York St, the church. The community was self-contained even to a railed enclosure in the square where the fashionable residents could take a promenade.

At the end of the Stuart monarchy, vacated private houses were taken over by the clubs which had originated in taverns, coffee and chocolate houses where men of similar calling, like interest, congenial company, made a practice of meeting regularly. The encounters developed into subscription groups with reserved quarters and finally took over the houses in which they met, employing the owner or publican as manager and enhancing the amenities, particularly the food for which many became famous. In the period of Beau Brummell (1778-1840) and the Prince Regent, the clubs were known as the resort of the wealthy and the fashionable and as infamous gambling centres. Numbers grew until by the turn of the 19/20C there were nearly 200 in the West End; now there are fewer than 30. Their character has also changed from 18C flamboyance, to 19C silence and reserve and now to a modified social function or gaming.

Berry Bros façade.

St James's has remained a masculine world of bespoke boot and shoemakers, shirtmakers and hatters, sword, gun and rod makers, antique and 18C picture dealers, wine merchants, cheese vendors, jewellers traditional and modern, fine art auctioneers. Although banking and property companies have invaded St James's St it is still the address of eight of London's principal clubs, Pall Mall of five.

St James's Sq*. – The square, with a Classical equestrian statue of William III (1807) beneath very tall plane trees, is encircled by modern offices and 19C residences except on the north and west sides where there are still Georgian town houses. Of them the most notable are no 4 of 1676, remodelled in 1725 – Ionic porch, rich cornice and continuous iron balcony; no 5 of 1748-51 with 18, 19C additions; no 13 of 1740 with faked mortar uprights to give an all-header effect to the blackened brick wall; no 15, Lichfield House, of 1764-5 – a perfect Classical stone façade with fluted columns marking the doorway and embracing the upper floors beneath a pediment (note also the continuous iron balcony); and no 20 built by Adam in 1775 with no 21 its 20C mirror image. No 32 was the town residence of the Bishops of London from 1771 to 1919. No 31, Norfolk House, where George III was born, was General Eisenhower's headquarters in 1942 and 1944.

No 14 (of 1896) is the **London Library,** no 12 with a stucco front and Tuscan pillared porch is possibly by Cubitt (1836) and nos 9-10, Chatham House, the Royal Institute of International Affairs (f 1920). The houses date from 1736 and no 10, in its time, has been the residence of 3 PM's: William Pitt, Earl of Chatham, 1757-61, Edward Stanley, Earl of Derby, 1837-54 and William Gladstone, 1890.

St James's Church*. – Wren, the automatic choice of architect in 1676 for the new parish church, built a plain basilica of brick with Portland stone dressings and balustrade and a square tower. Plain glass windows, segmental below and tall and rounded above, line the north and south walls and a tripartite and superimposing Venetian window fills the east end. The original entrance was placed in the south wall looking down Duke of York St to the square until 19C when the local emphasis had changed and new entrances were made on both sides of the tower.

The galleried interior is roofed with a barrel vault and entablature, richly decorated with plasterwork, fashioned from mouldings made from bomb damaged fragments. The organ case, surmounted by figures, is original as is the altarpiece of gilded wood with garlands of flowers and fruit, framing a pelican with her young, also a marble font in the form of a tree of life with Adam and Eve on either side, all carved by **Grinling Gibbons.** Several artists including the two van der Veldes are buried in the church (plaque in vestibule) which is the parish church of the Royal Academy. The outdoor pulpit against the north wall dates from 1902.

St James's St*. – The wide street, unnamed but clearly marked in early 17C maps as the approach from Piccadilly to the palace, developed as part of the quarter and by the end of the century was lined on either side by town houses including those of merchants who fled the City after the Great Plague and Fire of 1665 and 1666. It retains an atmosphere of quiet elegance with individual shops, restaurants and clubs. Starting from Piccadilly, the most famous buildings include:

White's Club (no 37): established in 1693 from a coffeehouse of the same name, this club, the oldest and Tory in character, occupies a house of 1788 to which the famous bow window was added in 1811. The façade was renewed in 1852;

Boodle's Club (28): dating from 1762, the club is in a house of stock brick and stucco of 1765. On either side are identical porches and at the centre a rounded Venetian style window with below a bay window added in 1821;

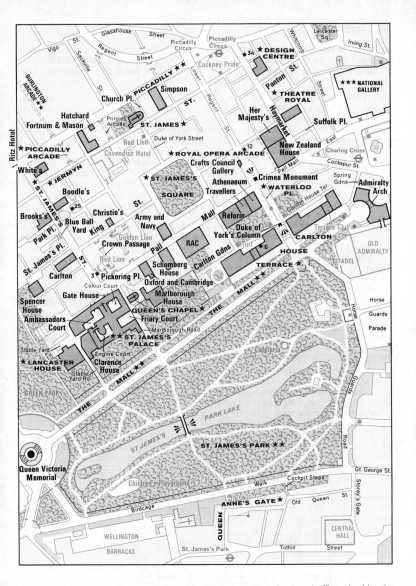

The Economist (25): the 1966-8 complex which houses a gallery, bank and offices, besides the journal, consists of three canted glass towers around a paved court;

Brooks's Club (61): founded as the rival Whig club to White's in 1764 by the politician Charles James Fox and the Duke of Portland, the club is in a house built of yellow brick and stone designed by **Henry Holland**, Robert Adam's rival, in 1778 in which year it took over the famous Almack's of Pall Mall;

Royal Overseas League (f 1910: 50 000 members): the brick buildings and annexes now almost fill the side street, Park Place. No 14 was formerly Pratt's.

Blue Ball Yard. – The far end of the gaslit yard is lined by stables of 1742, now garages, but still with round niches in the walls where iron hay baskets once hung. Above are the old tiled cottage quarters and, in the corner, the pink Stafford Hotel.

St James's Place. – The L shaped street is lined by 18C houses which become more ample and include decorative fanlights and continuous iron balconies as the street widens. **Spencer House** (1756-66) in the corner, overlooking Green Park, was designed by John Vardy and contains the earliest and most important neo-Classical interior in Europe; since the 1920s the house has been let as offices. Castlemaine House, of 1959-60, a block of flats, strongly horizontal in line, was designed by **Denys Lasdun**. At the street end (no 20) is the Royal Ocean Racing Club, a neat Georgian town house. On St James's St corner is a gunsmith (67a).

    Carlton Club (69): the club, which originated as "Arthur's", was formed in 1832 by the Duke of Wellington. It is now in an early 19C Palladian stone building which incorporates rooms once part of White's Chocolate and Gaming House.

    No 74, formerly the Conservative Club, was designed by **George Basevi** and **Sydney Smirke** in mid 19C, in modified Palladian style including a canted bay window.

    Constitutional Club (1883), the Savage (1857), the National, the Flyfishers were formerly at no 86, a club house in golden ochre stone, a magnificently Victorian building of 1862.

    At the end, relating to the corner opposite, are two buildings by **Norman Shaw** in terracotta brick and stone, with asymmetric gables, friezes and an angle tower. At the lower end also, are:

Byron House (7, 8, 9): 1960s on the site of the house in which Byron awoke one morning on the publication of *Childe Harold* in 1811 to find himself famous; **Lobb's** the bespoke bootmaker; **Lock's** the hatters (6) (the firm dates back to 1700, the topper in the window to 19C, the bow windowed shop to late 18C);

Berry Bros & Rudd (3): wine merchants "established in the XVII century". A half timbered passage beside the shop (note the wall plaque: the Republic of Texas legation 1842-5) leads to **Pickering Place,** a gaslit court of 18C houses, reputed to be the site of the last duel to be fought in London.

Pall Mall. – The ancient way from the City to St James's Palace is named after an avenue planted to its north which served as an alley for the game brought over from France early in the 17C and much favoured by the Stuarts. When St James's was developed, the avenue was cut down, the road lined with houses and renamed after the old alley. The dark red brick exterior of **Schomberg House** (nos 80-82) dates from 1698; Nell Gwyn lived next door at no 79, still the only freehold property on the south side of the street, which, since 19C, has been famous for its clubs: the **Travellers** (no 106) founded in 1819 with a rule that members must have travelled a minimum of 500 miles (now 1000) in a straight line from London outside the British Isles; the **Reform** (nos 104-5) established, in opposition to the Carlton, by Whig supporters at the time of the Bill in 1832, the latter on the renumbered site of Julius Angerstein's house and both in 19C Italian palazzo buildings.

The **RAC** is in a vast building of 1911 by the constructors of the Ritz; the **Oxford and Cambridge** (no 71), the last on the south side, was founded in 1830 by Lord Palmerston at the British Coffeehouse, in Cockspur St. The **Army and Navy** (f 1839), the only club on the north side, was rebuilt in 1963.

Crown Passage (beneath 59-60) leads away from such spaciousness up past an ironmongers, locksmiths, picture, coin and bullion dealers and the 19C Red Lion to King St where the Golden Lion, a Victorian pub, gleams with cut mirror glass and mahogany.

King St includes two world famous establishments: Spinks (no 5), specialists in coins, medals, and orders (besides antiques of all kinds) and **Christie's** (no 8), the fine art auctioneers, founded in 1766 at the time of the height of the grand tour.

Waterloo Place★. – The wide street, which swept straight down from Piccadilly to Carlton House (qv) as part of Nash's grand design, lost its climax when the house was demolished in 1829 although it gained a vista across the park to Whitehall. With the years it acquired the **Crimea Monument,** the **Duke of York's column** (qv) and Classical façades of the Athenæum (west) and the former United Services Club (east), now Institute of Directors. On the east side is the Duke of Wellington's mounting-block.

The **Athenæum** by Decimus Burton (1828-30), a square stucco block, in deference to the Club's foundation as a meeting place for artists, men of letters and connoisseurs, was given Classical touches in the torches, Roman Doric pillars supporting the porch, the gilded figure of Pallas Athene and the important Classical frieze.

The **Crafts Council Gallery** and Information Centre. Open Tuesdays to Saturdays 10am to 5pm, Sundays 2 to 5pm; closed Mondays, 25 and 26 December. The gallery puts on exhibitions and provides information through its bookshop and slide index (coffee bar).

British Travel Centre. – 12 Lower Regent St. The centre offers a whole range of services: tourist information, hotel and travel booking etc. covering the whole country. There is also a bookshop.

Haymarket. – (From the north end). No 34, a small bow-fronted Georgian shop, was for 201 years until 1981 the home of Fribourg and Treyer 'purveyors of fine cigars, snuffs and tobaccos since 1720' to royal and distinguished patrons.

Design Centre★. – (no 28). Open Mondays, Tuesdays 10am to 6pm, Wednesdays to Saturdays 10am to 8pm (Christmas Eve 4pm, New Year's Eve 6pm); Sundays, 1 to 6pm; closed 1 January, 25, 26 December. Shop and coffee bar.

The ordinary building of 1954-5 houses changing exhibitions of well designed products from machines to toys, textiles to fishing tackle, manufactured in Britain.

Panton St. – The street recalls Col Panton, card player and gambler, who in an evening in 1664 won enough to purchase "a parcel of ground at Piccadilly". This he laid out as a narrow street, lined with shops, one of which in 1770 was taken by William Stone, Wine and Brandy Merchant, eventually transformed into a coffeehouse and later a chophouse.

Theatre Royal, Haymarket★. – When **John Nash** designed the theatre in 1821 with a great pedimented portico, he resited it to stand, unlike its predecessor of 1720, in the axis of Charles II St and so enjoy a double aspect. The interior, which has been remodelled, is most elegantly decorated in deep blue, gold and white.

Her Majesty's. – Opposite, on the corner of Charles II St, is the fourth theatre on the site, a Victorian, French pavilioned, building with an ornate but efficient interior plan, constructed by Beerbohm Tree as his own in 1895-7.

New Zealand House. – Since 1957-63, the 15 storey tower above a 4 storey podium, 225ft in all, has stood sentinel at the bottom of the street. It is glazed overall, banded in stone, recessed at ground level to provide a canopy. Partially incorporated in the ground floor is the **Royal Opera Arcade★,** a delightful row of bow fronted shops designed by **Nash** and Repton in 1817 as one of three arcades surrounding the then Royal Opera-house to harmonise with other buildings opposite in the **Haymarket** and **Suffolk Place** (note the big corner house, now American Express). George III in bronze on horseback in Cockspur St, completes the scene – the future king was born in St James's Sq.

Piccadilly★★. – (For the north side of Piccadilly see p 116).

The shops have restrained displays of merchandise of such variety that window shopping is diverting – silk, leather, cashmere, tweed; wines and spirits, fruit and preserves; books; china, glass and kitchenware; military memorabilia; umbrellas, sticks; hairbrushes; rifles and guns.

Simpson's beautiful in proportion, simplicity, sophistication, dates from 1935.

Hatchard's, the bookshop in Piccadilly (no 187) which was established by John Hatchard in 1797 with a capital of £5, is still in the original 18C building with small paned bow windows on either side of the entrance.

In **Fortnum and Mason's** (founded 1707) shop assistants in tail coats add to the sense of luxury. Since 1964 Mr. Fortnum and Mr. Mason have emerged from the façade on the hour to bow to one another as the clock chimes high above the Piccadilly traffic.

The **Ritz Hotel** marks the end of the south side of Piccadilly. It was built at the height of the Edwardian era, in 1906, an early frame structure in the French classical style by Mewès and Davis. Inside all was gilded Louis XVI decoration and marble.

Jermyn St★ boasts shirtmakers, pipemakers, antique dealers, antiquarian booksellers, the original Walls sausage shop (no 113, now a restaurant), a chemist with real sponges, a provision merchant (Paxton and Whitfield, 93) selling countless varieties of cheese over a wooden counter, a perfumier (Floris, 89); modern jewels (Andrew Grima, 80), restaurants, bars, chambers and the Cavendish, a luxury hotel, on the site of the famous Edwardian rendez-vous. On the corner of St James's St, Davidoffs with its special Havana room, offers everything for the smoker from cigar cutters to humidors. Between Jermyn St and Piccadilly are two parallel arcades, Princes', and the **Piccadilly★**, bright, with bow fronted shops.

ST MARYLEBONE ★ (Westminster)

Map pp 118-119.

St Marylebone village had just begun to expand along the High St and Lane which followed the winding Tyburn River south through the fields, when, in the early 18C, Edward Harley, 2nd Earl of Oxford, began the development of Cavendish Square. By the end of the century the most complete grid layout of streets in any area of London had been superimposed on the village and the surrounding waste land; the two original streets, the **Lane** and the **High St,** are the only two between Oxford St and Regent's Park not to conform to the rectangular theme. In 1778 the pleasure gardens, set up in 1650 on land sold off by James I in 1611, were sold and the Manor House, a hunting lodge built by Henry VIII in his royal park of St Marylebone (east of the church) and used by him and Elizabeth I for entertaining important guests, was demolished in 1791.

■ THE SQUARES

Cavendish Sq. – The square was designed in 1717 as a focal point north of Oxford St with a chapel of ease, St Peter's to the west, dependent residential and service streets and a local market (the street name Market Place remains on the east side of Oxford Circus).

The square retains a pair of stone faced Palladian houses of the 1770s at the centre of the north side, which are now linked by a bridge against which stands a moving, dark bronze, *Virgin and Child* by **Jacob Epstein** (1950). There are late 18/19C houses, much altered, along the east side – no 5 was the home of Nelson in 1787 and, 100 years later, of Quintin Hogg (d 1903), founder of the London Polytechnic (Upper Regent St).

St Peter's Chapel. – *Vere St.* The attractive small dark brick church with quoins emphasising the angles and a square turret and open belfry, is unexpectedly spacious inside including galleries supported on giant Corinthian columns with massive entablatures. The architect was **James Gibbs**, the date 1721-4, making St Peter's, possibly the experimental model for St Martin-in-the-Fields. It is now the home of the London Institute for Contemporary Christianity.

Portman Sq★. – At the northwest corner there remain two of the finest houses that ever graced the square. No 20 by **Robert Adam** was built and furnished in 1775-6 for Elizabeth Countess of Home, now the **Courtauld Institute of Art** (London University). No 21, its pillared porch round the corner in Gloucester Place, houses the Drawings Collection of the British Architectural Library RIBA *(open by appointment only, ☎ 01-935 9292)* and the **RIBA Heinz Gallery** showing changing architectural exhibitions *(open during exhibitions Mondays to Fridays, 11am to 5pm, Saturdays 10am to 1pm; closed public holidays).* Both houses have curving, shallow stepped staircases, the Adam one being particularly fine.

Manchester Sq. – The last of the three principal squares dates from 1776 when the 4th Duke of Manchester built a town house on the Portman estate. Manchester Square developed to the south of the house during the next 12 years although the house itself became the residence of the Spanish ambassador who built a chapel, St James', in the adjoining street, henceforth known as Spanish Place. In 1872, the house was again sold, the new owner being Richard Wallace, Marquess of Hertford who renamed the property **Hertford House** and entirely remodelled it as the setting for his collection *(p 164)*. The square itself is attractive with late Georgian houses.

■ THE STREETS

Marylebone High St and Marylebone Lane wind south joining Oxford St near Stratford Place, which leads to the Palladian **Stratford House** (Oriental Club).

Of the network of over 100 streets and mews which intersect, always at right angles, north of Oxford St, seven, at least, are known for some special reason:

Wigmore St. – The street is one in which to look in the varied small shop windows, to wander off up Marylebone Lane, to pass through on the way to a chamber music concert or recital at the **Wigmore Hall**, to linger in the cafés and shops in St Christopher's Place – antiques, real and fake jewellery, fashion...

Gt Portland St. – The old street, rebuilt in 19/20C, was widely known in 1930s and again in 1950-60s as the Mecca of second-hand car dealers (no more). At the top end is the Royal National Institute for the Blind (no 224). At the east end of Mortimer St, stands the Middlesex Hospital, founded in Windmill St in 1745, since 1754 on the present site, entirely rebuilt in 1925-36 and extended in 1960s.

Portland Place. – *Page 127.*

Chandos St. – The street is named after the palatial residence the Duke of Chandos failed to erect because of the bursting of the South Sea Bubble in 1720. At the north end, facing down the street and resembling one of his own immaculate drawings, is the perfectly proportioned **Chandos House** (Royal Society of Medicine) designed by the Scotsman Robert Adam. Built of Portland stone in 1771, it is 4 bays wide, 3 floors high, and unadorned except for a narrow frieze above the second floor, the square porch, and the 18C iron railings and lamp holders, complete with snuffers.

Harley St. – Seemingly every door, three steps up from the pavement, is emblazoned with consultants' brass plates. Architecturally the street is a mixture, dating back from the present, through the terracotta brick and stone of mid 19C to the original Georgian. Nos 43-9, with a Tuscan pillared, stucco portico, is **Queen's College,** the oldest English school for girls, which was founded in 1848 initially to provide a proper training for governesses and counted Miss Beale and Miss Buss among its early pupils; Florence Nightingale lived at no 47.

Wimpole St. – Elizabeth Barrett, before her marriage to Robert Browning in St Marylebone Church in 1876, lived at no 50, demolished when the street was largely rebuilt at the turn of the century.

Baker St. – The wide thoroughfare was 100 years old when Sherlock Holmes in 1880s went to live at 221B – a number no longer fictitious since the street, originally in two sections and with 85 the top number, was united and renumbered in 1930! Hansom cabs, gas lamps, the fog, private houses with rooms to let, inevitably have vanished, romance remaining only in some of the small shops in the side streets, quiet in the twin early 19C squares to the west: **Montagu,** notable for the shallow ground floor bow windows, and **Bryanston,** for its long stucco terraces. The parallel Gloucester Place has attractive small doorways, ironwork balconies and railings towards the upper centre.

■ MARYLEBONE ROAD *(Map p 126)*

The line of Marylebone, Euston and Pentonville Rds was laid in 1756 as a by-pass from the City to Paddington and west London. For its first 100 years it was known as New Rd; the division into named sections came in mid 19C when it became absorbed into the surrounding areas. The principal landmarks today include: St Marylebone Station and Leyland House west of Baker St, the underground station with its Sherlock Holmes' decorative motif, Mme Tussaud's and the Friends Meeting House (nos 173-7) with its bookshop and garden.

Madame Tussaud's*. – *Open daily 10am to 5.30pm; closed 25 December only; £4.50, children £2.95. Joint ticket with the Planetarium (see below) £5.80, children £3.55.*

Mme Tussaud, born in 1761, perfected her modelling skill by "doing" the French royal family for the waxworks museum opened by her uncle in Paris in 1770. She lived through the Terror taking deathmasks of its victims – Marat, Robespierre... In 1802 she brought the waxworks, by then hers, and her children to England and for 33 years she travelled the country before settling in Marylebone in 1835 aged 74. At 81 she made a self portrait: a stiff, small figure, mercilessly revealed; at 89, in 1850, she died.

(By courtesy of Mme Tussaud's)

Madame Tussaud.

The **exhibition** begins with a wax attendant standing at the entrance to a series of halls: historical tableaux; the conservatory, where sports, film, TV personalities of the present stand; The Grand Hall which is peopled by historical, political, military, royal figures from Henry VIII and his wives to Lenin, General Montgomery, prime ministers, the Royal Family; the Chamber of Horrors, illustrating methods of execution, famous murderers in their appropriate settings and, in the cells, the most infamous 20C British "lifers". Illusion is carried further as one walks below decks aboard HMS *Victory* at Trafalgar with Nelson dying amidst the smoke, sound and fury. The exhibits are regularly up-dated to take into account personalities in the limelight.

The Planetarium. – *Performances daily from 11am to 4.30pm; closed 25 December only; £2.50, children £1.60. Joint ticket with Madame Tussaud's £5.80, children £3.55.*

Star shows project the moon, stars and planets on to the roof of the dome and probe the mysteries of the universe.

The Laserium. – *Performances at 6 and 7.45pm, Wednesday to Sunday, and at 9.15pm on Fridays and Saturdays; every night July and August; £3.75, children £2.75.*

A fantasy in music and light, combining the dazzling colours of the laser beam with music from classical to rock.

St Marylebone Church. – The church by Thomas Hardwick, was completed in 1817, a large balustraded building with a three stage tower ending in gilded caryatids upholding the cupola. Nash saw it as a potential focal point from the park in the axis of York Gate and ennobled Hardwick's edifice by the addition of a pedimented Corinthian portico.

The road continues with the Royal Academy of Music (north side), an attractive building in red brick and stone, with reclining figures in the large segmental pediment (1911) and the London Clinic (south side).

Opposite the academy on the south side of the road is a sculptured panel showing characters from the six principal works written by **Dickens** while living in a house on the site.

Beyond Park Square stands **Holy Trinity,** designed by **Soane** in 1826, its thin egg-shaped cupola rising from a pillared square base above a balustrade and Classical pedimented portico. The outside pulpit dates from 1891. In 1955 the church was sensitively converted into the bookshop and offices of the SPCK; services are still held in the apse on weekdays.

Behind the church is the **White House,** an early modern apartment-hotel block, erected in 1936 to a star shaped plan, 9 storeys tall and faced overall in white ceramic tiles.

■ **ST JOHN'S WOOD** *(Map pp 5-8, BC/V)*

St John's Wood developed rapidly in the first half of the 19C. Its rural character, dating back to the Middle Ages when it was the property of the Knights Hospitallers of St John, whence its name, was swept aside as Marylebone began to overflow and Nash's development of Regent's Park made it a potentially desirable residential area. It was, moreover, within three miles of the City and Westminster. Cleverly the developers departed from the current urban styles and erected Italian type villas, broad eaved, often in pairs. By 1824 when Edwin Landseer (d 1873) moved into a house in St John's Wood Rd, a colony of artists had begun to gather which much later included Sir Lawrence Alma-Tadema (d 1912) and W R Frith (*Derby Day:* d 1909).

The villas have now largely disappeared, replaced by apartment blocks and neo-Georgian houses; the small High St has been modernised. Two landmarks, however, do remain:

St John's Wood Church. – *Prince Albert Road.* The church is of the same date, 1813, and by the same architect, Thomas Hardwick, as St Marylebone Parish Church and like it has a distinctive, cupolaed turret.

Lord's Cricket Ground. – The first match to be played at Lord's was MCC (Marylebone Cricket Club) v Herts on 22 June 1814. The club, originally at the White Conduit in Islington moved to Marylebone and altered its name accordingly in 1787 when Thomas Lord leased a site in what is now Dorset Sq. In 1811 Lord lifted the sacred turf first to a field which proved to be in the course of the Regent's Canal and then to what, by purchase, has become the permanent ground. The first Test Matches at Lord's were played in 1884.

The **Ashes** (of a bail), portraits and cartoons, cricketing dress, memorabilia from batting lists to snuff boxes, can be seen in the **Memorial Gallery** *(Late April to late September, on match days only 10.30am to 5pm; the rest of the year, guided tours by appointment – ☏ 289 1611; £1, children and OAPs 50p).* The main gates were erected in memory of **Dr W G Grace** (d 1915) in 1923, Father Time (removing the bails) on the grandstand in 1926.

Saatchi Gallery of Modern Art. – *98a Boundary Rd. Open Fridays and Saturdays, noon to 6pm; closed 2 weeks at Christmas, 1 January, Good Friday and Easter weekend.* Housed in a converted warehouse, the gallery holds temporary exhibitions of works from the Saatchi Collection of Modern Art. The collection comprises paintings and sculpture by A. Keifer, A. Warhol, M. Morley, C. André, F. Stella and other artists.

SOUTH BANK ★ (Lambeth)

The area on the south bank remained rural until the construction of Westminster and Blackfriars Bridges and their approach roads in the mid 18C. The evolution of public transport developed the area from village to town and spa, where the modestly wealthy such as Henry Thrale built out-of-town residences. Finally the area became a suburb where squares and terraces were erected by Thomas Cubitt and lesser men, who agglomerated in a network of small streets between the major roads.

Industry. – An ordnance factory in Charles II's reign, the Vauxhall Plate Glass Works 1665-1780, the Coade Stone Factory in late 18C (the site now of County Hall), Doultons, lead shot foundries (a shot tower stood at the centre of the 1951 Festival), candle, vinegar, basket, brush factories, boatyards, breweries and distillers, multiplied as the population increased and labour became available. There were specialist workshops and potteries such as the one producing Lambeth delft. The war devastated acres of Victorian streets, slums, the Lambeth Walk, factories, enabling the authorities to rebuild on a vast scale and the then LCC, under Herbert Morrison, to clear the debris from the riverside for the 1951 Festival of Britain and future arts centre.

■ **SOUTH BANK ARTS CENTRE★★**

The buildings in the Arts Centre are connected by elevated walkways (shown in grey on plan). Access for cars is from the south; by train and underground, direct from Waterloo Station.

The Royal Festival Hall★. – The hall was the only permanent building erected that bright summer of the 1951 Festival of Britain, the occasion being seized to build a new concert auditorium for London, since the Queen's Hall had been gutted by incendiaries and the Albert Hall's acoustics were still troubled by an echo.

The building was planned by Sir Leslie Martin and Sir Robert Matthew, LCC architects, who worked, it was said, from the inside. Design began with the hall: first the acoustics; then visibility of the stage, which can hold a choir of 250; finally comfortable seating for 3 000 auditors. They succeeded both aesthetically and practically in the design of foyers, staircases, concourses, bars and restaurants, managing the space to avoid crowding, afford views of the river and inner perspectives of the building itself; finally the whole edifice was insulated against noise from nearby Waterloo Station. In 1954 an organ was installed. In 1962-5 the river frontage was redesigned to include the main entrance, and faced with Portland stone.

Queen Elizabeth Hall and Purcell Room. – In 1967 came the opening of the Queen Elizabeth Hall and Purcell Room, a smaller concert hall seating 1 100 and recital room for 370 – part of the second phase of building. The exterior is in unfaced concrete; the interior acoustics are superb.

Hayward Gallery. – The gallery, which houses temporary exhibitions of painting and sculpture under the auspices of the Arts Council, was opened in 1968. The building, a terrace-like structure of unfaced concrete, in fact "works" successfully to provide on two levels inside five large gallery spaces and three open air sculpture courts, together with views of the river.

National Film Theatre. – The NFT, which opened in 1951, was rebuilt in 1957 and enlarged in 1970 so that it now comprises two cinemas (seating 466 and 162). The NFT, one of the world's leading cinemathèques, organises the London Film Festival each year.

Museum of the Moving Image (MOMI). – *Open Tuesdays to Saturdays 10am to 8pm, Sundays and bank holidays 10am to 6pm; closed Mondays and 24 to 26 December. £3.25, children, OAPs £2.50.* Situated underneath Waterloo Bridge MOMI explores the story of cinema, television and their antecedents and previews technological developments with great attention to detail. It aims to involve visitors actively as they are given the opportunity to read the news, take part in an interview, work behind a camera... under the prompting of museum guides in the guise of a cinema commissionaire, a war veteran and other characters. Charlie Chaplin's hat and cane, Marilyn Monroe's black dress, Dali's lip-shaped sofa are among the prized exhibits. There are innumerable screens to view and buttons to push in 50 permanent exhibition areas.

National Theatre★. – *Guided tours Mondays to Saturdays at 10.15am, 12.30, 12.45, 5.30 and 6pm; closed Sundays; 1 1/4 hours; £2.50; advance booking by post or in person at Lyttelton Information Desk 10am to 11pm.* The theatre opens the third phase in the South Bank scheme, both by its position downstream from Waterloo Bridge and, more importantly, by its design. The architect, **Denys Lasdun,** has incorporated three theatres – the Lyttelton, with proscenium stage, seating 890, the Olivier, with large open stage, seating 1 100 and the Cottesloe, a studio theatre with a maximum capacity of 400 – workshops, bookshops, bars and buffets, within a construction in which the external height is cut by strata-like terraces which parallel the course of the river at the building's foot.

In front of the theatre stand a pleasing stone sculpture, Arena, by J. Maine (1983/84) and a bronze of London Pride by F. Dobson, a sculpture commissioned for the 1951 Festival and rediscovered recently.

IBM Building. – This five-storey building faced in concrete and granite, also designed by Sir Denys Lasdun (1983), harmonises in scale and structure with the National Theatre.

Next to it is the London Weekend Television building dominated by the IPC towers.

The riverside walk extends to Blackfriars Bridge. Beyond LWT is the Coin Street development which includes housing and gardens, the Gabriel's Wharf market, the Oxo tower (1928) and shopping arcade at Stamford Wharf. Further on is the distinctive river frontage of Sea Containers House.

The Old Vic. – The cradle of the National Theatre and, until 1976, its home, was built in 1818 as the Coburg. In 1880 it was taken by Emma Cons (d 1912), a pioneer of social reform, and run as the Royal Victoria Music Hall and Coffee Tavern with a programme of concerts,

temperance meetings and penny lectures, the last proving so popular that in 1889 the Morley Memorial College for Working Men and Women was founded within the theatre *(see p 139).* Under Lilian Baylis (d 1937), who succeeded her aunt, the theatre, now known as the Old Vic, became a centre for music, opera and drama, especially Shakespeare, with a company, in which virtually every British actor of note played at some time. The stage was difficult and draughty; the seats in the pit and the gods were hard and one had to beware of pillars, but prices were low – 4d in the gallery, 5s in the stalls – and the acting was excellent. In 1940 the Vic was bombed and the company moved to the New Theatre, returning after the war until 1976 when as the National Theatre Company it moved into the new National Theatre, leaving the old house to be taken over by the Prospect Company from 1979 to 1981. Now under new management and after refurbishment to restore its former Victorian music-hall appearance and provide better facilities, it is once again a thriving repertory theatre.

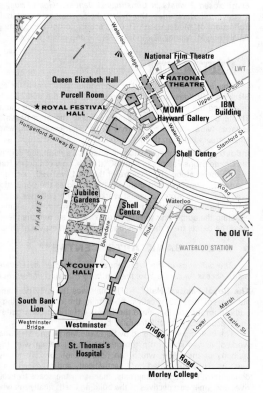

Shell Centre. – The Shell Centre, built between 1957-1962, comprises three blocks beside the Thames: the Upstream and Downstream stone-faced, 10 storey buildings and a 26 storey tower, 351ft high. As one of the biggest office blocks in the kingdom it has 43 acres of floor space, 7 000 windows, 88 lifts, 12 escalators, 240 telephone lines and 4 500 extensions.

Jubilee Gardens. – The gardens, on the site of the 1951 Festival and incorporating the flagpole from British Columbia, were opened in 1977 to celebrate the 25th anniversary of the Queen's accession. A bronze sculpture by I. Walters (1985) is dedicated to the International Brigade (1936-39). Nearby is the Jubilee Oracle, a smooth bronze by Alexander (1980).

County Hall★. – *Belvedere Rd.*
County Hall was the headquarters of the Greater London Council until its abolition in 1986.
The hall, a colonnaded arc 700ft in diameter and still, amidst all the new constructions, one of London's most distinctive buildings, was designed in 1908 by a 29 year old architect, Ralph Knott. The stone pile with Renaissance inspired, steeply pitched dark tile roof with a multitude of dormers, only completed in 1922, has since been trebled in size but always in compatible style.

The South Bank Lion. – The lion, 13ft long, 12ft high, carved out of Coade stone, gazes speculatively from a plinth at the foot of Westminster Bridge. Painted red, it was the mascot in 19C of the Lion Brewery until poised at the bridgefoot in 1952.

St Thomas's Hospital. – The red and white buildings have scarcely changed in outward appearance since being built in 1868-71. In the 1970s some of the eastern blocks were replaced by buildings of 7-14 storeys containing treatment centres, clinics, medical school...

From 13C infirmary to 20C teaching hospital. – The hospital, at first dedicated to St Thomas Becket, originated in an infirmary set up early in 13C in Southwark by the Augustinians of St Mary Overie Church, possibly immediately after the great fire of 1212. By 1228 the priory quarters were too small and a hospital was built opposite on a site which eventually extended the length of St Thomas St. In the 16C, although St Thomas's was caring for the sick, the orphaned and the indigent, it was forfeited, as a conventual establishment, to Henry VIII and closed, only to be rescued in 1552 by the City which purchased it for £647 4s. The story since is one of expansion, of removal to Lambeth in 19C, of research and development, of the foundation of the Nightingale Fund Training School for Nurses, of ten aerial attacks between September 1940 and July 1944 when at least one operating theatre was always open...

Westminster Bridge Rd. – The road which was developed in 1750 when the bridge was built, has a distinctive landmark in the white spire encircled by red brick bands of Christchurch, built in 1874 with funds from the USA. Further along is **Morley College,** (no 61), erected in 1920 when the college removed from the Old Vic, and rebuilt in 1958 to designs by Edward Maufe, with interior murals by John Piper and Edward Bawden. It has a strong musical tradition.

SOUTHWARK ★ (Southwark)

Southwark, which extends south from the Thames 7 1/2 miles to Crystal Palace, includes the Borough and Walworth, Bermondsey, Rotherhithe, Camberwell and Peckham, and Dulwich. Its history, layer upon layer, peels away to the Middle Ages and even Roman times, in documents and locations, for buildings and roads have been rebuilt on ancient sites. Its men – native born and adopted – have been diverse: Shakespeare, Ben Jonson, Marlowe, Burbage, Alleyn, Fletcher, Massinger, Lily Langtry, Chaucer, Blake, Browning, Dickens, Ruskin, Goldsmith, Faraday, Desenfans, Bourgeois, Passmore Edwards, Thomas Guy, John Harvard...

The Roman invasion to the Dissolution of the Monasteries. – The construction by the Romans of a bridge and the convergence at the bridgehead of roads from the south of England attracted settlers to the fishing village already established on one of the few sites relatively free from flooding on the low-lying marshlands of the Thames' south bank. By Anglo-Saxon times the bridge had become a defence against ship-borne invaders and the village, the *sud werk* or south work, against attacking land forces: Olaf of Norway's rescue of Ethelred from the Danes is commemorated locally in Tooley St (a corruption of St Olave's St); the Conqueror fired Southwark before he took London by encirclement. In the *Domesday Book,* Southwark was described as having a strand where ships could tie up, a street, a herring fishery and a minster or priory. In 1540, at the Dissolution, the priory reverted to the crown; Henry acquired from Archbishop Cranmer the Great Liberty Manor, granted to Canterbury in the 12C (which extended from the Old Kent Rd to the High St) and for good measure, Bermondsey Abbey (f 1082) among whose tenants were the Bishops of Winchester and the Knights Templar whose 100 acres had by the 15C become the famous Paris Garden. The bishops had erected a veritable palace, which they named **Winchester House,** and the notorious prison known as the Clink. Also along the main bank were stews (brothels) whose occupants were known as "Winchester geese".

There were also two hospitals, St Thomas's, originally at the priory gate and subsequently across the road, and the Lock or Leper Hospital in Kent St (Old Kent Rd) beyond the Bar or bounds of the medieval town (closed 1760).

The people of Walworth, Newington, Camberwell, grew and sold produce at the market first held on London Bridge, later in the High St and finally on the present site; Southwark people were also fishermen and boatmen. Industries developed such as plaster and mortar making (pollution from the lime burners was being complained of to the king in 1283), weaving, brewing (by refugees from the Low Countries) glassmaking and leather tanning (note the Bermondsey street names: Leathermarket, Tanner, Morocco and the windows in Christchurch, *p 143*).

For entertainment there were the midsummer Southwark Fair, the occasional frost fairs when the Thames froze over, the Elizabethan theatres, the brothels and taverns. Not all inns were licentious; many prospered as staging posts for the coaches going south and to the ports and as hostelries for travellers awaiting the morning opening of the bridge to enter the City.

The Dissolution to the 20C. – Henry rapidly sold off the monastery estates. The City increased its interests in Southwark but it never acquired jurisdiction over the Clink prison or Paris Garden which was therefore a popular location for theatres. The reign of the **Rose** (1587), the **Swan** (1596), the **Globe** (1599) and the **Hope** (1613) was however brief: those that had not already reverted or become bull and bear baiting rings were closed finally under the Commonwealth. The stews or brothels, particularly along the river bank, developed from early public bath houses, were so notorious by the 15C that a code of conduct was drawn up for them. Beneath their signs, the Boar's Head, Cross Keys, Swan, Saracen's Head, they continued until they became so infamous that they had to be closed by, of all people, Henry VIII. They re-opened, of course, but finally disappeared with the closure of the theatres.

In 18 and 19C, City merchants and businessmen began to build out-of-town houses in Camberwell and Dulwich. The area closer to the river, largely owned by the City and known as the Borough of Southwark, which time has shortened to the **Borough,** became heavily industrialised, following the building of the bridges, the 19C expansion of the docks and the coming of the railway. The introduction of the 1d workmen's return to London Bridge brought dense urbanisation to the fields where Robert Browning had once walked and to a village which gave its name to the Camberwell Beauty when that butterfly was first seen in England.

By the end of the 19C the last of the prisons had been demolished: the Clink, instituted for miscreants within the liberty, in 1780; the Marshalsea, where Dickens' father had been locked up for debt, in 1842; King's Bench in 1880 and Horsemonger Lane Jail in 1879.

Southwark, in 19C, became increasingly the area of Livery Company almshouses and charities and, in the 20C, of two pioneer ventures – **Clubland,** an educational and social youth centre founded by the Methodist, James Butterworth in the 1920s (*no 56 Camberwell Road* – the Chapel designed by Edward Maufe, was destroyed in 1939-45 war and rebuilt in 1962); and the

SOUTHWARK★

Peckham Experiment *(St Mary's Rd, Camberwell)* which from 1935-1945 was conducted as a social and recreational centre, concerned with preventive as well as curative medicine for an all-income, cross-section of the community.

In 1939-1945 came widespread devastation. Southwark is now after extensive rebuilding, an amalgam of the very old and the new, each area with its particular characteristic even to street furniture such as the Dulwich finger posts and the bollards made from sawn off cannon with a cannon ball in the mouth, inscribed Wardens of St Saviour's 1827, and Clink 1812.

■ SOUTHWARK CATHEDRAL★★ (St Saviour and St Mary Overie)

The history of the site records a progress from Roman building to Saxon minster, from Augustinian priory (1106) to parish Church of St Saviour (1540) in the Winchester diocese and, finally, to Cathedral (1905). The name, according to Stow, derived from the convent being endowed with "the profits of a cross-ferry" from which the church came to be known as "over the river" or St Mary Overie. The first sight of the present building, which lies below the level of London Bridge and Borough High St and is screened from its parish by a railway viaduct is of a solid square central tower, 14C below, early 15C above, with paired lancets surmounted by a chequer pattern and pinnacles. The view of the cathedral from the river is now unimpeded save for the newly built chapter house and restaurant which skirt the base of the building.

Interior. – *(Enter through the southwest door).* Immediately to the left is the Gothic arcading of the church rebuilt after a fire in 1206, for in addition to the succession of "owners" who altered, embellished, restored or neglected the church, it suffered disastrous fires. Against the west wall at the end of the north aisle are 12 ceiling **bosses** rescued from the 15C wooden roof when it collapsed in 1830: the pelican, heraldic sunflowers and roses, malice, gluttony, falsehood, Judas being swallowed by the devil... Nearby stands a black marble stoup with a gilt cover set in a frame. The nave was rebuilt in neo-Gothic style in 1890-97 to harmonize with the 13C chancel. There are fragments of a Norman arch in the north wall. More vestiges of the Norman church have been discovered behind a doorway near the north transept, also a holy water stoup of great antiquity. John Gower (1330-1408), poet and friend of Chaucer, with "small forked beard, on his head a chaplet of four roses, a collar of essex gold about his neck" lies, pillowed on his own works, beneath a canopy of red, green and gold. The north transept, with 13C Purbeck marble shafts set against 12C base walls, includes the allegorical Austin monument of 1633 showing a standing figure, Agriculture, between girls in large sun hats, fallen asleep in the harvest field, also the reclining figure, with gaunt face framed by a full wig, of the quack doctor, Lionel Lockyer (1672). Note also the Jacobean communion table with turned legs in groups of four in front and three behind, pulpit (1702) and wooden sword rest.

From the nave near the transept crossing where the great brass candelabrum of 1680 is suspended between the massive 13C piers which support the central tower, there is an uninterrupted view of the intimately proportioned, 13C chancel in true Early English style. The **altar screen** appears in sumptuous Gothic glory, framed by the virtually unadorned arches to the chancel aisles, triforium and clerestory. The screen, which was presented by Bishop Fox in 1520, remained empty until 1905 when statues were carved to people the niches; the lower register was gilded in the thirties. Funeral pavement stones commemorate the burial in the church of Edmund (d 1607), brother of William Shakespeare, and the Jacobean dramatists, John Fletcher (d 1625) and Philip Massinger (d 1640).

Adjoining the asymmetrical, stilted arch which opens the north chancel aisle is the **Harvard Chapel,** dedicated to John Harvard who was born in Borough High St and baptised in the church in 1607 (emigrated 1638). Mementoes include the American made window, a tablet to the Pilgrim Trust and a carved scallop shell, the pilgrim emblem. In the north chancel aisle is a smaller Jacobean communion table.

The wall monument with the colourful three-quarter figure is to John Trehearne (d 1618), "Gentleman porter to James I" (note the epitaph). Next to it lies a 15C stone effigy of a corpse in a shroud. Beyond, against the wall, is a rare figure of a knight, possibly a Templar, meticulously carved in oak (1280-1300). To the right is the free standing monument to Richard Humble and his wives in full 17C finery. The sparsely adorned retrochoir, 13C and square ended, is divided into four equal chapels by elementarily shaped piers; from 1540-1617 it served as tribunal, prison, billet, sty and bakery. Note the Nonesuch Chest (1588) of inlaid wood.

In the south chancel aisle near the altar is the free standing tomb of Lancelot Andrewes (d 1626), Bishop of Winchester, member of the commission which produced the Authorised Version, a figure in shallow ruff and ample deep blue robes, beneath a modern canopy, gilded and crested. Nearby is displayed a statue of a Roman Hunter God (*c*2-3C AD) found in excavations beneath the cathedral. In the south transept – mainly 14 and

(After photograph, Jarrold's, Norwich)

Alderman Humble and wives, 1616.

early 15C, with early Perpendicular tracery (renewed) in the three light windows, the large window ornately 19C – are, to the left, the red painted arms and hat of Cardinal Beaufort, 15C Bishop of Winchester, and on the right, a miniature recumbent effigy of William Emerson (d 1575), high above, a colourful half figure in gown and ruff, John Bingham (d 1625), saddler to Queen Elizabeth and James I. Note the tesselated paving from a Roman villa at the chancel step.

Against the wall of the south aisle is the memorial to Shakespeare – a 1911 alabaster figure, reclining beneath a modern Shakespearean window.

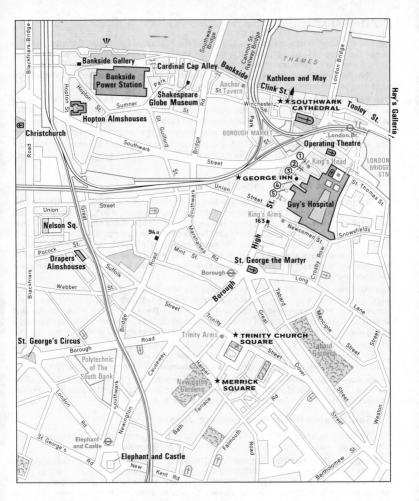

Westwards from Southwark Cathedral

A riverside walk extends from the Cathedral to Blackfriars Bridge.

Clink St. – To the west of the cathedral Winchester Walk and Winchester Sq, recalling the former Bishop's palace, lead into Clink Street. A plaque under the railway arches mentions the notorious prison which lay below the high tide water level and gave rise to the expression 'to be in clink'. The two 19C warehouses have been refurbished. The site of 12C Winchester Palace has been opened up: the excavated ground floor and the screen wall of the early 14C great hall of the palace with its graceful rose window are now on permanent view.

The adjoining office buildings in golden brick with rounded arches and passageways harmonize with the cathedral.

The trading schooner **Kathleen and May,** built in 1900 in North Wales, is berthed at St Mary Overy Dock. It has been restored by the Maritime Trust and gives a picture of life on board. It also presents an exhibition on coastal trading. *Open Mondays to Fridays 10am to 5pm, Saturdays and Sundays (except in winter) 11am to 4pm; £1, children, OAPs 50p.*

Bankside. – The Anchor Tavern was erected in 1770-75 on the site of earlier inns and is associated in its history not only with the river and the prison (truncheons, manacles etc in one bar) but also with Shakespeare and Dr Johnson and Boswell, through the Thrales who at one time owned it. More importantly Henry Thrale also owned a brewery in Park Street of which Johnson remarked, as executor, "We are not here to sell a parcel of boilers and vats but the potentiality of growing rich beyond the dreams of avarice". Recent excavations in the Park St area have revealed traces of a Roman warehouse.

The **Globe Theatre** (1599-1613) was located in the area. Work to build a replica of the Globe and a museum of Elizabethan and Jacobean theatre on Bankside is in progress.

Shakespeare Globe Museum. – *Bear Garden Alley. Open Mondays to Saturdays 10am to 5.30pm (4.30pm November to April); Sunday 1.30 to 6pm (4.30pm November to April); closed 1 January, 24 to 31 December, ☎ 01-928 6342; £1, children, OAPs, students 50p.* The museum, which is in a converted 18C warehouse on the site of the 16C bear baiting ring and later Hope Playhouse, houses a unique collection of material, including scale models, on the evolution of the Bankside Elizabethan theatre or **wooden O's,** the Globe, the Hope, the Swan and the first, the Rose (1587), also the bear and bull baiting rings and a diorama of Southwark at the time of one of the great Frost Fairs. Upstairs is a replica of the stage and tiring house of a theatre, designed in 1616 by Inigo Jones, which is used for occasional productions.

Two 18C private houses stand on either side of **Cardinal Cap Alley**. The first, no 49 Bankside, was built on the site of the Cardinal's Hat, a 16C stew. It bears a plaque which solemnly declares that it was where "in 1502 Catherine Infanta of Aragon and Castile and afterwards first Queen of Henry VIII, took shelter on her first landing in London" and also that it was where Christopher Wren lived during the building of the cathedral – all of which would appear unlikely as the house, although the oldest on Bankside, was built 50 years after the Great Fire. The houses, beyond the alley, now used as the Lodgings of the Provost of Southwark Cathedral, slightly larger and more stylised, are some 30 years later. Further west there is a **view** across the river of St Paul's and of Queenhithe, once London's most important dock above London Bridge.

The **Bankside Power Station,** a massive landmark among its peers with its single 320ft chimney, was designed by Giles Gilbert Scott (completed: 1964; closed: 1981).

The Bankside Gallery. – *48 Hopton Street. Open Tuesdays to Saturdays, 10am to 5pm, during exhibitions also Sundays; £1.* The Gallery, which opened in modern premises by the river in 1980, is owned by the Royal Societies of Painters in Water Colours (f 1804) and of Painter-Etchers and Engravers (f 1881) and used by five other clubs. Regularly changing exhibitions are held.

The Hopton Almshouses. – *Hopton St.* A group of two storey brick and tile cottages, the main wing pedimented, were built round three sides of a garden in 1752 and remain to this day bright with paint and still very rural.

Eastwards from Southwark Cathedral

The riverside area is undergoing extensive development. On the site of Hay's Wharf a new complex, London Bridge City, comprising offices, restaurants, pubs, a hospital, flats and shops, and retaining some of the original features is nearing completion. A site opposite the Tower has been identified as that of Edward II's Rosary Palace (14C). The Courage Brewery site by Tower Bridge is also being redeveloped along the same lines. Butler's Wharf is being converted and the Victorian warehouses are being refurbished to include a Design Museum. Concordia Wharf to the east which dates from 1885 has been carefully renovated to provide housing and other facilities taking full advantage of the riverside setting.

Hay's Galleria. –On the site of Hay's Dock which has been sealed over, the Galleria boasts a 90ft high glass barrel vault. The warehouses once full of tea, jute, spices and other exotic commodities now house shops, bars and restaurants. The stalls of the Wharf Market and entertainers add to the colourful scene. A monumental kinetic sculpture *The Navigators* by David Kemp, is a nostalgic reminder of the days when clippers docked at Hay's Wharf.

The London Dungeon. –*34 Tooley St. Open 10am to 5.30pm (4.30pm October to March); closed 24-26 December; 1hr; £4.50, children £2.50.* A gruesome parade of tableaux, with sound effects, of torture, witchcraft and early surgery in historical sequence – not for the squeamish.

Space Adventure. – *64-66 Tooley St. Open daily 10am to 6pm; closed 25 December. £3.50, children £2.* The dream of space travel comes true: a space craft takes off for an exciting journey to Mars via the Moon, a dramatic space rescue, a meteor storm...

Southwards down Borough High Street

The Borough, kernel not only of Southwark but of London south of the Thames, rings with historic street and inn names though many of the old buildings have now gone.

St Thomas's Old Operating Theatre. – *St Thomas St. Open Mondays, Wednesdays, Fridays 12.30 to 4pm and by appt* – ☎ *01-407 7600 Ext. 2739; closed Bank holidays; £1, children, OAPs 40p.* The entrance to the awesome early 19C operating theatre is through the tower door of St Thomas's Parish Church (now Southwark Cathedral chapterhouse – *not open*), formerly joined to the buildings of the original St Thomas's Hospital which extended east from the High St in three quadrangles. The hospital *(qv)* moved to its present site near Westminster Bridge in 1871. One wing of the old building still exists, set back off Borough High St, just north of St Thomas St, and is now occupied by the Post Office. St Thomas St itself was lined from halfway along by officials' houses of which the late 18C terrace remains (the wide gateway served as a hospital side entrance).

The church attic was already in use as a herb garret when, in 1821, the hospital committee decided to convert it into a women's operating theatre since it adjoined the Dorcas women's ward in one of the hospital's two front blocks. The theatre (rediscovered in 1956) is semicircular, about 40ft across with a 14ft amphitheatre ringed by 5 rows of "standings" for students. At the centre was the operating table, a sturdy wooden structure with upraised headpiece, and below, on the floor, a wooden box of sawdust which could "be kicked by the surgeon's foot to any place where most blood was running". In the corner was a small washbasin about the size of a large soup plate, in which surgeons washed their hands after – sometimes even before – operating. The theatre was last used in 1862 and is the only one of the period to be preserved in London.

Guy's Hospital. – The vast, 1 000 bed unit with one of London's tallest towers among its new buildings, retains the iron railings, gateway and square forecourt of its foundation construction of 1725. The court is flanked by the original tile roofed brick wings which lead back to the slightly later, Palladian style, centre range with a stone frontispiece decorated with allegorical figures by Bacon. In the court stands a bronze statue by Scheemakers of Thomas Guy (1644-1724), son of a Southwark lighterman and coal dealer, who began as a bookseller (Bibles), gambled successfully on the South Sea Bubble and other enterprises and then, like his 20C successor at Guy's, Lord Nuffield, who also rose from humble stock, became a munificent patron of medical institutions. In the chapel (centre of the right wing) is a full size memorial in high relief by John Bacon of Guy, portrayed before the 18C hospital into which a stretcher case is being borne. In the quads to the rear are a statue of Lord Nuffield and a mid 18C alcove from old London Bridge.

The Yards and the Inns of Southwark. – Several narrow streets and yards off Borough High St, south of St Thomas St, mark the entrances to the old inns which were the overnight stop of people arriving too late at night to cross the bridge into the capital. These inns were also the starting point for coach services to the southern counties and the ports. **King's Head Yard** ①: the King's Head, known as the Pope's Head before the Reformation, now a 19C building, sports a robust, somewhat supercilious, coloured effigy of Henry VIII. **White Hart Yard** ②: the pub (no longer in existence) was the headquarters of Jack Cade in 1450 and where Mr. Pickwick first met Sam Weller. **George Inn Yard** ③ *(closed 3 to 5.30pm):* the George Inn★, when rebuilt in 1676 after a fire, had galleries on three sides – only part of the south range remains but this still possesses two upper galleries outside and panelled rooms inside. Shakespeare is played in the cobbled yard in summer and open fires and traditional fare warm customers in winter. Note the Act of Parliament clock constructed in 1797 when a tax of 5s made people sell their timepieces and rely on clocks in public places – the act was repealed within the year.

Talbot Yard ④: recalled by Chaucer in the Prologue: "In Southwark at the Tabbard as I lay, At night was come into that hostelrie Wel nyne and twenty in a compagnye of sondrye folk... and pilgrims were they alle That toward Canterbury wolden ryde".

Queen's Head Yard ⑤: site of the Queen's Head (demolished: 1900) sold by John Harvard before he set out for America; Newcomen St: the King's Arms (1890) takes its name from the brightly painted lion and unicorn supporting the arms of George II (not George III as inscribed), a massive emblem which originally decorated the south gatehouse of old London Bridge.

A plaque at no 163 indicates the first site of **Marshalsea Prison** (1376 to 1811), the notorious penitentiary of which only one high wall remains on the later site (no 211). No 116 marks the location of the 16C palace of the Duke of Suffolk who married a daughter of Henry VII.

St George the Martyr. – *Open Mondays to Fridays, noon to 2pm.* The stone spire and square tower of the 1736 church on a 12C site mark the end of the first section of the High St. Dickens features the church in Little Dorrit, who is commemorated in the east window. The alms chest is a converted lead water cistern (1738), the pulpit the highest in London, the chandelier Georgian and the Te Deum ceiling unique, a replica of the late 19C Italian-style original, destroyed in the war, with cherubs breaking through a clouded sky accompanied by rays of glory.

London Fire Brigade Museum. – *94A Southwark Bridge Rd, SE1. Visit by appointment only* ☎ *01-587 4273.* The brave history of the fire fighting services is illustrated by fire marks, uniforms, medals, paintings, old fire engines as well as modern appliances.

Trinity Street (east of Borough High Street) marked by a contemporary pub, the Trinity Arms, leads into two complete, early 19C, squares. The first, **Trinity Church Sq★** is an unbroken quadrilateral of three storey houses, punctuated on the ground floor with round arched doorways, and united above by a narrow white course and coping. At the centre, in the garden, are a statue and a church. The statue, more than lifesize, is believed to have been brought in 1822 from Westminster Hall where it had stood in a niche for 450 years so making it the oldest statue in London: it is known as **King Alfred.** The church with a portico of colossal, fluted columns and a small openwork tower, built in 1824 and bombed, has been transformed (1975) into a studio for use by major orchestras. The adjoining and equally complete **Merrick Square★** of more modest houses, is named after the merchant who left the property in 1661 to the corporation of Trinity House. Both squares have distinctive and elegant lampstandards.

■ ST GEORGE'S CATHEDRAL, ELEPHANT and CASTLE

St George's Roman Catholic Cathedral. – *Lambeth Road; SW of St George's Circus.* St George's, one of the first major Roman Catholic churches to be built in England after the Reformation, was opened in 1848. It was designed by **A W Pugin** (1812-52), the impassioned advocate of the Gothic Revival (of the late 13C and early 14C English architectural style), who ended his days in the Bedlam hospital opposite, now the Imperial War Museum. The cathedral, destroyed by incendiary bombs during the War, was rebuilt to the design of Romilly Bernard Craze and reopened in 1958. Pugin's vision was never realised, so the stock brick exterior is characterised by a massive stump, the foundation of what is to have been a soaring spire.

Interior. – The new cathedral with an added clerestory is much lighter than the old: fluted columns of white Painswick stone support high pointed arches; plain glass lights the aisles, the only elaborate windows being those at the east and west ends which form jewelled pendants with rich red and deep blue glass. The new building's sole ornate feature is the high altar with its carved and gilded reredos. Statues are modern in uncoloured stone, memorials few but including the canopied figure of Cardinal Manning.

St George's Circus. – The circus, now a forlorn roundabout, was laid out in 1769 by act of parliament as London's first designed traffic junction with the obelisk to Brass Crosby *(qv)* marking the central island. Five, now six, roads converged at the centre of St George's Fields, long an open area crossed by rough roads where rebels had assembled (the Gordon Rioters), cattle grazed, a windmill turned, preachers roused crowds. In the vicinity are the **Drapers' Almshouses** (1820) two storey cottages with neo-Gothic windows and Nelson Sq where post war municipal housing adjoins a 1799 terrace. In Blackfriars Rd (no 27) stands **Christchurch,** the South London Industrial Mission, rebuilt in brick in a shady garden, which contains inside *(ring)* modern windows illustrating all the local trades including that of the Mrs Mops who in delighted return keep the church clean and polished.

Elephant and Castle. – The crossroads where the Roman Stane Street from Sussex was joined on its way to London Bridge by Watling Street from Kent and roads from villages where Lambeth now is, remained unnamed until the middle of 18C, when the corner smithy became a tavern and took as its sign the elephant and castle of the Cutlers' Co which, like so many other City companies, has associations with the area. Roads proliferated with the construction of bridges over the Thames in the 18 and 19C until congestion at the junction became notorious. Aerial devastation produced a new opportunity and in the 1950-60s, the 40 acre site was entirely redesigned and rebuilt except for the Metropolitan Tabernacle (1861) with its pillared portico rising majestically near the circus. In 1979 the Labour Party moved its headquarters from Smith Square, Westminster, to 150 Walworth Road *(map pp 5-8).*

■ CAMBERWELL and PECKHAM

The area offers an assortment of interests and buildings of 18, 19 and recent 20C. Grouped geographically they include:

Cambridge House *(131 Camberwell Rd),* early 19C houses, now the University Settlement; Camberwell Antique Market, 159-161 Camberwell Rd filled with lesser antiques, frippery and china; **King's College** and **Maudsley Hospitals** on either side of Denmark Hill and beyond, in Champion Park, behind the bronze statues of the General and his wife, Evelina, the **William Booth Memorial Salvation Army Training College** (1932).

Camberwell Grove off Camberwell Church St, is a wide avenue, closely planted, rising and lined by late 18, early 19C, Georgian town houses and terraces, Victorian cottages and villas. At the avenue's opening has long stood Mary Datchelor Girls' School, founded from monies left in 1726 in charity by Mary Datchelor who had been bequeathed a City coffeehouse by her father *(qv).* In 1863 the coffeehouse was sold for £30 000 and the school established in Camberwell where from late 19C it was endowed and administered by the Clothworkers' City Co; it closed in 1981. Near the avenue's top are Grove Chapel (1819) and opposite a small crescent of attractive stuccoed houses of 1830.

St Giles *(Peckham Rd)*, neo-Gothic with a towering spire, is remarkable for its gargoyles of Gladstone and other statesmen and inside, brasses dating from 1497 (Mighell Skinner) 1532...

Georgian Terraces *(nos 29, 30-34,* ie *both sides)*: the northerly of the two ranges, once known as Camberwell House was at one time a school attended by Thomas Hood; the southern asymmetrical terrace, east of Lucas Gardens, is preceded by a cobbled forecourt furnished with a contemporary gas lamp, iron gateway etc... Camberwell School of Arts and Crafts and the South London Art Gallery, Peckham Rd, combine massive elongated new buildings with the old school (1903), where caryatids guard the entrance, and the even older gallery (1897).

Nunhead Green *(southeast)* is marked by the rebuilt tavern, the Old Nun's Head, which claims a licence dating back to Henry VIII's reign and the **Beeston's Gift Almshouses** *(Consort Rd)*, erected in 1834 by the Girdlers' Co on land left them in the 16C by Cuthbert Beeston.

St John's *(Meeting House Lane)*, designed by David Bush in 1964, has a high, asymmetrical, brick end wall and an interior where roof lines, curving organ pipes, lead the eye to the bronze Christ, rescued from the bombed parish church and now high on the brick wall behind the altar; colour comes from the ground level window, a glowing abstract of blues, greens, yellows and from a joyous *Mother and Child* by Ron Hinton (1966). Turn left into Asylum Rd where set back round three sides of a forecourt, is a long, two storey, brick range with a central, pedimented portico, the Licensed Victuallers Benevolent Institution of 1827 (now Caroline Gardens).

STRAND – CHARING CROSS ★ (Westminster)

The Strand was an ancient track, midway between the highway west out of the City to Oxford in the north and London's main thoroughfare, the Thames; it was a street of great mansions and law students' hostels or inns from Plantagenet to Hanoverian times, the south side being especially favoured by provincial bishops for their town houses purchased, after the Dissolution, by the nobility. Between the big houses and down the lanes were hundreds of small houses, ale houses, bordels, coffeehouses – the Grecian, later the Devereux public house, when it was a favourite of Addison, is now the Edgar Wallace with an Edwardian decoration and interesting mementoes. **Twinings** (no 216) the tea house (small museum inside) with two Chinamen over the door opened in 1706 as Tom's Coffee House. There were also shops and from 1609 an arcade known as the **New Exchange**, patronised by James I and his Queen, Charles I and later Pepys who recounts how he bought gloves, linen, lace, garters, stockings and even books there – 76 of the 150 shops were milliners and mercers (demolished: 1737). In the late Victorian – Edwardian era, the Strand was known for its gaiety – a popular 19C music hall song was *Let's all go down the Strand.* – for its theatres, its hotels – the Cecil with 1 000 bedrooms (now Shell Mex), the Metropole, the Victoria, the Grand, besides those of today – and for its restaurants – no 222, a branch bank since 1895, was built in 1881 as a restaurant with electric lighting, elaborate ventilators and its own Artesian well and was decorated in 1886 with panelling in American walnut and sequoia, inset with Doulton tile pictures of chrysanthemums and characters from the plays of Ben Jonson who had frequented the Palsgrave's Head Tavern which stood on the site in 1612. Frederick Palsgrave and his wife, James I's daughter, Elizabeth, are pictured on panels beside the entrance.

Along the commercial thoroughfare of today, built and rebuilt in 19 and 20C, only the churches remain from the medieval period while street names recall the palaces and mansions of the past: Essex St and Devereux Ct after Robert Devereux's Essex House (later owned by another Elizabethan favourite, Robert Dudley, Earl of Leicester), Arundel St after the great house of the Howards. The name of George Villiers, Duke of Buckingham, to whom James I presented York House, one-time palace of the Archbishop, in 1624, is perpetuated in the streets east of the railway station, although Of Alley has now been renamed York Place. Hungerford Lane recalls the 15C house of a notorious family who replaced it with a market to pay off gambling debts and even built a footbridge in 1845 to attract customers, before finally selling up for Charing Cross Railway Stn to be built on the site. The famous town house of the Duke of Northumberland *(see p 147)* was demolished in 19C to make way for Northumberland Avenue.

St Clement Danes★. – *Open 8am to 5pm.* St Clement's, designed by **Wren** in 1682, with the open spire in three diminishing pillared stages, crowned by a small dome and turret added by **James Gibbs** in 1719, was burnt out in 1941 and rebuilt as the RAF church in 1955-8. To the Wren design of panelling and galleries beneath a tunnel vault richly decorated with coffered plaster work surrounding the Stuart coat of arms, have been added Air Force mementoes including 800 squadron and unit badges carved as slate keys and inlaid in the pavement, floor memorials of the badges of the Commonwealth air forces and the Polish squadrons. There are also a USAAF and other shrines and Memorial Books with 125 000 names. The grand pulpit is the original one by Grinling Gibbons, carefully restored after the war. In the crypt, a burial place till 1853, are the Norwegian Air Force font and the Netherlands Air Force altar.

Tradition has it that boats with oranges and lemons came up the Thames to land fruit for sale in Clare Market (on the site of Kingsway – Drury Lane) and paid a tithe in kind to the church; association is disputed *(p 53)*, but a carillon rings out the **nursery rhyme** at 9am, noon, 3 and 6pm on weekdays. Samuel Johnson was a worshipper, hence the statue overlooking Fleet St.

Royal Courts of Justice. – The Law Courts date from 1874-82 when the Perpendicular design of G E Street was constructed to replace the ranges erected around the courts' original seat in Westminster Hall. The centrepiece inside is the Great Hall, a vaulted arcade, 230ft long, 82ft high, decorated with foliated doorways, blind arcades, diapering and a seated statue of the architect. The early courtrooms and the majority still – there are more than 20 – depend from the hall which is marked outside by a needle spire, counterpoint to the long arched façade, the heavy tower and polygonal west end. There is a small exhibition of legal costumes *(open weekdays 10am to 4pm)* near the main entrance.

Aldwych. – The sweeping semicircle was laid out in 1905. The huge half moon island on the Strand is occupied by massive buildings – Australia House, India House (reliefs), the Citibank and, in the centre, the 1925-35 **Bush House,** base of the BBC External Services.

London School of Economics. – *Houghton St.* The school which numbers 3 700 full-time students and 500 part-time students (40 % postgraduates), was founded in 1895 under the auspices of Sidney Webb and has been part of London University since 1900. The British Library of Political and Economic Science, which contains some 2 750 000 items, including pamphlets and tracts, is also housed in the building.

The Registry of births, deaths and marriages. – *10 Kingsway. Public Search Rooms open Mondays to Fridays 8.30am to 4.30pm. Closed public holidays.*

Registration has been compulsory since 1837 and there are now some 250 million entries; nearly 4 000 people a week use the search rooms.

St Mary-le-Strand. – The second church on an island site is a Baroque miniature. It was designed by **James Gibbs** in 1714-17 with a semicircular, columned, west porch and columns above supporting a pediment. The tower immediately behind the porch, is in four tiers, the centre two columned beneath a final turret (*cf* St Clement Danes and St Martin-in-the-Fields). Inside the decoration is concentrated in the plasterwork roofing.

The church stands on the site of the Strand Maypole and has been known as the Cabby's church since Capt Bailey set up the first hackney carriage rank on the north side in 1634.

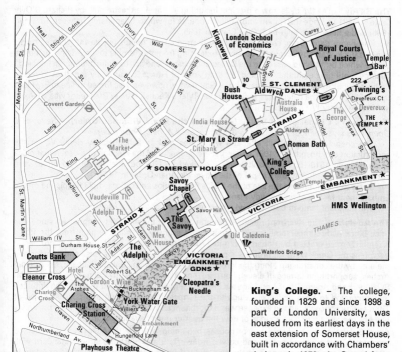

King's College. – The college, founded in 1829 and since 1898 a part of London University, was housed from its earliest days in the east extension of Somerset House, built in accordance with Chambers' designs; in 1970s the Strand front was renewed in an unrelated, modern style. The courtyard, long and narrow is terminated by the colonnaded pavilion which completes the Somerset House river front.

Roman Bath. – *5 Strand Lane. Visible through the window. For admission ring 01-798 2063-4.*

The bath, fed by a nearby spring, is long and rounded at one end; it is possibly Tudor, more likely 17C but certainly not Roman. Dutch 17C tiles, the traditional delft and a tulip design, panel areas of the walls.

Somerset House★. – The present building, foretaste in size of future ministries, was erected enduringly in Portland stone in 1776-86 to the designs of **Sir William Chambers;** it housed the Navy and Navy Pay Offices, the, then small, Tax and Excise offices and three learned societies: the Royal Academy, which Chambers was instrumental in founding and of which he was treasurer, the Antiquaries and the Royal Society.

The 18C building stands on the site of the palace begun by Protector Somerset in 1547 and still incomplete when he was executed in 1552. He had an obsession for building; to acquire additional land he demolished the 13C Mary-le-Strand, bishops' palaces and an Inn of Chancery; he collected (or failed to collect *p 172*) stone from buildings forfeited under the Reformation. He achieved a palace of entirely new appearance, which extended from

Somerset House : river front.

the Strand to the river and which, on his execution, passed to the crown and was given by each Stuart to his queen: Anne of Denmark (when it was known as Denmark House), Henrietta Maria, who returned to it at the Restoration, and Catherine of Braganza.

The building. – The narrow Strand façade, inspired by Inigo Jones' Palladian riverside gallery designed for Henrietta Maria, has a triple gateway and giant columns beneath a balustrade decorated with statues and a massive statuary group by Bacon. Inside is a vast courtyard nearly 120 yds long by just over 100 across: Chambers' gift lay in design on a more domestic scale and he treated the courtyard as a square of terrace houses. The Strand block, in which the societies were accommodated (the names are still over the doors) and which contains the so-called **Fine Rooms**, notable for their proportions and plasterwork, has two advanced wings and is the most elaborate. The Courtauld Institute Galleries *(qv)* are scheduled to move into the Fine Rooms in 1989. A continuous balustrade, punctuated by vases (supplied by Mrs Coade at 6 gns each!) unites the fronts. The riverside front, which is 800ft long including the later extensions, stands on a continuous line of massive arches which in 18C were at the water's edge.

Located in Somerset House today are the Board of Inland Revenue and the **Probate Registry** *(access to the index free; examination and copies of wills available on payment – Mondays to Fridays 10am to 4.30pm; closed on all holidays and 27, 28 December).*

The Savoy. – The Savoy is now a precinct including a chapel, a **theatre** built by Richard D'Oyly Carte in 1881 to stage the Gilbert and Sullivan operas (of which 13 appeared between 1875 and 1896) and a **hotel**, also built by D'Oyly Carte in 1889.

The name dates from 1246, when Henry III granted the manor beside the Thames to his queen's uncle, Peter of Savoy. On the acres extending from the Temple to the Adelphi he built a palace which by 14C had passed to the Dukes of Lancaster and as "the fairest manor in England" became, until his death, the "lodging" of King John of France, captured by the Black Prince at Poitiers (1356). The last owner, was John of Gaunt who, however, was forced to flee to Ely Place *(qv)* in 1381 when the palace was sacked by Wat Tyler's Kentish rebels. The manor was annexed in 1399 by Henry IV.

The Queen's Chapel of the Savoy (Chapel of the Royal Victorian Order). – *Savoy Hill. Open Tuesdays to Fridays 11.30am to 3.30pm; closed August, September.*

The chapel, largely rebuilt after the war, dates back to a bequest by Henry VII for the construction of a hospital for 100 "pouer, needie people" and the erection of a dependent place of worship in 1510-16. The hospital was dissolved in 1702 but the chapel and burial yard survived to be made into the Chapel of the Royal Victorian Order in 1937.

Savoy Hill is famous as the site of the BBC's first studios and offices: 1923-32 (plaque on the Embankment façade of no 2 Savoy Place).

The standard lamp in Carting Lane which never goes out is lit by sewer gas.

The Adelphi. – The riverfront retains the name although the massively ungraceful stone and brick block with cumbersome angle statues could scarcely be more remote from the Royal Adelphi Terrace erected by Robert Adam in 1768-72 (demolished 1937). The Adam brothers – *adelphi* is the Greek word for brothers – purchased the site on a 99 year lease and transformed the area by the construction along the foreshore of a towering embankment arcade, the Adelphi Arches, supporting a terrace of eleven houses. The row was framed by John (now John Adam) St, Robert and Adam Sts, the end houses in the latter, which overlooked the river, pedimented and decorated to form advanced wings to the terrace. It was the first and possibly finest of Thamesside concepts but the expense was exhorbitant and it was a financial failure; now only a few houses remain to give an idea of how the quarter must have looked in 18C.

Adam St: the east side has a run of houses beginning with no 10, Adam House, neat and compact with a rounded corner and curved ironwork; 9 and 8 are the street's standard with attractive, pilastered doors; no 7, in the axis of John Adam St, is a typical example of Adam in full decorative style with his favourite acanthus leaf motif on pilasters, cornice and ironwork *(illustration p 25).*

John Adam St: no 8 was built for the Royal Society of Arts (f 1754) in 1772-4 by Adam with a pillared porch surmounted by giant fluted columns framing a Venetian window; The delightful rear façade, surmounted by a slender water carrier, can be seen from the top of the steps leading up from Durham House St into the Strand, just west of New South Wales House.

The north side of the Strand backing on to Covent Garden, is notable for the narrow front of the Strand Palace Hotel (no 372), Stanley Gibbons stamp shop and Gallery (399), the Vaudeville and Adelphi Theatres and Coutts Bank, a modern glass insertion at the centre of a delightful pavilioned 19C façade (restored) in the style of John Nash.

Buckingham St. – 17 and 18C brick houses with pilastered, hooded and corbelled doorways still line both sides (nos 12, 17, 18, 20 date from 1670s). Pepys lived at no 12 from 1679-88. At the bottom of the street stands the **York Water Gate**, a triple arch of rusticated stone decorated with the Villiers arms and a scallop shell. It was built in 1626 at the water's edge but since 1864 has led into the **Victoria Embankment Gardens*** where music is played in summer. Opposite the gardens between the road and the river stands **Cleopatra's Needle,** erected in 1878. The dolphin lamp standards and decorated bench ends are appropriate to their riparian location.

Beneath the viaduct from Charing Cross Station to Hungerford Railway Bridge and connecting Villiers and Craven Sts (Benjamin Franklin lived at no 36) are Hungerford Lane where there is a Saturday coin, medal, stamp and Victoriana, market, The Arches where there are military and police paraphernalia and coin shops and, between the two, the **Players Theatre Club** *(members only)* in an old music hall. The area is undergoing extensive redevelopment. The **Playhouse Theatre** (Northumberland Avenue) reopened in 1987 thirty-six years after its last live performance. The Franco-Venetian interior resplendent with gilding, plasterwork and murals dates from 1906.

Charing Cross. – Where the Strand met the road from Westminster and the road north, there developed the village of Charing (from Anglo-Saxon *ceirring:* a bend) where in 1290 Edward I placed the last of the 12 **Eleanor Crosses** marking the funeral cortege of his queen to Westminster. The original Cross, octagonal and of solid appearance in marble and Caen stone, which stood where the statue of Charles I is now, was destroyed by the Puritans; the present one in the station forecourt is mid 19C. A mural (Northern Line) shows 13C cross abuilding.

Open April to September Sundays to Thursdays, October, Sundays only, noon to 4.15pm; £1.75, combined house and garden ticket £3, children £1.25 and £2 respectively.

The colonnaded east front of Syon House is visible across the river from Kew Gardens, the Northumberland Lion with outstretched tail silhouetted against the sky; a second beast, also from the model by Michelangelo, crowns the Lion Gate and graceful Adam screen on the London Rd (A 315). The plain castellated main front gives no hint of the rich ornamentation within.

The house's history. – On the walls inside are portraits of the men and women who built up the house and their royal patrons, by Gainsborough, Reynolds, van Dyck, Mytens, Lely and by unknown artists of the English 16C school. Two men were principally responsible for the construction: the Lord Protector, Duke of Somerset, brother of Henry's queen, Jane Seymour, in the 16C and Hugh Percy, 1st Duke of Northumberland in the 18C. Somerset was given the former monastery site in 1547 by his nephew Edward VI and erected a Tudor mansion in the plan of a hollow square, dined his monarch there in 1550, laid out gardens, including the first physic garden in England... but in 1552 he was charged with conspiracy and executed.

For the next two centuries Syon was a political storm centre as the owners intrigued, conspired and often died brutally: John Dudley was beheaded (1553) for promoting his daughter-in-law, Lady Jane Grey, as queen; Percys, Earls of Northumberland, were executed for supporting Mary Queen of Scots (1572), were found dead in the Tower (1585) and imprisoned for association with the Gunpowder Plot... With the marriage in 1682 of Elizabeth Percy to Charles, 6th Duke of Somerset, Syon returned to a descendant of its earlier owner, who also held office under the crown. By the 18C, the house and grounds, in the opinion of the new heirs, the Duke and Duchess of Northumberland, were in urgent need of remodelling: they commissioned **Robert Adam** and **Capability Brown** to produce designs.

The Great Hall. – Adam is at his most formal in the high, wide Hall, which has a black and white marble pavement reflected in the ceiling design, and an apse at either end, one framing a statue of the *Apollo Belvedere,* the other raised and screened by Doric columns, framing a bronze figure of the *Dying Gladiator.*

The Ante-Room. – The ante-room, by contrast, gleams darkly with heavy gilding, reds, blues, yellows, in the patterned scagliola floor, and green marble and scagliola pillars, which line the walls on three sides and stand forward from the fourth to "square" the room. Gilded statues gaze down from the entablature.

State Dining Room. – The long apartment with column screened apses at either end was the first to be remodelled by Adam: deep niches with copies of antique statues along the left wall were reflected in pier mirrors; frieze, cornice, ceiling, decorated half domes, beautiful doorcases and doors, afforded a perfect setting for the banquets given by the duke and duchess in late 18C.

Red Drawing Room. – Scarlet Spitalfields silk, blooming with pale gold roses, on the walls and at the windows, a carpet, signed and dated 1769, woven at Moorfields, door pilasters with ivory panels covered with ormolu, gilded ceiling studded with Cipriani painted medallions, provide great richness – but the room is, in fact, dominated by its Stuart portraits: Charles I (Lely), his queen, Henrietta Maria (van Dyck); his sister Elizabeth of Bohemia (van Honthorst); his elder brother who pre-deceased him, Prince Henry (van Somer); his daughter, Princess Mary of Orange (Hanneman), Henrietta, Duchess of Orleans (Mignard), Princess Elizabeth (Lely), his sons, Charles II and his wife Catherine of Braganza (Huysmans) and James II as Duke of York (Lely). The elegant mosaic-topped side tables are noteworthy.

The Long Gallery. – The long gallery of the Tudor house was transformed by Adam into a ladies' withdrawing room (far enough away from the dining room not to hear any masculine after dinner ribaldry!). It is 136ft long, 14ft wide and has a crossline decoration on the ceiling, grouped pilasters, wall niches, pier mirrors, so arranged as to disguise the length. Much of the furniture was designed, as throughout the house, by Adam, notably the veneered chest of drawers made by Chippendale.

The Print Room. – The furniture in this small room includes two remarkable walnut, marquetry inlaid cabinets of the late 17C; the walls are again hung with family portraits.

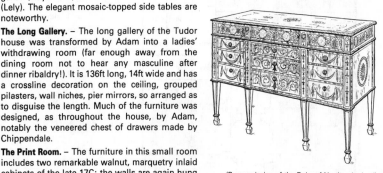

(By permission of the Duke of Northumberland)

Adam commode.

■ SYON PARK GARDENS ★

Open daily 10am to 6pm or dusk when earlier; closed 22-29 December; £1.50, children £1, combined house and garden £3, children £2. Garden Centre, car park, cafeteria.

Capability Brown assisted in designing the gardens, which extend to the river and maintain a tradition begun by Protector Somerset who planted many rare and imported trees; two of his mulberries still survive. In 1837 the gardens, world famous for their botanical specimens, were opened to the public. A vast **rose garden** *(separate entrance south of the house)* is in bloom from May to August.

Great Conservatory. – The conservatory, a beautiful semicircular building of white painted gun metal and Bath stone, with a central cupola and end pavilions was designed by Charles Fowler in 1820-27. Inside are cacti and an aquarium.

The London Butterfly House. – *Open daily 10am to 5.30pm (3.30pm in winter); closed 24, 25, 26 December, £1.90, children £1.10; shop.*

In a tropical greenhouse visitors may stroll among many varieties of brilliant butterflies. All stages of breeding may be observed. Another section displays live spiders and insects – locusts, crickets, ants and scorpions.

SYON PARK★★

Heritage Motor Museum. – *Open daily (except 25, 26 December) 10am to 5pm (October to February 4.30pm); £2, children, OAPs £1.*

Among the 250 vehicles, 100 of which are on display at one time, are such makes as Alvis, Lanchester, Wolseley, Riley and MG; also Lord Nuffield's own 6 cylinder bullnosed Morris (1921), Austin 7 Tourer (1922), Endcliffe Morgan (1924 Aero), the Millionth Austin (1948) autographed by every Longbridge employee, Morris Minor (1948) and Mini (1959).

South of Syon Park

Isleworth Parish Church of All Saints. – The church beside the river on the south outskirts of Syon Park has a square crenellated west tower of ragstone, dating back to 15C and containing two 18C monuments, one to a church benefactor. The church was bombed and on the site since 1970 has stood a well proportioned modern vessel of brick, wood and plain glass, with only small brasses rescued from the fire.

The London Apprentice. – The pub on the river dates back centuries, the present building some 200 years. The name is said to be after the 16/19C apprentices who rowed up the river on their annual holiday and made the inn their own for a day.

TATE GALLERY ★★★ (Millbank, Westminster)

Open daily 10am (Sunday 2pm) to 5.50pm; closed 1 January, Good Friday, May Day holiday, 24, 25, 26 December; for special exhibitions see the press or telephone: ☎ 01-821 7128.

The opening in 1979 of a major extension to the Tate enables about one eighth of the British and Modern Art collections of some 16 000 paintings, sculptures and prints, acquired in the ninety years since its foundation, to be shown at one time. The Clore Gallery for the Turner Collection, designed by James Stirling, opened in Spring 1987. New museums for sculpture, New Art and 20C art are planned and are being designed by James Stirling.

In 1967 the gallery's pictures were re-organised into the **British Collection** of works by artists born before 1860 active in Britain and the **Modern Collection** of painting and sculpture by artists of all nationalities born after 1860.

The British Collection arrangement *(on the left)* is generally static; the Modern *(on the right and centre)* is liable to considerable re-arrangement as subjects are frequently moved to accommodate acquisitions, to be displayed in special exhibitions, or to go out on loan.

Special exhibitions, always a feature of the Tate, are mounted in galleries 49-60. Sculpture is usually exhibited in Gallery 29.

Foundation to 1979 extension. – The Tate aims to illustrate the evolution and range of style, the contribution to a school of contemporary artists and the latest developments in art.

The Gallery developed because within 50 years of the purchase of the Angerstein collection and the founding of the National Gallery. in 1824, the nation had acquired a large number of pictures – notably through the Chantrey Bequest, for the purchase of works by living artists as well as earlier masters, two major collections (the Vernon and Sheepshanks), and the Turner

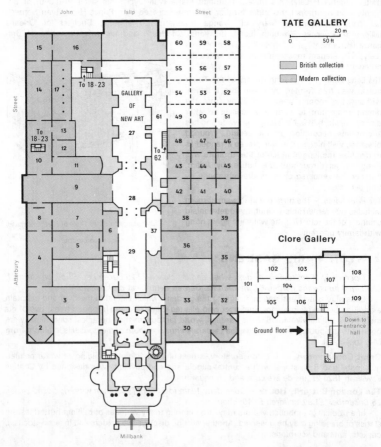

bequest of about 300 oil paintings and 20 000 water colours and drawings (1856). These pictures were shuffled between the National Gallery, V & A and Marlborough House until, in 1891 Henry Tate, sugar broker, munificent benefactor and collector of modern art, offered his collection to the nation and £80 000 for a building, if the government would provide the site. The government offered the site of the former Millbank Prison.

In 1897 the Tate opened as the Gallery of Modern British Art – "modern" being post 1790! Tate (d 1899) and the Duveens supplied funds for extensions; Sir Hugh Lane (d in the *Lusitania*, 1915) made a bequest of 39 paintings, including superb Impressionists, "to found a collection of Modern Continental Art in London" (despatched to Dublin, 1959); Samuel Courtauld, in 1923, funded the purchase of modern French paintings; in 1955 the Tate Gallery became legally independent of the National Gallery.

GALLERY	SUBJECTS, ARTISTS, TITLES

A free Gallery Plan, updated weekly, is available from the Information Desk.

3	**Early British (16, 17 and early 18C):** Bettes – *Man in a Black Cap, The Cholmondeley Sisters,* Johnson, Dobson – *Endymion Porter,* Lely, Kneller, Hogarth – portraits of bishops, *Children's Party, The Beggar's Opera,* Devis – *The James Family.*
2	**British:** Hogarth – self-portrait with his dog Punch, portraits; Verrio, Thornhill, Highmore *The Good Samaritan* and illustrations for Richardson's *Pamela..*
4, 5	**Late 18C:** George Stubbs *The Haymakers, The Reapers, Mares and Foals*; Gainsborough early landscapes, portraits of the Italian dancer, *Giovanna Baccelli,* and the brewer, *Ben Truman*; Romney, the young *Lady Hamilton*; Joshua Reynolds three *Self-portraits,* when young, in his prime and as a deaf man, and many others; Zoffany conversation pieces; Wilson landscapes; Benjamin West neo-classical heroic scenes; Joseph Wright of Derby *Sir Brooke Boothby.* Lawrence, *Kemble as Hamlet.*
6	**Painters of the Sublime and Exotic:** Fuseli, de Loutherbourg (also 8).
7	**William Blake:** dramatic presentation of the large colour prints and *Divine Comedy;* Samuel Palmer.
8	**Late 18C:** rustic scenes, landscapes and dramatic scenes by Loutherbourg *Avalanche in the Alps, Distant Hailstorm;* Hoppner *A Gale of Wind;* Copley *Death of Major Pierson;* portraits by Raeburn *The Allen Brothers, Lady Dalrymple,* Lawrence *Miss Caroline Fry, Lady Georgiana Fane.*
9	**19C.** Dramatic landscapes by Crome *Slate Quarries,* Palmer *The Waterfalls,* Turner *Coniston Fells,* J. Ward *Gordale Scar,* J. Martin *The Last Judgment, Plains of Heaven.*
10	**Constable:** *The Opening of Waterloo Bridge* and smaller paintings, studies – *Flatford Mill, Chain Pier, Brighton, Clouds.*
11	**Works on Paper.**
12	**Early 19C Landscape:** Crome *Yarmouth Harbour,* David Cox, Bonington *Near Boulogne, Le Pont des Arts,* Richard Dadd *The Fairy Feller's Masterstroke,* G. Lewis *Harvest Scene.*
13	**Sporting Art:** Stubbs, Sartorius, Herring.
14	*To be rehung.*
15	**Pre-Raphaelites:** Holman Hunt *Strayed Sheep,* Ford Maddox Brown *Lear and Cordelia, The Hayfield,* Arthur Hughes *The Tryst,* Millais *Ophelia, Beata Beatrix, Aurelia, The Annunciation.*
16, 17	**The Later Victorians:** *The Lady of Shalott* by J.M. Waterhouse, *Blossoms, A Garden* by Albert Moore, Alma Tadema, Frederick Leighton, G.F. Watts, Millais *The Vale of Rest,* James Tissot *Portrait,* J.S. Sargent *Carnation, Lily, Lily, Rose,* Burne-Jones' exploration of the medieval world in *The Golden Stairs* and Whistler's *Nocturnes in Black and Gold* and in *Blue-Green* indicate the profusion and diversity of the age.
18	**British Art early 20C:** Sickert *Portraits,* Orpen, M. Smith, Bomberg, A. John.
19	**British Art 1920s, 1930s** Nash, Burra *Harlem,* Spencer *Double Nude Portrait, St Francis and the Birds,* Nicholson *Painting 1932*; Wallis *The Blue Ship,* Hitchens *Autumn Composition.*
20	**British Art 1940-60** Bratby, Sutherland *Crucifixion 1946,* Ayrton, Nash *Dead Sea,* Freud *Girl with white Dog.*
21	**British Art early 20C** large works by Spencer *Resurrection series,* A. John *A Smiling Woman.*
22, 23	**British Art 1920-1940.** Dame L. Knight, B. Hepworth, Nicholson.
27, 28	Changing display of **20C art.**
30	**Cubism, Futurism, Vorticism:** Léger, Gris, Braque, Picasso.
31	**British Painting c1880-1920** G. John *Self-Portrait,* A. John, Steer, Bell, Fry. Grant, Spencer, Sickert *Ennui, La Hollandaise,* Gilman *The Artist's Mother.*
32-33	**Post-Impressionism:** Rousseau, Bonnard, Derain, Matisse, Gauguin, Cézanne.
35	**European Abstraction c1910-1940:** Mondrian, Kandinsky, Nicholson, Malevitch; smooth sculptures by Brancusi, Hepworth, Arp, Gabo.
36	**European Art c1945-1960:** Dubuffet *Monsieur Plume, The Busy Life,* Appel *People, Birds and Sun,* Jorn. Sculptures by César, Chillida, Fontana.
38	**European Painting:** Leger *Acrobat and his Partner;* Miro *Message from a Friend;* Matisse *The Snail;* de Staël, Chagall *Bouquet with Flying Lovers,* Rouault.
39	**German Art:** Munch *The Sick Child,* Nolde *The Sea,* Kirchner *Bathers at Moritzburg,* Kandinsky *Cossacks,* Beckman; Kokoschka; Schmidt-Rotluff *Two Women.*
40, 41	**American Abstract Expressionism:** Hofmann, Gorky, Kline, de Kooning, Pollock.
42	**Dada and Surrealism:** Ernst, Picabia, Duchamp, Dali.
43, 44	*New acquisitions.*
45	*Kinetic sculpture.*
46	**Giacometti** *Diego, Seated Man,* Balthus *Sleeping Girl,* Morandi.
47	**British and American Art 1950-1980:** Freud, Bacon, Kitaj, Kossoff, Moynihan, Auerbach.
48	**Pop Art:** Warhol *Marilyn Diptych,* Hockney, Blake, Johns *Zero through Nine,* Oldenburg *Soft Drainpipe,* Lichtenstein *Whaam.*
62	**Print Gallery:** *Changing displays.*

Clore Gallery. – A modern building houses the 300 paintings and 20 000 drawings bequeathed to the nation by J.W.M. Turner (1775-1851).

On the first floor are displayed 120 oil paintings which trace Turner's artistic development: large dramatic compositions (*Hannibal Crossing the Alps, Waterloo, Shipwreck, Mountain Scene*), sketches of the Thames, views of Italy and of Venice (*Bridge of Sighs, Ducal Palace and Custom-House*) and light effects (*Sunset, Snow storm, Norham Castle*). One room is reserved for watercolours.

The THAMES ★★

Regular steamer services began on the Thames in 1816 and by mid-century were carrying several million people: families and friends out for an evening trip or for an excursion, often to the estuary and seaside towns of Herne Bay, Margate, Ramsgate. In the week, the boats were crowded with workers crossing into the docks, boatyards, to the arsenal and south bank factories. Fares were a penny from one pier to the next. A riverbus service now operates between Greenwich Pier and Chelsea Harbour Pier at 15 minute intervals (30 minutes at weekends). For information ☎ 01-376 3676. An express service runs hourly between Charing Cross, Swan Lane and London City Airport.

Pleasure boat services

There are regular services all the year round: LTB River Information (01-730 4812); from Westminster down river (01-930 4097) (20 min intervals) to the Tower (01-488 0344) (20 mins), Greenwich (45 mins) and the Thames Barrier (01-930 3373) (1 1/4 hours) and from April to October up river (1/2 hr intervals) to Putney (40 mins), Kew (90 mins), Richmond (150 mins; up to 12.30pm only) and Hampton Court (225 mins; up to 12.30pm only).

London's Bridges. – 28 bridges span the tideway from Teddington Lock to the Tower: one footbridge, 9 rail bridges, 18 road bridges.

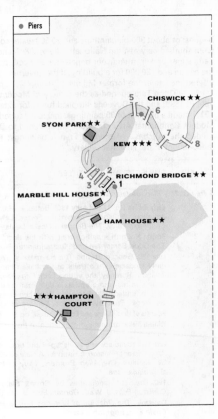

● Piers

CHISWICK ★★
SYON PARK ★★
KEW ★★★
RICHMOND BRIDGE ★★
MARBLE HILL HOUSE ★
HAM HOUSE ★★
★★★ HAMPTON COURT

NAME	DATE	ARCHITECT	HISTORY	CHARACTERISTICS
Richmond ★★	1774	James Paine	Toll bridge until mid 19C; painted by Turner.	Classical, stone, very handsome with 5 arches and parapet (widened 1937).
Richmond Rlwy	1848	Joseph Locke	Richmond-Staines-Windsor line.	Iron and concrete. Typical early railway style.
Twickenham	1933	Maxwell Ayrton		Concrete. 3 wide spans.
Richmond Footbridge	1894			Double footbridge. Forms the crest line of the 3 gate weir.
Kew (King Edward VII)	1903	Wolfe Barry and Brereton	Replaced an 18C bridge.	Stone. 3 spans with attractive solid outline.
Kew Rlwy	1869	W R Galbraith	Opened as part of the S W Rlwy.	Lattice girder. 5 arches.
Chiswick	1933	Baker		Concrete. 150ft wide centre span.
Barnes Rlwy	1849	Locke		Iron. Unique humpback outline.
Hammersmith	1884-1887	Joseph Bazalgette	Replaced the first Thames suspension bridge (1827).	Suspension. Lines ruined by typically Victorian pavilions.
Putney	1884	Bazalgette	Replaced a wooden toll bridge of 1729.	Cornish granite. The boat race starts just upriver.
Fulham Rlwy	1889	William Jacomb	Originally part of the District Rlwy.	Iron girder trellis. Footbridge parallels rail bridge.
Wandsworth	1938	E P Wheeler	Replaced a 19C bridge.	Concrete; flat, low lying, 3 spans.
Battersea Rlwy	1863		Still the only bridge to carry a railway line directly connecting north and south England.	Concrete.
Battersea	1890	Bazalgette	The ferry was replaced in 1771 by a wooden bridge lit by oil lamps in 1799, gas in 1824. Subject of Whistler's *Nocturne* painting.	Iron. Flat, decoratively painted but now spiked by emasculated sodium lamp standards.
Albert	1873	R W Ordish	Modified by J. Bazalgette.	Suspension cantilever. A cat's cradle, painted in 3 colours and illuminated at night. Spare bulbs are stored in the twin tollmen's huts at either end.
Chelsea	1934	Forest and Wheeler	Replaced an 1858 suspension bridge.	Suspension. Clean lined; typical of interwar bridges.
Victoria Rlwy	1859		Symbolised the immense importance of 19C railways.	Originally 900ft long × 132ft wide to accommodate 10 tracks to Victoria Stn; since widened.
Vauxhall	1900	Maurice Fitzmaurice	Replaced an earlier iron bridge.	Iron and stone; high iron parapet with figures, Engineering, Science etc, against the piers.

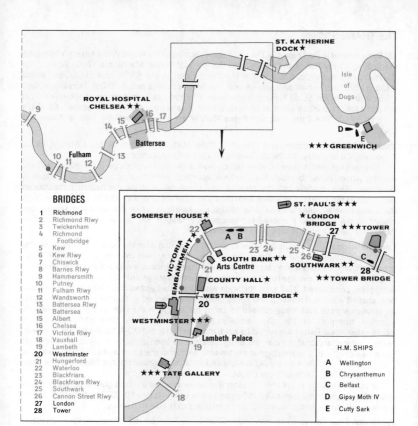

H.M. SHIPS

A Wellington
B Chrysanthemum
C Belfast
D Gipsy Moth IV
E Cutty Sark

NAME	DATE	ARCHITECT	HISTORY	CHARACTERISTICS
Lambeth	1932	G Topham Forest	The horse ferry was replaced by a bridge in 1862.	Steel; spanking scarlet and black parapet.
Westminster*	1862	Thomas Page	Successor to the stone bridge of 1750, the first to be built after London Bridge and where Wordsworth composed his sonnet (1807).	Stone. Flat with lanky piers, seven low arches.
Charing Cross Rlwy or Hungerford	1862		Replaced Brunel's suspension bridge (1845-subsequently incorporated in Clifton S. Br.)	Plain lattice girder structure (parallel footbridge).
Waterloo	1945	G G Scott	Replaced Rennie's 19C bridge.	Portland stone over concrete; sleek and white; 5 low spanning arches.
Blackfriars	1899	James Cubitt	Replaced an 18C structure.	Iron and stone. River bank footpath.
Blackfriars Rlwy	1886		Opened as part of the Dover line.	Iron; high parapet, coats of arms at either end, typify 19C rlwy prosperity.
Southwark	1919	Ernest George	Replaced Rennie's 1815-1819 bridge.	Iron; 3 arches. Referred to as the Cast Iron Bridge in Dickens' *Little Dorrit*.
Cannon Street Rlwy	1866	J W Barry J Hawkshaw		One vast structure with the brick train shed, crowned with twin pavilions.
London Bridge*	1973	Harold King	*see p 152.*	Concrete. 3 low arches balanced on slender piles.
Tower Bridge**	1894	Barry and Jones	*see p 152.*	Iron drawbridge. *(See cover illustration.)*

"Every drop of the Thames is liquid history"

The Thames provides work, has influenced the capital's size, the country's wealth. Throughout its 215 miles (from Thames Head, 3 miles from Cirencester, to the Nore) it is not scenically spectacular although the upper reaches near its source in the Cotswolds are extremely pleasant; it has mirrored ships of every type from men o'war to tugs, from the *Great Eastern*, Millwall (1856) to state barges and rowing shells; in its tidal waters it reflects the Houses of Parliament, the South Bank Centre, the Embankment (1864-70) spiked by Cleopatra's Needle (erected in 1878) and the RAF, eagle crowned, memorial, offices, wharves, pubs, parks, power stations, bridges, City and other churches, St Paul's, houses... the ebb and flow of London life.

If you take a boat up or downstream you will also see the bridges, HM Ships *(p 152)* moored along the Embankment and most spectacularly the Tower, Greenwich, Lambeth Palace, Syon Park, Hampton Court, as our forefathers saw them as they travelled London's main highway by leisured state barge or more modest craft.

The THAMES★★

HM Ships moored in the Thames. – The ships to be seen include a World War II frigate, Wellington, the floating Livery Hall of the Honourable Company of Master Mariners, a World War I sloop, Chrysanthemum, headquarters of the London division of the RNVR, and the cruiser **Belfast** (1938, 11 500 tons) which saw service with the Arctic convoys and on D-Day *(access via Hay's Galleria and Tooley St, SE1. Ferry from Tower Pier runs daily in summer, weekends only in winter; 11am to 5.20pm (4pm in winter); closed 1 January, 24, 25, 26 December; £3, OAPs, children £1.50).* The **Cutty Sark** and **Gypsy Moth IV** are in permanent dry dock at Greenwich *(qv).*

Tower Bridge★★. – *Open daily 10am to 6.30pm (4.45pm 1 November to 31 March); closed 1 January, Good Friday, 24, 25, 26 December; £2, OAPs, children £1.*

The familiar gothic towers, steel lattice-work high level footbridge *(lift – 200 steps)* and original power house beneath the southern approach were opened in 1982 as a museum. Diagrams, films, models and the original equipment demonstrate the hydraulic mechanism which raised the 1 100 ton bascules from the building of the bridge in 1886-94 by Sir John Wolfe Barry and Horace Jones until 1976. In 1952 a bus failing to notice the lights and signals, was caught on the bridge as it opened but successfully "leaped" the gap of several feet to safety. Panoramic views from the high level walkways.

London Bridge★. – London Bridge was the only crossing over the lower Thames until 1750 when Westminster was constructed. The Romans probably built the first bridge on the single gravel spit which exists in the clay; the Saxons certainly erected a wooden structure which had to be repeatedly rebuilt against the ravages of floodwater, ice and fire. In 1176-1209 a stone bridge was constructed, 905ft long 40ft wide with 19 pointed arches rising from slender piles on boat shaped wood and rubble piers. These blocked the river bed so that the water poured down as through sluices and many refused to shoot the bridge in the river boats which were the principal transport of the day; equally they enabled ice to form and the river to freeze, when great Frost Fairs would be held, most famously in 1683-4. On the bridge itself were houses, shops, a chapel – Peter the Bridgemaster had been chaplain to St Mary Colechurch (disappeared) – also a drawbridge at the seventh arch from the south and gatehouses which as part of the City defence were closed at night and which were where traitors' heads were exposed – Jack Cade (1450), Thomas More (1535).

In 1831, following an act of 1823, John Rennie constructed a robust granite bridge of 5 wide spans, 60yds upstream. It endured 150 years before being replaced in 1973 by the present, sleek crossing – Rennie's bridge was sold for £1 million and is now in Arizona.

Woolwich Free Ferry. – The ferry, now operated by 3 roll-on roll-off vessels each capable of carrying 1 000 passengers and 200 tons of vehicles on the 5 minute crossing, dates back to 14C and is the last regular service of hundreds which once plied the stream.

Tunnels. – The first tunnel under the Thames was begun in 1825 from Rotherhithe *(qv)* to Wapping. Together with five other tunnels it now belongs to the London underground network. There are also in use two pedestrian passages: the Greenwich Footway *(qv)* of 1902 and the Woolwich Foot Tunnel of 1912 for when bad weather stops the ferry; and five road tunnels: Blackwall, a pedestrian and road tunnel dating back to 1897 and its 1963 parallel, Rotherhithe of 1908 and the Dartford Road Tunnel, an 18C project realised in 1963 and doubled in 1977.

River flow control. – **Teddington Lock,** where some 1 200 million gallons pour daily over the weir, was built in 1912 as part of the system of 50 locks and 140 weirs devised to control the water level in the upper reaches. It marks the boundary between the non-tidal and tidal Thames – high tide is 1 1/2 hours later than at London Bridge – and is approximately 94 miles from the Tongue (opposite Margate) which is the seaward limit of the jurisdiction of the Port of London Authority. Above Teddington the river is controlled by the Thames Water Authority.

Thames Barrier. – *Access: By river bus from Westminster Pier (01-930 3373) (1 1/4 hours; round trip 2 1/2 hours); from Greenwich (01-305 0300) (25 mins). Cruises from the Barrier Pier half-hourly 10am to 4pm in summer; booked parties only in winter (01-854 5555). By train from Waterloo to Charlton. Buses Nos 51, 177, 180.*

Construction of the barrier at Woolwich was undertaken in 1972-82 to protect central London from being inundated by a surge tide. London is sinking on its bed of clay and Britain itself tilting – Scotland and NW are rising, SE is dipping by about a foot a century; tide levels have risen by 2ft at London Bridge in the last 100 years. The barrier is composed of 4 falling radial gates (3 to the north and 1 to the south) and 6 rising sectors gates, the 4 larger being 61m (200ft) long and weighing 3 300 tonnes and the 2 smaller being 31.5m (103ft) long and weighing 900 tonnes. Each sector gate is raised – rotating through 90° from its concrete sill in the riverbed — by two arms projecting from the barge-shaped piers in which the lifting machinery is housed beneath huge stainless steel cowls. There is a car park *(charge)* together with a landing stage (for visitors arriving by boat) and a visitors centre (audio-visual presentations, shop, restaurant) on the south bank. *Open 10.30 to 5pm (5.30pm weekends); closed 1 January, 25, 26 December.*

Shipping and the docks. – London grew to importance as a port and developed and remained for centuries the great centre of world trade. Ships were built downstream; traders, unable to sail beneath London Bridge and equally unable to approach the wharves on shore across the mudflats, moored in midstream and depended on the fleet of some 3 500 lighters and other craft for all their handling. There were thousands of boats of every size on the river as all the old engravings show; there were also thieves: River Pirates, Night Plunderers, Scuffle Hunters and Mudlarks. The 19C saw the construction of the first commercial dock, the West India, soon followed by others until by the end of the century there were 5 systems extending over 3 000 acres with 36 miles of quays and 665 acres of dock basins. In 1909 the enterprise, in urgent need of modernisation, was taken over by the newly instituted Port of London Authority as the controlling authority. The docks prospered throughout the first half of this century and served stalwartly despite bombing and fire raids (December 1940) during the war, but shipping activity has now transferred to Tilbury.

The decline of the area has been reversed following the setting up of the enterprise zone as part of the docklands development plan *(p 156)* Some of the basins have been filled in but the remaining ones are integrated into the new business and leisure schemes under consideration and will remain a characteristic feature of the area.

Open March to October 9.30am (2pm Sunday) to 5pm (4pm November to February closed Sundays); £4.80, OAPs, Students £3, children £2. Guided tours by Yeoman Warders at 30 minute intervals starting from the Middle Tower – exteriors only – about 1 hour. Weekdays are slightly less crowded than weekends, winter is by far the best time. Queues for the Jewel House move fast – do not be put off. The Tower is closed on 1 January, Good Friday, 24, 25, 26 December.

The realm of the Tower. – William I constructed the Tower to ensure that he remained "the Conqueror". The fortress, first of wood (1067) then of stone (c 1077-1097), was intended primarily to deter Londoners from revolt; additionally its vantage point beside the river gave immediate sighting should any hostile force approach up the Thames. Norman, Plantagenet and Tudor successors showed their approbation by extending the work until it occupied 18 acres; they built first one and then a second fortified perimeter, excavated moats, built a second chapel, barracks, transferred the royal residence to new (now demolished) palatial buildings. The last king in residence was James I.

From 1300 to 1810 the Tower housed the Royal Mint and briefly, the Royal Observatory; because of its defences it soon became the Royal Jewel House and also served for centuries as an arsenal for small arms. For a while it was used as a bank by City merchants until, in 1640, Charles I "borrowed" the commoners' deposits amounting in all to £130 000. From 13C until 1834 the Royal Menagerie was kept in the Lion Tower (demolished).

The Armour collection displayed in the White Tower was started by Henry VIII and increased under Charles II when suits and accoutrements from Greenwich, Westminster and Hampton Court were redistributed between Windsor and the Tower to make the latter one of the world's greatest collections.

The Tower served as a prison both for the many, such as the 600 Jews accused of adulterating the coin of the realm in 1282, and the individuals captured in battle or suspected of intrigue. Among the latter were David, King of the Scots (1346), King John of France (1356-60, captured at Poitiers), Richard II (1399), Charles, Duke of Orleans (1415-27, captured at Agincourt), Henry VI (1465-71), the Duke of Clarence, drowned in a butt of malmsey (1478), the Little Princes (Edward V and Richard of York, 1483-5), Perkin Warbeck (1499), Thomas More (1534-5), Anne Boleyn (1536), Thomas Cromwell (1540), Protector Somerset (1552), Lady Jane Grey (1554), Robert Devereux, Earl of Essex (1601), Sir Walter Raleigh (1603-15), Guy Fawkes (1605), James, Duke of Monmouth (1685) and, this century, Roger Casement and Rudolf Hess.

Jewel House. – *Closed February.*
British orders of chivalry and decorations for valour (robes and insignia), the coronation robe, maces and 10 silver state trumpets provide the ground floor introduction to the scene.

The Crown Jewels★★★. – The jewels date from the Restoration, all the earlier regalia, with the exception of the head (14C) of the ampulla or vessel in the form of an eagle and the anointing spoon (12C) believed to have been made for King John's coronation in 1199, having been sold or melted down by Cromwell.

The Crowns: St Edward's made from an old crown likely to have been the Confessor's for the coronation of Charles II and weighing nearly 5 lbs is now worn only at a monarch's coronation. **Imperial State,** made for Queen Victoria in 1838, is worn on state occasions such as the Opening of Parliament; the ruby is the one said to have been given to the Black Prince by Pedro the Cruel after the Battle of Najara 1367 and to have been worn by Henry V at Agincourt; the diamond incorporated centuries later, is the second largest of the Stars of Africa cut from the **Cullinan diamond** (mined 1905, presented to Edward VII in 1907); there is a total of 3 733 precious jewels in the crown. **Queen Elizabeth,** the Queen Mother's Crown made for the coronation of 1937, incorporates the **Koh-i-Noor** diamond, the 14C stone presented by the East India Co to Queen Victoria. Queen Victoria's small crown will be familiar to every stamp collector.

Orbs and Sceptres. – The **Royal Sceptre** contains the **Star of Africa,** at 530 carats the biggest diamond in the world. **Swords of State** and staffs lie beside equally beautifully worked bracelets, armills, spurs and plate, including Queen Elizabeth's salt, ewers and vast dishes. The display fascinates every time by its purity and brilliance, the timeless craftsmanship, mass of gleaming gold, chased, modelled, its symbolism and history.

Chapel of St Peter ad Vincula. – *Admission free to Sunday services: 11am (except August); otherwise in guided tours only.*
The chapel, consecrated on the feast of St Peter in Chains in 12C, rebuilt in 13 and 16C, is chiefly known as the burial place of "two dukes between the queens, to wit, the Duke of Somerset and the Duke of Northumberland, between Queen Anne and Queen Catherine, all four beheaded", to whom Stow might have added Lady Jane Grey, Guildford Dudley, her husband, Monmouth and hundreds more. Note the Tudor font and the carvings by G. Gibbons.

Tower Green. – The lawn was the burial ground, the square the site of the scaffold. Of the seven most famous victims all were beheaded with an axe except Anne Boleyn, who was executed by the sword. Although the bodies of those executed on the green and many of those on Tower Hill were buried in the Tower, the heads were placed on pikes and displayed for all to see at the southern gateway to London Bridge. A new block was made for each victim. The last used (1747) is displayed in the Bowyer Tower.

Middle Tower. – The 13C tower (rebuilt 18C) stood between 2nd and 3rd drawbridges and was originally preceded by a causeway (which included the 1st drawbridge) and the Lion Tower (demolished). The moat was drained and grassed over in 19C. From the bridge view of the outer wall.

Byward Tower. – 13C, the main gate – the portcullis and lifting machinery are still in position on 1st floor. Wall paintings include English Leopards and French *fleurs-de-lys*. After curfew, a pass word which is changed daily, is required for admission.

Bell Tower. – Elizabeth, while confined in the adjoining Lieutenant's Lodgings (now the Queen's House – *not open*), walked for exercise along the ramparts.

Traitor's Gate and St Thomas's Tower. – The 13C gateway served as the main entrance to the Tower when the Thames was London's principal thoroughfare; only later, when the river was used as a less vulnerable and more secret means of access than the road, did the entrance acquire its chilling name. The Tower contains an oratory named after Thomas Becket.

The TOWER of LONDON★★★

Bloody Tower. – The former Garden Tower, although, according to legend, the place where the Little Princes were murdered in 1485 *(see also the White Tower)* only acquired its lurid name in 16C, probably after the suicide of Henry Percy, 8th Earl of Northumberland. The longest, most famous "resident" was **Sir Walter Raleigh** who occupied the years from 1603-1615 writing a *History of the World* for Prince Henry (a copy is in the sitting room). The lower story is noteworthy for its original tile pavement and for the portcullis. Above are the bedroom, with a four poster and very finely carved small cupboard, and the ramparts and brief Raleigh Walk.

Wakefield Tower. – The tower in the Middle Ages, as well as a defence, served as a major junction between the palace and the river from which passengers would alight and, crossing by way of St Thomas's and the bridge (19C reconstruction), arrive in the vaulted chamber on the first floor of the Wakefield. This was adjoined by a small oratory – where Henry VI was discovered murdered in 1471 – and the palace Great Hall – where Anne Boleyn stood trial (demolished 17C). Part of the same defence are the 13C embrasured wall extending north to the Cold Harbour Gate (**G** – *visible as excavations)* and the east wall and perimeter towers. These replaced the Roman City Wall (**B** – still partly visible), incorporated in his stronghold by William I.

Wall Walk. – The walk along the curtain wall of the Inner Ward from the Wakefield to the Martin Tower provides fine views of the Tower's defensive system and the Thames. The displays illustrate the history and layout of the Tower.

Beauchamp Tower★. – The 13C tower now faced with Tudor brickwork, has served since 14C as a place of confinement and is probably named after an early prisoner, Thomas Beauchamp, 3rd Earl of Warwick (1397-99 freed). In the main chamber are dozens of carved graffiti and articles found during archaeological excavations.

White Tower or Keep★★★. – The White Tower, one of the earliest fortifications on such a scale in western Europe, was begun by William I in 1078 and completed 20 years later by William Rufus. The 100ft high walls of Kentish and Caen stone, erected in an uneven quadrilateral, are marked at the corners by three square and one circular tower. Two walls divide the interior into a large west gallery and two unequal, east chambers on every floor.

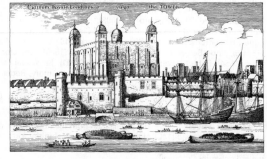

(After Hollar's engraving)

The Tower in 17 C.

In 1241 Henry III had first the royal apartments and then the exterior entirely white-washed from which time only it became known as the White Tower. In 17C when repairs were being undertaken and the windows on all but the south side enlarged, children's bones, thought to be those of the Little Princes, were discovered beneath an old staircase.

1st floor: Sporting and Tournament Galleries. – Crossbows, swords and firearms, heavy and angular or light and beautifully balanced, display the weapon makers' craftsmanship and also the jewellers' art, for many are enriched with gold and silver mounts, chasing and incrustations. The collection includes a brace of **pistols** with mountings of silver gilt made by Peter Monlong, a Huguenot who emigrated to London and by 1695, when the pistols were made, was Gentleman Armourer to the King. The Armour for the Tournament and for the Tilt – German, Italian and English – appears massive and weighty, made with incredible skill. In St John's Crypt are the carved wooden heads and horses used in the 17C Line of Kings display.

2nd floor: St John's Chapel★★. – The stone chapel, 55 1/2ft long rising through two floors, remains much as in 1080 when it was completed. An inner line of great round columns with simply carved capitals bear circular Norman arches which enfold the apse in an ambulatory and are echoed above in a second tier beneath the tunnel vault. Medieval monarchs passed the night in vigil in St John's before riding from the Tower to their coronation; some also lay in state there – Henry VI in 1471 – while Mary Tudor was betrothed there by proxy to Philip II in 1553.

Medieval and 16C Galleries. – The armour of the common soldier and knight in the field from late 14-16C – mail, back and breast plates, helmets and arms, show the rapid evolution in design before armour was superseded. There are also suits of parade armour and decorated firearms.

3rd floor: Tudor and 17C Gallery. – The great Council Chamber, which this top floor originally was, is filled with the presence of Henry VIII, four of whose suits stand in brave array: one of 1520 for the king aged 29, which weighs 94 lbs (a modern tin helmet weighs 2 1/2 lbs, a light flack jacket 10 lbs, a heavy one 16 lbs), one of 1540 of greater girth, a silvered and engraved armour for the king and his horse. Some suits were made at Greenwich as did those of Robert Dudley (c 1575) and Worcester (note the weight, without reinforcements, 110 lbs). Also displayed are a boy's 3/4 armour and a helmet and cuirass, probably made for Charles I as a boy (c 1610), and the ornate Stuart royal armours (c 1625-30).

Basement. – The area, the ground floor in fact, has been an arsenal since 18C and today houses helmets (English and foreign), swords, cuirasses, muskets, lances, halberds, "secrets" for felt hats... There are also 16, 17, 18C mortars and cannon, one raised from the *Mary Rose* (1545).

History Gallery (A). – Beneath an arcade *(south of the White Tower)* the history of the Tower of London is recounted on wall panels.

Royal Fusiliers Museum, New Armouries, Waterloo Barracks. – The Museum (**D**) *(25p)* traces the history of the regiment since its formation in 1685, the New Armouries (**C**) houses mid 17 – mid 19C British military weapons. The Barracks now contains the **Oriental Gallery (E)**, in which armour and weapons dating from 15-19C from China, Japan, Tibet, Burma, India, Turkey,

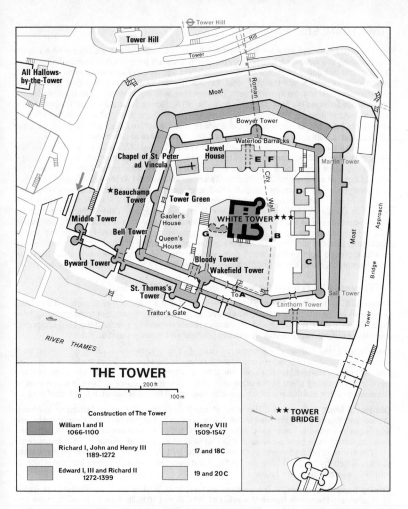

THE TOWER

Construction of The Tower

- William I and II 1066-1100
- Richard I, John and Henry III 1189-1272
- Edward I, III and Richard II 1272-1399
- Henry VIII 1509-1547
- 17 and 18C
- 19 and 20C

★★ TOWER BRIDGE

Labels visible on map: Tower Hill, All Hallows-by-the-Tower, Moat, Roman, Bowyer Tower, Waterloo Barracks, Jewel House, E F, Martin Tower, Chapel of St. Peter ad Vincula, City Wall, D, ★ Beauchamp Tower, Tower Green, WHITE TOWER ★★★, B, Middle Tower, Gaoler's House, G, Bell Tower, Queen's House, C, Byward Tower, Bloody Tower, Wakefield Tower, Sal. Tower, St. Thomas's Tower, To A, Lanthorn Tower, Traitor's Gate, Moat, Approach, Bridge, Tower, RIVER THAMES

Persia and North Africa can be seen in fine and fantastic array – even to an elephant's steel plating, and the **Herald's Museum (F)** *(closed October to March),* which explains the function and history of heraldry from its 12C origins, with displays of early Rolls of Arms, shields, extracts from Royal Charters, crowns, coronets and crests of Knights of the Garter and heralds' tabard.

The **Bowyer Tower** contains a collection of torture instruments.

Ceremony and Pageantry. – The **Yeoman Warders,** originally a detachment of the Royal Bodyguard founded by Henry VII on Bosworth Field (1485), is now made up of regular exservicemen. They wear Tudor uniform, embroidered with the sovereign's monogram (blue for every day, scarlet for ceremony) and may be seen on daily parade at 11am in the Inner Ward. The **Ceremony of the Keys** *(admission on written application only),* the ceremonial closing of the Main Gates, is enacted nightly at 10pm. The 31 boundary stones of the Tower Liberty are beaten every third year at Rogationtide by the choirboys of St Peter's, armed with long white wands, the Governor and Warders in procession (1990, 1993...).

Royal Salutes are fired by the HAC from 4 guns on the wharf: 62 guns for the Sovereign's birthday, accession, coronation; 41 for the State Opening of Parliament, birth of a royal infant... The **Ravens,** about which legend has it that if they die out the Tower will fall, now number eight.

TOWER HAMLETS (The City and Tower Hamlets)

Tower Hamlets, the East End, source of London's commercial prosperity from the 16 to the mid 20C with its shipping, wharves, docks, provider of fresh produce to the City through Spitalfields Market, of calico and silk (16/18C), of clothes and shoes and furniture, has always been, except for those who work or have lived there, a world apart, beyond the City wall. The Romans built a signal station at Wapping; in *Domesday* the odd manor is recorded; by the 12C the population, grouped in small communities, had grown to 800 and the area east as far as the Lea and north to Hackney Downs had been given into the charge of the constable and named Tower Hamlets (a name revived under the 1965 Act).

In 1598 Stow was describing the riverside, east from St Katarine, as a "continual street... or filthy strait passage, with alleys of small tenements or cottages, inhabited by sailors, victuallers almost to Radcliffe and Radcliffe itself hath been also increased in building eastward (to) Limehouse". The overcrowding became ever worse, intensified by the arrival of English craftsmen – woodworkers, boat-builders, masons, spinners and weavers and 10 000 ex-slaves who fled to the waterside to work as dockers. In 16C Dutch traders and craftsmen began to settle – leatherworkers, nail and locksmiths – closely followed by the line of refugees which continues to this day: Dutch and French Huguenots (13 000 French arrived in 1687), the Irish, Jews, Chinese, W Indians, Indians, Pakistanis... Houses, in 16/19C, were used as workshops and factories as well as dwellings, with families moving on as soon as they had the means to leave the terrifying conditions starkly described by Mayhew in his *Survey of the London Poor,* 1850.

100 years later the area fell into decline: the docks, bombed and set ablaze on so many nights during the war, were nearly deserted; the population once 600 000, numbered less than 200 000; the housing was 95% authority owned; cottage industry was virtually extinct. Only a few landmarks remain and the traditional, famous names: Whitechapel, Mile End, Commercial St (where the first university settlement, Toynbee Hall, was instituted in 1884), Stepney (where Dr Barnardo founded his first children's home in 1874), Sidney St, Middlesex St (*Petticoat Lane* with its Sunday market), Wapping, Limehouse, the Isle of Dogs, that tongue of land which may or may not have got its name as the place where "the Queen" or "her dad", as locals describe Elizabeth I and Henry VIII, kept their hounds when in residence at Greenwich.

The formation of the Docklands Joint Committee in the 1970s and of its successor the London Docklands Development Corporation in 1981 heralded the regeneration of the area – some 5 000 acres extending 8 miles east of Tower Bridge – by attracting private investment; the Isle of Dogs, where the new Billingsgate Market opened in 1981 in the West India Docks, has been designated an Enterprise Zone. A new financial centre is being built at Canary Wharf and new businesses, trade centres and workshops are opening up. Several Fleet St newspapers have moved to Docklands. Housing development is proceeding apace. Other schemes include an indoor sports arena in a 3 acre warehouse in Millwall Docks with a medical centre, hotels and leisure facilities (water sports, dry ski slope, restaurants etc), a Museum of London *(qv)* in Docklands. Modern communications are ensured with the siting of satellite dishes. Besides the new overground light railway which links up with the underground network, other transport improvements include a new bridge, a river boat service *(p 150)* and new access roads.

Tower Hill, Trinity Square *(Map pp 9-12*, RS/YZ*)*

Tower Hill. – The hill was from earliest times and is still a place of free speech and a rallying point from which marchers set out, nowadays, usually to Westminster. For three centuries from 1455, 75 years after Wat Tyler and the Kentish rebels summarily executed the Lord Chancellor and others outside the Tower, a permanent scaffold and gallows stood on the site.

Docklands Light Railway. – A computer-controlled railway service running on a raised track links Tower Gateway to Stratford and Island Gardens at the southern tip of the Isle of Dogs. The line is being extended to Bank in the City. It affords a unique opportunity to see the developments taking place in the docklands area. From Island Gardens there is a fine view of Greenwich on the south bank which is within easy reach by the Greenwich foot tunnel *(qv)*.

Old Royal Mint. – *Tower Hill*. The Mint, of which the Chancellor of the Exchequer is Master Worker and Warden, was installed in the Classical stone building in 1811 and transferred to new and larger premises in Llantrisant, near Cardiff, in 1968. The site has been redeveloped – the listed buildings have been retained and the remains of a Cistercian abbey (c 1350) excavated.

The first mint in London was under the Romans; by 11C there were 70 in various parts of the country which, by 14C, had been reduced to 2 and under Henry VIII devolved into one which, in mid 16C, was placed in the Tower.

Trinity Square Gardens. – The gardens enclose, from west to east: the **scaffold site** (railed enclosure), the **Mercantile Marine Memorials** of 1914-18 and 1939-45 Wars by Edwin Lutyens and Edward Maufe respectively, a 50ft section of the **Wall,** the upper part medieval, the base principally Roman, a monumental Roman inscription (original in the BM) to the procurator who saved London from Roman vengeance after the City had been sacked by Boadicea in 61AD, a statue presumed to be of Emperor Trajan (AD98-117) and the remains of 13C gate tower *(pedestrian subway leading to the north side of the Tower)*.

Trinity House. – The late 18C, elegant two storey building relieved by plain Ionic pillars (rebuilt after the war), is the seat of the Corporation of Trinity House (1514). Fine weathervane.

All Hallows-by-the-Tower. – *Page 51.*

The Riverside: St Katharine Dock, Poplar, Limehouse

St Katharine Dock★(SZ). – The present development is the third on the site. The first was the **Hospital of St Katharine by the Tower** founded in 1148 by Queen Matilda, first of an unbroken succession of royal patrons. The medieval community which traded from its own wharves developed into a hospital, travellers' shelter, and refugee settlement, being outside the City within which no immigrant might live. The first to seek shelter were the English forced to quit Calais in 1558, closely followed by Flemings, Huguenots... until by 18C the overcrowded community town numbered nearly 3 000. In 19C the site was sold and the nucleus of the community moved to Regent's Park from where it returned to the East End in 1920s and after being bombed out is now in Butcher Row in new buildings.

The St Katharine site was developed in 1828 by **Thomas Telford** with a series of basins surrounded by warehouses covering in all some 25 acres. The dock was the nearest to the City and for 100 years it prospered exceedingly.

After being bombed during the war, the dock was abandoned until 1968 when it was reorganised to provide moorings for private yachts; the warehouses were demolished except for Telford's Italia-

St Katharine Dock, Ivory House.

nate building, renamed Ivory House and converted into executive flats above a shopping arcade, and a pre-1820 timber brewery built of European redwood, now re-sited and converted into a three-storey restaurant and bar. Also overlooking the basins are the 1960s **World Trade Centre** (including the PLA offices), a large striated brown hotel with before it a leaping bronze fountain by David Wynne of a *Girl with a Dolphin* (1973) and modern blocks of flats. The **London Fox** (The Futures and Options Exchange) opened in 1987 at Commodity Quay, trades in futures for such commodities as cocoa, coffe and sugar.

Coronarium Chapel. – *Service Thursdays 1.30pm.*

Composed of seven Doric metal columns from a former warehouse erected in a circle round a plastic sculpture of an irradiated crown, the chapel was consecrated in June 1977 to commemorate the medieval hospice.

Wapping Wall and High St. – Wapping was the landing for generations of watermen, the setting for Dickens' novels along the densely populated waterfront cut by alleys, steps, stages and docks; Execution Dock was where condemned pirates and thieves – Captain Kidd in 1701 – were left for the tide to wash over them three times.

Today there is renewed activity as the docks are redeveloped but a few landmarks remain: **Wapping Pierhead**, a parallel terrace of 18C houses; the St John's Wharf and Gun Wharf warehouses now converted into luxury flats; the modern building of the **Metropolitan Special Constabulary** (Thames Division) or River Police, established in 1798, which patrols the 54 miles of waterway in 33 boats; the early 16C **Prospect of Whitby.** News International which publish *The Times* and *Sunday Times* have moved to new premises in Wapping.

Three local churches especially are interesting: **St Paul Shadwell** (Highway), known in 17/18C as the Church of the Sea Captains among whom was Captain Cook, **St Matthias** (Poplar *closed*), built in 1776 by the East India Co with 7 mighty masts and a stone column inside to support the roof and **St Anne's** (Limehouse), Hawksmoor's first East End church (1712-24) with a characteristically distinctive square tower.

Tobacco Dock. – *The Highway E1.* A new shopping and entertainments complex built around a former tobacco warehouse and replicas of two 19C sailing ships.

Further east along Wapping Wall an old pumping station is being converted for use as a rehearsal hall and recording studio by the Academy of St Martin-in-the-Fields. Shadwell Basin is used for water sports.

Whitechapel High St and Rd, Mile End and Bow Rds, Stepney

Whitechapel Art Gallery. – *80 High St. Open Tuesdays to Sundays, 11am to 5pm (8pm Wednesdays); closed Mondays, Good Friday, 25 and 26 December. Admission fee for major shows.*

The gallery of 1901, designed by C. H. Townsend, surmounted by twin angle turrets and decorated with contemporary arts and crafts reliefs, provides exhibition facilities for modern and contemporary art by non-established artists; Barbara Hepworth and David Hockney first showed their work here.

In the entrance of the adjoining Passmore Edwards library built in the same style, decorated tiles depict scenes from the Whitechapel Hay Market which flourished for over three hundred years along the road.

A few doors on (no 90) is **Bloom's Kosher Restaurant,** famous for its salt beef sandwiches.

By Aldgate East underground station, the Sedgwick Centre's annexe, a distinctive gleaming white building, houses a conference centre, a sports complex and the Chaucer Theatre.

Great Synagogue. – The famous Great Synagogue of Duke's Place, Aldgate, dating back to 1722, was totally destroyed in the war; the synagogue which replaced it in 1958 closed in 1978 as have ten others in the neighbourhood, reflecting the decline in numbers of the community which in 1900 numbered 125 000 and today 12 000. There remains on the traditional site an institute, library, after-care association to act as the Jewish centre (no 96).

Nathan Mayer Rothschild *(qv)* is buried in the now disused cemetery in Brady St.

Whitechapel Bell Foundry. – *34 Whitechapel Rd.* The foundry, whose records go back to 1570 and which may be 150 years older, has been on its present site since 1738. It has cast, and after the 1666 Fire and last war, recast Bow Bells, St Clement Dane's, Big Ben...

The London Hospital. – *Whitechapel Rd.* The "London" has been extending and modernising its building around the 18C entrance ever since it opened in 1757. It was conceived by a young surgeon, John Harrison, and six others in a tavern in Cheapside in 1740 and began as the London Infirmary in a house near Bunhill Fields. It soon removed to occupy first one then five houses with 68 beds in Prescot St (by the Mint) and when that was insufficient moved again to Whitechapel which afforded 161 beds. Two centuries later the number is 1 350.

Trinity Almshouses. – *Mile End Rd.* The almshouses, built by the Corporation of Trinity House in 1695 for "28 decay'd Masters and Comanders of ships" or their widows, form a terrace of basement and ground floor cottages around three sides of a tree planted quadrangle.

A statue (1979) of General William Booth on Trinity Green, marking the site where he began the work of the Salvation Army *(qv)*, commemorated the 150th anniversary of his birthday.

Queen Mary College. – *Mile End Rd.* The college, incorporated in London University in 1905, originated in the mid 19C as the Philosophical Institute. A grand building and library (costing £20 000 in all) failed to arouse continued interest and the Drapers' Company took over and reconceived the institution as a **People's Palace** where education would be combined under one roof with gymnastics, swimming, music... The educational side prospered, merged with the adult education Bromley and Bow Institute to form the East London College and become part of the university; it took its present name in 1934 upon receiving a Royal Charter. On the site of the recreational halls stand '50s buildings of glass, brick and concrete as typical of their period as is the terracotta brick and stone institutional building erected in 1885 at the back of a wide forecourt on the main road.

St Mary, Stratford Bow Church. – *Bow Rd.* The church, which dates back to 14C, stands on an island site in the middle of the road, a little west of where Queen Matilda's single arched, "bow" bridge, which gave the area its name, spanned the Lea.

St Dunstan and All Saints. – *Stepney*. The church on an early Christian site and with a dedication to the contemporary 10C mayor, Dunstan the great divine – is now an amalgam of rebuildings dating from 13C with memorials inside as ancient.

St George-in-the-East. – *Cable St (open)*. St George's, with a two tier octagonal lantern squarely buttressed and crowned by a balustrade and flat topped sculptured drums, is Hawksmoor's and the East End's most distinctive tower. Consecrated in 1729, it was bombed and fired in 1941. A smaller modern church has been built within the 18C exterior.

Bethnal Green, Spitalfields, Shoreditch (*Map pp 5-8*, H/VX)

Bethnal Green Museum of Childhood. – *Map p 15 (UY). Cambridge Heath Rd. Open Mondays to Thursdays, Saturdays, 10am (Sundays 2.30pm) to 6pm; closed Fridays, 1 January, May Day holiday, 24, 25, 26, December.*

The museum houses the Victoria & Albert Museum's collection of toys, dolls, dolls' houses, games, puppets, toy theatres and toy soldiers, as well as a collection of children's clothing, furniture and other artefacts of childhood.

The **building,** the oldest surviving example of the type of prefabricated iron and glass construction utilised by Paxton (now with a brick encasement), was originally erected to contain items from the 1851 Exhibition retained to form the nucleus of the V & A; it was re-erected and opened on the present site in 1872.

Englefields (London) Ltd. – *Reflection House, Cheshire St. Conducted tours Mondays to Fridays 10.30am and 2.30pm; closed public holidays and 8 to 19 August.* ☎ *01-739 3616.*

The oldest craft pewter manufacturers in London. Visitors will see craftsmen at work using traditional methods; some of the moulds are nearly 300 years old.

St John's Church. – *Cambridge Heath/Bethnal Green corner.* The west tower of the church (1825-8) by Soane, though not high, is an easily distinguished landmark as it rises from a square, clock stage, through a drum with blind arches to a vaned cupola.

Spitalfields Market. – The fruit, vegetable and flower market takes place in two large hangar like buildings of 1900 and 1935 respectively and in the surrounding streets (8 acres in all) in the early hours of weekday mornings; *all is over by 9am*. The market was granted a royal charter by Charles II in 1682 and acquired by the City Corporation in 1902. The area is undergoing extensive redevelopment.

Christ Church. – *Spitalfields. Open during lunch times and for services on Sundays at 10.30am and 6pm.*

Hawksmoor's spire still dominates the area almost as it did when built in 1714-30, although now more starkly having been rebuilt in 19C without the original dormers on each face, corner crockets and stone finial. It rises above a Classical west portico through an echoing interplay of ascending circular bays and arches, dramatically cut by the horizontal lines of entablature, cornice... At the east end a Venetian window is framed by paired niches beneath a pediment.

Note the doorways of the mid 18C merchants' and weavers' houses in Fournier St; the spacious glass-fronted reception area revealing older buildings round the cobbled yard of Truman's Brewery in Brick Lane.

Geffrye Museum*. – *Kingsland Rd, Shoreditch. Open Tuesdays to Saturdays and holiday Mondays 10am (2pm Sundays) to 5pm; closed Mondays, 1 January, Good Friday, 25, 26 December. The museum, under ILEA, caters especially for school parties; advance booking essential* ☎ *01-739 9893.* The **almshouses** and chapel were erected around three sides of an open court and the plane trees planted in 1712-19 by the Ironmongers' Co with a bequest left by Sir Robert Geffrye, Lord Mayor. The two storey brick buildings, perfectly proportioned, are decorated only with continuous modillioned eaves and at the centre, marking the chapel, stone trimming, a pediment and niche in which stands the periwigged figure of the founder.

Inside a series of rooms illustrate furniture and furnishings from Tudor times to 1930s: including John Evelyn's Closet of Curiosities, several Georgian shopfronts and a woodworker's shop with bench and tools and, at the back, an open-hearth kitchen.

St Leonard's Parish Church. – *119 Shoreditch High St. Open daily noon to 2pm, Sundays 10am to noon.* ☎ *01-739 2063.*

The mid 18C church with 192ft spire is on the site of an earlier church within whose precincts were buried: **James Burbage** (d 1597) a joiner by trade and the head of Lord Leicester's players who in 1576 built in Shoreditch the first English playhouse, **The Theatre;** Cuthbert Burbage (d 1635), his son who in 1599 built the **Globe** *(qv);* **Richard Burbage** (d 1619), also his son, the first actor to play Richard III and Hamlet; William Somers (d 1560) court jester to Henry VIII; Richard Tarlton (d 1588), one of Queen Elizabeth's players; Gabriel Spencer (d 1598), a player at the Rose Theatre; William Sly (d 1608) and Richard Cowley (d 1619), players at the Globe.

To the north, Holy Trinity, Trinity Rd (1849), has been known since Grimaldi's day as the Clowns' Church and holds an annual service for circus folk.

TWICKENHAM (Richmond upon Thames)

Twickenham, which in the 20C, on occasions, echoes to the cheers of English and French rugby fans (Stadium, Rugby Rd), in the 19C, saw Louis-Philippe, cousin of Louis XVI and future King of France (1830-1848), three of his five sons, several descendants and a number of sympathisers, living in as many as nine houses in the immediate vicinity. Of these four remain: Bushy House, now the residence of the Director of the National Physical Laboratory (Teddington); Morgan House, Ham Common, now part of the Cassel Hospital and York House.

York House. – *Richmond Rd. The house (council offices) is closed; the gardens open.*

The Yorke family lived on and worked a farm on the site in the 15 and 16C; successors, who from 1700 altered and rebuilt the house, retained the name including, in 19C, members of the exiled French royal family and, this century, an Indian merchant prince.

The house has a terrace at the rear overlooking the walled garden. A footbridge leads to a cascade and rose garden preceding a shrubbery and grass terrace beside the Thames.

Sion Rd. – The road by York House leading to the river, is joined halfway down, at the rounded Waterman's Lodge, by Ferry Rd, a close of "two down, two up" cottages. Beyond is **Sion Row,** a terrace of 12, three storey houses built in 1721, in ordered lines with a uniform cornice, three lights and off centre entrances, personalized by individual doorways. At the end, parallel to the river *(passenger ferry 10am to 6pm daily except 25 December to Ham House),* is a straggling line of houses of all periods: a pub, all corners and balconies, the Ferry House, three floors of white stucco with a slate roof, and Riverside House (1810), a rambling two storeys beneath broad eaves.

Orleans House Gallery. – *Open Tuesdays to Saturdays 1pm (Sundays, holiday Mondays 2pm) to 5.30pm (4.30pm October to March); closed Good Friday, 24, 25, 26 December.*

Orleans House itself was demolished in 1926, only the **Octagon,** added in 1720, ten years after the house was first built, still remaining. This wing by James Gibbs has a brick exterior and splendid plasterwork, including fireplace, door pediments, figures and ceiling.

Marble Hill House*. – *Open daily including public holidays 10am to 5pm (4pm November to January); closed 24, 25 December.*

Marble Hill House was built in the mid 1720s by Henrietta Howard, with monies settled on her by her royal lover, the future George II. She acquired a parcel of land beside the river; plans were sketched by the Architect to the Prince of Wales, Colen Campbell. It was 1731, however, before Henrietta, now Countess of Suffolk and Mistress of the Robes, could "often visit Marble Hill" and several years more before she took up residence there with her second husband, George Berkeley. She was an active hostess and received politicians, lawyers, and men of letters, including Alexander Pope and Horace Walpole. The most famous of later residents was another royal mistress, Mrs. Fitzherbert, who lived there briefly in 1795.

The gardens, now disappeared but in the 18C considered integral to the house's design, were, from 1724, the preoccupation of **Alexander Pope,** a near neighbour at Crossdeep, in a house of which nothing remains and gardens of which only a grotto survives.

The House. – The Palladian style, stucco, house is three storeys high with the centre advanced beneath a pediment and an insignificant, 18C, entrance.

From the small hall, the square mahogany staircase leads directly to the Great Room, a 24ft cube splendidly rich in white and gold with carved decoration and copies of van Dyck paintings upon the walls. Lady Suffolk's bedchamber *(left),* divided by Ionic pillars and pilasters to form a bed alcove, is completed, like the other rooms, by a rich cornice and ceiling decoration. Though the actual furniture and furnishings were dispersed, an almost exact reconstruction is being successfully achieved from a detailed inventory made on her ladyship's death in 1767. Some items have been successfully traced: overmantel and overdoors by Panini and carved table in the Great Room. Fine collection of 18C paintings (Hogarth, Wilson, Hayman, Kneller).

A stone staircase leads to the restored second floor *(access on conducted tours only)* where is displayed a collection of chinoiserie.

The stable block *(north east)* dates from 1825-7. Close by is an 18C terrace, Montpelier Row.

Strawberry Hill*. – *Twickenham (St Mary's College, Waldegrave Rd). Tours Wednesday and Saturday afternoons during term-time, on written application –* ☎ *01-892 0051 Ext 222.*

"A little plaything... the prettiest bauble you ever saw". – Horace Walpole, Cambridge and Grand Tour graduate, MP with few prospects although the son of the former PM, man about town, historian, antiquarian, diarist, and letter-writer extraordinary, was truly delighted when in May 1747 he acquired a 50 year old cottage at Strawberry Hill on the outskirts of Twickenham.

The great houses in the vicinity were Classical: Marble Hill, York, Orleans, ... Walpole announced that as "Grecian columns and all their beautiful ornaments look ridiculous when crowded into a closet or a cheesecake house... I am going to build a little Gothic structure at Strawberry Hill". The resulting battlements, cloister, round tower, turret and gallery made it so different that, though by no means the first building to include Gothic features, it became the chief influence in 18/19C **Gothic Revival.**

Under *The Committee of Taste,* established by Walpole with two friends, the interior also was transformed to incorporate Gothic features. The original designs were reproduced more or less exactly but in an utterly dissimilar context. The chimneypiece in the Holbein room was modelled on the tomb of Archbishop Warham at Canterbury; in the Round Room on the tomb of Edward the Confessor, while the ceiling reflects a window in Old St Paul's; the chapter house at York is recalled in the Tribune ceiling and the fan vaulting in the Long Gallery was copied from the Henry VII Chapel in *papier maché.* Against this fanciful setting Walpole displayed his "profusion of rarities" – it was an age of collectors: Sir Hans Sloane, Angerstein, Sir John Soane and the 1st Marquess of Hertford, Walpole's cousin and correspondent, who was acquiring the nucleus of the future Wallace Collection. Walpole, a bibliophile who set up his own printing press, had a very fine collection of enamels and miniatures – missal illustrated by Raphaël, a Holbein portrait of Catherine of Aragon – as well as lesser items such as Cardinal Wolsey's hat.

Walpole died in 1797. By 1841, by way of a great niece, Strawberry Hill had come into the possession of the 7th Earl of Waldegrave and his wife, Frances, and the collection was auctioned at a sale which lasted 32 days, was attended by 50 000 and realised £33 468.

In 1847, Frances Waldegrave remarried and became a prominent political hostess. She embarked on restoration and refurbishing (1855) which in her own words made "Strawberry more like a fairy place than ever" but the house proved too small and an extension was added. Under her aegis Strawberry Hill in the 1860s and '70s became a meeting place for those in politics, letters, the arts and society. When she died in July 1879 the house dimmed into obscurity. In 1925 St Mary's College moved from Brook Green to new buildings in the grounds.

Interior. – The main door, adjoining a small cloister, leads into the hall and staircase described by Walpole as "the most particular and chief beauty of the castle" with its rose "paper painted in perspective to represent Gothic fretwork", staircase balustrade after Rouen Cathedral, "adorned with antelopes (our supporters) bearing shields" and star spangled vault. The light, as in many parts of the house, is filtered to Gothick obscurity through painted Flemish glass.

Above are the Blue, or breakfast room, the library, where books are ranged behind ogee arches and the ceiling is in Tudor style, and the Long Gallery. The Waldegrave wing opens with the anteroom to the Drawing Room which served the beautiful Lady Waldegrave, whose portrait hangs at one end, as banqueting hall or resplendent ballroom beneath glittering chandeliers.

Open daily except Fridays 10am (Sundays 2.30pm) to 5.50pm; closed 1 January, May Day holiday, 24, 25, 26 December; donations. Restaurant, photography permitted. Galleries may be closed at short notice owing to reorganisation or shortage of staff.

Origin. – The 1851 Exhibition was the parent of the V & A as of the neighbouring Kensington museums *(qv)*. The collections which derived from purchases of contemporary works manufactured for the Exhibition (and displayed from 1852 in Marlborough House) and items of all periods accumulated by the Government School of Design at Somerset House, have, since 1909, been exhibited in the idiosyncratic building by Aston Webb of brick, terracotta and stone with a pierced central tower, crowned by a figure of Prince Albert. Gifts and bequests from its earliest days and subsequently purchases, have transformed the originally disparate agglomeration of items to the present collection with its vast brief of "the fine and applied arts of all countries, all styles, all periods".

The museum's treasures are displayed in **art and design galleries** where a wide variety of arts afford an idea of a period or a civilisation, and in **materials and techniques galleries,** such as the ceramic rooms, where, for example, the development of individual factories may be studied in detail. In all there are some 7 miles of galleries. The guide-index and plan below are designed to help you pinpoint what interests you in the maze-like interior. Two new developments opened in the 1980s: the Henry Cole Building for the display of paintings, prints and drawings and a new gallery *(lower ground floor)* for temporary exhibitions of 20C and contemporary art and design. The V & A also administers branch museums at Apsley House, Ham House, Osterley Park and the Bethnal Green Museum.

ART AND DESIGN GALLERIES

LEVEL A (Ground Floor)

Room 43: Medieval Treasury
– 400-1350: Ivory carvings, gold and enamel work (Gloucester candlestick, Eltenberg reliquary), Limoges and other *champlevé* enamels; textiles; Rouen Treasure *c*1350, glass: Syrian, Roman; Syon cope (English 14C).

Rooms 22-25: Europe 1100-1450
Room 22. – Italian Sculpture: G. Pisano *Prophet;* N. Pisano *Wooden Angel;* reliefs, metalwork, maiolica, embroidery.
Room 23. – Capitals, tympanum, columns, reliefs, Angel, Virgin and Child; Easby Cross (9C).
Room 24. – French sculpture and chests; English and German sculpture in painted wood, terracotta, stone; alabasters; church furnishings, altarpieces.
Room 25. – Spanish earthenware; reliquaries, pyx, chalices, altarpiece of St George.

Rooms 26-29: Renaissance Art 1450-1550
– 16C Northern Europe: embroidery, silver **(Burghley nef),** metalwork (Marquart clock 1567); decorated altarpieces; German plate; enamels; brasses; stone ware; stained glass.

Room 38: Gothic Tapestries
– French (Arras, Tournai) 15C hunting scenes; Trojan War; Flemish 16C The Triumphs of Petrarch; pastorals *(millefleurs).*

Morris, Gamble and Poynter Rooms
– Three refreshment rooms added from 1866 onwards with wallpaper and stained glass by William Morris, furniture by Philip Webb and Burne-Jones, stained glass and ceramics by Gamble, tile panels, and an iron and brass grill *(in use until 1939)* by Sir Edward Poynter.

Rooms 11-20: Italian Renaissance 1400-1500
Rooms 11-16. – Inlaid folding door, intarsia panel, chests, shields; bronzes by Riccio and Antico; **maiolica,** *Adoration of the Magi, Assumption of the Virgin, Stemma of Rene of Anjou,* roundels (labours of the months) by the Della Robbias; *Dead Christ* and *Chellini Madonna* by Donatello; painted tile pavement.
Rooms 17-20. – Shields, chests, maiolica; Lombard ceiling fresco; Rossellino *Virgin with the Laughing Child;* Verrocchio *The Rape of Europa;* marble figures and reliefs (*Virgin and Child* by Crivelli); metalwork, Venetian glass; Paduan fireplace.

Rooms 21-21A: High Renaissance – Europe 1500-1600
– 1500-1600: Spanish, Italian, German, French metalwork; **small bronzes** (Cellini); marble sculpture by Francavilla; Giovanni Bologna *Samson and the Philistine;* wax models by Michelangelo, Sansovino, Bologna; Italian red and white marble altarpiece; earthenware by B. Palissy.

Room 51: Neo-Classical Sculpture 1780-1820: 18-19C English, Italian, French – Canova, Chantrey.

Hall *(Exhibition Road entrance):* Rodin sculpture. *Access to Henry Cole Wing. Information Desk.*

Room 40: Costume. – European fashions 1600-1988.

Room 40A: Musical Instruments. – Early keyboard instruments: spinets, virginals, harpsicords; early string instruments; recorders, a serpent; cylinder musical boxes, symphonions, a barrel organ. Collection of clocks, sundials, watches.

Rooms 38 a, 41 and 47A-B: Indian Art and South East Asia. – *Reorganisation in progress.* Mughal arts, 16-19C: 17C carved rock beaker; paintings; carpets (Fremlin – floor centre); cotton paintings, jewellery; golden Chair of State; **Tipu's Tiger.**
Indian sculpture and bronzes; God Shiva in a circle of flames.
Textiles; scroll paintings; betel nut containers; Burmese 19C gold ware, Nepalese divinities; musical instruments.

Rooms 42 and 47 C: Islamic Art. – Turkish and Persian tiles, pottery (lustreware, Kufik decoration); damascened brassware (ewer) and bronze (lamp); Syrian enamelled gilt glass; Persian and Turkish carpets, textiles, Ardabil Carpet (1540; 30 million knots); Egyptian mosque pulpit; Persian enamelled gold dagger and sheath, dish.
Persian, Mesopotamian pottery; Egyptian glass.

The collection. – French 17 and 18C furniture from the workshops of the master cabinet makers **Boulle** (1642-1732), **Cressent** (1685-1768) and **Riesener** (1734-1806), also 18C French clocks are to be seen throughout the house.

- Old masters and English portraits: Gallery 19 and entrance hall
- French 18C pictures, porcelain, furniture and gold boxes: staircase, landing and Galleries 11, 12, 21, 22, 23, 24, 25
- Flemish and Dutch pictures (interiors, landscapes, still life paintings, portraits): Galleries 15, 16, 17, 18, 19
- Armour: Galleries 5, 6, 7, 8
- The Boningtons: Gallery 10 and corridor
- Early Italian paintings and works of art: Gallery 3
- Miniatures: Galleries 20, 21
- Medieval and Renaissance works of art – the maiolica and small bronzes: Galleries 3, 4 and corridor
- The Canalettos and Guardis: Gallery 13
- Sèvres porcelain: Galleries 2, 12, 14.

The wrought iron and bronze staircase balustrade, chased and gilt, was made c 1735 for the Palais Mazarin (now the Bibliothèque Nationale); it was sold for scrap-iron in 1855, rescued by the 4th Marquess and adapted to the present staircase by Wallace. Note the interlaced Ls, sunflowers and cornucopias.

GROUND FLOOR

GOLD BOXES

18C and principally French, the 89 boxes are in multicoloured gold, hardstone, mounted with Sèvres porcelain, jewelled, enamelled, painted, incorporating tortoiseshell, oriental lacquer, miniatures, square, oblong, oval, round, with oblique corners, shell-shaped... and quite exquisite – Galleries 12 and 25.

PAINTINGS

ARTIST	TITLES and GALLERIES
Boucher	*Mme de Pompadour, The Rising* and *The Setting of the Sun:* 22 and staircase
Canaletto	*Venice:* 13, 14
Philippe de Champaigne	*Adoration of the Shepherds, Marriage of the Virgin, Annunciation:* 19
Clouet, after	*Mary Queen of Scots:* 3
Foppa	*The Young Cicero reading:* 3
Fragonard	*The Swing, Souvenir, a Boy as Pierrot:* 21, 25
Gainsborough	*Mrs Robinson – Perdita, Miss Haverfield* (a small girl in a large hat): 19
Greuze	*Mlle Sophie Arnould:* 25
Guardi	*Venice:* 13
Frans Hals	*Laughing Cavalier:* 19
Horenbout	Portrait of Holbein *(miniature):* 21
Hoppner	*George IV as Prince of Wales:* entrance hall
Lancret	*La Belle Grecque:* 21
Lawrence	*George IV, Countess of Blessington:* 19, 1
Murillo	Religious paintings: 12, 19
Nattier	Portraits: 12, 25
Rembrandt	*Titus – the artist's son,* two groups, *Self-portrait, Good Samaritan:* 19, 16
Reynolds	*Mrs Carnac, Nelly O'Brien, Perdita,* two children's portraits – *The Strawberry Girl, Miss Jane Bowles:* 19, 23
Salvator Rosa	*Landscape with Apollo and the Sybil:* 19
Rubens	*Isabella Brandt, Sketches, Landscape with a Rainbow, Holy Family:* 11, 15, 16, 19
Titian	*Perseus and Andromeda:* 19
Van Dyck	Full length portraits: *Philippe Le Roy* and his wife: 19
Velazquez	*A Lady with a Fan,* also court pictures: 19
Vigée-Le Brun	*The Comte d'Espagnac* (boy in a red coat): 25
Watteau	The pastorals – *Halt during the Chase, Fête in a Park; The Music Party, The Music Lesson, A Lady at her Toilet:* 21

FURNITURE

MAKER	ARTICLES and GALLERIES
Boulle (1642-1732)	Cabinet, wardrobe, pedestal clock and other fine pieces; wardrobes (pair); toilet mirror: 2, 11, 24
Cressent (1685-1768)	Chest of drawers, veneered with gilt bronze dragon mounts: writing table; gilt bronze clock case, cabinet: 13, 21, 24
Riesener (1734-1806)	3 drop front secretaires (made for Marie-Antoinette); 2 chests of drawers; Comte d'Orsay's roll-top desk with marquetry work and bronze mounts; chased and gilt corner cupboards (for Marie-Antoinette); mahogany cylinder top desk; oval secretaire: 12, 21, 23, 25

Surprisingly to many, reminders of the locality's medieval history, its 17 and 18C associations and its 19C development are still apparent.

Wandsworth began as a Surrey village straggling along the banks of the **Wandle,** a river which rises west of Croydon, is only 10 miles long and in addition to the "fishful qualities" noted by Izaak Walton, neither dries up in summer nor freezes in winter. As early as 1602 its waters were harnessed to work corn and iron mills. Potters, calico bleachers, fullers, launderers, printers, coppersmiths, all of whom needed a constant water supply, swelled the population and were joined in late 17C by silk weavers and felt hat makers, many of whom were Huguenot and whose presence is recalled in **Huguenot Place** *(Trinity Rd/Wandsworth Common Northside),* the Huguenot Burial Ground (St Anselm's RC Church), which formerly served English and French Protestants and contains stones dating from 1697 and, in the road off the west side of Streatham Common, **Factory Gardens.** The factories referred to were silk weaving mills and felt hat making shops, the latter a Huguenot specialty and, specialty of specialties, cardinals' red hats! It was said that a cardinal caught in a shower could only be certain of not getting a red face if his hat had come from Wandsworth.

All Saints Parish Church, on an ancient site, is 18C with 19C additions, St Ann's *(St Ann's Hill),* the Pepperpot Church, 1820's and the Friends' Meeting House, 1778, in place of a 1697 building (burial ground).

The "1723 House", Wandsworth Plain, is a terrace of six fine, three storey, brick houses with short flights of steps up to Corinthian pilastered front doors, a central pediment and wall sundial. Armoury Way, at the back, recalls Tudor times when every parish had its armoury.

Wandsworth Prison, Heathfield Rd, has, a contemporary opinion commented in 1851, "nothing to recommend it to the eye".

The beautiful black Shire horses to be seen delivering beer locally are from Young's Ram Brewery in the High St. *All visits by arrangement only.*

GREEN TOURIST GUIDES

Picturesque scenery, buildings
Attractive routes
Touring programmes
Plans of towns and buildings.

■ PALACE OF WESTMINSTER★★★

Access restricted; tours on application to an MP only.

Princely palace to Mother of Parliaments. – "King William I built much at his palace, for" according to Stow, he found the residence of Edward the Confessor "far inferior to the building of princely palaces in France". Aggrandised and embellished but, unlike the Tower, never strongly fortified, William's palace continued for centuries, never actually being demolished but gradually disappearing beneath frequent rebuildings caused by fires of which the most devastating were those of 1298, 1512 and finally 1834. Of that early period there remain Westminster Hall, St Stephen's Crypt, the later (1526-9) two storey St Stephen's cloister and the Jewel Tower. Hemming in the palace on all sides were houses for members of the court, knights and burgesses, who, as representatives of local communities or commons, began from 1332 to meet apart as the House of Commons.

Parliament's opening ceremony took place in the presence of the monarch, as it does now, but in those days it was held in a richly ornamented hall known as the Painted Chamber. The Lords then adjourned to the White Hall while the Commons remained or adjourned to the Chapterhouse or even to the monk's refectory.

After the fire of 1512 Henry VIII did not rebuild the old palace and, until he confiscated Wolsey's York House in 1529, had no royal residence at Westminster. Among the buildings to survive was St Stephen's, the king's domestic chapel, which was granted by Edward VI in 1547 to the Commons as their chamber. It was while they were in St Stephen's that King Charles came to arrest and impeach Hampden, Pym and three others (1642) and it was there that they continued to sit until 19C. The Lords, so nearly blown up in the **Gunpowder Plot** of 1605, continued to meet in the White Hall until the night of 16 October 1834 when cartloads of notched tally sticks (old Exchequer forms of account) were put into the underground furnace which overheated... In hours what had come to be known as the Houses of Parliament had been burnt almost to the ground.

The buildings. – **Charles Barry** and **Augustus Pugin** together won the competition of 1835 for a new design, stipulated as being either Elizabethan or Gothic in style: Barry was a Gothicist by necessity, Pugin by innermost fervour.

Barry's ground plan is outstanding in its apparent simplicity: the two chambers are on a single, processional axis – the throne, woolsack, bars of the two chambers and Speaker's chair all in line. At the centre is a large common lobby which the public enter through St Stephen's Hall; libraries and dining rooms, in parallel to the main axis, overlook the river. Above the central lobby rises a lantern and slender spire (originally part of the ventilation system); at either end a tower, one over the royal entrance, the other housing a clock. This plan, executed in Yorkshire limestone (badly quarried and in constant need of repair), is equally remarkable in its exterior for the interplay of symmetry and asymmetry: the towers balance but are totally unlike, the St Stephen's turrets are not a pair; in contrast the long waterfront is entirely regular with Gothic pinnacles and windows extending from end to end with medieval tracery, carving, niches and figures, individually designed by Pugin in the Perpendicular tradition. The foundation stone was laid in 1840, the Victoria Tower completed by 1860; there were over 1 000 rooms, 100 staircases, 2 miles of corridors spread over 8 acres; construction had united the work of hundreds of painters, sculptors, craftsmen; Barry was knighted, Pugin died in Bedlam, both in 1852.

INTERIOR

Royal entrance and staircase (1). – The route through the Victoria Tower, where the sovereign is met by high officers of state on the Opening of Parliament, proceeds up a flight of stairs, lined on state occasions by the Household Cavalry, to the **Norman Porch** (2). This is square in shape, Perpendicular in style with gilded vaulting.

The Robing Room★. – The room where the sovereign assumes the Imperial State Crown and crimson parliamentary robe, presents, with the Lords' Chamber, Pugin's most remarkable concentration of decorative invention – every inch of wall space and panelled ceiling is ornamented with sovereigns' badges, patterned and gilded, coloured, carved, is hung with flocked paper and pictures, frescoed after the legend of King Arthur...

The Royal Gallery. – The gallery, the sovereign's 110ft processional way, is decorated with frescoes by Maclise, gilt bronze statues of monarchs from Alfred to Queen Anne and portraits of every sovereign and their escort from George I. In the **Prince's Chamber,** which follows, are the Tudor monarchs and their wives – all six of Henry VIII.

House of Lords★★. – The "magnificent and gravely gorgeous" chamber is the summit of Pugin's achievement; a symphony of design and workmanship in encrusted gold, gilding and scarlet. The throne and steps beneath a niched and finialed Gothic canopy mounted on a wide screen, all in gold, occupies one end of the chamber. The ceiling is divided by ribs and gold patterning above the red buttoned leather benches (the one with arms is for the bishops – said to prevent those who have dined too well from rolling off) and the woolsack ("most uncomfortable"). The cross benches lie

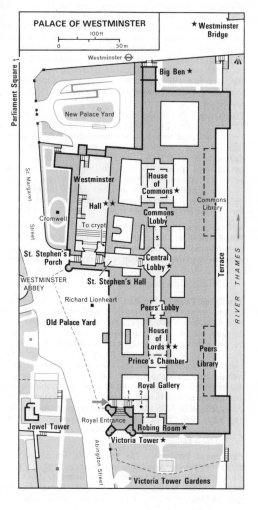

between the clerk's table and the bar of the house behind which the Commons stand when summoned by Black Rod to hear the speech from the throne. Looking down from between the windows are statues of 18 barons who witnessed King John's assent to *Magna Carta*.

Central Lobby★. – The 75ft high, octagonal lobby through which everyone passes, is where one waits for one's MP. If parliament is in session one spots faces, if the house is in recess one notices the Perpendicular arches encircling windows and entrances decorated with English sovereigns, the life size 19C statesmen, the mosaics over the doorways, the gilded and patterned roof ribs, the chandelier, all by Pugin.

Corridor (3) and Commons Lobby. – The lobby, destroyed in the 1941 air raid, has been reconstructed to incorporate stones from the old fabric in a newly named **Churchill Arch** which is flanked by his statue in bronze by Oscar Nemon and that of Lloyd George.

House of Commons★. – The chamber, also destroyed in the 1941 raid, was rebuilt simply, without decoration, the benches in the traditional green hide, running parallel beneath a plain Gothic timber structure. There is seating for 437 members out of the 635 elected. At the end is the canopied Speaker's chair with before it those of the Clerks and the table of the house with the bronze mounted despatch boxes and the mace. Red stripes on either side of the green carpet mark the limit to which a member may advance when addressing the house – the distance between the stripes is reputedly that of two drawn swords. The government sits on the Speaker's right, the PM opposite the despatch box. When a division is called, members leave for the tellers' lobbies past the Speaker's right for Aye and through the far end for No – the Lords divide similarly but vote "Content" or "Not Content".

Libraries. – The libraries, overlooking the river, are oases of silence, the Lords' again the more remarkable for Pugin's decoration. Note in the Lords' Library the warrant signed by Cromwell and the council for Charles I's execution.

The Terrace. – The terrace, reserved for MPs and their guests, is one of London's most special places for tea.

WESTMINSTER***

St Stephen's Hall. – The long narrow hall *(public entrance)* was reconstructed by Barry to look like the 14C chapel with ribbed vaulting springing from clustered piers and at the end two superimposed arches, the uppermost filled with a mosaic of St Stephen between King Stephen and Edward the Confessor. Note the brasses on the floor delimiting the old Commons chamber (60 × 30ft; *see also the Derby relief below).*

Westminster Hall★★. – The hall, scene throughout the Middle Ages of royal Christmas feasts, of joustings, ceremonial and congregation, was added to his father's palace by William Rufus in 1097. It was repaired by Thomas Becket, flooded in 13C "when men did row wherries in (its) midst", and re-roofed by command of Richard II in 1394. In 1401, however, before rebuilding was complete, the king was arraigned there before parliament and deposed. Sir Thomas More (1535), Somerset (1551), Northumberland (1553), Essex (1601), Guy Fawkes (1606) and Charles I all stood trial in the hall. This century monarchs and Churchill have lain in state there.

When peripatetic courts following the king were decided to be no longer practical, the Great Hall, already a place of pleadings and trial, was appointed the permanent seat of justice with the floor space divided between courts of Common Pleas, Chancery and King's Bench, bookstalls and shops.

The interior. – The master mason, Henry Yevele, and carpenter, Hugh Herland, commanded in 1394 to re-roof the 240 × 70ft hall, rebuilt the upper walls and erected what is probably the finest timber roof of all time, a superb **hammerbeam**★★★. It weighs more than 660 tons, which is the reason for the exterior buttresses, and rises to 90ft at the crest; it depends on projecting hammerbeams 21ft long × 3ft 3ins × 2ft 1in thick, held on curving wooden braces resting on carved stone corbels. The now steel re-inforced beams, which support the vertical posts on which the superstructure rests, are carved with great flying angels.

Nine light Perpendicular windows occupy the north and south ends, the latter set back in 19C by Barry to effect a dramatic junction up wide flights of steps with St Stephen's Porch. Flanking the arch are six 14C statues of early English kings.

St Stephen's Crypt (Chapel of St Mary). – The domestic chapel built by Edward I between 1292-7 was on two levels, the upper being reserved for the royal family. After St Stephen's had been granted to the Commons, the lower chapel was used for secular purposes until the 19C when the medieval foundation was redecorated as a chapel.

EXTERIOR *(Map p 175)*

The Clock Tower – Big Ben★. – The 316ft tower, erected close to the site of the old palace clock tower which had existed from 1288-1707 and at one time had the staple or wool market at its foot, was completed by 1858-9 with clock and bell. The name Big Ben, probably after Sir Benjamin Hall, First Commissioner of Works and a man of vast girth, applied originally only to the bell which after recasting at the Whitechapel Foundry weighs 13 tons 10 cwts 3 qtrs 15 lbs, measures 9ft in diameter and 7ft in height and early on developed a 4ft crack. The clock mechanism (electrically wound) weighs about 5 tons. The dials of cast iron tracery are glazed with pot opal glass and are 23ft in diameter; the minute spaces 1ft sq; the figures 2ft long. The minute hands of copper are 14ft long, weigh 2 cwts, and each travel over 100 miles a year. The mechanism proved reliable, except for minor stoppages, for 117 years until it succumbed to metal fatigue in 1976 and major repairs were required. Big Ben was first broadcast on New Year's Eve 1923. The light above the clock remains lit while the Commons is sitting.

A Jubilee fountain of heraldic beasts, sculpted in iron, was opened by the Queen in May 1977 in New Palace Yard.

Parliament Square. – The square and Parliament St, laid out in 1750 when the first Westminster Bridge was being built, was most recently redesigned in 1951. The bronze statues are of **Churchill** by Ivor Roberts Jones, **Smuts** by Jacob Epstein, **Palmerston**, Derby – note the pedestal reliefs: the old Commons in 1833 – **Disraeli, Peel, Canning** and **Lincoln. Boadicea** can be seen heroically riding her chariot by Westminster Bridge.

(After photograph, Kardorama, London)

Palace of Westminster.

Middlesex Guildhall, described as *art nouveau* Gothic, is richly embossed with figures beneath a turreted tower. Nearby is the new Queen Elizabeth II conference centre.

From above the small east door of St Margaret's the head of Charles I looks across the street to **Oliver Cromwell,** one of London's most telling statues, by Hamo Thorneycroft, before Westminster Hall. **Richard the Lionheart** sits astride his horse in Old Palace Yard.

Jewel Tower. – *9.30am to 6.30pm (4pm mid-October to mid-March); closed Sundays, 1 January, 24, 25, 26 December.*

The L shaped tower with a corner staircase turret, dates from 1365 when it was built with a moat surrounding it as the king's personal jewel house and treasury – there is a brick vaulted strongroom on the first floor with a later iron door (1612). When Westminster ceased to be a royal palace, the tower, with windows renewed in 1718, became the archive for parliamentary papers *(see below)* and subsequently the weights and measures office – Standards of Weight and Length are displayed in the top chamber. In the vaulted lower chamber are the tower's rediscovered ancient wooden foundations, bosses from Westminster Hall and capitals.

Abingdon Garden is adorned with a sculpture, *Knife Edge to Edge,* by Henry Moore (1964).

Victoria Tower★. – *Members of the public may consult the records on application in writing to the Clerk of the Records, House of Lords, London SW1A OPW.*

The tower, the taller of the two at 336ft, was designed as the archive for parliamentary documents – previously kept in the Jewel Tower and therefore saved from the 1834 fire. Among the 3 million papers are master copies of acts from 1497, journals of the House of Lords from 1510, the Commons from 1547, records of the Gunpowder Plot, Charles I's attempted arrest of Hampden, Patents of Nobility, the Articles of Union of 1706...

Victoria Tower Gardens. – In the gardens stand a cast of the great bronze group by Rodin the **Burghers of Calais** (who ransomed themselves to Edward III in 1347), a slim statue of Emmeline Pankhurst, the suffragette, and a bronze medallion of her daughter, Christabel.

Smith Square. – The square now synonymous with politics or music, began to develop in 1713 with the erection at the centre of **St John's** by **Thomas Archer.** The tall, Baroque church, rising by colossal columns and open pediments and balanced by four ornate corner towers, is said to have been compared by the queen to an up-turned footstool and is known to many as Queen Anne's Footstool. It was badly bombed but has been restored with giant Corinthian pillars beneath a deep cornice, Venetian windows and 18C chandelier, to serve as a concert hall.

In the square's southwest corner is Conservative Central Office.

The four streets which enter the square midway along each side, the square itself and the streets to the north, include among inevitable rebuildings, many of the original Georgian houses, most notably nos 6-9 Smith Sq, Lord North Street entirely except its northern end and the south end of Cowley St (occasional date stones 1722, 1726).

■ WESTMINSTER ABBEY★★★

Open daily 8am to 6pm. Choir, transepts, Royal Chapels: Mondays to Fridays 9am to 4.45pm; Saturdays 9am to 2.45pm and 3.45 to 5.45pm); Royal Chapels: £2, children, OAPs £1. Chapter House and Museum see below.

Monastery Church to Royal Peculiar. – The Westminster Abbey in which **William I,** the first king ever to be so, was crowned on Christmas Day 1066, had been built by Edward the Confessor in the Norman style; only with the Plantagenet Henry III's rebuilding in 13C did it acquire its Gothic appearance. **Sebert,** 6C King of the East Saxons is credited with building the first church and monastery, or abbey, on Thorney Island, a triangle formed by the twin outflows, some 700yds apart, of the Tyburn into the Thames. **Edward the Confessor** "built it of new", intending to make the church his sepulchre and indeed died and was buried in it within a week of the dedication on 28 December 1065. He also built the parish church of St Margaret's outside the precincts and a royal palace. The now important centre soon became known as Westminster: the minster in the west, as opposed to the cathedral in the east, St Paul's.

In 1220, inspired by the Gothic style of Amiens and Reims, came **Henry III's** rebuilding, beginning with the Lady Chapel to provide a noble shrine for the Confessor who had been canonised in 1163. When the Lady Chapel was complete, construction continued west over the existing building which was demolished as the new construction replaced the old: by late 13C, the east end, transepts, choir, the first bay of the nave and the chapter house were complete; progress then halted and it took another two centuries to finish the nave.

When **Henry VII** came to construct his chapel, Gothic, in its Perpendicular form, was still the ecclesiastical style and he produced the jewel of the age (1503-19). Later additions, notably the west towers (1722-45) by Wren and Hawksmoor, and repairs by Scott and others have kept to the Gothic spirit: heavenward vaulting, soaring windows between slender, buttressed, walls, flying buttresses, gabled transepts with traceried rose windows surmounting doors with enriched covings, and, at the east end, the long chancel culminating in the Henry VII chapel, more delicate, more finely niched and pinnacled than any other church.

Dissolution in 1540 meant the confiscation of the abbey's treasure, forfeiture of its property but not destruction of the buildings. The 600 year old Benedictine community of some 50 monks was disbanded; the abbot, enjoying both temporal and spiritual power, with his own lavish household, was dismissed as were those supervising the widespread property or serving on missions abroad. In 1560 Elizabeth I granted a charter establishing the Collegiate Church of St Peter, with a royally appointed dean and chapter of 12 prebendaries (canons), and also the College of St Peter, generally known as Westminster School, replacing the monastic school.

Although the detail in the vaulting and medieval carving is inexhaustible, the abbey should be viewed as built, as the setting for state occasions when it is brilliant with colour, resounds to the music of coronations and royal weddings (since the marriage in 1923 of the future George VI and Queen Elizabeth). It is no longer a royal mausoleum.

The abbey dimensions are: west door to east window inside, 511ft 6in of which the nave is 166ft, Henry VII's Chapel, 104ft 6ins; the nave, including the aisles, is 72ft wide and 102ft high; the height outside to the topmost pinnacles of the west towers is 225ft, the lantern 151ft. The fabric is Caen and Reigate stone.

INTERIOR

Nave and transepts. – The soaring vaulting remains in the beauty of its conception; the carving on screens and arches, in spandrels and covings is delicate, often beautiful, sometimes humorous; the ancient tombs in Henry VII's, St Edward's and the ambulatory chapels (broadly beyond the high altar), making no pretence of portraying the living, are dignified, and, on occasion, revealing in expression (a few are derived from death masks). The 18 and 19C surfeit of monuments in the transepts and aisles has become a byeword even though sculpted by the great names of the day – Roubiliac, the Bacons, Flaxman, Le Sueur, Westmacott, Chantrey.

It is at the dean's discretion who is buried in the abbey and to whom memorials may be erected – situations not synonymous since 18C when the custom developed after several of like calling had been interred, of commemorating others of equal standing: the most famous result is **Poets' Corner★** *(see after tour of Royal Chapels)* where Chaucer (1), who as Clerk of Works was associated with the palace and abbey, and the statues of Dryden (2) and Ben Jonson (3), court poets, have been joined by Shakespeare (4) (a "preposterous monument" in Horace Walpole's opinion), Milton (5), Blake (6) (bust by Epstein, 1957), Burns (7), Longfellow (8), so that by 18C, Addison (9) was commenting "In the poetical quarter I found there were poets who had no monuments and monuments which had no poets". Plaques and stones are now more the order of the day – Auden, Hardy, Gerard Manley Hopkins were added in 1975-6; Dylan Thomas and Lewis Carroll in 1982 (10). Of all the pavement stones, however, the most famous will always be that in the nave, surrounded by Flanders Poppies, to the **Unknown Warrior** (11).

The nave west end, north aisle and north transept are chiefly filled with politicians, philanthropists and commanders. Note against the first south pier the famous **painting of Richard II** (12) and in the north aisle, low down, the small stone which covered the upright figure of the playwright "O rare Ben Johnson" (13) (misspelt!). The choirscreen, a 13C structure of stone, lierne vaulted in the arch between the nave and the choir, was richly redesigned in 19C with gabled niches.

Choir and Sanctuary. – In the choir, re-embellished in mid 19C – the eye is led immediately to the gilded blaze of 19C high altar screen and the altar before it. This area, the **Sanctuary,** is approached by a low flight of steps marked on the left by a gilded and blackwood 17C pulpit and is laid with a 13C Italian pavement of porphyry and mosaic. It is where the crowning is performed in the **coronation** ceremony and the sovereign receives the peers' homage. To the right hangs a 16C tapestry behind a large 15C altarpiece of rare beauty. Beyond is an ancient 13C sedilia painted with full length royal figures (Henry III, Edward I and a bishop).

On the left are three tombs, each a recumbent figure on a chest beneath a gabled canopy – Aveline of Lancaster (14; d 1274) a great heiress and a great beauty; Aymer de Valence, Earl of Pembroke (15; d 1324) cousin to Edward I; and Edmund Crouchback (16; d 1296), youngest son of Henry III, husband of Aveline.

North ambulatory chapels. – The chantry chapel of Abbot Islip is known for its rebus – an eye and a slip or branch of a tree clasped by a hand, also a man slipping from a tree; the **Chapel of Our Lady of the Pew,** in the thickness of the wall, contains a modern alabaster Madonna and Child *(p 173);* St John the Baptist's and St Paul's Chapels, medieval tombs in decorated recesses or beneath ornate canopies with highly coloured effigies and elaborate gilded wall memorials with helms at the crest.

From the ambulatory note the small gilded kings and queens on Crouchback's tomb (16).

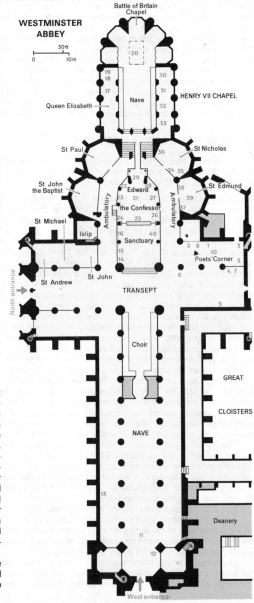

WESTMINSTER ABBEY

30 ft
0   10 m

Battle of Britain Chapel

Nave

HENRY VII CHAPEL

Queen Elizabeth

St Paul

St Nicholas

St John the Baptist

Edward the Confessor

St Edmund

Ambulatory

Ambulatory

St Michael

Islip

Sanctuary

Poets' Corner

St Andrew

St John

North entrance

TRANSEPT

Choir

GREAT

CLOISTERS

NAVE

Deanery

West entrance

Queen Elizabeth Chapel. – In the north aisle of Henri VII Chapel is the tomb of **Queen Elizabeth I** (17) in white marble, ruffed, austere, the only colour the regalia, lions and the overhead canopy; beneath is the coffin of Mary Tudor without any monument. At the east end are memorials to two young daughters of James I, Princess Sophia and Princess Mary (18) and in a small sarcophagus, the bones found in the Tower in 1674 and presumed to be those of the Little Princes (19).

Henry VII Chapel***. – The fan-vaulted roof is superb, the banners of the Knights Grand Cross of the Order of the Bath still and brilliant, the stall pinnacles surprising with their crowning helmets and coifs, the stalls patterned with the heraldic plates of former occupants and their esquires and witty with inventive 16/18C misericords. (The chapel was first used for the knights' installations in 1725 when George I reconstituted the order.) The great double gates at the entrance are made with wooden frames in which are mounted pierced bronze panels of the royal emblems of Henry Tudor and his antecedents: the roses of Lancaster and York, the leopards of England, *fleur-de-lys* of France, the falcon of Edward IV, father of Elizabeth, Henry's queen. At the east end is the tomb, of Henry VII and Elizabeth of York (20).

The 1947 Battle of Britain Chapel with a many faceted, brightly coloured memorial window, records the badges of the 68 Fighter Squadrons which took part.

Chapel of Edward the Confessor**. – The chapel, with the Confessor's shrine (21) at the centre, ringed by the tombs of five kings and three queens, is also known as the Chapel of the Kings. The shrine itself is in two parts, the lower, prepared by Henry III, is of Purbeck marble, the upper is a stepped wooden construction made after the original had been looted at the Dissolution. On either side are **Queen Eleanor of Castile** (22; d 1290), she of the crosses, slender and serene, in gilded bronze by the master goldsmith **William Torel; Henry III** (23; d 1272), in gilded effigy, builder of the chapel who spent more than all the money he possessed in constructing the abbey; **Edward I,** Longshanks (24; d 1307), the first king to be crowned in the present abbey (1272) and who, as the Hammer of the Scots, brought the Scottish regalia and the Stone of Scone south in 1297.

Coronation Chair and Screen (25). – The carved stone screen, which closes the west end of the chapel was completed in 1441. At the centre stands the Coronation Chair made of oak and once brightly painted and gilded with, below the seat, the **Stone of Scone.** For coronations the chair is moved into the sanctuary.

On the chapel's south side are **Richard II** (26) who married **Anne of Bohemia** in the abbey in 1382 and raised her tomb there in 1394. In the centre is the gilt bronze figure of Edward III (27; d 1377) on an altar tomb of Purbeck marble, surrounded in niches at the base, by bronze representations of his children, of whom 6 remain (towards the ambulatory) including the Black Prince. Beyond, carved in white marble once painted and gilded, lies his queen, **Philippa of Hainault** (28; d 1369) who interceded for the Burghers of Calais. Finally, at the end on a Purbeck marble tomb, is the oak figure, once silverplated, of the young Henry V (29; d 1422) and above, the king's chantry chapel in which Catherine of Valois is now buried.

(After photograph, Jarrold's, Norwich)

The Coronation Chair.

South aisle, Henry VII Chapel. – Here are buried, without sculptured memorials, in a royal vault (30), Charles II, William III and Mary, Queen Anne and her consort, George of Denmark. Three grand tombs occupy the centre, all effigies upon tomb chests: Lady Margaret Beaufort (31; d 1509), mother of Henry Tudor, in widow's hood and mantle, her wrinkled hands raised in prayer, her face serene in old age, **Torrigiano's** masterpiece in gilt bronze; **Mary Queen of Scots** (32) in white marble, like Elizabeth but beneath a much grander canopy and with a crowned Scottish lion in colour at her feet; and Margaret Douglas, Countess of Lennox (33; d 1578) niece of Henry VIII, mother of Darnley and grandmother of James I – a beautiful woman carved in alabaster.

South ambulatory chapels. – St Nicholas' chapel contains the tomb of Philippa, Duchess of York (34; d 1431) with wimple and veil about her expressive head, the vault of the Percys (35) and the tomb of Anne, Duchess of Somerset (36; d 1587), widow of the Protector. In St Edmund's Chapel are the tombs of William de Valence (37; d 1296), halfbrother of Henry III, the figure remarkably carved with clothes and accoutrements powdered with crests, and the marble effigy of John of Eltham (38; d 1337), 2nd son of Edward II. In the centre, on a low altar tomb, is the abbey's finest **brass:** Eleanor Duchess of Gloucester (39; d 1399) beneath a triple canopy. Note, in the ambulatory Sebert's tomb (40) and the sedilia painting of the Confessor.

Chapter House**. – *Open 9.30am (Sundays 2pm) to 6.30pm (4pm in winter); combined ticket with the Chapel of the Pyx and museum: £ 1.50, children 40p.*

The chamber (1248-53), used at one time as a royal treasury, is octagonal, 60ft in diameter, with vaulting springing from a slim central pier of attached Purbeck marble columns, encircled by two shaft rings. At each of the eight angles the lierned ribs descend on to a single marble column which reaches to the floor; marble shafts reappear at the windows and bearing the trefoiled blind arcade which circles the house and provided seating for the monks in chapter; the walls are partially decorated with medieval paintings of the Last Judgment and the Apocalypse. The windows show the transition – not followed in the body of the church as it would have spoilt the architectural unity – to the massive glazing characteristic of the mid Gothic style; each bay rises nearly 40ft to quatrefoils and cusped circles. The floor tiles are original (1255).

Chapter House as Parlement. – The King's Great Council met under Henry III in the chapter house in 1257 confirming that it was intended from the first to accommodate secular assemblies as well as the 60-80 monks of St Peter's. Under Edward I it became the Parlement House of the Commons and continued after the Dissolution, when the hall passed into the direct ownership of the Crown. By 19C it had become an archive for state papers: the floor had been boarded over, a second storey inserted. In 1865 the building's condition necessitated complete restoration and a century later, after wartime damage, reglazing, enabling a return to be made to clear glass, decorated with the coats of arms of sovereigns and the arms and the devices of the two medieval master masons, Henry de Reyns who designed Henry III's abbey and Henry Yevele who built the nave (southwest and southeast windows).

Chapel of the Pyx. – *See Chapter House for opening times and admission.*
    The chamber built between 1065-1090 as a monastery chapel and retaining the only stone altar in its original position, was converted into the monastery treasury in 13/14C. At the Dissolution it passed to the Crown and was used as the strongroom in which gold and silver coins were tried against the standard specimens kept there in a box or pyx. There is a display of church plate from the abbey and from St Margaret's. Note also a 17C cloth of gold cope and a late medieval oak cope chest.

Library. – It is housed in part of the former monks' dormitory which has a fine late 15-early 16C hammerbeam roof. The collections include manuscripts, incunabula, printed books and bibles. On display are the Litlyngton Missal, a 13C bestiary, the Charter of Offa, King of Mercia AD 785, the oldest document among the muniments.

Westminster Abbey Museum. – *Open daily 10am to 4pm; combined ticket with the Chapter House and Chapel of the Pyx; £1.50, children, OAPs 30p.*
    The museum in the low Norman undercroft with two of the several pillars in its 110ft length still decorated with 11C carving, contains historical documents, gold plate, reproductions of the coronation regalia, a number of unique wax and wood funeral effigies. Edward III and Catherine of Valois, both full length, are of wood. Of the 11 wax effigies, the contemporary figure of **Charles II** in his Garter robes is unforgettable though not carried at his near clandestine funeral. Among the women are Catherine, Duchess of Buckingham, natural daughter of James II and wife of John Sheffield, builder of Buckingham House, who had her effigy made during her lifetime, and Frances, Duchess of Richmond and Lennox who was the model for Britannia on the old penny piece. **Nelson,** of whom it was said by a contemporary "it is as if he was standing there", was purchased by the abbey in 1806 in an attempt to attract the crowds away from his tomb in St Paul's!

Jericho and Jerusalem Chambers. – *(Not open).* Both are in the former abbot's, now the dean's, lodgings. The Jericho Parlour has linenfold panelled walls of early 16C and is 150 years older than the Jerusalem Chamber where Henry IV died in 1413 (H IV Pt II v).

The Bells. – There are 12 bells which ring out on great occasions and some 25 days of festival and commemoration including 25, 26, 28 December, 1 January, Easter and Whit Sundays and the Queen's official birthday, generally between noon and 1pm.

The Sanctuary. – The right of sanctuary, extended in the monastery's time over a considerable area, became so abused by vagabonds, thieves and murderers, and the quarter so overbuilt with squalid houses, that it was first restricted and finally abolished, in all but name, under James I. On the site of the Gatehouse (demolished: 1776), in which **Sir Walter Raleigh** spent the last night before his execution and **Richard Lovelace** penned the line "stone walls do not a prison make...", stands a red granite column in memory of former pupils of Westminster School (Old Westminsters) who died in the Indian Mutiny and Crimean War. Nearby, on the opposite side of Gt Smith St, stood the almonry where Caxton set up his press in 1476 using as his imprint William Caxton in the Abbey of Westminster.

Dean's Yard. – At the centre of the Sanctuary buildings, designed by Sir Gilbert Scott, the gateway leads into the Dean's Yard, once the heart of the Abbey precinct but now a tree-shaded lawn reserved for Westminster School. Down the west side are parliamentary offices and the 20C Abbey Choir School. The south side is filled by **Church House,** completed in 1940, containing the Hoare Memorial Hall, where the Commons met during the war, and the large circular Convocation Hall where the General Synod of the Church of England meets. The eastern range of buildings, some medieval, some Georgian, is pierced by the entrance to Westminster School, which extends east round Little Dean's Yard to the Palladian College, the mid 17C brick Ashburnham House, incorporating part of the 12-13C Prior's Lodging, and School (the Great Hall), part of the late 11C monastic dormitory and until 1884 the school's only classroom, now rebuilt and again emblazoned with the arms of former headmasters and pupils. College hall, formerly the abbot's state dining hall, is now the refectory for the 470 boys.
    At the north east corner of the Dean's Yard is the entrance to the **Cloisters,** where there is a large **brass-rubbing centre** *(open daily except Sundays 9am to 5pm; from £2.50),* and to the 900 year old **Abbey Garden** *(open Thursdays 10am to 6pm (4pm October to March); band concerts 12.30 to 2pm August to mid September).*

ENVIRONS *(Map p 175)*

St Margaret's★. – *Open daily 9.30am to 4.30pm except during services.* The church was erected originally by Edward the Confessor to serve local parishioners. In mid 14C the establishment of the wool staple, or market, at Westminster (close to the site of Big Ben) increased local prosperity and the now dilapidated church was rebuilt and yet a third time in 1488-1523. Scarcely completed by the Reformation, it was saved from becoming building stone for Protector Somerset's palace in the Strand by parishioners who "with bows and arrows, staves and clubs and other such offensive weapons... so terrified the workmen that they ran away in great amazement". Radical restoration and renewal by Sir Gilbert Scott in mid 19C gave the church much of its present late Perpendicular appearance.
    Inside all thought of the august surroundings vanishes and one is in a parish church with a rich assemblage of Tudor monuments: sympathetic old Blanche Parry, Chief Gentlewoman of Queen Elizabeth's privie chamber, the behatted wife and cloaked figure of Thomas Arnway (d 1603) who left money to be loaned to the young to set them up in business, a Yeoman of the

Guard (d 1577 at 94), Richard Montpesson, kneeling by his wife's tomb... There are two plaques (by the east door) and fragments of a window (north aisle) as memorials to Caxton, buried in the old churchyard; Walter Raleigh executed in Old Palace Yard on 29 October 1618 and buried beneath the high altar is commemorated in a tablet near the east door and in the west window, presented in late 19C by citizens of the USA. The east window is unique: it was made in Flanders in 1501 at the command of Ferdinand and Isabella of Spain to celebrate the marriage of their daughter, Catherine, to Prince Arthur; but by the time it arrived Arthur was dead, the widowed princess affianced to the future Henry VIII. The window was despatched outside London and only retrieved in 1758 when the House of Commons purchased it for 400 guineas and presented it to the church. The carved limewood reredos of 1753 is based on Titian's *Supper at Emmaus.*

St Margaret's is the House of Commons' church not only through the Palace of Westminster lying within the parish but by a tradition inaugurated on Palm Sunday 1614 when the Commons met for the first time for corporate communion and, being mostly Puritans, preferred the church to the abbey.

A **Garden of Remembrance** flowers in November each year in the churchyard.

■ WESTMINSTER ROMAN CATHOLIC CATHEDRAL* *(Map pp 5-8 DY)*

Open daily 7am to 8pm (6pm public holidays, 4.30pm 25 December). Bell tower lift open 9.30am to 4.30pm or dusk if earlier (closed in winter), 70p, children, OAPs, students 30p.

Christian Byzantine in 20C Victoria. – The land was in disuse in 1884 when Cardinal Manning purchased it as the site for a new cathedral. It had been a derelict marsh centuries before when the Benedictines of Westminster Abbey had originally taken it over to establish a market and fairground; following the Reformation it was occupied by a maze, garden, bullring, house of correction and finally a prison which during the Commonwealth held 1 500 Scots taken prisoner at the Battle of Worcester, 1651, pending their deportation.

Cardinal Manning and his successor, Cardinal Vaughan, determined on early Christian inspiration for the architecture of the new cathedral in that age of neo-Gothicism, perhaps in part because, in a second building in Westminster, they had no wish to emulate the style in which the great abbey had been achieved centuries before.

The architect, **J F Bentley** travelled widely in Italy before producing in 1894 Byzantine-Italian plans which promptly began to be executed (1895) and by 1903 had been completed so far as the fabric was concerned. Within the seven years 12 1/2 million bricks had been laid and there had arisen a building 360ft long × 156ft wide, distinguished by a domed campanile 273ft high.

The interior. – The initial impression is of vastness and fine proportions – the nave, the widest in England, is roofed with three domes. The decoration has still to be completed and unpointed bare brick walls, awaiting mosaics, rise above the lower surfaces and piers, faced with coloured marble and granite. The eye follows the successively raised levels of the nave, chancel and apse. The altar, beneath its baldachino with yellow marble columns, is dominated by a suspended crucifix. On the main piers are the 14 Stations of the Cross, distinctive low reliefs over beautifully incised lettering by Eric Gill (sculptor and type face designer).

The second chapel in the north aisle contains the body of the English martyr, John Southworth, hanged, drawn and quartered at Tyburn in 1654. In the south transept are an early 15C statue of the Virgin and Child, carved by the Nottingham school in alabaster, which originally stood in the abbey (replica now there), was removed for five centuries to France and returned in 1955, also a bronze of St Teresa of Lisieux by Giacomo Manzu and a Chi-Rho, executed in flat headed nails, by David Partridge. The cathedral is known for its music.

ENVIRONS *(Map pp 5-8 EY)*

Victoria St. – The street is lined with 20C buildings: tower blocks in steel and brown glass, faced with marble, stone and concrete, containing government offices and international oil and chemical companies. The street was cut through the Georgian slums to link Parliament to Victoria Station (1862).

On the south side a long shopping arcade is punctuated by Strutton Ground (street market) continuing as Horseferry Road to Lambeth Bridge which replaced the old horse ferry linking Lambeth and Westminster, by Artillery Row leading to Vincent Sq *(see below)* and by Ashley Place, a modern piazza before Westminster Cathedral.

On the north side, grouped round a former churchyard shaded by plane trees and adorned with a monument to the suffragette movement by E. Russell (1974), are **New Scotland Yard,** (1967), London Transport's headquarters (1927-9) by Charles Holden with decorative statuary groups by Jacob Epstein and reliefs by Eric Gill, Henry Moore and others, and **Caxton Hall** (1878) once famous for registry office weddings. The delightful square red brick building in Buckingham St was erected in 1709 to house the Blewcoat Charity school, founded in 1688. Three theatres mark the west end of the street: Westminster *(Palace St),* Victoria Palace (1910) and Apollo Victoria *(Wilton Rd).* **Little Ben,** a 30ft high model of Big Ben, stands outside **Victoria Station,** which was constructed in the 1870s on the site of the Grosvenor Canal. The present buidings date from the turn of the century. The Grosvenor Hotel (1860-61) was designed by J. T. Knowles. In Stag Place, a great bronze stag marks the site of the Stag Brewery (closed 1959).

Vincent Sq. – The large square was laid out in 1810 on part of the former Tothill Fields in order that its centre might provide playing fields for Westminster School. Along the length of the northeast side are **Westminster Technical College** (1893 with post-war extensions) and the high square brick building of the **Royal Horticultural Society** (f 1804), with at the back the New Horticultural Hall (1923-8), famous for its monthly flower shows *(open to non-members).*

Greycoat School. – *Greycoat Place.* The grey uniform of this Westminster Charity school, founded in 1698, can be seen on the small wooden figures in niches contrasting puritanically with the brilliantly coloured royal coat of arms set between them on the pedimented stucco; it is now a girls' school. Greencoat Place, nearby, housed a green liveried school (1633).

Queen Anne's Gate*. – *(Map p 133).* The street dates from when the queen was on the throne and is decorated with a statue of her as a very young woman. It is as built with substantial 2 1/2 bayed, three storeyed, terrace houses of now darkened brick on either side. The sash windows are square beneath continuous eaves and wide courses, the pilastered doorways, in several instances, protected by flat hoods richly carved and decorated with angle and centre pendants. The street's hall-mark is the satyrs' white masks set in place of tablet stones above the ground and first floor windows of every house. No 15, at the southeast corner, avoids the right angle with a canted wall, and around a second corner, between blocked windows, provides the background for Queen Anne.

Beyond Cockpit Steps, leading down in the days of Whitehall Palace to the pit and now to Birdcage Walk, is Old Queen St, incomplete but with several 18C houses still – note the rounded hood on corbels at no 28.

Central Hall. – Designed in 1912 by Rickards and Lanchester as a Wesleyan church with the third largest dome in London, it is also hired out for various public events.

WHITEHALL – TRAFALGAR SQUARE ★★ (Westminster)

Palace of Whitehall. – Henry's confiscation of Wolsey's London palace in 1529 was a matter of convenience as well as concupiscence. The property dated back to mid 13C when it had passed by bequest to the See of York; in 1514 Wolsey made it his personally, rebuilding, enlarging and enriching it, adding to the grounds until they occupied 23 acres. Henry VIII continued building and increased the royal precinct until it extended from Charing Cross to Westminster Hall, from the river to St James's park.

Always respected by the early owners of Whitehall was Scotland, a parcel of land until 16C the site of a Scottish royal palace but later built over and the streets named Little, Great **Scotland Yard** etc. The newly formed Metropolitan Police, given an office there in 1829, became known by their address and retained it when they moved in 1890s along the Embankment and later, in 1967, to Victoria St.

Tudors and Stuarts continued after Henry to live in and alter Whitehall Palace but William and Mary disliked it and bought Kensington and, after a disastrous fire in 1698, did nothing to restore it. Today there remain Tudor walls and windows behind the Old Treasury (visible from Downing Street), the end of Queen Mary's Terrace, (a riverside quay and steps built in 1691 by Wren; south end of Horseguards Av), **Henry VIII's Wine Cellar** *(open Saturday afternoons April to September on written application to the Dept of Environment, ☎ 01-921 4849)* and the highly decorative Banqueting House.

Nowadays Government offices and buildings line Whitehall and Parliament Street linking Westminster Abbey and the Houses of Parliament with Trafalgar Square.

Old Home Office, Foreign and Commonwealth Offices and Treasury. – The two Victorian-Italian palazzo style buildings of 1868-73 and 1898-1912 are best known for the Treasury door on St George St, from which the chancellor goes to the House on Budget Day, and the former Home Office balcony, from which members of the Royal Family watch the Remembrance Day service.

Cabinet War Rooms. – *Clive Steps, King Charles St. Open 10am to 5.50pm; closed 1 January, 24, 25, 26 December; £3, OAPs, children £1.50.*

The underground emergency accommodation provided to protect Winston Churchill, his War Cabinet and the Chiefs of Staff of the armed forces from air attacks was the nerve centre of the war effort from 1939 to 1945. Nineteen rooms are on view including the Cabinet Room, the Transatlantic Telephone Room for direct communication with the White House, the Map Room with the original maps left in place, the Prime Minister's Room, and the room from which Churchill made direct broadcasts to the nation.

The Cenotaph. – The slim white monument by Lutyens (1919) is without any effigy; the horizontal lines are very shallowly arced, the verticals converge 1 000 ft up in the sky; flags stir in the wind on either side.

On Remembrance Sunday *(November)* a service is held at which those who died in battle are remembered.

Downing St. – No 10 has been the residence of the PM since 1731 when Sir Robert Walpole accepted it *ex-officio* from George II. The "four or five very large and well built houses, fit for persons of honour and quality, each having a pleasant prospect of St James's Park", were erected in 1680s by Sir George Downing, diplomat, courtier and general opportunist of the Commonwealth and Restoration. The speculation was successful. The row was rebuilt in 1720s. No 10 contains the **Cabinet Room** and staircase, on which hang portraits of each successive resident. The building was thoroughly restored from 1960 to 1964.

Old Treasury. – Treasuries have stood on the site since 16C. The present one of 1845 by Barry, utilising the columns from the building by his predecessor, Soane, was the first of the phase of government building which has continued to 20C. The current style is exemplified in the monolithic **Ministry of Defence** opposite.

The small, jaunty, bronze before the MoD is of **Sir Walter Raleigh**, beheaded nearby. Next to him stands **'Monty'**, a 10ft solid bronze statue of Field Marshal Lord Montgomery of Alamein by Oscar Nemon, unveiled in 1980. Richmond Terrace was designed by Thomas Chawner in 1822. The façade has been restored to its original design and the Fine Rooms reinstated.

Scottish Office (Dover House), **Welsh Office** (Gwydyr House). – The 18C houses, both named after 19C owners are, in the latter case, open to the street, the only ornament a Venetian window above a tripartite door and in the former, a tall screen with an advanced porch designed by Henry Holland for the then owner, Frederick, Duke of York, in 1787.

Banqueting House★★. – *Open Tuesdays to Saturdays 10am (Sundays 2pm) to 5pm; closed 1 January, Good Friday, 24, 25, 26 December; 80p, students, OAPs 60p, children 40p.*

The hall, the third on the site, has been called a memorial to the Stuarts: it was built for James I in 1619; Charles I commissioned the sumptuous ceiling paintings from Rubens in 1629 and stepped on to the scaffold in Whitehall through one of its windows on 30 January 1649; Charles II received the Lords and Commons in the hall on the eve of his restoration on 29 May 1660; after James II's flight in 1689, William and Mary received within it the formal offer of the crown.

Banqueting houses served many purposes: as a setting for court ceremonial and revelry, for the reception of royalty and embassies, state banquets, the distribution of Royal Maundy, touching for the King's Evil, for dancing, music-making and courtly masques.

Inigo Jones, King's Surveyor and famous masque designer, constructed for James I at the centre of the Tudor palace, a Palladian inspired, building. Although the exterior has been refaced in Portland stone (1829 by Soane) and a new north entrance and staircase were added by Wyatt in 1809 (lead bust of Charles I over the door and bronze of James I by **Le Sueur** inside) and although the interior was used as a chapel and a museum from 18/20C, it now looks as splendid as in 17C and still serves superbly beneath the chandeliers for occasional official functions.

Exterior. – The building stands two storeys high above a rusticated basement with an open balustrade at the crest. Note the details: windows alternately pedimented and, above, straight hooded; framing pilasters, advanced centre; balconies, cornice and ornamented frieze.

Interior. – Inside it is empty – a gilded space awaiting players. It has the distinction of being a double cube – 110ft × 55ft × 55ft – with a delicate balcony, supported on gilded corbels on three sides; above, richly decorated beams quarter the ceiling decorated with Rubens' flamboyant **paintings** in praise of James I. In Stuart times the lower walls would have been hung with Mortlake and other tapestries.

Horse Guards★. – *The guard is ceremonially mounted daily at 11am (10am Sundays) on Horse Guards Parade in summer and in the courtyard in winter by the Queen's Life Guard (the Guard can also be seen riding from and to Knightsbridge); inspection on foot 4pm. For Trooping the Colour; p 30.*

The low 18C stonefaced edifice designed symmetrically by **William Kent** around three sides of a shallow forecourt, is pierced by a central arch and marked above, like its mid 17C predecessor on the same site, by a clock tower. The building,

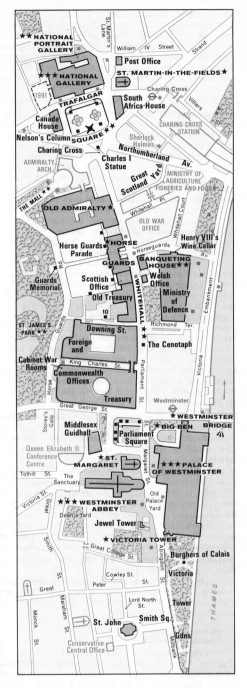

without adornment, is completed by the statuelike presence of the Household Cavalry sentries: the Life Guards in scarlet tunics and white plumed helmets, the Blues and the Royals, in blue with red plumes. On the parade where the Colour is Trooped are two memorials, the **Guards'** (1926) and **Cadiz,** (1812) incorporating an original French mortar supported on the back of a winged and scaly dragon!

Old Admiralty★. – The Old Admiralty of 1722-6 was, in Horace Walpole's phrase "deservedly veiled by **Mr. Adam's** handsome screen" in 1759-61, a single storey, blind porticoed wall with angle pavilions and a central arch crowned by a low balustrade between winged seahorses. (In 1890s vast terracotta brick additions were made to the rear.)

Trafalgar Square★★. – The square was laid out by Nash in 1820 as part of a proposed north-south communication between Bloomsbury and Westminster. It was placed on the open space at the meeting of the Strand and King St, later Whitehall, an age old site on the edge of the village of Charing which had been marked in 1290 by the last of the Eleanor Crosses (destroyed by the Puritans in 1647) and since 1675 by the statue of Charles I. It was overlooked from the southeast by the early 17C Northumberland House, medieval and magnificent with a lion over the gateway (p 147), and from the north by St Martin-in-the-Fields and the Royal Mews, soon replaced by the National and National Portrait Galleries. Of Nash's proposed connecting roads Pall Mall East was built, St Martin's Lane was straightened at the north end and Charing Cross

WHITEHALL – TRAFALGAR SQUARE★★

Rd laid (1880s). The square, begun in 1829, was completed only in 1840s when Charles Barry levelled it and constructed the north terrace as a frontispiece to the National Gallery and the column itself was erected. The clover-leaf fountains are best seen at night when floodlit.

The square is associated with political rallies; 50 000 can mass around the column at a time.

Since the war each year the Norwegian nation has sent a **Christmas Tree** which stands in the square from about mid December and is lit up at night. The first lighting is performed by the ambassador accompanied by Norwegians in national costume who open the carol singing which continues nightly around the tree and a crib until Christmas.

On New Year's Eve revellers congregate at midnight to hear the chimes of Big Ben.

The monuments: Nelson, a small man in life, is here three times lifesize in a sculpture 17ft 4 1/2 ins tall. The monument including the pedestal decorated with bronze reliefs cast

from French cannon, fluted granite column, bronze capital and the admiral, stands 185ft overall. The lions by **Landseer** (20ft long, 11ft high) were mounted in 1867, twenty years after the column was erected. Against the north terrace wall are Imperial Standards of Length and busts of 20C admirals, on the south corner plinths, two 19C generals (also to the south two lamps from or after those on the *Victory* – the east one on a police observation post). The northwest pedestal is empty, the northeast one occupied by an equestrian figure of George IV, commissioned by the king for Marble Arch. The bronze never made the arch and only reached the square in 1843!

Charles I was cast by **Hubert Le Sueur** in Covent Garden in 1633 (date and signature on left forefoot) where it stood until discovered in St Paul's crypt by Cromwell's men in 1655. It was sold "for the rate of old brass, by the pound rate" to a brazier who made a fortune from "relics" in theory made from the statue which actually he kept intact. Eventually it was purchased for £1 600 by Charles II and set up overlooking the execution site (wreath-laying 30 January (11am) by Royal Stuart Society). Mileages from London are measured from this point *(plaque in pavement behind statue)*. Before and behind the National Gallery are **James II** by Grinling Gibbons, **George Washington** after Houdon (marble in Richmond, Virginia) and Henry Irving. On the island (NE) is Nurse **Edith Cavell.**

Charles I.

The buildings. – The square is flanked by **South Africa House** *(east)*, designed by Herbert Baker in 1933, and **Canada House** *(west)*, a classical building of golden Bath stone (1824-7) by Sir Robert Smirke for the Royal College of Physicians *(qv)*. The **Post Office** *(24-28 William IV St)* – there are long queues for first day covers – is open from 8am to 8pm Mondays to Saturdays *(poste restante etc.).*

St Martin-in-the-Fields★. – The church is known not only for its spire but as the church where actors' memorial services are often held and, since the 30s, as a shelter for the down-and-out.

Gibbs, in 1722-6, designed the present church which is at least the third on the site, one being mentioned in 1222 and a rebuilding recorded in 1544. The steeple, towering in 18C above the surrounding slums, rises by 5 stages to a pillared, octagonal lantern and concave obelisk spire. Before the west front, he set an outstanding Corinthian portico, crowned by a triangular pediment bearing the royal arms – Buckingham Palace stands within the parish. Inside the galleried interior is dark beneath a barrel vault; the pulpit is by Grinling Gibbons.

The London Brass Rubbing Centre. – *In the crypt. Open daily 10am (Sundays noon) to 6pm; closed Good Friday and 25 December.*

The centre has replicas of brasses from churches in all parts of the country and from abroad *(average fee: £2.50 including materials and instruction; average time: 30 mins).*

The crypt also houses a bookshop, visitor centre and restaurant. There is a colourful arts and crafts market in the courtyard.

WIMBLEDON (Merton)

The earliest known inhabitants of Wimbledon occupied the iron age hill fort on the south west side of the Common known erroneously as **Caesar's Camp.** The village developed in Saxon times along the High Street and around the church, first coming to prominence in 1588 when Thomas Cecil, Lord Burghley, then Lord of the Manor, built a mansion with turrets and gables, set amid terraced gardens on a slope north east of the church. Before its destruction in 1720 it was visited by Queen Elizabeth and King James I. The only building surviving from this period is **Eagle House** (1613) in the High Street which was built by Robert Bell a native of Wimbledon and a founder of the East India Company. The Manor subsequently passed to Queen Henrietta Maria, to Sir Theodore Janssen, a financier who built a new house west of the church but was ruined in the South Sea Bubble, and then to Sarah, Duchess of Marlborough, who also built a new house linked to detached servants quarters by an underground passage which still exists.

The 18C saw several large mansions rise round the Common; **Lauriston House** (1724; destroyed 1959), home of William Wilberforce; **King's College School** (1750) with adjoining Great Hall in Gothic Revival style (note the hexagonal pillar box of 1872); **Southside House,** *Woodhayes Road* (1776: *Guided tours of historic rooms 1 October to 31 March, Tuesdays, Thursdays, Fridays, each hour between 2 and 5pm; £2, children £1)*; **Gothick Lodge,** *Woodhayes Road* (1760) owned by Capt. Marryat in 1820s; **Chester House** (1670); famous for the Sunday parties of the Revd John Horne Tooke whose election to Parliament in 1801 provoked the Act which made the clergy ineligible; **Westside House** (1760); **Cannizaro** (1727, rebuilt in 1900) owned by Viscount Melville from 1887 who laid out the gardens and entertained William Pitt, Edmund Burke and Richard Sheridan *(gardens open to public);* **Stamford House** (1720) and **The Keir** (1789). The **Round** or **Old Central School,** an octagonal building, was built in 1760 to educate 50 children of the deserving poor and is now incorporated in a primary school *(Camp Road).*

The **Crooked Billet** and the **Hand in Hand,** public houses in the south west corner of the Common, are 17C. Stage coaches set out from the **Rose and Crown** and later from the **Dog and Fox** in the High Street, although the road over Putney Heath was infested with highwaymen.

St Mary's Church. – Wimbledon church was mentioned in Domesday; parts of a 13C rebuilding remain in the chancel. The present nave, tower and spire were designed in 1843 by Sir Gilbert Scott. Several famous people – William Wilberforce, Sir Theodore Janssen, and J. W. Bazalgette *(qv)* – are buried in the churchyard. To the north stands the **Old Rectory** (1500) the oldest house in Wimbledon and probably a priest's house until the Reformation. Near the churchyard entrance stands a small white house, **Stag Lodge,** with the hinges on which the gate to the later Manor House was hung still visible on a post at the side.

The **Well House** in Arthur Road dates from 1761.

The **Village Club** in the Ridgway, built in 1858 to provide the working and middle classes with enjoyment and improvement through a reading room, library, lectures and instruction, now houses a small local **museum** *(open Saturdays 2.30 to 5pm).*

Wimbledon Common. – In 1871, after 7 years of legal dispute with Earl Spencer, Lord of the Manor, who wanted to enclose the Common and develop some 300 acres for housing, Wimbledon Common was transferred to the Conservators to preserve in its natural state. Whereas Lord Spencer asserted that the land was boggy with noxious mist and fogs arising from it, Leigh Hunt wrote of the "furze in full bloom making a golden floor of all that fine healthy expanse". The horse racing, duelling and drilling of soldiers of earlier days have given way to horse riding, cricket, rugby and golf. 'Every person playing golf' is required by the Conservators 'to wear a red outer garment'. From 1860 the National Rifle Association held their annual shooting competitions on the Common, even setting up a horse drawn tramway for the spectators, before moving to Bisley in 1889.

Wimbledon Windmill Museum. – *Open Easter to September, Saturdays, Sundays and bank holidays, 2 to 5pm; 30p, child 15p.* The windmill, a hollow post mill built on the Common in 1817, has been converted into a museum illustrating the story of windmilling in pictures, models and the machinery and tools of the trade. In the neighbouring miller's house Lord Baden-Powell began to write 'Scouting for Boys' in 1907.

Wimbledon Lawn Tennis Museum. – *Church Road. Open Tuesdays to Saturdays, 11am (Sunday 2pm) to 5pm. Closed Mondays and bank holidays. During the championships open only to those attending the tournament. Admission £1.50, OAPs, children 75p.*

Displays depict the development of tennis and include sections on dress, equipment and the Wimbledon Champions from the early days in Worple Road to the modern era. The historic Centre Court can now be viewed from the Museum.

Polka Children's Theatre. – *240 The Broadway. Open Tuesdays to Fridays, 10am to 4.30pm, Saturdays noon to 6pm; closed September.* A full programme, with performances and workshops for children, is supplemented by exhibitions of puppets etc and a playground.

■ MERTON

The village of Merton dates back to 1114 when Merton manor was granted to Gilbert the Knight. In 1117 he founded an Augustinian priory which was dissolved in 1538.

The arrival of the railway in 1838 transformed the village into a London suburb in fifty years. From 4 600 in 1861 the population grew to 55 000 in 1911. Rows of mainly small terraced houses covered parts of the Manor House park and the area round the station. In 1867 John Innes, a successful business man, began to develop **Merton Park**, the original garden suburb, with tree-lined roads, holly hedges and interestingly varied houses. He was a keen farmer and in his will endowed an agricultural institute which has since produced composts and fertilisers bearing his name. From 1801 to his death in 1805 Nelson lived at Merton Place, now built over by rows of houses: Hamilton, Hardy, Nelson, Victory and Trafalgar Roads.

St Mary's Church. – Built by Gilbert the Norman in 12C St Mary's has a stunted shingled steeple above a fine medieval roof and contains the seat from Nelson's box pew and his funeral hatchment. The south aisle windows, a memorial to John Innes, are by the firm of William Morris which occupied premises at Merton Abbey.

The **Norman Arch** *(west of the church)* is probably the gateway (re-sited 1935) of the guest house of Merton Priory where Thomas à Becket and Walter de Merton, founder of Merton College, Oxford, were educated and where royal courts were held; the Statute of Merton, the oldest in English law, was drawn up here in 1236.

▆ WOOLWICH (Greenwich)

Woolwich. – The fishing village was transformed firstly by the Tudor monarchs into the most important naval dockyards in the country (*Great Harry* was built there in 1512 in Henry VIII's time) and secondly in 1716-7, when the gun casting works were transferred from Moorfields and it became the **Royal Arsenal** (maximum extent 1914-18: 1 200 acres, 80 000 men and women).

Royal Artillery Museums. – The town is now the base of the RA which occupies, besides barracks, the 720ft long, arcaded former **Royal Military Academy** (f 1741; amalgamated with Sandhurst 1964). **R A Regimental Museum** – history of the regiment: *open noon (Sundays 1pm) to 5pm (4pm October to March); closed 1 January, Good Friday, 24 to 26 December.*

The **Museum of Artillery in the Rotunda,** up the hill, traces the development of artillery from medieval days to the present time: *open daily noon to 5pm (October to March 4pm); closed 1 January, Good Friday, 24, 25, 26 December.*

This most elegant of small museums began as a campaign tent designed by John Nash for the somewhat premature celebration of the defeat of Napoleon organised by the allied sovereigns in St James's Park in 1814. In 1819 the Prince Regent ordered the tent's reerection at Woolwich "to house military curiosities".

Thamesmead. – The architecture of the new town, only 11 miles from the centre of London on 1 500 acres of marshland with a 3 mile river frontage and an estimated population of 50 000 by the year 2000, has been described as "persistent – sharp and invigorating".

The London ZOO ★★★ (Regent's Park, Westminster)

Open daily (except Christmas Day) 9am (10am November to April) to 6pm (7pm Sundays and holiday Mondays) or sunset if earlier; adults £4.30, children £2.60; children's zoo free.

Noah's Ark. – The Zoological Society of London and the Zoo developed from the aim proposed to an audience of scientists by Sir Stamford Raffles in 1826 of founding a society for "the advancement of Zoology and Animal Physiology and the introduction of new and curious subjects of the Animal Kingdom". The first part has been so far achieved that conservation of species in the wild state and even their re-introduction where extinct is now a major objective. Landmarks along the way have been the contribution by members and the zoo's staff to systematic anatomy, the establishment in 1962 and 1964 of the Wellcome Institute of Comparative Physiology and the Nuffield Institute of Comparative Medicine to study reproductive physiology (including human fertility), biochemistry and disease which affect diet, health and husbandry.

The second part of Sir Stamford's phrase has resulted, since 1828 when the society opened on a 5 acre site in Regent's Park with a small collection of animals looked after by a keeper in a top hat, bottle green coat and striped waistcoat, in today's collection of over 8 000 animals of 945 species on a 36 acre corner of the park, cared for by a staff, including research workers, of more than one hundred. A large proportion of the animals are now bred in Regent's Park and at Whipsnade *(qv)*.

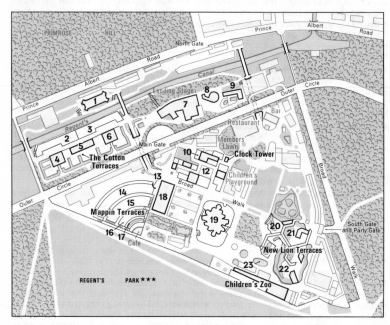

1 Snowdon Aviary	**8** Great Apes	**16** Wild Pigs
2 Deer	Breeding Colony	**17** Pelicans
3 Antelopes	**9** Insects	**18** Reptiles
4 Horses and Cattle	**10** Giant Panda	**19** Elephant and Rhinoceros
5 Giraffes and Zebras	**12** Apes and Monkeys	**20** Tigers
6 Camels and Llamas	**13** Aquarium	**21** Big Cats
7 Mammals and	**14** Sheep and Goats	**22** Lions
Moonlight World	**15** Bears	**23** Penguins

Housing. – The gardens were originally laid out by **Decimus Burton** who also designed several buildings of which there remain the Ravens' Cage on the Members' Lawn, the Clock Tower and the Giraffe House. The Reptile House dates from 1902 and the Insect House from 1912. Houses for all animals from tropical climates were kept heated and closed until the turn of the century when Carl Hagenbeck at the Hamburg Zoo revolutionised contemporary practice by providing paddocks for tropical animals and surrounding enclosures not with bars but moats and ditches; this led to the construction of the Mappin Terraces (1914) in London and to the creation of Whipsnade (1931) on 480 acres of derelict Bedfordshire farmland:

Since 1930s the Zoo has been the setting of often highly innovative architecture: the Great Apes Breeding Colony (1933) and the Penguin Pool (1934) with intersecting spiral ramps, both by Lubetkin (the pool, the first example of such use of pre-stressed concrete, is now a scheduled building).

In the last twenty years there have been the Cotton Terraces (1963), which in new pavilions and Burton's altered Giraffe House, house giraffes and zebras, camels and llamas, horses and cattle, antelope and deer (Père David herd); the distinctively roofed Elephant and Rhino Pavilion by Casson (1965); the 150ft by 80ft high Snowdon Aviary (1965), which in summer contains as many as 150 birds in natural surroundings and through which the visitor passes on an elevated walkway, and the £200 000 Charles Clore Pavilion for Small Mammals (1967) with its **Moonlight World,** where one sees animals active only at night.

In 1972 there arose the Michael Sobell Pavilions for Apes and Monkeys (gorillas; also the giant panda Chia-Chia – on loan to Mexico Zoo) and in 1976, the New Lion terraces, an extensive complex of tree and greenery planted enclosures from which the big cats survey all lesser mortals.

Plans for redevelopment include a coral reef aquarium, new enclosures for the Mappin Terraces and a new children's zoo.

IDEAS FOR AN EXCURSION

Last admissions to most properties are between 1/2 and 1 hour before closing time.

Ascott House★★ (AC). – Wing, SW of Leighton Buzzard (A418). Anthony de Rothschild collection of paintings, French and Chippendale furniture, Oriental porcelain; topiary sundial. *Open: House and Garden 19 July to 18 September, Tuesdays to Sundays 2 to 6pm, August holiday Monday 2 to 6pm, closed following Tuesday. Gardens only: Thursdays and last Sunday each month April to September, 2 to 6pm. House and Garden £2.20, children £1.50; Gardens £1.40, children 70p. NT.*

Audley End★ (BC). – Saffron Walden, Jacobean mansion with additional Adam decoration; wooded park by Capability Brown. *Open Good Friday to mid-October, Tuesdays to Sundays, holiday Mondays, 12 noon (house 1pm) to 5pm; closed ordinary Mondays; £2.50, children £1.25.*

Ayot St-Lawrence (AC): **Shaw's Corner.** – GBS' home 1906-1950. *Open April to October, Wednesdays to Sundays 2 to 6pm, Sundays and holiday Mondays noon to 6pm; closed Good Friday; £1.80. NT.*

Bekonscot Model Village (AC). – Warwick Rd, Beaconsfield. Miniature town – houses, shops, farms etc with rivers, lake and working railway laid out in 2 acre-garden. *Open March to October 10am to 5pm (Sundays and holidays 10am to 5.30pm); £1.60, children 80p.*

Bluebell Rlwy (BD). – Sheffield Park Station, Uckfield. Standard gauge steam trains to Horsted Keynes *£3 rtn, children £1.50; platform, museum, engine sheds £1, children 50p; June to September daily; March, November and December weekends; January and February Sundays; April weekends and 1st week; May Wednesdays, weekends and last week; October weekends and last week.*

Chartwell★ (BD). – Westerham (B2026). Sir Winston and Lady Churchill's country home; mementoes; gardens (golden roses). *Open March and November, Wednesdays, Saturdays and Sundays 11am to 4pm, April to October Tuesdays to Thursdays, Saturdays, Sundays, holiday Mondays (closed following Tuesdays) 11am (12 noon weekdays) to 5pm; gardens and studio, April to October, 11am to 4pm; £3, garden only £1.20, studio 40p. NT.*

Chessington World of Adventures★ (AD). – On A 243 between Surbiton and Leatherhead. 1 000 animals and birds, miniature rlwy, summer circus, boating, amusement park. *Open all year (winter; zoo only), 10am to 6pm (4pm in winter; closed 25 December); £6.25, children £5.25.* ☎ 03727-27227.

Chiddingstone Castle★ (BD). – E of Edenbridge. Late 18C Gothic castle displaying Royal Stuart, Egyptian and Japanese swords and lacquer collections. *Open April to October, Wednesdays to Saturdays 2pm (Sundays and holiday Mondays 11.30am) to 5.30pm; mid June to mid September, Tuesdays also; April and October, weekends only; closed Mondays; £2, Sundays and holidays £2.50, children £1.25* ☎ (0892) 870347.
In the **village** are 15-16C half timbered houses *(NT)* opposite 14C church with funeral hatchments and masons' marks.

Chislehurst (BD). – On A 222. Prehistoric chalk caves. *Open Easter to September daily (October to Easter weekends only) 11am to 5pm; "ordinary" 35 minute tour – £1.50, children 70p; "long" 1 1/2 hour Sundays and holidays only 3pm tour – £2, children £1.*

Clandon Park★ (AD). – West Clandon, Surrey. Unusual Palladian house by Giacomo Leoni, containing Gubbay bequest of 18C English furniture and English, continental and oriental porcelain. *Open April to mid October, Saturdays to Wednesdays 1.30 to 5.30pm, holiday Mondays, (closed Tuesday following) and preceding Sunday 11am to 5.30pm; £2.50. NT.*

Claydon House★ (AC). – Middle Claydon, NW of Aylesbury. 18C rococo state rooms, marquetry staircase; Florence Nightingale mementoes. *Open April to October, Saturdays to Wednesdays, 2pm (holiday Mondays 1pm) to 6pm; closed Thursdays and Fridays; £2, children £1, NT.*

Cliveden★ (AC). – E of Maidenhead. B 476. 19C house surrounded by formal, rose, water gdns; herbaceous borders. *House (3 rooms only) open April to October, Thursdays and Sundays 3 to 6pm; timed ticket 80p; gardens open March to December 11am to 6pm; £2.40. NT.* ☎ (06286) 5069.

Eton College★★ (AD). – 15C King's Chapel, School Yard (founder's statue: Henry VI), grounds; *open April to early October, daily 2 to 4.30pm (10.30am in holidays) £1.80, children £1.20.*

Flamstead (AC). – West of Harpenden. Attractive village with 14 and 15C church with consecration crosses, Perpendicular rood screen and 13C wall paintings.

Greensted-juxta-Ongar (BC). – St Andrew's Anglo Saxon church of 850 AD: only surviving example of split oak trunk construction; 17C shingled spire.

Greys Court★ (AC). – Rotherfield Greys, Henley-on-Thames. 16C house with 18C furniture and plasterwork; medieval ruins, gardens, symbolic maze. Tudor donkey water wheel, 19C horse wheel. *Open April to September, closed Good Friday; house Mondays, Wednesdays, Fridays; gardens Mondays to Saturdays 2 to 6pm; house and gardens £2.40; gardens only £1.60. NT.*

Hatfield House★★ (BC). – Splendid Jacobean mansion and surviving Tudor palace wing; gardens and parkland; famous portraits and relics of Queen Elizabeth. *Open late March to mid October, daily (except Mondays), 12 noon to 5pm, Sundays 1.30 to 5pm, holiday Mondays 11am to 5pm; closed Good Friday; £3.20 children £2.25.*

Hughenden Manor★ (AC). – N of High Wycombe. Rebuilt by Disraeli in 1847 as his country seat; Victorian furniture, letters, portraits etc. *Open March weekends 2 to 6pm; April to October Wednesdays to Saturdays 2 to 6pm or dusk if earlier, Sundays and holiday Mondays 12 noon to 6pm; closed Good Friday: £2, NT.*

179

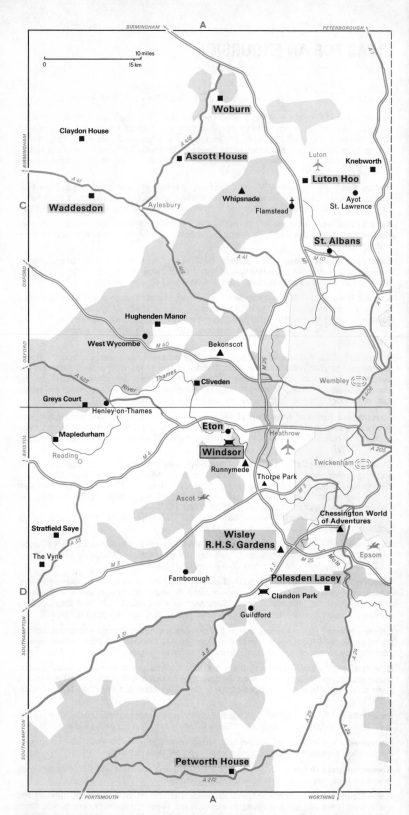

Hunting Lodge (BC). – Chingford, A1069. Henry VIII's lodge, a Tudor, timber framed building; Epping Forest museum. *Open Wednesdays to Sundays and holiday Mondays 2 to 6pm (or dusk if earlier); closed 25 and 26 December; 25p.*

Ightham Mote★ (BD). – Ivy Hatch. SW of Sevenoaks. 600 year old moated manorhouse. *Open April to October, daily except Tuesdays and Saturdays, 12 noon to 5.30pm (Sundays and holidays 11am to 5.30pm); £2.50 children £1.20.*

Kent and E Sussex Rlwy (BD). – Tenterden. *Open weekends April to December, also Wednesdays, Thursdays, June, July, daily in August 11am to 4.30pm; £2.70 rtn.* **Ellen Terry Museum,** Small-hythe Place. *Open late March to October daily except Thursdays, Fridays, 2 to 6pm or dusk if earlier £1.40.*

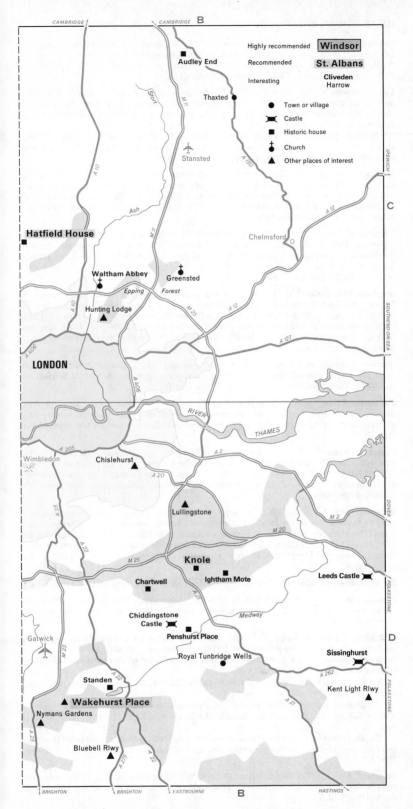

Knebworth House★ (AC). – W of M1, S of Stevenage. Tudor mansion remodelled in 1843 by Sir Edward Bulwer Lytton, Edwardian garden; deer park; skate park; narrow gauge rly; adventure playground. Delhi Durbar exhibition.

Open daily April to late May, weekends and school holidays; late May to mid-September Tuesdays to Sundays; closed Mondays except holiday Mondays; house 12 noon to 5pm, park 11am to 5.30pm; £3, children £2.50.

Knole★★ (BD). – Sevenoaks. Vast 15C house: Jacobean interior; 17, 18C furniture, paintings; wooded deer park. *Open April to October Wednesdays to Sundays, holiday Mondays, Good Friday 11am (Sundays 2pm) to 5pm; closed November to March; £2.50. NT. Connoisseurs' day Fridays (not Good Friday). £3. (NB: many rooms have no electric lighting.)*

IDEAS FOR AN EXCURSION

Leeds Castle* (BD). – SE of Maidstone. M20-B2163. The island "castle of the medieval queens of England"; water and woodland gardens; aviary. *Open April to October daily 11am to 5pm, November to March, weekends only, 12 noon to 4pm; grounds £3.80, OAPs £2.80, children £2.30; castle £4.80, OAPs £3.80, children £3.30. No dogs.*

Loseley House* (AD). – W of Guildford. Elizabethan mansion of stone from Waverley Abbey; painted panelling from Nonsuch Palace, plasterwork; grounds, dairy farm. *Open June to September, Wednesdays to Saturdays and holiday Mondays, 2 to 5pm; £2.80, children £1.50, farm tour 4pm £1.50, children £1.30.*

Guildford Cathedral of the Holy Spirit, 1936-61 by Sir Edward Maufe in simplified Gothic style in local brick; 20C work by artists and craftsmen. *Open daily 8.30am to 5.30pm.* **University of Surrey,** 1966. **Yvonne Arnaud Theatre,** by the River Wey, 1965.

Lullingstone (BD). – Off A 225 south of Dartford. **Roman Villa** with painted walls and extensive mosaics (under cover). *(Closed during 1989 for major renovation.)* **Castle:** Tudor manor house and gateway with Queen Anne additions and connections; gardens. *Open April to October, weekends, Good Friday, holiday Mondays, 2 to 6pm; £2.50 children £1.* Extensive park. Medieval church: rood screen (1510) and 18C portable font.

Luton Hoo ** (AC). – Exit 10 off M1, A6 and Park St. Wernher collection of pictures (Dutch, Italian), tapestries, English china (Bow, Chelsea, Worcester); medieval ivories, jewels (Fabergé, Renaissance), small bronzes, silver; mementoes of Russian Imperial Family; park by Capability Brown. *Open: house and gardens mid-April to mid-October, Tuesdays to Sundays, holiday Mondays, 2 to 5.45pm; £2.50, children £1.25; café.*

Mapledurham House* (AD). – NW of Reading off A 4074. Elizabethan house beside the Thames; moulded plaster ceilings, oak staircases, 16, 17, 18C paintings. *Open weekends and holiday Mondays 2.30 to 5.30pm from Easter Sunday to September, £2, children £1.* 15/18C working **watermill** grinding flour for sale; *open Easter Sunday to 30 September, 1.30 to 5pm, also Sundays in winter, 2 to 4pm; 90p, children 45p.* Access also by river from Caversham Bridge, Reading, leaving 1.45pm.

Nymans Gardens (BD). – Handcross, south of Crawley (A 23). Walled gardens, topiary work, rare trees, shrubs, bulbs. *Open April to October, Tuesdays to Thursdays, Saturdays, Sundays and holiday Mondays 11am to 7pm; closed Good Friday; £2.* NT.

Penshurst Place* (BD). – Tonbridge (B 2176). Great hall of 1340. Birthplace of Sir Philip Sidney; state rooms, furniture, picture gallery; toy museum. Tudor gardens, venture playground. *Open April to first Sunday in October, Tuesdays to Sundays, holiday Mondays, 12.30 to 6pm; £2.90.*

Petworth House ** (AD). – Petworth junction A 272 and 283. Late 17C mansion (19C alterations) in 700 acre deer park by Capability Brown. Important collection of paintings; Grinling Gibbons carvings. *Open Tuesdays to Thursdays, Saturdays and Sundays, April to October, holiday Mondays 1 to 5pm; £2.70. NT. Connoisseurs' day, Tuesdays (except after holidays) £3. No dogs. Park open daily.*

Polesden Lacey ** (AD). – NW of Dorking. Off A 246. Regency villa with Edwardian alterations: pictures, tapestries, furniture; famous gardens – roses, herbaceous plants, clipped hedges, beech walks. *Open: house, March and November weekends only 1.30 to 5.30pm; April to October, Wednesdays to Sundays 1.30 to 5.30pm, holiday Mondays and preceding Sunday, 11am to 5.30pm; garden all year daily 11am to sunset; house and garden £2.50 (holidays and Sundays £3), garden only £1.20. NT.*

Royal Tunbridge Wells (BD). – The Pantiles: arcaded parade of Beau Nash and 17C dandies.

Runnymede (AD). – Northwest of Staines, off A 308. Watermeadow (188 acres) where King John signed Magna Carta in 1215; President Kennedy memorial (1965), Commonwealth Air Forces Memorial *(hill top).*

St Albans ** (AC). – **Cathedral,** 11C to 20C; warmly majestic in brick, flint and stone in parkland setting; vast asymmetrically arched nave, 15C reredos, brasses, 13C wall paintings, 13 and 15C decorated wooden ceilings. *Open daily 7am (Saturdays and Sundays 8am) to 6.45pm (5.45pm in winter and Sundays).* 14C Abbey gateway.

In the city: old houses, alleys, pubs; Saturday and Wednesday market; museum: 19C trade workshops (blacksmith, cooper, wheelwright).

Verulamium: Roman theatre, excavations, hypocaust and museum. *Open daily 10am to 5.30pm, Sundays 2 to 5.30 (4pm November to March); closed, 25 and 26 December; £1, children 50p.*

Kingsbury Watermill: *open Wednesdays to Sundays and holiday Mondays (closed 25 December and 1 January) 11am to 6pm (5pm in winter; Sundays and holidays 12 noon to 6pm); 60p, children 30p.*

Standen* (BD). – SW of East Grinstead (B 2110). 19C house and garden by Philip Webb with William Morris interior. *Open April to October, Wednesdays to Sundays 1.30 to 5.30pm; £2.40, garden only £1.20. NT.*

Sissinghurst Castle* (BD). – NE of Cranbrook. A 262. The gardens created by Vita Sackville West and Harold Nicolson – spring, rose, cottage, moat, white and herb, and the "purple border"; Tudor manor house (tower and long library). *Open 24 March to 15 October, Tuesdays to Fridays, 1 (weekends and Good Friday 10am) to 6.30pm; Tuesdays to Fridays £3, Saturdays, Sundays and holidays £3.50. NT. No dogs.*

Stratfield Saye* (AD). – S of Reading, off A 33. Carolean house presented to Duke of Wellington 1817; paintings, mementoes, funeral carriage (museum); State Coach. *Open daily except Fridays, May to September 11.30am to 5pm; £3, children £1.50.* **Wellington Country Park.** Boating, fishing, nature and fitness trails, adventure playground, miniature steam rly; riding, camping. *Open daily March to October and winter weekends 10am to 5.30pm or dusk, £2, children £1.*

Thaxted (BC). – Old wool town, spacious parish church (14C-15C) and 15C guildhall of three overhanging storeys.

Thorpe Park (AD). – Near Chertsey (M3). Theme park featuring adventure rides, water sports facilities and other attractions. Cafeterias and picnic areas. *Open late-March to late October; admission charge.* ☎ *(0932) 56233.*

The Vyne (AD). – N of Basingstoke. A 33. Diapered early 16C red brick mansion, 17C portico, oak gallery with linenfold panelling, Palladian staircase; grounds. *Open 24 March to mid October daily except Mondays and Fridays; 1.30 to 5.30pm; holiday Mondays, 11am to 5.30pm, closed following Tuesday; £2.30, Sundays and holidays £2.60. NT.*

Waddesdon Manor★★ (AC). – NW of Aylesbury (A 41). 19C French Renaissance house of Baron Ferdinand de Rothschild; French 17C, 18C furniture, carpets, panelling; English, Dutch, Flemish, Italian paintings; porcelain; costume, lace, button collections; grounds, aviary. *Open mid March to late October, Wednesdays to Sundays 1 to 5pm (weekends and holidays 6pm) (grounds: Wednesdays to Saturdays 1pm, Sundays 11.30am), Good Friday and holiday Mondays all open 11am to 6pm; house and grounds closed Wednesdays after holiday Mondays; £3, grounds only £1.50. (House will be closed during 1990 for major refurbishment) NT.*

Waltham Abbey★ (BC). – Norman abbey church with limited 19C restoration. Burial place of King Harold in 1066. 15C wall painting; Burne-Jones stained glass.

Wakehurst Place★★ – N of Ardingly, B 2024. 250 acres of lawns, lakes and woodlands – exotic trees, shrubs and plants – managed by Kew Gardens. *Open daily 10am to dusk; closed 1 January, 25 December; £1.50, children 60p. NT.*

West Wycombe★ (AC). – West of High Wycombe. The **village** main street retains half-timbered and oversailing, brick and stucco buildings of 15 to 19C *(NT)*; **West Wycombe House:** Palladian mansion with two-storey colonnade containing fine 18C furniture, paintings, set in landscaped garden and park (farm and forest trail). *Open June to August, Sundays to Thursdays, 2 to 6pm; £2.60, children £1.10; grounds only £1.60, children 80p. NT.* **St Lawrence Church:** 13C with 18C interior, paintings, golden ball crowned tower; beneath are 1/4 mile of **caves** (18C waxwork scenes and commentary): *open March to late May 1 to 6pm, late May to early September, daily 11am to 6pm; early September to October 1 to 6pm; November to March, Saturdays and Sundays, 1 to 5pm; £2, children £1.*

Whipsnade★ (AC). – Dunstable (MI junction 9). Founded 1931 as the country quarters of the London Zoo; over 2 000 animals and birds in beautiful surroundings; steam rly. *Open every day except Christmas Day, 10am to 6pm (7pm Sundays, bank holidays) or sunset if earlier; £3.90, children £2.40; cars extra charge.*

Windsor Castle ★★★ (AD). – **Precincts:** *open daily (except for Garter Ceremony in June) 10am to 7.15pm (5.15pm late March to April, September to late October, 4.15pm late October to late March).* **St George's Chapel:** *open during British Summer Time daily 10.45am (2pm Sundays) to 4pm (3.45pm in winter); closed January, 24, 25 December; £1.50, children 60p; free admission to services. Times subject to alteration at short notice.* **State Apartments:** *open (when the Queen is not in residence – see press) 10.30am (1.30 pm Sundays) to 5pm (3pm in winter); £2, children £1.* **Queen Mary's Dolls' House** (1920s by Lutyens) and exhibition of dolls, **Exhibition of Drawings** (Holbein, Leonardo), **Royal Mews Exhibition:** *open during*

(After photograph, Pitkin Pictorials)

St George's Chapel, Windsor Castle.

BST daily 10.30am to 5pm (Sundays 3pm); in winter Mondays to Saturdays, 10.30am to 3pm; closed Sundays in winter, 1 January, Good Friday, 23 to 31 December; £1 each.

Great Park: *open all year, sunrise to sunset;* **Savill Garden,** *near Englefield Green: open March to December 10am to 7pm (6pm weekdays, 5pm in winter); £1.80, OAPs £1.60, children free (accompanied); car park 80p;* **Safari Park** *(lions, elephants, llamas, dolphins etc) open daily 10am to dusk; closed 25 December; £5.95, children £4.95.*

Royalty and Empire Exhibition. – Windsor Central Station. Exhibition portraying the 1897 Diamond Jubilee celebrations of Queen Victoria: wax works and audio-visual shows. *Open daily except 25 December 9.30am to 5.30pm (4.30pm in winter); £3.55, OAPs and children £2.55.*

Wisley, RHS Gardens★★ (AD). – Near Ripley (A3). Superb gardens. *Open February to October 10am to 7pm or sunset, (4.30pm November to January) (Sunday; members only); closed 25 December; £2.50, children £1. No dogs.*

Woburn Abbey and Wild Animal Kingdom★★ (AC). – Northwest of Dunstable on A5. 18C house: French and English furniture, silver, porcelain; model soldiers; 16-17C portraits; Canalettos, Rembrandts, Gainsboroughs, Reynolds...; state apartments. **Park and game reserve;** antiques centre (20p); children's amusements; pub etc. *Abbey open April to October daily 11am to 5pm (5.30pm Sundays and holidays); January-March, weekends only 11am to 4pm; closed November, December; £4, children £1.50; deer park £1.70 cars.* **Wild Animal Kingdom:** *open mid-March to 1 November 10am to 5pm; £4.50, children £3.50.*

183

INDEX

Churches, squares, almshouses and pubs have been grouped and galleries also listed together since artists' works, with a few famous exceptions, have not been indexed under the painters' names. Statues are under the subject portrayed. The index is not exhaustive.

Place, street and building names are in roman characters ; people, familiar names, historical events, rhymes, etc., in italics *eg* Middlesex St, *Petticoat Lane,* Westminster Abbey, *The Dissolution,* Bank of England, *South Sea Bubble.*

MANUFACTURE FRANÇAISE DES PNEUMATIQUES MICHELIN

Société en commandite par actions au capital de 875 000 000 de francs

Place des Carmes-Déchaux - 63 Clermont-Ferrand (France)

R.C.S. Clermont-Fd B 855 200 507

© Michelin et Cie, Propriétaires-Éditeurs 1990

Dépôt légal 1er trim. 1990 – ISBN 2 06 015 435-9 – ISSN 0763-1383

Printed in France - 01.90.35

Photocomposition : COUPÉ S.A., Sautron – Impression : LAZARE-FERRY, Paris 12e, n° 10256